BUSHPEOPLE'S GUIDE TO

BUSHWALKING IN
SOUTH-EAST QUEENSLAND

SECOND EDITION

Completely Revised, with over 100 Additional Pages

BUSHPEOPLE PUBLICATIONS

Second Edition completely revised 1991.
First Edition published 1987, then titled
The Bushwalk Book of South-East Queensland.

Published by BUSHPEOPLE PUBLICATIONS
P.O. Box 365, Goodna. Qld. 4300. Australia.
Telephone: (07) 814 2556.

Copyright © Bushpeople Publications 1991
ISBN 0 646 03753 6

Printed by James Ferguson Pty Ltd,
37 College Street, Hamilton. Qld. 4007.

Typesetting by Brown Business Services,
7 Lawrie Drive, Collingwood Park, Qld. 4300

Cover design and artwork assistance by Graphic Litho Pty Ltd,
20 Priority Street, Wacol. Qld. 4076.

Maps prepared by Rob Canty. Artwork assistance and illustration on
page 2 by Anne Lahey. Unless otherwise credited, all text and
photographs are by Ross and Heather Buchanan, proprietors of Bushpeople Publications.

Advertising and Editorial Policy: Bushpeople Publications has a policy
of only including selected advertising which provides a genuine reader service.
All advertising and other publication content must be compatible with conservation
and equal opportunity principles. This book has been written without the use of
gender specific language.

EDITORIAL: CONSERVING THE DIVERSITY OF RECREATIONAL EXPERIENCES

Although south-east Queensland lacks extensive national park areas such as occur around cities like Hobart and Sydney, one of the great assets of our bushwalking regions is the diversity of landscapes and bushwalking experiences. South-east Queensland must surely be the only region in Australia that can offer, within 200km of a major city, natural landscapes ranging from superb rainforests, spectacular gorges, serene waterfalls, steep mountain ranges and precipitous rocky pinnacles, to dramatic granite architecture, red arid landscapes and the outstanding beauty of Fraser Island's freshwater lakes.

The range of bushwalking experiences is equally diverse. While there is no true wilderness in this region (i.e. as defined by the academic criterion of minimum size), there are many areas which have notable wilderness qualities, with pristinity and solitude values that are no longer offered in some of Tasmania's so-called "wildernesses". There is also a wide range of other equally legitimate bushwalking experiences. These include possibly the most significant graded track system in Australia, an immense variety of off-track bushwalks and several localities offering walks up to three weeks in duration.

But this situation is not static. There are continual pressures for the development of national parks and other bush areas, with public and political perceptions often regarding national parks simply in terms of the tourism and recreation facilities they can support. Development proposals range from picnic areas and walking track systems to full scale tourist resorts. Considered in isolation, some of these proposals may have minimal effect on the overall range of recreation opportunities available, but you need to consider the overall effect of all such proposals on the region as a whole. For instance, the creation of a new camping area and walking track system on the Scenic Rim may only affect the immediate surrounds, but four or five new developments scattered around the Scenic Rim may completely alter the recreational nature of the entire region.

It is important to realise that the richness of national park recreation opportunities depends substantially on the diversity of the recreation types available, and that all types of conservation-compatible recreations have an equal right to exist. One of the objectives of recreational planning should be to ensure the continued viability of various recreation forms, and developments should not be merely a reaction to the commercial interests of local shires and development pressure groups. If possible, we should try to find planning solutions which suit all interests. If not, planning should conserve as many future options as possible.

In south-east Queensland, an issue of great concern is the future of wilderness style bushwalking, particularly with regard to the management of the Scenic Rim. Many people are unaware how easily this recreation opportunity could be lost. Probably the greatest threat are the continued proposals for the establishment of an official Scenic Rim walking trail (rather than the current unofficial route), a single initiative which would destroy some 50% of wilderness style bushwalking opportunities in the region. The uncertain future of wilderness bushwalking can be further illustrated by reference to the draft (and now discredited) 1989 Scenic Rim management plan, which proposed a number of ill-conceived developments. Many bushwalkers failed to realise at the time that had this plan come into effect in combination with the Scenic Rim trail proposal, wilderness style bushwalking opportunities in south-east Queensland would have virtually ceased to exist.

Consequently, if south-east Queensland bushwalkers wish to ensure the future of their recreation opportunities, it is critical that they take an active interest in national park management planning and adopt a watchdog role to assess development proposals. Graded tracks, picnic areas and the like may all be legitimate in certain areas, but it is also important that we conserve the opportunities for wilderness-orientated recreation activities.

PREFACE

The first edition of this book was released in 1987 and was then titled *The Bushwalk Book of South-East Queensland*. The book was well received by the public and bushwalking community, but after a while it became evident that significant improvements could be made. Consequently, this edition has been completely rewritten and restructured. The major changes are as follows:

(1) Most route descriptions have been completely revised to provide far greater detail and accuracy, with nearly all information in this edition being written from direct personal experience. In addition, the route gradings have been reviewed and a number of small but significant errors in the 1987 book have been corrected.

(2) Nearly all chapters have a considerable amount of new information, with new bushwalking opportunities at Brisbane Forest Park, Sundown National Park and Back Creek being particularly notable.

(3) The book has been designed to be used in a variety of different ways i.e. as a "100 Walks" style guide, as an encyclopaedia of bushwalking features and routes, or as an instruction manual for bushwalking skills.

(4) Locality illustration maps have been included for quick reference purposes.

(5) Greater direction and guidance have been provided for inexperienced bushwalkers.

(6) Nearly all chapters were reviewed by the local national park and/or forestry rangers prior to publication. This has not only helped ensure up-to-date information, but has assisted in achieving compatibility with management practices.

We hope that readers will appreciate these changes and that the book brings you many satisfying and enjoyable bushwalking ventures.

ACKNOWLEDGEMENTS

We wish to express special thanks to Rob Canty for his massive and painstaking effort in preparing the maps. This has provided one of the major improvements since the first edition. We are also grateful to Anne Lahey for preparing the cartoon illustration on page 2 and for assistance with the illustrations in Chapter 6.

Thanks are due to the various national park and forestry rangers who reviewed the manuscripts. Martin Fingland of Brisbane Forest Park deserves special recognition, having been almost singlehandedly responsible for discovering and providing information on numerous new bushwalking routes in that area.

In addition, we wish to thank all those people (too many to name individually) who over the years have provided numerous odd snippets of advice and information that have helped to improve the book.

WARNING NOTE

Readers are warned that it is almost impossible to ensure that a bushwalking guidebook of this size is entirely free of errors, despite great care having been taken when compiling the route descriptions. All bushwalkers should be prepared to use their own skill and judgment at all times when bushwalking, and should not rely too critically on any guidebook. Please refer to Chapter 1 for more details.

Corrections and Comments: Readers who find any information in this book misleading or out-of-date are invited to send corrections to the publisher. In general, payment or acknowledgement cannot be made for corrections, but honest efforts will be made to remedy faults in future editions.

CONTENTS

Editorial, Preface, Acknowledgements
Warning Note, Corrections and Comments

PART ONE
INTRODUCTION AND SKILLS

Track Marking and Walking Practices/page 80
 Track Marking, Party Size
General Issues/page 82
 *The Philosophy of Non-Disturbance; Machetes and Axes;
 Firearms and Domestic Animals; Sound Pollution and Other Impacts*

PART TWO
REGIONAL DESCRIPTIONS

PART ONE
INTRODUCTION AND SKILLS

Bushwalking can mean glorious moments on high peaks watching the sun rise and set. It can mean gazing at stars on a dark night, visiting remote pristine lakes, swapping yarns with friends around a camp fire, and viewing spectacular waterfalls and landmarks which few others ever see. Generally bushwalking is also a very safe recreation, provided you use care and commonsense and progress gradually from easy to harder trips.

However, if you treat the activity recklessly, or venture into rugged areas ill-equipped or unprepared, bushwalking will become a gamble with the terrain and weather. It is as well to remember that bushwalking can involve discomfort and great fatigue, being scratched by bush and thorns, facing freezing rainstorms or sweltering heat, and occasionally being confronted with dangerous situations.

To a great extent, how well you avoid or cope with the difficulties will depend on how well you have understood and planned for the conditions beforehand. It is in your own interests to learn how to bushwalk safely and so avoid the worst risks and discomforts. The first seven chapters of this book deal primarily with topics related to safety and preparation, together with minimum impact bushwalking ethics which will allow you to visit the bush with the least environmental impact.

CONTENTS OF PART ONE

1

HOW TO USE THIS BOOK
(Important Reading for Everyone)

This guidebook differs in philosophy and approach to most Australian bushwalking guidebooks, giving much more direction on safety and environmental conservation than is usual in such texts. In this respect, it is hoped that it will give a lead to guidebooks of the future. This book is also designed so that it can be used in at least four quite different ways:

• **One Hundred Suggested Walks:** The trip suggestions in Chapter 8 can be used to discover new places to visit and new things to do. In particular, less experienced bushwalkers are encouraged to use the book in this manner. These "100 walks" are arranged with a graduated scale of difficulty to facilitate a safe progression from easy to harder trips.

• **A Bushwalking Encyclopaedia:** The book can be used as an encyclopaedia of the region's major bushwalking localities i.e. to find out detailed information on bushwalking features and routes which are already known to readers, or which you have "picked off the map" or "observed on the skyline".

• **Learning Bushwalking Skills:** You can also use the book to learn bushwalking skills. The skills information is not totally comprehensive, but in combination with the *One Hundred Suggested Walks* and the route grading system, the material can greatly assist in the development of your bushwalking abilities. If you apply the skills information as you progress gradually from easy to harder trips, ability, fitness and experience will develop together.

• **Inspiration to Dreamers:** Lastly and not entirely illegitimately, the book can stay on your bookshelf, and be simply brought down when you want to imagine you are out in the wilds or wish to recall a favourite bushwalking trip or feature.

SPECIAL ADVICE TO READERS

Whichever way you use the book, it is not intended that you simply pull it from the bookshelf and head off on a trip. This type of approach often gets inexperienced bushwalkers into serious difficulties. To make sure you are prepared for the conditions you may encounter, there are a few pages of the book which are considered essential preliminary reading, and a few major points to note.

IMPORTANT SECTIONS TO READ

There are several sections (totalling only about a dozen pages) which should be considered prerequisite reading prior to using the book on any bushwalks. These are:

- All of Chapter 1.
- The short sections on *The Nature of Bushwalking* and *Assessing Your Level of Fitness* in Chapter 3 (pages 19 and 21).
- The information on bushwalking preparation and safety practices in Chapter 5 (pages 35 to 38).
- The information about how to use the grading system in Chapter 2 (pages 8 to10).

In addition, it is strongly recommended that readers acquire at least a basic familiarity with the following as early as possible in their bushwalking careers (preferably before embarking on their first trip):

- *Bushwalking Conditions in South-East Queensland* (Chapter 4; page 24).
- *Minimum Impact Bushwalking* (Chapter 7; page 71).
- The introduction to *One Hundred Suggested Walks* (page 85).
- *Permits and Private Landowners* (pages 12 to 15).

N.B. It is suggested that you read these sections again after you have completed a dozen or so walks, as you will discover much information you missed on the first occasion.

THE BASICS OF CHOOSING AND PLANNING WALKS

There is a great deal of information in this book about bushwalking safety and preparation. Here is a brief summary about how it is recommended that you use the book, and how to choose and plan walks.

(1) Read this chapter entirely, together with those sections which are listed above as "prerequisite reading".

(2) Objectively assess your fitness and experience on the basis of the information in *Assessing Your Level of Fitness* at the end of Chapter 3 (pages 21).

(3) Unless you have had at least 20 days bushwalking experience in a variety of off-track terrains, start out by using the *One Hundred Suggested Walks* to choose trips appropriate to your fitness and experience (Chapter 8; page 85).

(4) Buy a good quality topographic map of the area you intend to visit and ensure that you can clearly identify the route on the map (information is given on page 59 about where to purchase maps, and all map titles are listed in the relevant chapters, usually with appropriate recommendations).

(5) Be sure that you are aware of what conditions to expect (don't only refer to the route description, but also to the chapter's *Special Notes* and to the information in Chapter 4). Don't tackle walks in areas where navigation is difficult unless somebody in the party has the necessary navigation skills, and don't tackle walks

in rugged areas unless everybody in the party has the necessary scrambling skills.

(6) Prepare for the walk properly and be aware of general bushwalking safety practices (see pages 35 to 39).

(7) Carry appropriate and adequate equipment e.g. on day walks it is generally recommended that you always carry a map, watch, torch, water bottle, basic first aid kit, compass, parka, pullover, hat and a little extra food (such as chocolate or sweets that have high energy value).

(8) Don't set out alone. There are quite a number of walks suggested which don't require previous bushwalking experience (see page 86), but even on these trips it is recommended that you walk with a small group of friends (or you might wish to consider joining a bushwalking club - see page 19).

(9) Tell a responsible person about your route and intended time of return.

(10) To preserve the environment, ensure that you follow minimum impact bushwalking practices on all trips. This book has a considerable amount of information on this subject. Your aim should always be to leave the places you visit unmarked and unaltered.

SPECIAL POINTS TO NOTE

In addition to the above, it is important to note that:

• The maps in the book are intended for locality illustration only, and detailed topographic maps are essential on the majority of trips described (even most of those which are noted as requiring only basic navigation skills). Many route descriptions also make extensive use of grid references, and consequently will make little sense without a topographic map (refer to page 59 for advice on where to purchase maps). N.B. Experience has shown that attempts to provide detailed topographic maps in guidebooks are rarely satisfactory, and often only encourage inexperienced walkers to venture into the bush without adequate maps.

• You must always be prepared to use your own skill and judgment. Considerable effort has been made to use "average" standards of fitness and ability in the route descriptions, but the standards will not suit everybody. Due to different levels of fitness, skills and experience, people vary immensely in their perceptions of bushwalking obstacles and difficulties.

• Do not rely on the information in the book being precisely correct on all occasions, especially since bushwalking conditions change with time. There may also be occasional inaccuracies in the text at the date of publication, despite great care having been taken in the compilation of the route descriptions. The nature of bushwalking is such that it is virtually impossible to ensure that a guidebook of this size is precisely correct in every respect, or that the standards used are totally consistent.

• On some very rugged routes, only summary information is given. On these routes skill and judgement are far more valuable than any guidebook information, and you should not attempt these trips until you have gained adequate experience.

• Most route descriptions have been compiled from personal experience, but sometimes general reports among the bushwalking community and/or long distance field observations have also been included (usually to illustrate exploratory possibilities). These are evident in the text and extra care should be taken when using this information.

- Provided you use care and commonsense, and progress gradually from easy to harder trips, bushwalking is normally an exceptionally safe recreation. However, if you treat the activity recklessly, or venture into rugged areas ill-equipped or unprepared, bushwalking will become a gamble with the terrain and weather. It is in your own interests to learn to bushwalk safely and so avoid these risks.

CODE OF BUSHWALKING ETHICS

SAFETY

Before you leave, advise a responsible person of your route and intended time of return. Prepare well, ensure you know the nature of the country, that you can find your way and that you have ample time for the trip. On all trips carry a good map, compass, watch, matches, torch, first aid kit, hat, water and adequate food and clothing of a type suitable for unexpected cold or wet weather. Carry a whistle for use in emergencies.

When walking, constantly keep track of your movements and position. Don't act foolishly, take unnecessary risks, or dislodge rocks. Inexperienced people should not walk alone, be made to tackle tasks beyond their ability, or be left without experienced leadership.

CONSERVATION

Rubbish: Carry out what you carry in, and don't litter the bush in any way. All walkers should carry a plastic bag for their rubbish. It is particularly important not to leave non-degradable items such as aluminium foil, cans, plastic and glass. Don't leave any rubbish in fireplaces, even small items such as aluminium foil, matches and cigarette butts. Remember that the old rule of "Burn, Bash and Bury" for disposing of cans no longer applies. Bury only easily biodegradable food scraps in areas where they won't be uncovered.

The Environment: Rocks, vegetation, animals and archeological features should be left undisturbed. Nothing should be damaged, defaced, removed or interfered with in any way. Carry aluminium tent poles, never cut them from the bush.

Camp Fires: Use existing fireplaces if available, and only use wood fires in non-fragile areas where wood can be easily collected from the ground in the near vicinity. Where wood is scarce, bushfire danger high, or vegetation communities fragile (e.g. in most heath regions), use gas or liquid fuel stoves instead of fires. When you do have a camp fire, use wood sparingly. Collect only fallen branches for firewood. Never damage live vegetation or even dead standing timber.

Fire Safety: Use stringent fire precautions and check whether fire restrictions are in force. Don't leave fires unattended, and ensure that your campfire is thoroughly extinguished at night and when you leave camp. Preferably use water to extinguish fires (in particular note that covering fires with dry sand is often ineffective). Take care if burning toilet paper or scattering the ashes of campfires.

Camping: For minimum impact in popular areas, camp on previously used campsites. Avoid camping on fragile vegetation. Don't dig trenches or construct tent platforms or bed sites. Leave the campsite in as natural condition as possible. In pristine areas especially, try to leave no sign of your visit at all.

Water Supplies and Hygiene: Keep water supplies clean. Don't use soap or detergents in or near rivers and lakes, and if possible, wash utensils, clothing and bodies well away from watercourses. All human waste and toilet paper should be well covered and away from tracks, possible campsites, streams or drainage channels.

Party Size: Restrict the party to an acceptable size, having consideration to both the ecological fragility of the area and your impact on the enjoyment of other bushwalkers.

Walking Practices: Use formed tracks where they exist, and avoid making new parallel tracks. Avoid track marking, especially in pristine areas. If track marking is necessary, use only methods which don't damage the vegetation or cause disturbance, such as coloured tape. Don't nail markers to trees. Machete blazing should never be used.

Utensils and Domestic Animals: Axes, machetes, firearms and domestic animals have no place in bushwalking (in thick scrub, garden gloves and gaiters are superior to hacking implements in any event).

LANDOWNERS

Obtain the relevant permits for national parks and forestry areas, and permission from the owner if you wish to traverse on private land. Be courteous to landholders, and do not help yourself to private conveniences or water tanks unless invited.

Go through, not over, gates and fences, or cross at a post. Use gates if available in preference to going through fences, and leave gates and slip rails as you find them. Be careful not to disturb stock, and take stringent precautions with fire.

COURTESY AND THE SPIRIT OF WALKING

Respect the presence of others in all your activities - cooking on communal fires, planning tent sites and fireplaces, use of wood and water etc.

In the bush, the sounds of the natural inhabitants should predominate. Noise from radios or other electronic or mechanical devices are not in keeping with wilderness.

Be self-reliant. The wilderness visitor should be fully self sufficient and should not use any form of mechanised transport for travel once in the bush (i.e. transport is by foot, skis, or hand or sail powered boats, not trail bikes etc). Supply your own equipment and accommodation - don't construct shelters or utensils from the bush.

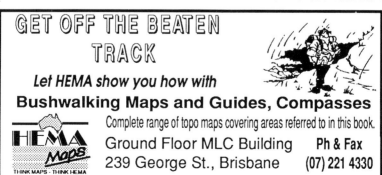

2

GRADING SYSTEM, ROADS, PERMITS AND PRIVATE LANDOWNERS

This chapter explains how to use the grading system, how to obtain permits for camping in national parks and state forests, and how to approach landowners if you wish to travel across private lands.

USING THE GRADING SYSTEM

To assist people choose trips appropriate to their level of experience, most bushwalking routes in this book have been graded on a scale ranging from 1/2 (very easy) to 7 (extremely hard). However, to use the grading system safely, you need to understand how the system works and realise its limitations.

BASIS OF GRADINGS

The grading system was introduced in the first edition of this guidebook to provide a more refined method of indicating route difficulty than the system of "easy", "medium" and "hard" that had been used in some previous guidebooks. A system with 14 different levels (seven categories with half grades) simply has to be more accurate than a system with three. Despite this, readers should realise that all attempts at grading bushwalking routes are somewhat subjective and approximate.

The difficulty of bushwalking routes depends on a number of factors, the main ones being:

• The physical fitness and effort required.
• Scrambling and climbing difficulties.
• Navigation difficulties.

- Miscellaneous hazards and problems such as the density of vegetation.
- Variable conditions such as weather and seasonal vegetation growth.
- The individual's fitness, skill and experience.
- The time available.

Of these, the first two factors - the physical effort involved and the scrambling and climbing difficulties - have been the primary considerations when deciding the route gradings in this book. Navigation and vegetation difficulties have also been considered, but usually their effect on the gradings is relatively minor. This is partly because navigation difficulties in the bush are highly variable, and to significantly alter the gradings for problems which may not be encountered could give erroneous impressions about the grading standards. However, potential navigation difficulties are usually mentioned in the text.

Note that low gradings should not be interpreted as indicating absence of serious hazards. The grading system is not able to reflect the potential dangers of bushwalking routes, since it is virtually impossible to "measure" danger in a numerical rating. There are too many variable factors such as the conditions at the time and the individual's experience and mental attitude. Many localities which statistically have the worst safety records are technically relatively easy, reflecting the fact that most bushwalking mishaps result as much from overconfidence and lack of preparation as from terrain hazards.

LIMITATIONS AND CONSISTENCY

Inevitably any bushwalking grading system must have significant limitations. This system is primarily based on a balance of two different and often unrelated factors - the physical effort involved and scrambling difficulties. This is satisfactory if both fitness and scrambling ability increase with bushwalking experience, but, of course, there are many variables. Bushwalkers with poor rock skills or with a particular fear of heights may find that routes in rugged areas are harder than the gradings indicate, while those with good rock skills may find the difficulties overstated. Similarly, people lacking agility may find that rockhopping trips are more difficult than expected.

It is also not possible to achieve total consistency in any grading system, because bushwalking conditions (either when readers visit the area or during the authors' visits) are highly variable. Consequently, a number of routes with the same grading will rarely be precisely the same level of difficulty. Rather, the gradings should be interpreted as indicating that the routes have a **broadly comparable** level of difficulty in normal conditions and circumstances.

GRADING STANDARDS

Bearing in mind the preceding information, the following is an approximate guide to the grading standards used in this book:

Up to Grade 1 1/2:	These routes should be suitable for unfit beginners provided they have a basic level of medical fitness.
Grade 2 to 2 1/2:	These routes are generally suitable for beginners, provided they have a good basic level of physical fitness. The walks usually include some steep hill climbs and some require rock-hopping and navigation skills. If there are navigation difficulties, an experienced leader will be necessary.

Grade 3 to 3½:	These routes need a good level of fitness and agility. They usually involve some scrambling and/or navigation problems, some of which may require a significant level of skill and judgment.
Grade 4 to 4½:	These routes nearly always require a high level of fitness and agility, together with good navigation and scrambling skills. A capable experienced leader is essential.
Grade 5 and Harder:	These routes are of extreme difficulty, usually requiring good climbing skills (not just scrambling skills), as well as excellent navigation ability and a very high level of physical fitness.

SOME GUIDELINES ON APPROACH

Some route gradings have been adjusted since this book's first edition, reflecting refinements in the system. In addition, feedback from readers has suggested some useful ideas about how to make the most effective use of the system.

A Psychological Perspective: One problem that became evident with release of the first edition is that many inexperienced bushwalkers, noting that the grading system ranged from 1 to 7, automatically assumed that the midway point (3½) represented a walk of average difficulty. For most readers, this is simply not the case. It is important to realise that only a small minority of readers will ever undertake trips harder than grade 5, and the proportion who do so in their first few years of bushwalking is very small indeed (most experienced bushwalkers only tackle these trips occasionally). Consequently, it is better to consider the grading system as extending from 1 to 5 instead of 1 to 7. By using grade 5 as the psychological "ceiling" of the grading system, you will be less likely to underestimate the difficulty of trips.

Gradual Progression: Because the grading system is never a perfect indication of the difficulty of a walk, don't assume you are competent on routes of a particular grading on the basis of one trip's experience. It is suggested that you undertake at least four walks at a particular level of difficulty before tackling harder trips.

ROAD DIRECTIONS AND DRIVING CONSIDERATIONS

ROAD NAVIGATION

For ease of reference, most road directions have been grouped together in the respective chapter, prior to the route descriptions. Often a particular access road can be used for many different bushwalks.

Like the route descriptions, the road directions are intended to be used with a map and traced out on the map beforehand. In most instances any recent good quality regional road map will suffice, although state maps of the whole of Queensland are unlikely to be adequate on the back roads.

The quality of the road directions varies depending on the detail shown in available road maps and the extent of signposting in the region. In some cases it is useful to use a topographic map in combination with a road map.

When navigating on the back roads, keep careful note of the kilometre reading on your odometer (speedometer), especially on rough roads and at night. When you are forced to drive slowly due to rough roads, or if you are cold or tired, distances become misleading, and you can easily overestimate the distance travelled if you don't note the odometer.

ROAD STANDARDS

Generally the road standards are indicated in each chapter, although remember that rain considerably influences the trafficability of dirt roads. If the year has been wet, expect washouts and extra rough creek crossings on the back roads. If the recent weather has been wet, expect the back roads to be slippery and possibly even untrafficable.

Provided you drive slowly and use care, two wheel drive vehicles are able to negotiate most roads in dry conditions. However, low clearance vehicles may be at a disadvantage on the back roads. Four wheel drive vehicles are essential for most localities in the coastal sandmasses.

OTHER VEHICULAR CONSIDERATIONS

Mechanical Aspects: No special vehicle standard is required for bushwalking, but obviously a car in reasonable mechanical condition is preferable. Some localities are a long way from sources of mechanical assistance, so it is advisable to carry a basic set of spares e.g. a fully inflated tyre, jack, fan belt, set of radiator hoses, tow rope, jumper leads, large water bottle and basic tool kit. Drivers with short-range cars should check petrol requirements if travelling outside of standard shop hours.

Generally, higher than normal tyre pressures preserve tyres on rough roads and help prevent blowouts. It is important to keep tyre valves capped, since grit in the valves is a common cause of flat tyres when driving on dirt roads.

General Driving Safety: People who are mainly accustomed to driving in city and highway conditions often need to modify their driving habits when on forestry tracks and country roads. In particular, the narrowness of these roads requires a number of driving concessions. For example:

- Ensure you keep to the left of the road on the crests of hills and when driving around blind bends, and don't park or stop close to a crest or sharp bend.
- Unlike highway driving, there aren't usually many overtaking opportunities, so often a tailing car cannot overtake unless the leading car pulls over. Even if there are occasional passing opportunities, overtaking is often a lot safer and easier if the leading car slows down or pulls over. Remember to monitor your rear vision mirror so that you notice if cars are following you.
- At night, assist overtaking traffic by using your high beam until the other car is level with you (it is almost impossible to overtake safely if the leading car is constantly using low beam).
- Turn on your headlights (on low beam) when driving in dust or with the sun behind you.
- Slow down (to a crawl if necessary) if stock or wildlife are on the sides of the road, since animals frequently move out in front of cars at the last minute. At night, constantly search ahead for animals along the roadsides.

Muddy Roads: Sometimes rain during a weekend will make the drive out after a bushwalk far more difficult than the drive at the start. In wet mud, it is generally better to employ low engine revolutions and high gears, since high revolutions and power will simply rip up the roads and break traction. Use a gentle touch on the accelerator, sufficient to maintain momentum, but not so great as to break traction or bog. On rare occasions (mainly when driving uphill on slippery surfaces) it is necessary to use higher power and engine revolutions to maintain momentum. The most dangerous time when driving on wet muddy roads is when going downhill. Sometimes if caught in such a predicament you may have no option but to stop and wait for conditions to dry out. If you do attempt descent, stay in low gear and idle down, and manoeuvre the car by gentle acceleration rather than braking if you start to skid. Any deceleration in such conditions will be likely to break traction, and once this occurs it is very difficult to regain control. Descents on muddy roads can be very dangerous if the gradient is steep.

PERMITS FOR NATIONAL PARKS AND OTHER CROWN LANDS

QUEENSLAND NATIONAL PARKS AND STATE FORESTS

The introduction of camping fees for Queensland national parks and state forests in the late 1980s has increased the complexity of organising trips and arranging permits in these areas, especially in the more popular parks. The following explains the procedures at the beginning of 1991.

General Procedures: You can obtain camping application forms and national park and state forest camping guides from the Brisbane offices of the Queensland National Parks and Wildlife Service and the Division of Forestry (see page 299 for addresses and telephone numbers). The guides and forms are also available from other outlets, so enquire by telephone if these localities are inconvenient to you.

The permit applications and accompanying fees are sent to the local national park or state forest office. In popular parks, bookings and payments often have to be made a long time in advance (sometimes up to four months ahead for base camps in holiday times). In other cases booking isn't required and it is acceptable to pay your fees on arrival. It is always advisable to check booking arrangements with the local rangers well before your trip, since they will have no option but to turn you away if you simply turn up and the camp ground is full. The telephone numbers of the local national park and forestry offices are listed at the end of each chapter.

At the time of writing, you need to give at least seven days notice of cancellation to obtain any refund on camping fees.

Base Camps for Large Groups: The difficulty of organising permits for base camps increases with the popularity of the park, the size of the group and if you wish to visit during peak holiday times. Most national park offices nowadays accept provisional bookings (i.e. tentative bookings not accompanied by the relevant camping fees), but if they don't then the problems of making group bookings at popular parks become very difficult. In this situation you may need to finalise numbers and collect fees many months in advance.

Throughwalks: At the time of writing, management plans are being prepared for many national parks in south-east Queensland, and it is likely that most of these will include number limits on the size of throughwalking parties. The limits may possibly be as low as six people in some areas. Don't assume that permits will always be granted. A few places have restrictions, which may vary seasonally or with recent usage. Enquire with the local national park offices for latest details.

Permit applications for throughwalks are made in the same way as for base camps. Among other information, the rangers will need to know:

- Your name and address.
- Party size.
- Car registration numbers of vehicles intended for use.
- Proposed itinerary (in summary), including dates and length of trip and overnight camping locations. N.B. In some national parks, you may be asked to complete a "safety form" recording various details about your trip and the membership of your party.

NEW SOUTH WALES NATIONAL PARKS

At the time of writing, the New South Wales national parks discussed in this book do not have camping fees and it is only necessary to book in advance during peak holiday times. However, always obtain the latest information by telephoning the relevant offices before your trip.

OTHER CROWN LANDS

There is a variety of other types of crown lands near bushwalking areas, including water reserves and prison reserves. Normally entry to water reserves is prohibited, but if you make enquiries with the local water board, short term access permits can sometimes be obtained in special circumstances. The prison reserves at Numinbah Valley and Palen Creek are for low security prisoners and permission to walk through the outskirts can usually be obtained by enquiring with the prison authorities. Conditions vary for other types of crown lands, but generally access is allowed if the lands haven't been set aside for a specific purpose.

PRIVATE LANDOWNERS

Many bushwalking features in south-east Queensland must be accessed across private lands, while some other features are located totally within private lands. These situations have always caused some difficulties, since the attitudes of farmers and graziers vary considerably. Some readily accept bushwalkers, while others are likely to prosecute for trespass if you do not have permission to traverse. Members of the public also vary considerably in the amount of care and responsibility they take. Consequently, there is potential for ill feeling on both sides if bushwalkers don't follow correct procedures when intending to walk on private property.

Generally most landholders allow bushwalkers on their lands if permission is sought first and the landowners are satisfied with their bona-fides. Most problems are caused through ignorance.

What you should do: It is preferable to ask permission well before the trip by telephoning or writing to the owner, then drop in and confirm your presence at the start of the walk. The correct procedure involves courtesy, commonsense and communication. There are three steps:

• Locating the landholder.
• Approach.
• Behaviour on the property.

LOCATING LANDOWNERS

Your first problem is finding out who owns the land. In most of south-east Queensland, the best first point of enquiry is the local office of the National Parks and Wildlife Service. Regional national park rangers are familiar with the local rural communities and are usually able to advise on access conditions affecting national parks. Even when a bushwalking feature is located wholly on private lands, the local ranger can often give you some direction.

Failing the national park ranger being able to supply information, the enquiry process becomes more laborious. The best method is usually to enquire at various farm houses in the vicinity. However, respect the occupants' right to privacy and security by not arriving out of normal daylight hours, especially in remote areas.

Other Methods of Locating Landowners: Shire councils can often assist but usually charge a small search fee. Some bushwalking clubs may also be able to provide information, but with their own reputations to protect, may be reluctant to advise people whose bona-fides are unknown to them.

APPROACHING LANDOWNERS

Typically people dislike approaching landholders, because quite simply it may be difficult to know what to say. Sometimes bushwalkers are also wary about whether they will be well received. Landholders are most likely to react well if the request is simple, open and polite.

You need to say:

• Who you are (you may have to provide your name and address, and the name and address of any club or group that you represent).
• That you wish to request permission to bushwalk on their lands.
• Where and when you intend to go, and for how long.
• The number of people and vehicles in your party.

If you are a member of an organisation such as a bushwalking club, be prepared to provide proof such as a letter on letterhead. Since clubs can be held accountable for the actions of their members, it increases your accountability also. In turn, this means that the landowner is more likely to trust you.

If landholders refuse permission for access, there is little point in "arguing the toss". Sometimes the credibility of landholders' reasons for refusing access may be suspect, but argument is only likely to make the situation worse in the future. It is worthwhile remembering that landholder attitudes often change, being influenced by their recent experiences with members of the public and by what they hear in the rural community of other landowners' experiences.

BEHAVIOUR ON PRIVATE LANDS

It may seem obvious that you need to act responsibly on private lands, but are you aware specifically what is required? Some actions, seemingly unimportant to bushwalkers, can be of greater significance to landholders.

Fences and Gates are obvious examples. They are costly to build and maintain, and landholders like them to last as long as possible. Climbing over gates and fences often strains them, weakening the hinges and stretching fencing wire. You should preferably go through gates and climb between the wire strands of fences. If you must cross over a gate or fence, do so at a post.

Naturally you should leave gates as you found them, whether open or shut. It is not acceptable for the first member of a large party to open a gate and leave it for the last person to close, since confusion may result. The person who opens the gate must stay until the end to shut it, or, if the party is scattered in groups, each should open and shut the gate separately. Neither is it good enough to "close the gate if in doubt", since you may be shutting the stock off from water.

Fires: If you think you might be using a camp or billy fire, ask the landholder first in case of objection. In addition, take stringent precautions.

Stock: Landholders are particularly sensitive about stock disturbance. This can sometimes be caused quite unwittingly e.g. by people camping at a waterhole in a dry season, or by a large strung-out group of bushwalkers walking diagonally across a paddock and cornering stock against a fence. Particular care must be taken if cattle are unused to humans. There have been cases where strung-out groups of people have unintentionally frightened wary cattle hundreds of metres away, causing them to stampede through fences. In these circumstances, it is preferable for large groups of bushwalkers to stay close together so that the cattle have plenty of opportunity to escape.

Litter: Landowners will want their lands left clean, so be scrupulous to observe all the normal ethics of minimum impact bushwalking. Carry out all rubbish and be hygienic in sanitary practices.

Looking north from Mt Mitchell to Mt Castle

3

STARTING BUSHWALKING: BASIC QUESTIONS ANSWERED

This chapter is intended to provide special advice to people who haven't bushwalked before. It answers the most common questions beginners ask about bushwalking and briefly describes the types of conditions you may encounter. It also gives suggestions about how to assess your fitness before embarking on your first walks. Most importantly, however, there is a section to familiarise readers with the very broad range of bushwalking experiences that are possible. This is frequently a source of considerable misunderstanding, and often leads to inexperienced bushwalkers choosing walks inappropriate to their fitness and expectations. The impressions people gain on their first few walks usually decide whether they take up bushwalking as a recreation or are turned off the activity for life, so it is important to learn how to choose appropriate walks.

TEN COMMON QUESTIONS

(1) Is Bushwalking Difficult? Bushwalking can be as easy or challenging as you want to make it. The critical questions are: What type of experience are you seeking from bushwalking, what are your physical abilities in terms of fitness and agility (and possibly your mental determination in the event of problems or discomforts), and how do you find walks that match your abilities and expectations?

Of these, you firstly need to give some thought to the type of experience you are seeking. The next section of this chapter, titled *The Nature of Bushwalking*, highlights how the common term "bushwalking" describes a wide variety of activities and experiences. People's expectations of what bushwalking involves vary greatly according to their prior perceptions.

The difficulty of bushwalks varies immensely. There are plenty of easy bushwalks in south Queensland (some suggestions are given in Chapter 8), and there are also some extraordinarily hard walks. To ensure that bushwalking turns out to be the experience you want it to be, you need to:

- Know what type of experience you are seeking (refer to page19).
- Realistically assess your fitness (refer to page 21).
- Prepare well (refer to page 35), and
- Progress gradually from easy to harder walks.

(2) Is Bushwalking Dangerous? Serious bushwalking mishaps are rare, although when they do occur the intensive publicity often gives the public an exaggerated impression of the dangers. Statistically, bushwalking is one of the safest forms of recreation, and is certainly far safer and less injury prone than physical contact sports. However, the chances of a major accident increase greatly if you act rashly. Of those serious mishaps that do occur, probably 80% or more are caused by foolishness or lack of preparation. Consequently, the likelihood of serious physical injury is largely dependent on the care you take yourself. With a responsible and careful attitude, the time of greatest risk will probably be the driving to and from the walk.

Of course, even with the best precautions you can never eliminate all possibility of a serious accident, but you run this degree of risk in most activities of daily living. There are also likely to be occasional scrapes and scratches, and from time to time there may be minor accidents such as sprained ankles. However, these are barely significant in comparison with the enjoyment and satisfaction that can be gained from this rewarding form of recreation.

(3) How Fit Do I Need To Be? Good fitness is an advantage, but it is not a prerequisite. When you are starting bushwalking, the problem is not so much one of needing to be fit as choosing walks appropriate to your level of fitness. There are numerous easy bushwalks available for unfit people (refer to the suggestions in Chapter 8).

Fitness will develop if you become a regular bushwalker. Many people who take up bushwalking are not particularly fit, but still make a success of it. The first few walks are usually the hardest. Those who discover that their initial bushwalks are very tiring usually also find that they "break the barrier" after three or four trips, after which they feel progressively more comfortable with their performance on each walk. There are also different sorts of fitness. Some experienced bushwalkers would be hard pressed to jog a kilometre without stopping, but are quite capable of carrying heavy packs up steep hills. Usually it is just a matter of bushwalking being the best training for bushwalking, so the more bushwalking you do, the better you get. However, any sort of regular physical exercise will help.

Of course, a basic level of medical fitness is required. If you have any doubts in this regard, obtain proper medical advice. In addition, it will be all the more important to start out with very easy walks and build up gradually, within your doctor's guidelines.

(4) What Types of Difficulties are There? The full list of potential difficulties is quite long. Possible terrain challenges which require physical fitness and agility include steep hills, long distances, creek rockhopping and scrambling and climbing difficulties. In addition, you will need to develop skills and knowledge to be able to solve all the problems of navigation. There is also a variety of other potential problems and discomforts, such as thick vegetation, occasional scratches and bruises, cold, wetness, heat, dehydration, ticks, leeches, thorns, stinging plants and various camping hassles. However, despite the lengthy nature of this list, experience will bring the necessary knowledge, skills and fitness to meet the challenges. In addition, it is usually possible to select and plan your walks so that you only encounter the challenges you choose to.

(5) How Do I Start Bushwalking? It can be as simple as reading Chapter 1 of this book, choosing an appropriate day walk from Chapter 8, gathering some friends and basic items of equipment, and setting out. There are also other options, such as joining a bushwalking club (see page 19), going on some of the Brisbane Forest Park's *Go Bush* activities (see Chapter 9), undertaking day walks while staying at a camping ground or guest house, or joining a commercial bushwalking tour. If you like, you can even get your local paper to help you form your own suburban bushwalking club.

(6) What About Snakes? The greatest fear of many Australians considering a walk in the bush is snake bite. This is a genuine concern, since Australia has by far the most venomous terrestrial snakes in the world. However, the incidence of snake bite is very rare, especially among genuine bushwalkers (most snake bites seem to be in places such as semirural suburbs). You are certainly likely to see snakes if you go bushwalking in non-winter seasons, and occasionally walkers have close encounters. However, the authors are unaware of any genuine bushwalking snake bite incident in south-east Queensland in the 21 years between 1970 and 1990 (i.e. in genuine remote bushwalking areas, rather than in areas close to camp grounds, guest houses, tourist localities etc). In this time, club bushwalkers alone have spent at least 200,000 "person-days" on bushwalking trips in this region. This is not to say that a snake bite won't occur in the future, but the statistical indications are that you'd have to be unlucky. See page 32 for more details.

(7) What Sort of Gear Will I Need? The main day walk items are a day pack, water bottle, map, compass, watch, basic first aid kit, parka, pullover, hat, lunch and snacks. Of these, a map and compass are the main specialised purchases. See page 47 regarding appropriate footwear, and page 52 for a full equipment checklist.

As you become more involved in bushwalking and start undertaking base camps and throughwalks, you will need to acquire items such as sleeping bags, tents etc. Comprehensive advice on equipment is given in Chapter 5.

(8) Is Bushwalking Expensive? The cost depends on what sort of bushwalking you want to do, how committed you become and what equipment you want to buy. Day walking is extremely cheap since you don't need much specialised gear at all, and many people spend years happily going on day trips with very little expense. For base camping and throughwalking you will eventually need to buy some costly equipment, although you can often purchase this gear progressively by hiring, sharing or borrowing particular items. In addition, many people make do with household items instead of specialised equipment in the first year or so of their bushwalking careers, particularly for base camps where weight is less important. A final point to note is that although major items of bushwalking gear are initially expensive, they usually last many years. Bearing all these factors in mind, the long term cost of bushwalking is less than most recreations, and it is certainly much cheaper than activities such as boating, sailing or motor sports. Refer to page 40 for more information about buying equipment.

(9) How Do I Learn Bushwalking Skills? There are various ways - attending training sessions organised by bushwalking clubs and other groups, attending training courses by commercial trainers (e.g. T.A.F.E. colleges), reading, experimenting, practising, talking to other bushwalkers, etc. You will probably need to use several of these methods to become fully proficient.

(10) How Do I Join a Bushwalking Club? There are about a dozen bushwalking clubs in south-east Queensland, including clubs at the Gold and Sunshine Coasts and Toowoomba. The majority are listed in the yellow pages of the local telephone directories under the title "Clubs - Bushwalking" (if necessary a full list can be obtained from the Queensland Federation of Bushwalking Clubs, at G.P.O. Box 1573, Brisbane, Qld 4001). Club activities cover a great range of interests and endeavours, and most clubs allow visitors to participate in several outings before having to pay membership fees. It is recommended that you consider joining a club when you are starting bushwalking, since clubs generally provide a much safer and more organised learning experience than setting out alone.

THE NATURE OF BUSHWALKING

TYPES OF BUSHWALKING EXPERIENCES

It is interesting to ask a variety of people what they imagine when they hear the term "bushwalking", since it conjures up all sorts of visions to the uninitiated. To some a kilometre walk on a graded track is a bushwalk, while others envisage scrambling up lofty peaks or battling through scrub. Many people imagine beautiful natural spectacles in pristine remote areas, but give little thought to the problems involved in reaching them. Some include related recreation activities such as canyoning, climbing and canoeing. All these may be legitimate interpretations of the term "bushwalking" when used in its broadest sense. However, it is important to realise that one person's use of the word will not always equate to another's, and that people's expectations vary greatly according to their previous perceptions.

If you are starting out bushwalking, it is a valuable exercise to clearly identify the types of bushwalking experiences you are seeking. For example, how do your personal expectations compare with the following?

• Some people are seeking full day walks, involving a reasonable expenditure of energy, but wish to avoid difficulties and dangers such as awkward navigation and scrambling.

• Many people enjoy some level of adventure and challenge, provided it is kept "within limits".

• Some people seek a "wilderness experience", undertaking overnight walks (or longer trips) to remote and pristine areas. Usually wilderness enthusiasts place great importance on the solitude and pristinity values of the bush i.e. they don't like to be among large groups of people and they don't like the bush to show signs of human impact or previous visitation. Trips of this nature often involve some hardships and challenges.

• A few bushwalkers are primarily interested in the challenge of bushwalking, and wish to test themselves physically and mentally on very difficult and arduous trips.

• For some people social contact is an important part of bushwalking, while others wish to avoid unfamiliar groups of people.

To help determine your bushwalking expectations, refer also to the information on page 20, and to page 24 regarding particular types of bushwalking experiences available in south-east Queensland.

THE NATURE OF BUSHWALKING TRAVEL

Types of bushwalking travel are often best distinguished by whether or not you follow any sort of track. The following will give you some indication of the different types of travel that may be involved in bushwalking. The categorisation is in approximate order of difficulty.

Graded Track Walking: Graded tracks are official walkways constructed by earth moving methods, just like miniature roads. They are designed to meet specific gradient standards, with the maximum steepness typically about 1 in 10 (hence the term "graded"). They provide the easiest bushwalking conditions, eliminating the need for steep climbs and scrambles as well as the majority of navigation difficulties. The graded track concept of bushwalking is possibly better known in south-east Queensland than most parts of Australia, since Lamington National Park has one of the most extensive graded track networks in the continent. See pages 22 and 127 for further information on graded track walking opportunities.

Other Official Walking Tracks: Not all official walking paths are graded tracks. Often management authorities provide walking tracks which are steeper than the standards used to prescribe a graded track, but which are nevertheless officially maintained and signposted.

Unofficial Tracks and Off-Track Bushwalking: There is a huge variety of unofficial bushwalking routes (i.e. those routes not recognised or maintained by management authorities). Most of these involve either steep hill climbs and/or difficulties such as rockhopping, scrambling or thick scrub (see below), although the amount of challenge varies considerably.

In south-east Queensland, most unofficial bushwalking routes follow ridges and creeks. These routes often develop into rough tracks if they receive sufficient usage. Some people also mark these tracks with coloured tape or by other means, although for both safety and environmental reasons modern bushwalking philosophy disapproves of most forms of track marking (refer page 80).

It is important to realise that there are no maintenance programs for unofficial bushwalking routes. A route well worn or taped on one occasion might be almost indiscernible six months later (this is partly why track marking methods are contentious; refer page 80). Often seasonal factors influence track clarity. In southeast Queensland, many footworn tracks become faint during the spring and summer months, although the paths usually form again through winter (see page 29 and 58 for more details).

Partly due to the fickleness of tracks, and partly for the challenge, some bushwalkers prefer not to rely on track systems and mainly plan their walking routes by the physical features of the land. This is the most classical form of bushwalking travel - walking without recourse to any tracks, route marking systems or other signs left by people. This type of bushwalking is well catered for in south-east Queensland, but requires good navigation skills.

Vegetation and Navigation Difficulties: Unofficial bushwalking routes have a variety of vegetation and navigation challenges. Some vegetation types allow easy travelling with good visibility to assist navigation, while some obstruct progress and/ or create great navigational problems (see pages 26 to 27 for more information).

Rockhopping: Many off-track bushwalking routes travel along creeks, and if the banks are steep (as they are along the majority of south-east Queensland creeks) you will probably have to travel along the creek bed itself. This is usually done by rockhopping - stepping and jumping from rock to rock along the creek bed - but sometimes wading is also necessary. Rockhopping is always a slow form of travel (usually less than 1 1/2km per hour), and progress can become extraordinarily slow if conditions are wet and slippery (occasionally as little as 500m per hour). In difficult conditions, rockhopping can also be quite hazardous. Conditions affecting rockhopping are partly seasonal. In autumn when the weather is often wet, and in winter when the rocks are shaded due to the low angle of sun, algal growth is greatest and the creek rocks become very slippery. The algae is driest in spring and early summer, so that unless there has been recent rain, these seasons usually provide the best rockhopping conditions.

Scrambling and Climbing: There are plenty of bushwalks in south-east Queensland which don't involve rock scrambling, but it is important to realise that there are also many off-track walks which do include scrambling difficulties. Some problems are relatively small and minor, but once again, the amount of challenge varies considerably. Probably 50% to 60% of off-track routes can be undertaken by people with an average level of scrambling ability. Most other routes can be undertaken by capable parties with good scrambling skills, provided the leader is experienced and competent with a safety belay. However, the hardest bushwalking routes are very precipitous and require great care and skill.

If you wish to learn rockclimbing and ropework skills, seek instruction from a qualified experienced instructor. Do not try to teach yourself, and do not experiment with book-learnt methods without the aid of an instructor. A responsible instructor will ensure that you always use a safety belay from above until you are very experienced.

N.B. Readers should refer to comments on page 9 about use of the route grading system in rocky and precipitous areas.

ASSESSING YOUR LEVEL OF FITNESS

Most people starting bushwalking lack a realistic view of their fitness and ability in the bush. Bushwalking competence depends on many factors, including physical fitness, muscular strength, depth and range of walking experience, navigation skills, climbing and ropework skills, and even planning and analytical abilities. Which of these are important or critical will depend on the route in question, but one fact is certain - you are likely to lack many of these qualities when you're just starting out. It is important that you learn to assess your abilities rationally and objectively. Assessing your physical fitness is the first step.

An apt example of how inexperienced people often choose walks inappropriate to their level of fitness is the South Ridge of Mt Barney. This has the reputation of being the "easy" route on the mountain, so many people who don't get regular exercise set out to climb the peak without any previous bushwalking experience. Consequently, it is not uncommon for experienced bushwalkers descending the ridge to meet somebody at 2 or 3 o'clock in the afternoon, less than half way up, asking "How much further to the top - can't be far now, hey?"

In this case, the word "easy" is quite misleading. The ridge is certainly much easier than most other routes on the mountain, but the simple fact is that there is just no "easy" way to climb a 1360m high peak. Try walking up a dozen flights of stairs in a city building and you will soon learn that gaining sheer elevation is hard work in anybody's terms. Unless you play sport regularly or exercise frequently, you will simply not be fit enough to climb Mt Barney on your first bushwalk, even by the easiest route.

Some questions to consider about your fitness when choosing your first bushwalks are:

(1) Do you get regular physical exercise?

(2) How strenuous is your regular exercise? All exercise will help, but a 2km walk around suburban streets every morning is not likely to equip you to tackle harder bushwalks. You will still need to build up gradually.

(3) What is your age? In particular, middle aged people need to carefully assess their level of fitness, since they are often unaware of their lack of fitness.

(4) In your past, have you played sport or been involved in the type of physical activity that would give you the muscular and cardiovascular development needed for more strenuous bushwalks?

After considering these questions, refer to the grading standards given on page 9 and 10 to decide the types of bushwalks you should tackle initially.

POTPOURRI

Graded track systems: Graded track walking has already been mentioned on page 20. South-east Queensland has one of the most extensive graded track systems in Australia. Most notable is the system in northern Lamington between Binna Burra and O'Reillys, where there are some 150km of excellently constructed tracks (page 127). Other notable track systems occur in national parks at Girraween, Cunninghams Gap and Springbrook. Most track systems can be visited on either day trips or base camps.

Graded tracks give excellent opportunities for people starting out walking, visiting some of the most spectacular features of the areas and eliminating the need for steep climbs and scrambles. Sadly, the graded tracks don't receive the usage they deserve. Some people berate graded tracks as too easy, but graded track walking can be made as easy or hard as you like by simply varying the distance.

Guest houses: For those who lack camping equipment, guest houses such as O'Reillys and Binna Burra provide opportunities to enjoy the graded track systems, together with motel style accommodation. Many people have been introduced to bushwalking in this manner. There are also camping grounds near both guest houses.

Bushwalking clubs: Refer to page 19 (Question 10).

The "Go Bush" Program: "Go Bush" is a program of organised bushwalks and nature-orientated activities operated by Brisbane Forest Park. The program provides another excellent means of starting out bushwalking. Refer to Chapter 9 for full details.

THROUGHWALKING

Throughwalking is the name bushwalkers use for overnight trips carrying a full pack. Throughwalking is harder than day walking, but the rewards are more memorable. Events and experiences seem all the more vivid and enriching if they have involved a major sacrifice of kilojoules and comforts. It is often at the campsite, or in the light of the setting sun and early morning, that the mind and spirit receive their greatest fulfilment. In the bushwalking calendar, winter is often referred to as the through-walking season, for this is the time when Queensland's weather becomes cool enough to allow the hardest and longest trips.

Many people who enjoy bushwalking convince themselves that they lack the muscular strength and fitness needed for throughwalking. However, it is possible to select easy throughwalks initially and build up gradually to harder trips (refer to the suggestions in Chapter 8). It is also possible to use "super-lightweight" bushwalking techniques to greatly limit the weight of your pack (see below).

Your first few throughwalks are likely to be tiring, but if you persevere you will gradually become fitter and more confident. The best training for carrying a pack is carrying a pack. Everyone has to start somewhere, and if you never try throughwalking you may never gain the fitness that you think you need.

The Super-Lightweight Approach: Those who specialise in super-lightweight backpacking often achieve remarkable results e.g. a two day pack under 12kg. Not every bushwalker practices these techniques, but it is important for beginners to be aware of the approach since it will usually take some time to develop the strength to carry heavy packs. The idea is to limit the weight of your pack by critically examining every item you intend to carry. Some people even cut part of the handle off their tooth brush. This may be a little extreme, but it serves to demonstrate what some people will do to save weight.

Measures which super-light backpackers commonly recommend include weighing everything on the kitchen scales before packing to eliminate every unnecessary gram, using ultra-lightweight gear, sleeping in your warm clothing so that you can make do with a lighter sleeping bag, using hutchies or bivvy bags instead of tents, carefully estimating your exact food requirements (measuring, say, your muesli by the spoonful), using solid fuel stoves instead of normal (liquid fuel) stoves, eliminating comfort clothing, eliminating other comfort items, eliminating any item which hasn't been used at least once on the last three trips, and leaving loose coins in the car.

Traps of the Super-Lightweight Approach: The super-light approach does not suit everybody and there are some traps. One is that many super-light walkers cut out too many safety items. This may be fine if you are mentally prepared for the potential discomforts and difficulties and have the experience to improvise to solve different types of bushwalking problems, but this is often not the case. Some super-light walkers are simply inadequately prepared and get into difficulties if the trip does not go as expected. They may also end up being "carried" by their bushwalking companions i.e. they may end up repeatedly borrowing items from first aid kits and the like, crowding into other people's tents if the weather is worse than expected, or being an emotional burden by complaining about their discomforts. Another problem of the super-light approach is that, if you don't try, you may never develop the physical strength or mental confidence to carry heavier packs (in particular, lack of mental confidence to carry a heavy pack is surprisingly common among some groups of experienced super-light bushwalkers). Therefore, the best approach for many people is a balance, starting out on easier walks with a light pack, then gradually building up to heavier packs and harder walks.

4

BUSHWALKING CONDITIONS
IN SOUTH-EAST QUEENSLAND

This chapter gives a detailed description of the types of bushwalking experiences available in south-east Queensland, and the terrain conditions and problems you can expect to encounter. The information is not only intended for people who haven't bushwalked before, but also for experienced bushwalkers who are visiting or have just moved to the region. Like other regions of Australia, south-east Queensland has its own peculiar combination of bushwalking hazards.

TYPES OF BUSHWALKING EXPERIENCES

South-east Queensland offers many types of bushwalking experiences, including:

Graded Track Walking: Graded tracks provide the easiest bushwalking conditions, and south-east Queensland has far more graded track walking opportunities than most regions of Australia. Refer to pages 20 and 22 for full details.

Off-Track Walking: There is a large range of off-track walking opportunities, with many different types of terrain and many different degrees of difficulty. Refer to the next section, *General Terrain Conditions* (page 25), and to page 20 for more details.

Throughwalking is the name bushwalkers use to refer to overnight walks carrying a full pack (see page 23). South-east Queensland's most famous throughwalking regions are contained in the Scenic Rim, an arc of mountains extending some 200km from Coolangatta to Laidley (see chapters 10 to 15). However, the granite and coastal regions (chapters 17 and 20) also provide many outstanding throughwalks. The most popular throughwalking itineraries are from 2 to 5 days in length, but longer walks (up to 3 weeks) are also available.

Rockhopping is very common on off-track bushwalks in south-east Queensland, with Lamington, Springbrook, Mt Barney, Brisbane Forest Park and the Conondale Ranges being particularly notable. Rockhopping trips also provide many of the region's best summer off-track bushwalks, although it is advisable to avoid wet conditions. Refer to pages 20 and 21 for more details.

Scrambling and Climbing Trips: Many off-track bushwalks in this region involve rock scrambling difficulties, ranging from quite easy problems to extremely precipitous terrains. See page 21 for more details.

Base Camping opportunities in south-east Queensland are mainly centred around national park and state forest camping areas, although this leaves no shortage of options. There are official camping grounds in most regions discussed in this book (refer to the *Special Notes* of each regional chapter). There are also a few unofficial base camping sites in undeveloped state forest areas and some other places.

Trips with Bushwalking Clubs: There are about a dozen bushwalking clubs in south-east Queensland - refer to pages 18 and 19 for details.

Day Trips from Guest Houses: This is yet another type of bushwalking experience available in this region, combining bushwalking with the luxuries of resort style accommodation. In particular, Lamington National Park's two major accommodation centres (O'Reilly's Guest House and Binna Burra Resort) offer excellent opportunities of this style. See also pages 22, 121 and 131.

Bushwalks with Commercial Tours: This is a small but expanding activity in south-east Queensland. Details of available tours can be obtained from various travel agents.

Canoeing, although obviously a different type of recreation from bushwalking, is nevertheless popular among bushwalkers. The only canoeing trips discussed in this book are on the Noosa River in Cooloola National Park, although canoeists also visit less pristine rivers in south-east Queensland as well as the popular northern New South Wales canoeing rivers.

GENERAL TERRAIN CONDITIONS

Brisbane probably has a greater variety of bushwalking terrains within easy reach than any other capital city in Australia. In the very rugged terrains of the Scenic Rim, there are spectacular mountain vistas, high rocky peaks, deep wet gorges, superb waterfalls and serene rainforest creeks. To the south-west, the granite regions exhibit spectacular domes and balancing rocks, while Sundown National Park displays stark arid vistas more typical of places such as the Flinders Ranges. In contrast to all of this, the coastal sandmasses have wide sandy beaches, magnificent freshwater lakes and spectacular coloured sands. A final contrast is the style of human influence. The bushwalking regions vary from areas with extensive graded track systems to rugged terrains showing little sign of previous human presence. While south-east Queensland lacks the vast remoteness of wilderness areas such as in south-west Tasmania and far northern Australia, this variety provides it with its own peculiar bushwalking character.

This book has divided south-east Queensland into twelve separate bushwalking regions, each of which is distinct in the nature of its terrain. Three different levels of terrain ruggedness are evident. Mountainous regions, which should be considered rugged by Australian standards, include the six regions of the Scenic Rim, many of the Boonah/Ipswich peaks and the Glass House Mountains. In contrast, the coastal sandmasses almost totally lack dangerously steep terrain, being mainly undulating coastal dunes. In between these extremes of ruggedness are the Granite regions, the Conondale Ranges and Brisbane Forest Park.

VEGETATION CONDITIONS AND HAZARDS

INFLUENCE ON BUSHWALKING TRAVEL

In your route planning for off-track trips, it is necessary to be aware of the problems associated with different vegetation types. The most common natural vegetation types in south-east Queensland's bushwalking areas are subtropical rainforest, wet sclerophyll forest, open dry sclerophyll forest, sclerophyll woodland, different types of heath (both coastal and montane) and various types of sclerophyll/heath mixes. In addition, logging and agricultural regrowth may be encountered in some areas.

Rainforest: In Australia, the term "rainforest" is broadly used to refer to any luxuriant terrestrial forest with a complete canopy cover, provided that it does not have a significant component of eucalypt species. The regions discussed in this book contain the most extensive areas of subtropical rainforest in Australia. Most notable in this regard is the eastern Scenic Rim, which is typically wet and lush in character. As one proceeds westwards to the central Scenic Rim and the Main Range, the vegetation becomes drier in character, although there is still a major component of rainforest.

Rainforest is commonly imagined as dense and impenetrable, but this is not necessarily the case. If totally undisturbed by storms or human influences, mature rainforest in flat terrain (e.g. along ridge tops or creeks of gentle gradient) is usually relatively open, with very little understory growth. However, where storms, logging or steep slopes allow light to penetrate the canopy, the understory may become very dense indeed.

There are many different types of rainforest communities, so it is not possible to make an all-encompassing statement about how rainforest affects off-track bushwalking travel. In good conditions travel is generally between 1km/hour and 2 1/2 km/hour, although progress may be much slower in dense vegetation. One common problem is that rainforest nearly always presents significant navigation problems (see page 29). Another is that rainforest usually harbours a variety of stinging and thorny plants which provide for painful encounters (see pages 27 to 29).

Wet Sclerophyll Forest is typically a luxuriant forest dominated by tall eucalypts and/or brush box, with a dense understory of either rainforest and/or wet heath species. Wet sclerophyll forest often occurs in the vicinity of rainforest, but this is not always the case. Generally, similar comments can be made about travel in wet sclerophyll areas as apply to rainforest.

Dry Sclerophyll Forest and Woodland: The difference between forest and woodland is simply its height. The main trees in these vegetation communities are often eucalypts, but acacias and other species are also common. Walking difficulty mainly depends on the density of the understory, which is typically composed of heath species (see below).

Heath: The word "heath" is used in this book in its broad sense i.e. to refer to any vegetation type that tends to be relatively low, scrubby and resilient, with tough sclerophyllous leaves. There are literally scores of different heath vegetations in south-east Queensland. Montane heath is common in the rockier and drier mountain areas, such as at Mts Barney and Maroon. Here it mostly occurs as an understory to sclerophyll forest or woodland, although montane heath also sometimes occurs as a dominant vegetation form (e.g. Daves Creek at Binna Burra). In the coastal sandmasses, heath vegetation is the most common vegetation type, occurring both as an understory and as a dominant vegetation type. Brilliant wildflower displays are characteristic of most types of heath vegetation.

Rate of travel in heath vegetation varies enormously. Possibly the thickest heath communities are in coastal areas, where "dodder vine" sometimes binds the plants together, making the scrub almost impenetrable. In extreme cases, travel can be slowed to 400m per hour. However, the density of heath vegetation varies greatly, and some heath types have very little effect on travelling rate. The density is also dramatically influenced by recent bushfire history, so the conditions may differ considerably from year to year.

Regrowth Scrub: Although popular bushwalking routes tend to avoid logged areas, most bushwalking regions in south-east Queensland have some regrowth scrub in their peripheries. This may be due to either logging, pastoral or agricultural disturbance. In addition, a few regions such as the D'Aguilar and Conondale Ranges have been logged very extensively, so there is always a danger of encountering regrowth scrub in these areas. In many logged areas, the extent and thickness of nettles, stinging trees, lawyer and lantana is extreme, even thirty or forty years after the cessation of logging. For these reasons, you always need to plan your trips carefully if there has been previous logging or clearing activities in the region.

SPECIFIC FLORA HAZARDS

It is valuable for bushwalkers in south-east Queensland to become familiar with specific flora hazards as early as possible in their bushwalking experience. The plants are listed below in approximate order of severity. With the exception of stinging trees, which have a wide variety of habitats, most of the following are typically associated with disturbed localities such as old logging sites, and are rarely profuse where there has been no previous disturbance.

Stinging Trees (also called gympie trees) are the most serious hazard to note, since severe stings cause intense pain which may recur for hours, days or even weeks. The trees are found in rainforest and some wet sclerophyll areas, being most common in disturbed localities and along creeks. They are recognised by their heart-shaped leaves, which are typically (but not always) bright green and perforated by insect holes. The leaves range in size from very small to over 30cm across, with the youngest leaves normally having the most painful sting. The trees have a light coloured bark and vary in size from miniature seedlings to massive forest giants. There are several species, the most common having leaves covered in fine hairs which deliver its potent toxin. However, the sting from the smooth-leaved stinging tree (which also has hairs, although they may be difficult to see) can be just as painful, often more so.

If stung by a stinging tree, the painful and recurring nature of the sting makes a lasting impression. An accidental brush against a leaf is all that is required to deliver a painful sting, so always be alert for these plants. Most bushwalkers receive occasional minor stings and alertness soon becomes second nature. Despite the painful nature of the stings, most fade within a day. Severe stings may recur for a somewhat longer period, but it is very rare for any sting to have long term consequences. However, you need to take special care to avoid leaves at face height.

There is no widely accepted remedy if you are stung, although it helps to apply skin irritation ointments which contain an anaesthetic and to avoid frequent washing of

Stinging tree leaves

the area. One treatment which may assist if applied promptly is the "sticky plaster method". This involves applying strongly adhesive plaster dressing to the sting site, and then pulling it off. Repeat the process several times, tearing the plaster off in a different direction each time. The treatment is reported to remove many of the plant's tiny stinging hairs (as well, of course, as any natural hair on the skin, which may also be painful).

Lawyer (Wait-a-While) Vine: This plant belongs to the only genus of Australian palms which has a vine habit. It grows in rainforest, often in dense thickets but also as an individual plant (the former normally where there has been previous canopy disturbance). It has inconspicuous tendrils laden with numerous tiny thorns, and the tendrils have an almost lecherous habit of grabbing the most tender of places - face, legs and numerous places in between. Tough skin and clothing are useful to withstand the onslaught of this formidable plant. If "grabbed," the fine thorns will cause local inflammation, although this can be avoided if you remove them promptly with a sterile needle and tweezers.

Lantana: This is an introduced noxious plant which forms thickets in disturbed localities such as old logging and agricultural areas. Fortunately, severe lantana infestations are mainly restricted to the peripheries of most bushwalking regions in south-east Queensland, although there are still localities where it presents major problems. The branches are rather scratchy, but the main difficulties for bushwalkers are its sheer density and extensiveness. Some infestations are major impediments and may cause extremely slow progress. The worst infestations are found in Brisbane Forest Park, the Conondale Ranges and the valleys east of Springbrook.

Raspberry and Barb Wire (Smilax) Vine: These plants are typically found in wet sclerophyll forest and rainforest edges. Both are barbed vines, and both are frequently encountered looping through low vegetation around knee height. They are often responsible for cuts and scratches to the legs. A number of other vines of similar nature inhabit disturbed rainforest areas.

Stinging Nettles typically grow at knee height in the same types of situations as stinging trees. However, although they are initially painful, the sting fades quickly.

Other Plants: There are many other thorny plants in rainforest areas, such as thornwood, which is a common name for a variety of trees with thorny spikes covering their trunks. The thorns cause local inflammation similar to a severe splinter, but can be removed with a sterile needle and tweezers.

NAVIGATION HAZARDS

Navigation is the skill of finding your way and arriving at your destination on time. To navigate safely, you need to understand and be able to predict what difficulties you might face.

Navigation hazards result from three main environmental components - the terrain, the vegetation and the weather. Navigation hazards can also be considered from two different perspectives - disorientating hazards, which cause you to lose the route or actually become lost, and travelling rate hazards, which may cause your party to be delayed and perhaps overdue.

Vegetation is the main navigation hazard in south-east Queensland. Many people new to bushwalking in this region are unaware of the difficulties of navigating in thickly vegetated areas, especially in rainforest which is often very extensive and usually blankets out all views of reference landmarks. There are places in Lamington National Park where you can walk for days without views. Even in less extensive regions, rainforest has frequently been responsible for parties becoming disorientated and overdue, with search and rescue operations resulting. If you lose track of your position or become disorientated in rainforest, it is especially difficult to relocate the route or find your position. An additional problem is that tracks often become obscured, particularly in late spring (when there is heavy leaf fall) and summer (when vegetation growth is fastest and walking activity least). Refer to page 58 for further information about the problems and skills of rainforest travel.

As well as the danger of disorientation, the sheer thickness of some types of vegetation can be a navigation hazard, causing unforeseen delays. As well as rainforest, heath vegetation (both coastal and montane) may present significant problems in this respect.

Terrain Hazards: The principal terrain hazards in south Queensland lie in precipitous areas, where there may be a danger of becoming cliffbound or losing the route amongst cliffs or crags. You need to take care in precipitous regions that you always have a means of retreat, especially if you are unsure of the exact route.

Weather can also be a navigation hazard if it obscures views of landmarks or causes disorientation e.g. mist or cloud. However, this danger is more typical of the open alpine areas in southern Australia than the relatively vegetated terrain in south-east Queensland. In this region, it is unlikely that weather conditions alone would cause long term disorientation, although they could become serious in combination with terrain hazards e.g. if you were caught in mist or cloud when you were trying to find your way in a very precipitous area without a recognised route.

WEATHER CONDITIONS AND WATER AVAILABILITY

While south-east Queensland does not have as many weather hazards as the far north and far south of Australia, both heat and cold can present serious problems if you are poorly prepared. People are often ignorant about the weather extremes that may be encountered.

HEAT AND DEHYDRATION

With the exceptions of Lamington and Springbrook, the terrains of most south Queensland bushwalking regions have a considerable amount of open vegetation. Consequently, heat, glare and sunburn can be significant problems in the hotter months. Many localities are not recommended for summer walking, and a few routes would be almost intolerable during this time. Winter is the preferred season for harder trips, and even in spring and autumn you must sometimes allow for the prospect of being delayed by hot conditions. In hot weather, rainforest areas provide the main bushwalking opportunities.

The hottest conditions occur on northern slopes with open vegetation, and in rocky and sandy terrains which have high reflectivity. Refer to the *Special Notes* in each chapter for detailed information about which areas are likely to have hot conditions. A good hat is essential in all regions.

Heat is most dangerous if coupled with dehydration, in which case you need to be wary of heat stroke, a potentially lethal condition. Sometimes people visit bushwalking localities in hot weather with little thought given to water availability, which is foolish. Many bushwalkers also fail to drink sufficient water when the opportunity arises, and consequently suffer "dry horrors" at night and occasionally more severe illness. If you feel affected by the heat, rest in the shade and drink plenty of water, and avoid travelling again until conditions cool off. Always carry ample water supplies.

WATER AVAILABILITY

South-east Queensland is not a dry region in Australian terms, but there are still times and places where water is difficult to find. The Lamington and Springbrook regions and parts of the coastal sandmasses are the only areas where water is relatively plentiful. In other places water may need to be carried in some quantity. On day walks it is typical to carry between 1 and 2 litres per person, depending on season. Many water points on throughwalks are soaks requiring a cup to fill bottles, and often there is only one water pick-up each day. In these conditions it would be typical to carry from 3 to 5 litres per person in winter, and somewhat more in warmer months. Some throughwalking routes are not practical in summer for this reason.

Water Quality is usually good, although in the cattle areas which surround some of the bushwalking regions, you may wish to carry water purification tablets or drink only boiled water. At Lamington people unused to drinking creek water sometimes suffer mild diarrhoea, but this is rarely serious. In the coastal sandmasses much of the water is stained deep reddish-yellow by tannins, but this does not affect its drinking qualities.

Finding Water: Creeks and soaks in south-east Queensland are wettest from mid-autumn to early winter and driest from spring to midsummer. Provided there have been normal autumn rains, most recognised water points continue to flow well during winter, despite this normally being a dry season. However, some water points on northern slopes dry up quickly after August.

Recognised water points are described in the text, although in most regions it is possible to find other water points by applying a few basic principles. Look for creeks and gullies on your map where:

- Creeks drain southern slopes, especially if the map indicates a wetter type of vegetation.
- Creeks have large catchments (some creeks which run parallel to ridge systems have large catchments while still being close to the ridge crest; this phenomenon is especially common along the border route between Wilsons Peak and Tweed Trig).
- Several small creeks or gullies join close together.
- There is a sudden change in the slope of the creek bed. While this is the least reliable indicator, pools are often found in creeks immediately before a sudden steep section, or where a creek levels out suddenly at the base of a steep slope.

In the coastal sandmasses, emergency water can often be found by digging at the base of large dunes.

COLD AND HYPOTHERMIA

Queensland is a relatively warm state, so many people underestimate the threat of cold weather. It is important to realise that extremes of cold are possible in most of the bushwalking regions discussed in this book. Winter night temperatures in the valleys around the Scenic Rim may drop to minus 5 degrees or lower, and light snow falls have occurred in mountain areas several times in the last decade (on one occasion the snow fall was quite notable). In addition, the mountain regions are often wet in summer and autumn, and in these conditions unfit or ill-equipped bushwalkers could place themselves in some risk. There have been definite cases of preliminary hypothermia in summer at Lamington, and in winter hypothermia would certainly be possible if you were caught out overnight in the mountains without proper equipment. The main reason why south-east Queensland is not a high risk region is that the winter is normally a dry season.

Conditions which contribute to hypothermia are cold, wetness, wind chill, lack of fitness, lack of proper clothing and equipment, fatigue and low blood sugars. It is general bushwalking practice to be prepared for cold and wet weather on all trips. This means carrying suitable clothing even on summer day walks. If you are caught out ill-equipped in cold wet weather, it is particularly important that you not exhaust your blood sugars. Keep eating sweets and don't push yourself to the point of severe fatigue. It is normally safer to seek shelter and stay put than continue travelling when you are very cold.

STORMS AND LIGHTNING

Thunderstorms generally increase in severity as one travels north in the continent, and many southern visitors are surprised at the ferocity of those in south-east Queensland. The worst storms tend to occur in spring and summer after hot days. Hailstorms are also encountered in these conditions and can bring sudden cold conditions.

If lightning is evident, avoid high peaks, knolls and open areas. If you decide to shelter under overhangs or caves, avoid positions immediately under the lip or where you would be touching against wet rock. When lightning strikes a wet vertical feature, much of the charge flows down on the outside of the rainsoaked rock. Similarly, when trees are struck it tends to flow down through the bark. It is preferable to avoid sheltering under trees, but if you do, you might reduce the danger by keeping well clear of the trunk.

FAUNA HAZARDS

Australia has few dangerous terrestrial animals, but it does have a considerable number of extremely venomous snakes. The other main fauna hazards in south-east Queensland are leeches and ticks, although in unusual circumstances animals such as spiders and bees could be of some concern.

SNAKES

The greatest fear of many Australians considering a walk in the bush is snake bite. This is a genuine concern, since bushwalkers are often a long way from sources of help and Australia has by far the most venomous terrestrial snakes in the world. However, snake bite is very rare, so don't let snake paranoia mar your enjoyment of bushwalking.

The most important thing to remember about snakes is to watch for them and avoid them. There is never a reason to kill a snake that is not near civilisation. Attacking a snake is one of the most serious ways of putting yourself at risk. If you surprise a snake at close quarters, retreat immediately and quickly. If you cannot walk around it, wait a few moments and it will usually move. A most important protective measure is to always wear good footwear.

In the mountain regions of south-east Queensland it is rare to see venomous snakes in winter, which eases the concerns for winter bushwalkers. However, they are active in all non-winter seasons (between late August and May), and are occasionally seen in the coastal regions during the cooler months.

How Common is Snake Bite? The authors are unaware of any snake bite incident in a genuine remote bushwalking area in south Queensland in the 21 years between 1970 and 1990. In this time, the number of "person-days" of bushwalking by club walkers alone would be at least 200,000. Most snake bites seem to occur in places such as semirural suburbs. There have also been occasional snake bite incidents in national park localities in south Queensland close to camp grounds or tourist areas, but these account for only a handful of mishaps in two decades. Of course, this is not to say that a snake bite won't occur in the future, since occasionally bushwalkers do have close encounters. However, the statistical indications are that you'd have to be unlucky.

Common Snakes in South-east Queensland: Tiger snakes are the most common dangerous snakes in the mountain regions of south-east Queensland, being frequently seen on the graded tracks at Lamington and other areas of the Scenic Rim. In Queensland they are mainly restricted to rainforest, wet sclerophyll forest and nearby environs, but around Cooloola and Gympie they occur in a variety of other habitats. Compared to their counterparts in southern Australia, most tiger snakes in south Queensland's mountain regions are relatively small, being typically slim and less than a metre long (this does not mean they are not dangerous). Their banding is also usually less evident, so that they may initially appear a dull brown. However, large and/or classically-banded specimens are occasionally encountered. Other dangerous snakes which may occur include taipans, rough-scaled snakes, brown snakes and death adders.

Red-bellied black snakes are also common. These beautiful snakes are not as venomous as the other species mentioned, but are still dangerous. There is also a variety of nonvenomous snakes such as carpet pythons and tree snakes. The former are common in all seasons and are sometimes aggressive in warmer weather. Pythons are often very large, and in threatening posture the snake presumably believes that its size makes up for lack of venom, a theory with which few bushwalkers disagree when faced with three metres of angry carpet snake.

Snake Identification: Snake colour is highly variable and is the least reliable indication of a snake's identity. For example, tiger snakes, taipans, brown snakes and several other species may appear similar, with common colouring being brown or black. However, in the unlikely event of a bite, identification can be made by venom analysis.

SNAKE BITE FIRST AID

It is recommended that you read a proper first aid manual for a comprehensive description of snake bite first aid. The following summarises the procedure:

- Do not attempt to kill the snake.
- Apply roller bandages to the bite area and as much of the limb as possible, bandaging firmly to constrict the lymph vessels.
- In order to further restrict spread of the venom via the lymph system, immobilise the limb with a splint and do not let the patient move.
- Do not cut the area or wash the bite.
- Seek help and medical evacuation urgently.
- Use cardiovascular resuscitation if necessary.

Antivenene is available for all species of snakes and is very effective in most cases.

LEECHES AND TICKS

Leeches and ticks are both common in south-east Queensland. They usually only cause local pain and swelling, but occasionally more serious reactions are experienced. A strange fact about these pests is that some people attract them more than others.

Leeches are mainly a problem in rainforest regions. They are most common after rain, and sometimes can be extremely numerous. The best means of repelling these pests is a rub-on insect repellent smothered over the boots and socks. Apply the repellent when your boots are dry at the start of the walk, since it lasts much longer if it soaks into the dry leather than if the leather is already wet. If necessary, reapply the repellent on the walk itself.

If leeches attach themselves, apply salt or insect repellent or simply pull them off. A tight band-aid will stop any bleeding. If they attach to your finger as you are pulling them off, use the index finger of your other hand to flick them away. Ensure that you do not flick them onto other people. The occurrence of the AIDS virus has raised the question whether leeches could spread blood diseases. Although it seems highly unlikely, this possibility has never been entirely eliminated, especially in situations where a leech fed on one person and then quickly reattached to another.

Ticks: Ticks usually cause more serious inflammation than leeches, but are not as common. Different types of ticks differ notably in their toxicity, and people also differ markedly in their sensitivity to the bites. Their frequency varies considerably, apparently according to seasonal conditions. You might not pick up a tick for years, then pick up several on one walk. Contrary to popular misconceptions, they are quite common in rainforest areas as well as sclerophyll forest.

Application of insect repellent to boots and socks will help control ticks, although not to the same extent as with leeches. Ticks can be removed by pulling or with tweezers but, if deeply embedded, it is better to kill them first with kerosene. Avoid squeezing the tick since this will inject more poison. A quick clean extraction is preferable. This is particularly important if the tick is in a vascular area such as the scalp, or near the face or neck, since an allergic swelling could potentially interfere with the breathing passage. Some ticks are very small and it is useful to carry a magnifying glass and an extra fine pair of tweezers. The smallest ticks often bring the worst reactions.

OTHER FAUNA PROBLEMS

Although none are likely to present significant threats to bushwalkers, other possible fauna hazards include spiders, scorpions, centipedes, ants, bees, wasps and platypus.

Spiders, Scorpions, Centipedes etc: At the time of writing there is no historical evidence of these creatures being a serious threat to bushwalkers in south-east Queensland. However, scientific research suggests that the arboreal species of funnel web spider found here is extremely venomous, and the toxicity of many other spider venoms is unknown. In the unlikely event of a spider bite resulting in a serious medical problem, treat the patient as you would for snake bite. Scorpions give a painful sting but it usually doesn't last more than a few minutes. Many of these animals are active at night, so a tent with a sewn in floor and well designed doors is an advantage.

Platypus occur in some creeks and the male has a poisonous spur attached to each back leg. Its sting is extremely painful, although it is unlikely that anyone would be stung unless they tried to handle the animal.

Ant, Wasp and Bee Stings are rarely considered serious threats. However, in most cases of animal stings there is a remote possibility of a severe allergic reaction, called anaphylactic shock. This causes general collapse of the victim who may die unless the cardiovascular system is maintained. Expired air resuscitation and cardiac compression may be required to achieve this. Bee stings in particular seem to be associated with anaphylactic shock, although this is undoubtedly largely because of the frequency of bee stings in Australia. In addition, in 1980 there was a freak bushwalking accident in south-east Queensland in which a party was savagely attacked by a swarm of feral bees, after their hive (a log) was accidently dislodged. To treat bee stings, promptly remove the sting by scraping lightly with an implement such as a blunt knife or long fingernail, moving it underneath and upwards. Do not squeeze the sting during the removal process.

5

PREPARATION SAFETY AND EQUIPMENT

The last event that anyone wants to encounter when bushwalking is an injury or serious mishap. Thankfully, accidents can usually be avoided. Genuine accidents, over which people have little control, account for only a minority of bushwalking misfortunes. Most mishaps result from lack of preparation or people taking foolish risks. Preparation is the first key to bushwalking safety, and also the most important.

This chapter describes how to prepare for a bushwalk, and provides advice on the range of equipment and skills you will need. While some information here is specifically applicable to south-east Queensland, much is relevant anywhere in Australia.

PREPARATION: THE KEY TO SUCCESSFUL BUSHWALKING VENTURES

The fundamental principles of bushwalking safety are:

- Being prepared, both in terms of knowledge and equipment.
- Using care and sound judgment.

However, that familiar scout adage, "be prepared", has a broader meaning than many people realise. It relates not only to your equipment and the skills you should possess, but also to what you know about the area you intend to visit, and the information you provide to others.

In relation to the area you intend to visit, your primary task is information gathering. You should learn as much as possible about the nature of the terrain and vegetation, including:

- The ruggedness of the area, and if there are cliffs, gorges or similar features in the region.

- The types of vegetation, and whether it will impede travel or obscure views of landmarks.
- The potential hazards of the country, including navigation hazards caused by the terrain, vegetation or weather.
- The weather extremes possible (either cold or hot).
- The location of recognised routes and campsites
- The nature and quality of tracks.
- The location of nearby settled areas.
- Where water can be found.
- Whether permits or the landholder's consent are required to travel or camp on any public or private lands.

This information can be acquired from a variety of sources - this book, other guidebooks, maps, the National Parks and Wildlife Service, other bushwalkers, and bushwalking clubs. Canvass a range of opinion since often one source will not provide a balanced picture, but be wary of advice from anybody with excessively casual or "gung ho" attitudes. These people often give unrealistic advice and underestimate difficulties. **Remember, your need is to predict how YOU will find the country**. Your experiences will not necessarily be identical to those of other walkers, since conditions and personal capabilities differ.

In your preparation, you should consider what action to take in the event of delays and emergencies. Is it possible to shorten the route if you are delayed? Do your maps show sufficient area around the intended route in case you have to vary it, or find a short emergency route to civilisation? All members of the party should be aware of the planned itinerary, and preferably everyone should carry their own map and compass and have at least basic navigational skills. It is important to plan the trip to be within the abilities of the weakest party member, not to match the average abilities of the group as a whole.

Once you know the extremes of conditions possible, you should consider what skills and equipment you will require. These topics are discussed later in this chapter. You also need to plan the route (refer pages 55 and 56).

Before you depart, advise a responsible person of your route and intended time of return. This is an important part of your preparation. Don't just inform them verbally, but give them a detailed written note or mark your route on a map or a photocopy. They should be sufficiently responsible and caring to check if you return on time, and they should know what action to take if you are overdue. Once you are on the track, do not vary significantly from your planned route unless quite unavoidable.

SKILLS AND SAFETY PRACTICES

SKILLS

Many bushwalking skills are learnt by sheer experience, for it is only by experience that you learn the range of conditions and problems that may confront you, and techniques for tackling them. With experience, individual bushwalkers develop their own preferred techniques for dealing with the numerous small problems that may be encountered on any bushwalk. These "little problems" can range from how to pitch your tent on rough ground, to cooking or how to treat blistered feet. Sometimes these "little problems" are not so minor e.g. badly blistered feet can be incapacitating. It is partly for these reasons that novices are advised to develop their bushwalking prowess gradually.

However, not all skills can be learnt by experience alone. For subjects such as navigation, first aid, survival procedures and rock and ropework skills, you should take the initiative by learning from formal training courses or good texts. There is no room in this guidebook to discuss these topics fully, although some basic concepts of navigation are outlined in Chapter 6. With respect to other skills, there is only space for brief comments:

First Aid is best learnt at an official ambulance course. It is desirable for all bushwalkers to have at least a basic knowledge of first aid, but if necessary one or two capable first aiders in a party will suffice.

"Survival Skills": It is recommended that all bushwalkers have some knowledge of what to do in the event of hazards such as bushfires, flooded creeks and hypothermia. Readers are referred to general bushwalking texts (available in most bushwalking shops) regarding these subjects.

Rock and Ropework Skills are briefly discussed on page 21.

GENERAL SAFETY PRACTICES

While readers are referred to other texts for the majority of information on bushwalking skills, there are nevertheless a few basic safety conventions of which all bushwalkers should be aware:

The "Tail-End-Charlie" Principle: This simply means that, in large groups, an experienced bushwalker should be positioned at the end of the party to ensure that slower members are not left behind or do not lose their way. Regular regroupings and head counts should be performed with large parties. It is also good practice to make it everyone's responsibility to keep in clear visual contact with the person *behind* them. This ensures that the group remains together.

Map and Compass: Another convention is that all party members should carry their own map and compass and keep track of their progress and position, in case they become separated from the main party or the leader makes an error. Navigation is not just the leader's responsibility.

Party Size: The optimum size for a bushwalking party is probably between 4 and 10. Much larger parties may be acceptable from the safety viewpoint, provided stragglers are controlled and the party has sufficient experienced people (depending on the location, there may be environmental objections - refer to page 81). A party of only 2 people would have problems if there was a serious injury, for the patient would have to be left unattended while the other sought help. **Never walk alone unless you are very experienced and have an intimate knowledge of the terrain**.

Children: You have a special responsibility if you are intending to take children or inexperienced walkers into the bush. If you are not certain about the nature of the terrain or your navigational ability, reconnoitre the route beforehand. On such "recces", enlist the aid of an experienced bushwalker or another capable adult.

Don't Unduly Coerce people into tackling obstacles beyond their limits, and don't adopt the misconception that climbing and rockhopping ability depends primarily on mental attitude and confidence. There is only a minimum of truth in this common belief. Ability and confidence are mutually dependent qualities which develop hand

Wilsons Peak from Teviot Falls (Walk 50)

in hand. Scrambling, climbing and rockhopping activities require fitness and athletic agility, and lack of confidence is often the result of lacking these qualities, rather than the reverse. Although there are many advantages in encouraging people to develop their abilities, ultimately each individual is responsible for determining their own development and deciding their limits.

Rockfall Dangers: Never purposely roll rocks down slopes or over cliffs, and if you accidentally dislodge any stones, yell a loud warning "ROCK" to anyone who may be below. If your party is on a steep slope where rockfall is a danger, adopting a diagonal course across the slope will help minimise the threat.

Packs: Never leave your packs in the bush without ensuring you can relocate them, especially in thick vegetation.

Camping Hazards: Always check overhead for tree branches before choosing your tent site. Against popular belief, eucalypt trees aren't particularly suitable for shading tents. Preferably avoid any eucalypt limbs above your tent, since even live branches can drop unexpectedly. In particular, cold windless nights seem to prompt eucalypts to shed apparently healthy limbs. However, you should certainly avoid pitching your tent beneath any dead limbs of any species of tree.

RISKS AND DECISION-MAKING

Commonly, accidents occur in the bush as a result of taking risks. Mishaps of this nature often involve a gung ho attitude to some particular venture or obstacle, but sometimes the mishap is a genuine accident. It should be quite evident that you need to act with some degree of self discipline to ensure your safety when bushwalking, but naturally it is not possible to avoid all risks once you venture "off-the-track". For example, there may be occasions when you must decide whether to climb a rocky obstacle or take a long circuitous route around the feature. Or you may have to decide whether to tackle an ambitious day walk at the risk of being caught out overnight without appropriate equipment.

Such decisions are best left to experienced bushwalkers, and beginners should always be prudent in all matters involving risk-taking in the bush. A good rule is that if you are unsure whether you are capable of a particular climb or venture, you probably lack the necessary experience. If you must take risks, do so intelligently and don't rush in blindly. The principles of assessing risks and making decisions are much the same for bushwalking as for any other activity:

1. Investigate the risk or decision (gather **all** the necessary information)
2. Know your own abilities.
3. Identify and recognise limitations (both personal and external).
4. Plan ahead (use the right equipment under the right conditions).
5. Work out all the available options (think flexibly).
6. Assess the options.
7. Examine the consequences of failure (if the consequences of failure are serious, you must ensure that the chances of success are high).
8. Have a number of back-up plans for different circumstances.
9. Remain alert (accidents sometimes occur in easy terrain at the end of a walk).
10. Retreat if your plans come unstuck.

EQUIPMENT

Few bushwalking topics cause such a diversity of opinion as equipment. To many beginners, equipment is a major topic of concern, and indeed some experienced bushwalkers are forever buying the best and latest gear. Other people, including a notable proportion of novices, give equipment very little thought at all. The best approach lies in a balance between these extremes (as with most topics of discord), although it is best not to underrate the role of equipment in comfortable and safe bushwalking.

Advice on individual items of equipment is given later in this chapter, but readers should note that the comments are only basic guidelines on the use, purpose and purchase of gear. Follow-up reading with other texts is recommended before buying expensive items. Some comments here are limited to noting qualities that are specifically important for south-east Queensland conditions, which may be over-looked in general bushwalking texts.

GENERAL GUIDELINES

Should you buy expensive equipment, or a great deal of equipment, or can you make do without this expense? Good bushwalking equipment is, without doubt, costly. The answers to these questions will depend on how much and what type of bushwalking you intend to undertake. However, it is generally preferable to buy only a few items at first, and borrow, rent or share some specialised items.

Many bushwalking clubs rent out packs, tents and sleeping bags to prospective members (you will need to provide an inner sheet to hire sleeping bags). In addition, items such as tents and stoves can often be shared or borrowed, and household items may be able to replace many other specialised items if you are not undertaking hard trips. Although you will soon need to consider purchasing packs, sleeping bags, stoves and tents if you are serious about bushwalking, initially footwear is probably the only major item that is essential to purchase.

The first step in purchasing equipment is to decide the type of walking you intend to undertake, since this dictates the purpose that the equipment must serve and the standard of equipment required. In south-east Queensland, environmental conditions are not as severe as in many other parts of Australia, so if walking in this region alone the equipment standard required is not as great. However, conditions can still be severe in some circumstances, so do not underestimate the quality of gear required.

Before purchasing important items of equipment, it is good practice to compare the advice and products of several specialist retail outlets. The general rule is to buy quality gear from specialist bushwalking shops. This does not mean that you always have to buy the best - rather it means buying gear that is amply good enough for its intended purpose. This will ensure that it lasts well and that it can cope with unexpected severe conditions. Penny-pinching when purchasing gear generally results in dissatisfaction with the service provided by the product, and/or a short service life. N.B. The equipment retailers advertised in this book are all specialist bushwalking outlets.

NAVIGATION EQUIPMENT

Navigation equipment usually comprises your:
- Maps
- Compass/protractor
- Guidebook
- Watch
- Map protector
- Notebook, pen and pencil

Maps: Detailed good quality topographic maps are available for almost all bush-walking areas in south-east Queensland. Information on available maps is given in each chapter. Generally the best maps are at the 1:25 000 scale, since these give the best compromise between detail and extent of coverage. Maps of 1:50 000 and 1:10 000 scales (if the latter are available) will also suffice for many areas. However, 1:100 000 maps do not usually provide sufficient detail for bushwalking purposes.

Ensure your maps cover a wide area around your route in case you are forced to vary your plans. Sometimes it is advisable to carry a combination of two maps, with different scales or publishers. Preferably all members of the party should carry their own maps but, as an absolute minimum, there should be two sets of maps in the party.

Compass: You don't need to buy the most expensive model, but do buy a quality item. Cheap compasses often have poor lubrication of the needles and housing. Bushwalking compasses incorporate a protractor, with the base plate doubling as a scale and ruler. The more basic models are usually quite satisfactory, but for bushwalking navigation the base plate should be reasonably large (at least 10cm long).

Watch: Many bushwalkers don't carry watches, but a watch is a valuable item of navigational equipment. You need to be able to keep track of time, know how much daylight is left and calculate your rate of progress. Few people can estimate the time from the sun, especially when tired and during bad weather when your need to monitor time is greatest. In these conditions a watch is a critical safety item.

Map Protector: Always carry your map in several layers of clear plastic bags to protect it from moisture, or use one of the special transparent map protectors now sold in bushwalking shops. If you fold your map appropriately, you can read it without removing it from the plastic.

Notebook, Pen and Pencil: While these items are not strictly essential, they allow you to record information on your route and progress or, in an emergency, leave notes behind about your intended route. In the event of a mishap, it is preferable for someone to seek help with a written record of the situation rather than rely on memory in a possible state of panic.

41

PACKS

Packs are an item where major design advances have been made in recent years, and there are now a myriad of brands and models available. The criteria of choice are size, quality, height, width, back length and cost. Shop assistants can usually advise you of the advantages of each design.

As a general rule, internal framed packs are superior to the old H-frame designs, with some qualification. Internal framed packs are available in a huge range of specialised forms. Greater carrying efficiency and comfort are achieved because the weight hugs the body and is close to your centre of gravity. They usually have adjustable webbing which can be rigged individually for different people.

One disadvantage of internal frame packs is that they are hotter to wear than H-frame packs. This can be important in summer in south-east Queensland. Another disadvantage is that some models of internal framed packs were designed for carrying heavy loads in open alpine areas, and may not be suited to the scrubby conditions in much of Australia. Packs with loose webbing, and those that are very high or very wide, tend to get caught in thick scrub. However, this also depends on individual walking style. Some people who find that high packs get snagged easily in thick scrub are relatively unperturbed by wide packs, while other people have the exact opposite experience.

Packing Rucksacks is an art in itself. Enclosing everything in waterproof plastic bags and cramming gear into all the small spaces is the usual strategy. Compactness means greater carrying efficiency. Items which are bulky for their weight, such as sleeping bags, are generally best packed at the bottom. Items which are heavy for their volume, such as water bottles, are best packed close to your back where they are near your centre of gravity. Such items are also usually better at the top of the pack, but this may depend somewhat on your body's strength characteristics and if you intend doing any climbing or scrambling. Packing weight high in the rucksack places greater stress on your shoulders and, in extreme cases, can decrease stability. However, packing the weight low causes you to bend over further and may increase back strain.

SLEEPING BAGS AND SLEEPING MATS

While you don't need the best or most expensive sleeping bag for walking in south-east Queensland, a cheap lightweight bag is unlikely to suffice in winter. Even here temperatures can fall well below zero on frosty nights. The apparent warmth of a bag will vary with individuals - some people are warm sleepers while others are cold sleepers. Nowadays the product information provided by manufacturers is much more reliable than in the past, but cold sleepers are still advised to assess manufacturers' claims cautiously.

Do use a sleeping mat with your sleeping bag, especially if your bag is down-filled. Down only insulates when it is not compressed. A foam or inflatable mat will greatly increase warmth as well as comfort. People with back ailments will probably find inflatable mats superior to the foam types, although they are heavier and more expensive.

Bags are made in different shapes. "Mummy" shaped bags are more efficient than rectangular bags on a warmth to weight ratio, although their reduced leg room may be uncomfortable on hot nights. If you only ever intend to buy one bag, a side zip is recommended (preferably full length and two-way) to allow ventilation for hot nights. A hood is an important consideration. The cheaper models which lack hoods are only suitable for mild conditions. The design of the quilting is a further feature which affects warmth.

Material choices for sleeping bags are straightforward in south-east Queensland, since wet conditions are rare in winter. Therefore, unless you are allergic to down, there is little advantage in synthetic bags which are much heavier and bulkier. Nylon is now the standard material used for the covering shell, although the older japara styles, while heavier, have superior durability.

STOVES

In southern Australia, stoves are a safety necessity. Even in parts of south-east Queensland, stoves are often regarded as essential, for it is almost impossible to light a fire with rainforest wood in wet conditions. Of course, there are many meals which can be eaten cold, but if you need to cook to prepare your meal, you will often be advised to carry a stove.

Despite such advantages, environmental factors are most responsible for the upsurge in stoves. More and more, the carrying of stoves is seen as a symbol of environmental responsibility, since firewood collection around many popular campsites has had a catastrophic effect on the environment.

Purchasing Criteria: There are a large number of stoves available. Factors influencing choice include weight, cost, simplicity of operation, safety of operation, versatility, heat control and fuel efficiency.

If you only ever intend to do weekend walks in south-east Queensland, the simpler, cheaper types of stoves which use methylated spirits or solid fuel are clear winners on most of these criteria. While lacking somewhat in heat control, they are simpler, safer, cheaper and, for short trips, much lighter than their kerosene and shellite rivals.

The more expensive types of stoves become advantageous if undertaking longer trips or walking in southern Australia. Most types perform satisfactorily, with some qualification. Don't simply assume that high cost means suitability for your needs. Models which have been primarily designed for fuel efficiency when melting snow may have poor heat control in comparison with many others. Also, avoid the more complicated types of stoves if you lack the confidence and "mechanical minded-ness" to operate them. It is a fact of life that some people are not mechanically minded, and you should never be shamed or coerced into buying a stove that you cannot operate competently. Indeed it is hazardous to try to use a stove on a bushwalk if you cannot operate it perfectly.

Safety: Regardless of your choice of stove, you should become thoroughly familiar with its operation and particular "idiosyncrasies" before using it on a bushwalk. Most stove designs have peculiarities in their method of operation. In all cases, safety of operation depends totally on studying the instructions thoroughly, and following them religiously. This is particularly the case with shellite stoves. Shellite is basically standard petrol and is just as explosive if misused. Use methylated spirits instead of shellite for priming stoves, and never use shellite for lighting fires.

Nasty accidents sometimes occur with stoves, but most result from a lack of alertness or poor observance of the detailed operating instructions. Carry fuel securely in the special lightweight canisters designed for the purpose and label fuel bottles clearly and obviously. One nasty accident apparently resulted from a walker using a fuel bottle, thought to contain water, to fill a billy on a fire. As a general rule, it is better not to attempt to repair stoves yourself, for the internal needles and jets are precision located. Don't use stoves in tents unless you are very experienced.

TENTS

For many short throughwalks, it is possible to make do with a small hutchie of the type sold in disposals stores. This saves weight and expense. However, sooner or later you will want to buy a tent. It is worthwhile considering your choice carefully, since good tents are expensive and many designs are intended for specific conditions.

There is a huge variety of tents available nowadays, which adds to the confusion of the buyer. Some tents are "single-skinned" (one layer of fabric), but most modern tents are "double-skinned" (outer and inner tent, or tent and fly, combined in one design). Unfortunately, some shop assistants don't understand the designs, and consequently buyers often receive incorrect advice and purchase tents inappropriate for their needs.

The first advice regarding tents is to avoid the very cheap supermarket versions. These will do little more than keep you dry in a heavy dew.

After acceptable weight, cost and quality, the most important consideration when buying a tent is the climate of the region where you intend to walk (this is frequently overlooked). Most design features on tents are intended for specific climate and weather types, so before you become carried away with all the trendy features that are apparently available, consider the functionality of the shape and design. Many "copy-manufacturers" make tents (normally in the cheap to medium price range) mixing cold and hot weather features simply to make a visual impression. Don't buy a tent simply because it looks impressive or incorporates the latest shape or features.

For cold regions you need a tent which retains heat and will withstand wind, rain and storms. In such tents, the outer goes right to the ground. This stops warm air escaping and prevents the wind catching underneath the tent and pulling it from the ground. However, such tents may be very hot in warmer conditions. For hot weather, ventilation is important. The breeze must be able to circulate easily through the tent and preferably there should be large doors on opposite sides to allow cross flow ventilation. Consequently, if you intend walking in both northern and southern Australia, or in both summer and winter in south-east Queensland, you would ideally use two tents. However most walkers choose one intermediate tent, or sacrifice weight and choose a tent with features which allow it to be pitched either closed-up or open to the breeze.

It is important to ensure that the sleeping compartment is of adequate size. Any tent, whether double-skinned or single-skinned, will give moisture problems in rainy weather if inadequate space means that the occupants are continually touching the walls. Remember to check both the length and width of the sleeping compartment. Cross-ridge and cross-tunnel tents in particular often seem to have inadequate length.

Any tent you choose will be a compromise, so to some extent personal preference will dictate the choice of designs, materials and additional features. Most modern tents are made of nylon or similar synthetic material. The older styled japara tents have superior durability, but japara is heavier than nylon (especially when wet) and is generally only used on single skinned tents of simple design. Single skinned tents are satisfactory for most south-east Queensland conditions, although double skinned tents, if of appropriate design, are superior in both very cold and very hot conditions.

44

Most people prefer the advantages of floors, mosquito nets and annexes. Floors are not the be-all and end-all for keeping out water, but have the advantage of keeping out leeches and ticks. One disadvantage is that they keep water in if they leak - a small sponge is handy to avoid this problem. It is common practice to protect tent floors by placing a groundsheet under them, but if you do this, fold any protruding edges under the outer tent. Otherwise they will collect and channel rain under the sleeping compartment. Anyone who has spent a night plagued by mosquitoes will appreciate the value of insect netting in tents, but note that the quality of insect netting varies considerably. Annexes - areas enclosed by the outer tent but outside of the inner tent - are ideal for storage of equipment. A cross ridge or cross tunnel tent, with two annexes to allow people to separate their equipment, is often regarded as an ideal. Sadly such tents tend to be heavy.

Weight is a critical factor for most walkers. Weight mainly depends on materials and size. If you want a super lightweight tent, you generally have to compromise with size and headroom. The best lightweight tents are usually very expensive for their size, since top quality materials are used and the designs may be very complex.

High storm resistance is particularly important if you intend walking in southern states. Storm resistant tents generally have either low rounded profiles and/or heavy frames, as well as as a large number of anchor points. However, it is worthwhile noting that many types of snow tents are designed to flap in the wind to shed snow. This can be extremely noisy, and may be a considerable nuisance if you never intend to use the tent in snow conditions.

Ease of pitching is another consideration. Ideally, tents should pitch easily, simply and quickly, and shouldn't be excessively susceptible to wind in the pitching stages.

Most tents are sold with poles and pegs. However, if you purchase a design which does not have these provided, you should buy them as additions. Poles and pegs should never be cut from the bush. If you have guy ropes, use white or yellow cord to enhance their visibility and reduce the chance of tripping over them at night. Some tents are designed without guy ropes, but these are often difficult to pitch on uneven or rocky ground. One method of combating this problem is tie a small length of tape in a series of loops to each peg eyelet on the bottom of the outer tent. This allows the peg to be placed in more than one position if the tent is pitched on uneven ground.

OTHER ITEMS

Other items are mostly evident from the checklist at the end of this chapter. However, here are a few general notes.

Spare Matches should always be carried, carefully wrapped in plastic to keep them dry.

Water Bottles can be aluminium or plastic, and can range from 1 litre to 4 litres depending on the conditions (see page 30). Generally two smaller water bottles are preferable to one large container, allowing for better weight distribution in your pack and providing some security against accidental breakage. It is sometimes advisable to carry a spare. Canvas buckets or large expanding water bottles are handy. An empty wine cask bladder will suffice for this purpose if handled carefully.

A Torch, with spare batteries and bulb, should always be carried. Candles are not recommended because of their extreme danger in modern tents.

A Whistle is recommended. If a distress call is necessary, whistle blasts carry further than voices in the bush. Three or six blasts in succession at five to ten second intervals are recognised distress signals.

A Groundsheet is usually considered necessary, although a large sheet of plastic will suffice for short trips if you wish to reduce cost.

Plastic Bags, in various numbers and sizes, are an essential component of the modern bushwalking pack. In wet conditions, maps, clothing, food and sleeping bags can be kept dry, encased in plastic bags. Many walkers use a large plastic bag to line the inner of their pack. It is also possible to completely enclose a pack with very large plastic bags if you have to swim across a water obstacle, although remember that even tiny holes will leak substantial quantities of water.

First Aid Kits should, at a minimum, contain bandaids, bandages, plaster tape, headache type pain killers, two pairs of tweezers (one very fine), scissors and safety pins. This is often combined with a repair kit, containing needle, tough thread and additional tape.

Insect Repellent, smothered on your boots at the start of a walk, will help repel leeches and ticks.

CLOTHING AND FOOTWEAR

CLOTHING

General Walking Clothes: Almost any durable clothing will suffice, although in summer it may be preferable to sacrifice durability in favour of lighter cooler fabrics. Shorts are preferable for most walking since the weather is rarely very cold during the day, but on scrubby trips long loose fitting trousers are useful. Trying to walk in tight trousers or jeans is both difficult and tiring. Gaiters are handy for keeping muck out of your socks and boots and for protecting your shins against cuts and thorns, but are not essential. On overnight walks it is recommended that you carry a spare set of clothes for night wear or in case you get wet.

Parka: The purpose of a parka is to keep out the wind and rain, which is especially important if the weather is cold. Mountain areas can become cold and wet at all times of the year, so a good parka is recommended, even on day trips. N.B. In the past there have been claims that bushwalkers don't need to prepare against the cold in Queensland, but these are quite erroneous. Night winter temperatures in the mountain areas of the Scenic Rim are usually well below zero, and at Lamington there have been definite cases of preliminary hypothermia in summer (see page 31).

Warm Clothing: Material which stays warm when wet is essential for bushwalking. Traditionally this has been wool, but in the last decade modern synthetic fabrics specially developed for this purpose have begun to dominate. Such garments are sold in bushwalking shops. Depending on season, one or two wool shirts or similar synthetic garments should be carried when bushwalking in the mountain areas of south-east Queensland. However, these garments won't be fully effective in wet or windy conditions unless you also have a parka.

In winter, it is recommended that you carry long trousers for night. Accessories such as mittens and balaclavas are useful for winter nights and mornings, but are not strictly essential unless you particularly feel the cold in your extremities.

Hat: A good hat is essential for bushwalking in south Queensland, since heat, dehydration and sunburn are just as much a problem as cold (see page 30).

Socks: Normally two pairs of socks are worn, one thick woollen outer set and one thin inner set. They should be in good condition. Carry spares, at least on longer trips.

Garden Gloves are handy in scrubby conditions, and are much superior to hacking implements such as machetes (which should never be used) for pushing through thick scrub.

BOOTS AND OTHER FOOTWEAR

Choosing footwear, like other items of equipment, usually means deciding on a balance between a range of factors - cost, comfort, sole quality and suitability for different conditions. Nobody has yet designed the perfect bushwalking footwear. What suits some people may not suit others.

Types of Footwear: Your choice of footwear will depend considerably on the bone structure and robustness of your feet - some people's feet and ankles are far more tolerant of different types of footwear than other people's. While some bushwalkers maintain that sandshoes and specialised "track" shoes are satisfactory, others recommend the additional ankle support and sole protection afforded by boots.

Those people who are able to use sandshoes and "track" shoes usually have well structured feet and no history of ankle sprains. The most common types of "track" shoes used for bushwalking are those that are specifically designed for walking or orienteering. Normal running shoes are often unsuitable due to lack of tread.

As a general rule, people who have had any significant or recurrent problems with their feet or ankles - such as fallen arches, frequent ankle rolling or even serious one-off sprains - are advised to wear good quality boots when bushwalking. Remember that most bushwalking terrain is far rougher underfoot than any other terrain you are likely to encounter, and even minor foot injuries can have serious consequences in the bush.

Bushwalking Boots and Work Boots: Specialised bushwalking boots have undergone major changes in recent years. Mostly these changes have been for the better, but there have been some detrimental effects. One is cost. Good boots are now exorbitantly expensive.

To avoid the cost, many beginners consider work boots as a cheap alternative to bushwalking boots. Work boots may suffice if you only intend one or two walks, but they are rarely designed for bushwalking conditions and are often not made to a high degree of comfort. The soles are often poor, sometimes made for hard floors, and composed of either very hard rubber (for durability) or very soft rubber (for comfort). Do not be influenced by the apparently rugged tread patterns on many work boots. Tread pattern is the least reliable indicator of a sole's performance - rubber type and grip on wet rock are much more critical. To be fair, the suitability of work boots varies considerably with the make and design of boot and the wearer's foot. For some people work boots may prove quite satisfactory. However, in general work boots are not recommended if you are serious about bushwalking, but by all means consider them (with due care) if your interest is only casual.

Size: The most critical feature when purchasing boots is to ensure they are of adequate size, sufficient to wear two pairs of socks (one thin set and one thick outer set). With many modern designs, which don't tend to stretch with usage and waterlogging as did older styled boots, this requirement is even more critical.

Sole Design: Most soles on modern bushwalking boots are designed for mud shedding and have relatively shallow treads, although this quality is not so important in south-east Queensland. In this region good grip on wet rock is of much greater importance, since much off-track bushwalking involves rockhopping in wet slippery creeks. Unfortunately, some of the soles on modern styled boots use rather hard rubber, necessary to compensate for the shallowness of the tread. Sadly this often reduces the grip on wet rock, and many modern soles perform rather poorly on this quality in comparison with the soles that were once traditionally installed on Australian and New Zealand made boots. There is no simple solution to this problem, since the old types of soles are rarely available nowadays. However, by consulting a range of shops and shop assistants you will still be able to make a decision balancing the various advantages and disadvantages of different types of boots.

Other Factors to consider include weight and comfort. A good deal of energy is expended moving the feet up and down, so lighter boots have a definite advantage, especially for smaller people. It is also imperative that your feet are comfortable. The more traditional styles of boot often lack the comfort features present in the more sleek designs, and they are certainly heavier. When you buy new boots, wear them in gradually before attempting hard trips or long walks. Some boots need little wearing-in, while others require a great deal.

FOOT PROBLEMS

Blisters: Blisters can be a problem in any type of terrain if your boots are not worn in properly or are of incorrect fit. Steep uphill climbs generally rub the heels while downhill sections rub the toes. However, blisters (and other foot problems) are generally of greatest concern in flatter terrains where you are covering long distances. The golden rule with blisters is to prevent them from the outset. Immediately you feel the rub point, cover the skin with several layers of smooth plaster tape. To increase the plaster's adherence, round the corners with a pair of scissors or wrap plaster completely around the foot. If a blister starts to become a serious concern, apply the same treatment but use multiple layers of tape. Don't break blisters except as a last resort.

Fallen Arches and Orthotics: Despite common perceptions, fallen arches are rarely an impediment to recreational bushwalking if you have good boots, especially if the type of walking you tackle involves steep ascents and descents rather than long distances. However, people who wear orthotics (a sort of inner sole prescription-made for a person's foot by a podiatrist, often worn for fallen arches and other foot problems) sometimes find difficulty with the devices in bushwalking footwear. Lack of friction on the inner sole when walking in rough terrains and unusual rub points when walking long distances are two common problems. Until you are thoroughly familiar with the devices in a range of bushwalking conditions, it is advisable to carry a spare set of inner soles so that the orthotics can be removed if necessary. Fitting of orthotics to footwear usually involves cutting the inner soles into shape, but this is not recommended with the specially designed inner soles of bushwalking boots. Since orthotics require only the front part of the boot's inner sole (the rest is cut away), a cheap inner sole from a sporting goods shop will suffice to cushion the front of the foot. This allows you to keep the good inner soles intact in case you experience problems with the orthotics.

Foot Ache is an occasional problem when bushwalking, mainly when covering long distances. There is little that can be done about it on the walk except for periodic resting and possibly bathing the feet in water if the ache is particularly severe. It is important to work up gradually to long distance walks to avoid this problem.

FOOD AND COOKING

Food for bushwalking is often a subject of some concern for beginners, but it need not be. There are many misconceptions on this subject.

DAY WALK AND BASE CAMP FOODS

A lunch of sandwiches is the normal fare for day walks, with high energy foods such as chocolate being carried for mid-meal snacks (see comments on page 50). For base camps, menus can be as basic or elaborate as you like. Those who are content with basic dietary habits can eat as they would on a throughwalk (see later comments). If you prefer, however, an ice box will allow you to eat much the same as you would at home, depending somewhat on your cooking skills and preferences for more gourmet delights.

THROUGHWALKING FOOD

Dinners: It is commonly considered that bushwalkers must eat dried food, or specialised packaged foods of the type sold in bushwalking shops. While specialised dried foods certainly save weight, they are not strictly essential for most weekend bushwalks in Australia. In winter in south-east Queensland, almost all foods will keep unrefrigerated for the duration of a weekend.

Furthermore, there is a good deal of choice available even within the dried food range. With a little imagination all sorts of rice and pasta dishes can be prepared on the track without the need to resort to preservative-ridden prepackaged meals. A simple packet white sauce or dried tomato paste, together with a few fresh vegetables, can be used to spice up a rice or pasta dish. Of course, if you don't mind eating prepackaged meals, your choice is greater.

Naturally, dried foods are only an advantage if water is available to add to them. In very dry conditions, you may be better off with other foods, even tins.

Burning is a common problem when cooking dried food in the bush, especially on open fires. The secret is prevention through constant deep stirring.

Beginners in particular should be conscious of weight when choosing foods, since they are unlikely to have developed the strength to carry heavy packs. They may wish to make do with dried meals for dinners rather than more lavish meals. However, if weight isn't a severe factor, there is a range of other options available for bushwalking dinners.

One technique is to precook meals such as casseroles and simply heat them up at night. This allows for home-cooked quality with a minimum of fuss on the actual walk. Simplicity is an advantage for bushwalking foods, since you often feel too tired after a day's walk to be troubled with extensive food preparations.

Precooking is also a means of carrying steak, since if unrefrigerated it usually lasts longer cooked than fresh.

Sometimes frozen meat and other frozen foods can be carried, but are best wrapped in copious layers of cloth e.g. in the centre of a tent or sleeping bag. This will insulate them and sometimes you may find them still frozen a day later. If carrying any type of moist food, ensure it is well sealed in several new plastic bags to guard against spillage in your pack. Be careful with any twist ties used to seal plastic bags, since the wire ends often pierce the plastic and even tiny holes can leak considerable fluid into your pack. Also note that frozen foods have a very limited life once they thaw.

Soups and Desserts are other foods to consider, and both can be either dried or tinned depending on your weight restrictions. After a hard day, a hot soup on a cold night is a great reviver. Dried apricots or apple, stewed and perhaps topped with custard, is a good dessert on a lightweight trip. Of course, there would be digestive reminders of the aroma of such a meal during the following night and day (if you're the only party member to dine on stewed fruit, be prepared to be tail-end-charlie next day).

Breakfasts on bushwalks will probably be similar to what you normally eat. Muesli, or any other cereal which doesn't crumble, is usually a satisfactory breakfast.

Although it is possible to carry long-life milk on walks, weight restrictions usually dictate that dried milk be carried. To avoid lumping of dried milk in coffee or muesli, mix it thoroughly with the other dried ingredients before adding water. Many people carry a plastic shaker to dissolve cold dried ingredients such as milk, the shaker doubling as a cup. However, **do not use shakers with hot fluids**, since if air is present, the sudden vaporisation usually causes the shaker to burst the lid and spray out hot fluid.

Porridge makes a delicious bushwalking breakfast on cold mornings, but most people prefer a sweetened recipe in such conditions. One recipe is (per serve) a half cup of rolled oats and a cup of cold water, plus a good handful of dried sultanas and a heaped tablespoon of sugar. Bring to the boil and simmer several minutes until the oats are swelled. Remove from the heat and stir in five dessert spoons of dried milk. Some amount of experimentation may be necessary to get a good consistency, but it is intended for the mixture to remain fluid when it is cooking to allow stirring and prevent burning. Dried milk added at the end thickens the mixture to the proper consistency.

Lunches and Snacks: If weight is a serious limitation, lunches will usually comprise biscuits, jams and spreads. However, if weight is less critical, there is nothing wrong with carrying fresh bread and salad vegetables. Fragile items, such as tomatoes, can be packed in cloth inside billies.

If the trip is long or the weather is hot, cheese is better wrapped in cheese cloth than plastic. Provided you avoid the strong flavoured varieties, both cheese and salami will usually keep unrefrigerated for many days in non-summer seasons.

Most bushwalkers carry a supply of sweets or chocolate which they nibble several times a day to maintain their energy levels. Carrying of these high energy foods is common bushwalking advice, especially in cold regions where there is a risk of hypothermia. Some people argue that bushwalkers shouldn't need to rely on these foods in normal circumstances, but it is certainly advisable to at least carry a reserve supply so as to be prepared for fatigue or unexpected emergencies.

There is a great deal of publicity nowadays about the benefits of low salt diets for cardiovascular fitness. However, if you are unused to strenuous exercise on a daily basis, and especially if the weather is hot, bushwalking can cause a short term loss of salts. An electrolyte supplement drink such as Staminade is the most effective means of combating this problem, and is superior to simple table salt.

Dampers: A common bushwalker's damper is based on 1 to 11/2 cups of self-raising flour per person. Some people add small quantities of dried milk and dried egg, and most add sugar and a good deal of dried mixed fruit. Mix then knead, gradually adding water, but ensure that the finished mixture is not too wet. It should sit up in a dry lump, being only just wet enough to gather all the dry ingredients. Put in a greased vertical sided cake tin and fry on very low coals at the side of the fire for thirty minutes, rotating the utensil occasionally. Remove, turn the beast over, regrease the tin, and bake another thirty minutes on the opposite side. Eat.

UTENSILS AND CONTAINERS

With the possible exception of a cheap tin billy, most beginners make do with household items for cooking utensils and food containers. Household utensils are actually quite suitable for many applications, although in time bushwalkers tend to buy the more specialised items, principally to save weight. Lightweight cutlery and plastic cups are normally used. However, if weight isn't critical, enamel cups may be preferable since they don't retain the taste of previous food as does plastic.

Aluminium billies are much superior to tin billies for bushwalking purposes, but they are much more expensive. Two billies in the 1/2 to 21/2 litre range is a popular selection, although with careful choice of foods you may make do with one billy. Alternatively, two people sharing a menu can share billies to save weight.

Your use of other cooking utensils largely depends on weight limitations, and your menu and imagination. Frypans, grills, jaffle irons, toasters, large cake tins and even woks can be used successfully on bushwalks if their weight isn't prohibitive. Specialised billy tongs ("billy lifters") are recommended, especially if cooking on an open fire.

Most bushwalking foods can be carried successfully in plastic bags, including flour, dried milk, tea and coffee. However, in case of piercing, place them in multiple layers of plastic bags and pack them carefully. For jam and spreads, you can use either small plastic or aluminium containers or the specialised reusable tube containers sold by bushwalking shops.

PERSONAL NOTES

....

....

....

....

....

....

....

EQUIPMENT CHECKLIST

In the following checklist, "p 43" indicates the page number of items discussed in previous pages, "Y" indicates items that are normally required, while an "O" indicates optional, questionable or purely comfort items.

ITEM	Comment	Day Walk	Base Camp	Through Walk
Pack/day pack	p 42	Y	Y	Y
Tent, with poles & pegs	p 44		Y	Y
Tent fly			O	O
Groundsheet	p 46		Y	Y
Sleeping bag	p 42		Y	Y
Sleeping mat	p 42		Y	Y
Inner sheet			Y	O
Pillow (air)			O	
Pack raincover		O	O	O
Pack liner		O	O	Y
_____				
_____				
Boots/footwear	p 47	Y	Y	Y
Socks and spares	p 47	Y	Y	Y
Gaiters	p 46	Y	Y	Y
Walking clothes (shorts, shirt, trousers, underclothes)	p 46	Y	Y	Y
Spare clothes (as above)	p 46		Y	Y
Parka	p 46	Y	Y	Y
Warm clothing (including wool shirts)	p 46	Y	Y	Y
Mitts, balaclava	p 46		O	O
Hat - wide brim	p 47	Y	Y	Y
Garden gloves	p 47	O	O	O
Personal Items (wallet/money, watch, hankies, personal toilet items etc)		Y	Y	Y
Toiletries (soap, toilet paper, tooth brush and paste, dental floss, comb, etc)		O	Y	Y
Towel		O	O	O
Sunburn cream		Y	Y	Y
Insect repellent	p 46	Y	Y	Y
_____				
_____				
Maps	p 40	Y	Y	Y
Compass	p 41	Y	Y	Y
Guidebook		Y	Y	Y
Map case	p 41	Y	Y	Y
Watch	p 41	Y	Y	Y
Notebook, pen & pencil	p 41	Y	Y	Y
_____				

ITEM	Comment	Day Walk	Base Camp	Through Walk
Torch, with spare batteries & bulb ...	p 45	Y	Y	Y
Pocket knife		Y	Y	Y
Spare cord		Y	Y	Y
Whistle	p 46	Y	Y	Y
Spare plastic bags	p 46	O	Y	Y
First aid kit	p 46	Y	Y	Y
Repair kit	p 46	O	Y	Y
Camera and film		O	O	O
Belay gear/rope		O	O	O
_____........................				
_____........................				
Cutlery		O	Y	Y
Cup and/or shaker	p 50	O	Y	Y
Plate			Y	O
Stove	p 43	O	Y	Y
Fuel and funnel		O	Y	Y
Priming fluid and/or fire starters		O	Y	Y
Matches and spares	p 45	Y	Y	Y
Water bottle	p 45	Y	Y	Y
Canvas bucket/wine cask bladder	p 45		Y	Y
Can opener		O	O	O
Billies (1 or 2)	p 51	O	Y	Y
Frypan/other cookware	p 51		O	O
Billy tongs			O	O
Pot scourer			O	O
Rubbish bag		Y	Y	Y
Food		Y	Y	Y
_____........................				
_____........................				
Gas stove			O	
Gas lantern			O	
Barbeque plate			O	
Binoculars			O	O
_____........................				
_____........................				

PERSONAL NOTES

....

....

....

....

6

BASIC BUSHWALKING NAVIGATION

Navigation is the skill of finding your way and arriving at your destination on time. It is essential that bushwalkers understand at least the basics of navigation. While not all bushwalking routes require advanced navigation skills, most need an understanding of maps and route planning. These are not difficult subjects to learn. Walking in the more rugged and heavily vegetated areas also requires a knowledge of compasses and directions. While these are more complex topics, most walkers can become adept in the skills given a gradual progression to harder trips.

For reasons of space, the information presented in this chapter is limited, it only being intended to help you avoid the worst predicaments and to give you basic knowledge in case you get into difficulties. Readers should refer to other texts for comprehensive information on bushwalking navigation techniques.

PLANNING AND OBSERVATION SKILLS

The initial key to good navigation is how you plan the trip and make observations during the journey. For important background information on these subjects, refer to pages 4, 5, 20, 21, 29, 35 and 36.

CHOOSING THE ROUTE

The first and most important step in navigation planning is information gathering. This involves accumulating every scrap of information possible about the area and proposed route. A full list of the information you need to gather, and other preparatory notes, is given on pages 35 and 36.

The next step is choosing the route and planning the length of the trip. In this task, you will principally be guided by the features you wish to visit, road access points,the time available, and known tracks, campsites and water points. However, the following principles should also be noted:

Left: Orienting the map on Mt May. Mt Barney in background.

- As a general rule, allow yourself as a safety margin one quarter to one third more time for the trip than what you think is strictly necessary. Alternatively, ensure your itinerary can be substantially shortened in the event of difficulties or slow progress.
- Provide a generous allowance for rest stops and lunch breaks, especially if there could be weather extremes or if the party is inexperienced or unfit. Most people find that five or six hours of actual walking time is all that will be achieved in an eight or nine hour day. Furthermore, an eight hour day - covering perhaps 15 to 20km in easy terrain and maybe half this in normal conditions - is ample for many people.
- Physical features such as ridges and creeks normally provide the easiest means of travel if venturing away from tracks. For information on ridge and creek travel, refer to pages 57 and 58.

RATE OF TRAVEL

Bushwalkers need to have a good idea of travelling rates for different terrains in order to estimate the time needed for any particular trip.

For reasonably fit people, a rough formula for calculating time requirements is to allow one hour per 5km of distance, plus 10 to 15 minutes for every 100 metres of uphill climbing. Alternatively, in steep uphill terrain, it may be preferable to use ascent rates. Allow an hour for every 200m to 300m of elevation if carrying a moderate pack, and for every 300m to 500m of elevation with day trip gear. Considerable variation is possible. Lack of fitness, heavy packs, scrub, heat, loose rock and thick grass will decrease speed, while fit parties could achieve better rates in favourable conditions. Often faster ascent rates are achieved on steeper slopes, provided you do not take excessively long or frequent rests.

Descent rates are much more variable than ascent rates. Commonly descents take about two-thirds of the time needed for the corresponding ascent, but on low and very high gradient slopes the difference reduces. Descents in very steep terrain can be more arduous than the corresponding ascents.

Many beginners are surprised at the possible variations in travelling rates. The following table shows some typical travelling speeds under different conditions, representative of a reasonably fit and agile person carrying a light throughwalk pack. This may help you predict travelling times, but remember that it is only a guide and that travelling speed depends greatly on fitness and conditions. A generous allowance for stops is required if using these rates to calculate the time needed for a trip, since rest stops and lunch breaks are not provided for. A throughwalk pack will generally slow your travelling rate to between half and three-quarters of your walking rate with day trip gear (depending on hills, weight etc.)

Speed	Conditions
6 to 7km/hour	On a flat graded track at a fast pace.
4 to 5km/hour	On a flat graded track at a normal pace (see also page 127 regarding walking speeds on graded tracks), or on hard beach sand (low tide) at a fast pace.
3km/hour	Over undulating country with a good track, or flat open country with a rough track, or on hard beach sand (low tide) at a normal pace.

| 1 to 2km/hour | In steep or scrubby terrain (but not extreme), or creek rockhopping on dry rocks in good conditions. |
| 1/4 to 1km/hour | Rockhopping on wet slippery rocks, travelling in very steep, precipitous or scrubby terrain, walking on soft beach sand at high tide, or travelling in country or weather conditions which present extreme difficulties. |

Your knowledge of travelling speed can be developed further on every trip simply by timing your progress. Note your walking time between two points several kilometres apart, and calculate your walking rate. Repeat the exercise in both easy and hilly terrains, and calculate your ascent rates on steep routes. To further develop your skill, try to predict when you will encounter various features along your route.

OBSERVATION SKILLS

Observation skills are important for safe and efficient bushwalking navigation. In particular you should always monitor your progress, direction and position. This involves a simple compass check of your direction of travel at least every fifteen minutes, and noting features passed over or beside. Do not underestimate the value of small landmarks. Minor ascents, descents, knolls, changes of slope and even changes of vegetation can all be related to features on the map. Study the map beforehand so that you know what landmarks to watch for, and by your knowledge of travelling rates try to estimate when you should reach various features.

Following foot tracks also requires careful observation. Footworn tracks are often frustrating, since they may divide, fade out and reform without rhyme or reason. Always monitor the direction of tracks, since often it is easy to miss junctions and take the wrong path. If a track divides but there is no actual route junction, don't automatically assume that the most worn path is the correct way. Sometimes false trails form where people miss a bend in a main track and walk straight ahead, and often these trails are well worn initially. Therefore check your direction of travel at such divisions and proceed with care.

If you lose a track, it is better to adopt a systematic approach than wander about wildly looking for a new path. Firstly retrace your steps a short distance and look for a possible track division. If this fails, search in the direction where you estimate the track should lie. If all else fails, the party can fan out and search for the path, but don't become separated and never leave your packs unattended in thick scrub.

RIDGE TRAVEL AND CREEK TRAVEL

From the navigational viewpoint, ridges and creeks are usually much easier to follow in one direction than the other. Ridge navigation is normally easier on ascent, because the various spurs and minor ridges converge in that direction i.e. various spurs may join on either side, but the upwards direction remains evident. In contrast, when descending ridges the spurs divide, and if you don't take care you are likely to take the wrong route. Consequently, unless the ridge is very obvious or you can see your objective, compass bearings usually need to be followed when descending ridges. This is particularly important in heavily vegetated areas.

The converse phenomenon occurs with creeks, which converge on descent and diverge on ascent. An additional problem along creeks is that often the landmarks are hidden from view, or if they are seen, are viewed piecemeal so that they aren't easily identified. When navigating along creeks, it is necessary to count the small spurs and tributaries which join on either side, as well as keep a constant eye on the direction of the creek. You will often find that creeks make subtle changes of direction not shown on maps, but by combining these techniques you are usually able to keep track of your position.

RAINFOREST NAVIGATION

Rainforest is the most common navigation hazard in south-east Queensland. There are three main problems:

• Rainforest usually blankets out all views of reference landmarks. If you lose track of your position or become disorientated, it may be extremely difficult to reorientate yourself or find your position on a map. In turn, this means that you will often be unsure which way to go.
• In some areas the rainforest vegetation is very extensive e.g. in parts of Lamington National Park it is possible to walk for several days without obtaining views.
• The sheer thickness of some rainforest vegetation may slow progress to a tedious rate, which can cause walking parties to become overdue.

It is important to appreciate that rainforest navigation hazards are not consistent. One time there might be a good track which makes a trip straightforward, but this may be absent a few months later. The clarity of tracks depends on season, recent usage and sometimes sheer luck. Do not become overconfident if you find that a particular walk is easier than expected, and be wary of advice from anybody who claims that navigation in a particular rainforest area is easy. Be careful about the advice you give to others if you do a rainforest trip but don't personally experience difficulties.

In south-east Queensland, footworn tracks are usually easiest to follow in late winter. The seasons which present most difficulty are late spring, when heavy leaf fall temporarily obliterates some tracks, and late summer and autumn when usage is least and vegetation growth is greatest.

Rainforest navigation uses normal bushwalking navigation techniques, except that the degree of care required is much greater. The lack of views not only makes the task of monitoring your position much more important, it also makes it much harder. In rainforest (and in any other conditions where visibility is limited), you need to:

(1) Ensure you have plenty of time for the trip.

(2) Carry the best and most detailed maps available.

(3) Constantly use your map and compass.

(4) Be rigorous in keeping track of your position and progress.

(5) Constantly monitor your direction and rate of travel.

(6) Be meticulous in your route observations.

(7) Train yourself to observe minor features, since you often need to rely on small features to monitor your progress.

The hardest navigation will occur if you lose the route or become badly disorientated. If you lack navigation experience, an otherwise straightforward trip can become a nightmare in these circumstances (refer to *Navigation Emergencies* at the end of this chapter).

A fundamental safety principle is never to walk alone unless you know the terrain intimately. As well as the obvious safety advantages if a mishap occurs, this practice will help prevent you becoming lost. The reasoning power of two or more people confronted with a problem is greater than that of one, and there is less tendency to panic.

FIELD OBSERVATIONS IN STEEP TERRAIN

It is useful to note that long distance field observations of steep terrain are often misleading. When viewed faced on, steep routes often appear even steeper due to foreshortening of the perspective, especially if the terrain is rocky. Often you will find that routes which appear very difficult when viewed face on from some distance away are much easier in reality. Nevertheless you should use caution in all steep terrain. N.B. The foreshortening effect is caused by the horizontal dimension being less visible to the plane of sight and thereby being condensed to the eye, while the vertical dimension (which is across the plane of sight) retains a strong impact, especially if there are dramatic vertical features.

The converse situation sometimes occurs when you are looking straight up at a steep slope from immediately below it. Care needs to be used in these circumstances because the slope may not look as steep as it is. The reason is similar to the above situation, except that the vertical dimension is condensed and horizontal terrain (e.g. small ledges) appears more prominent than it is in reality.

MAPS

Maps are a most important key to bushwalking navigation. Maps are used for predicting terrain, and for determining your route and position at various stages of the journey. Five elements of maps of particular importance to bushwalkers are the legend, scale, contour system, grid system and north points. The map's legend is self-explanatory. The remaining subjects are briefly discussed here.

Always remember that there are practical limits to a map's accuracy, so don't expect every detail to be shown. For example, on a 1:100 000 map the symbol for a house represents an area 80m square, so houses close together will be marked by one symbol. Two terrain features which are often represented poorly are cliffs and vegetation types. It is almost impossible to ensure that a map shows all the cliffs in an area, and older maps in particular often show wildly inaccurate vegetation information. The date of survey of the map will give some clue to its accuracy, but even recently published maps will have some inaccuracies.

Where to Buy Maps: There are many map retailers, although SUNMAP (pages 139 and 298) and HEMA Maps (page 7) are particularly notable. Other outlets include outdoor shops, bookshops, SUNMAP agents and surveyors. You can also look under *Maps and Mapping* in the Yellow pages. See page 40 about how to choose maps.

SCALE AND DISTANCE

A map's scale is the ratio of distances on the map to the distance between corresponding features in the field. By measuring distance on the map and using its scale, distance in the field can be calculated.

Scales can be expressed as ratios, such as 1:25 000, or fractions, such as 1/25 000. In both cases the meaning is the same - in this case, that 1cm on the map represents 25 000cm, or 250m, in the field. The most common scales on bushwalking maps are 1:25 000, 1:50 000 and 1:100 000, although 1:10 000 and 1:32 000 maps are available for a few areas.

Estimating Distances by Formulae Method: There are several ways of using a map's scale to calculate distance in the field. One is by simply remembering some standard formulae, such as:

Scale	1cm on map represents:	10cm on map represents:
1: 10 000	100 metres in the field	1.0km in the field
1: 25 000	250 metres in the field	2.5km in the field
1: 32 000	320 metres in the field	3.2km in the field
1: 50 000	500 metres in the field	5.0km in the field
1:100000	1000 metres (1km) in the field	10.0km in the field

Linear Scales: Alternatively, you can use the map's linear scale to avoid all types of calculations. A typical linear scale is shown below. Simply measure the distance between two features on the map against the side of a compass, hold the compass against the linear scale and read off the field distance. A twig or piece of string can be used instead of a compass, string being useful for winding features such as creeks. However, note that many linear scales have the zero point located part way along the scale, not at the end. This is sometimes a source of error for beginners.

SCALE 1 : 50 000

Figure 7.1

Estimating Distances by Grid Method: A very quick system for estimating approximate distances from maps is by use of the grid squares. Each grid square represents an area on the ground 1km by 1km, with 1.41km across the diagonal.

"Large" Scales and "Small" Scales: The terms "large scale" and "small scale" often cause confusion. It is commonly assumed that "large scale maps" cover large areas or that "large scales" have "large" numbers (such as 100 000), but both assumptions are incorrect. Scales should be compared as expressed in fraction form. For example, 1/25 000 is a larger fraction than 1/100 000, and hence 1:25 000 is the larger scale. The larger the scale, the greater is the detail shown on the map and the smaller is the coverage of the map.

CONTOURS AND RELIEF

On most topographic maps, contours are used to represent relief. These masses of wriggly brown lines may be confusing at first, but there are general principles which can help you understand them. A contour is simply a line which joins points of equal elevation above sea level. For example, if contour lines were drawn across the hill in the left hand diagram of figure 7.2, when viewed from above they would present a pattern similar to that shown at the right.

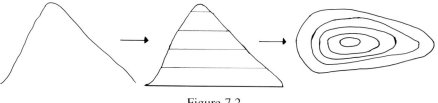

Figure 7.2

Some principles to help you interpret contours are given below.

(1) Direction of Slope: The slope always runs precisely at right angles to the contour lines. Sometimes it is difficult to tell from casual inspection which direction is uphill, but if this occurs look for creeks in the vicinity which mark gullies or valleys, or for the oval and circular contours which mark the hill tops and summits. Alternatively, trace along several contour lines to their elevation markings (see Point 5 below).

(2) Steepness of Slope: The steeper the slope, the closer are the map's contour lines e.g. concave and convex slopes appear as in Figure 7.3. This also means that areas of intense relief stand out because of the intensity and frequency of the contour lines. Special symbols are used to represent cliffs, with the contours merging into the symbol at both ends (Figure 7.4).

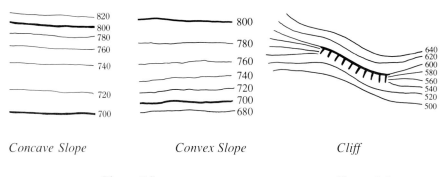

Concave Slope   *Convex Slope*   *Cliff*

Figure 7.3   Figure 7.4

(3) Contour Interval or Vertical Interval: This is the difference in elevation between the contours (refer Figure 7.2) and is stated in the margins of the map. With some exceptions (see point 9 below), it is consistent across the map.

(4) Line Intensity: On most maps every fourth or fifth contour line is printed more heavily for ease of map reading. Often this occurs at even one hundred metre intervals.

(5) Elevations above sea level can be interpreted from any point on the map, although sometimes you may need to trace along the contour line some distance to find an elevation marking. Alternatively, count contours either up or down the slope from an elevation marking on another contour, adding or subtracting the vertical interval on each occasion.

(6) Cliffs: Approximate cliff height can be discerned from the elevations of the top and bottom contours merging into the cliff symbol, as shown in Figure 7.4.

(7) Ridges and Valleys both typically have V-shaped contours. To distinguish between them, search for creeks in the vicinity which mark gullies or valleys, or for the oval or circular contours which mark the hill tops and summits. Alternatively, trace along several contour lines to their elevation markings.

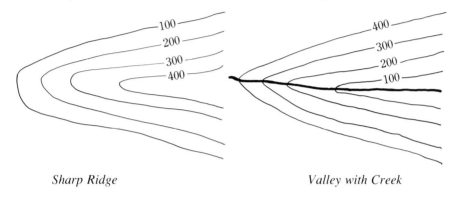

Sharp Ridge   *Valley with Creek*

Figure 7.5

(8) Typical Contour Patterns: Contours adopt similar patterns for particular types of features. Some of the most common patterns are shown in Figure 7.6.

(9) Contour Irregularities: Some maps in south-east Queensland have irregularities in their contour presentation. For example, in the Conondale Ranges certain maps have the lighter intermediate contours omitted in areas of intense relief, so that the contour interval in these areas is much greater than on the rest of the map. At Moreton Island some maps have additional contours provided in areas of low relief. Always check to see if the contour interval is consistent over the map.

GRID REFERENCES

A map's grid system is simply the set of black lines which crisscross the map vertically and horizontally, forming a system of squares. Most good topographic maps have a grid. Grid references are the most convenient way of defining and communicating positions on maps, and are also useful for measuring distances and bearings. Although initially grid systems may appear confusing, they are actually quite simple to learn and use.

National Mapping Grid: There are two types of grid system which you may encounter - the official system based on true north, and magnetic grids. Most maps recommended in this book use the former, although a few state forest and national park maps use magnetic grids. These are described briefly at the end of this section. N.B. Orienteering clubs also use magnetic grids.

In principle, positions on maps are defined by referring to the intersection of two grid lines, and using the reference number of each grid line for identification.

The grid lines running up and down the map can be regarded as running from true

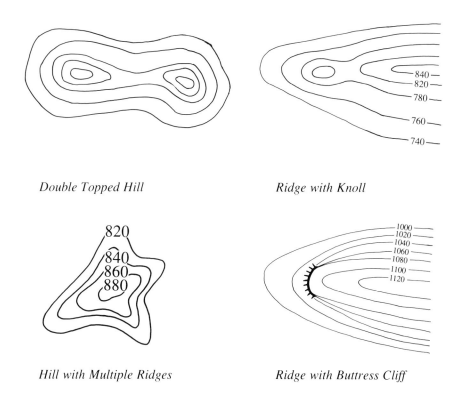

Double Topped Hill

Ridge with Knoll

840
820
780
760
740

820
840
860
880

Hill with Multiple Ridges

1000
1020
1040
1060
1080
1100
1120

Ridge with Buttress Cliff

Figure 7.6

north to true south, and those running across the map from true east to true west (this is not precisely the case, but the difference is so slight that it is irrelevant for bushwalking purposes).

The lines running up and down the map are called "eastings". This may be confusing because the lines in fact run north-south. However, the reference numbers of the lines are used to define the how far east each line lies; hence the title "eastings". Similarly, those that run across the page (west to east) are called northings, because the number of the line is a measure of how far north the line is.

Positions on maps are described by reference to the intersections of the eastings and northings. The procedure is usually outlined in the border of the map. It is illustrated below, with respect to the house shown in figure 7.7.

(1) Firstly obtain the number of the vertical line to the left of the object - 81.

(2) Next estimate how far the house is towards the next line to the right (in this case line 82), measured in tenths - i.e. 7 tenths.

(3) Hence the eastings reference is 817, and tells how far east the house lies.

(4) Similarly the northings reference is 627, telling how far north the house lies.

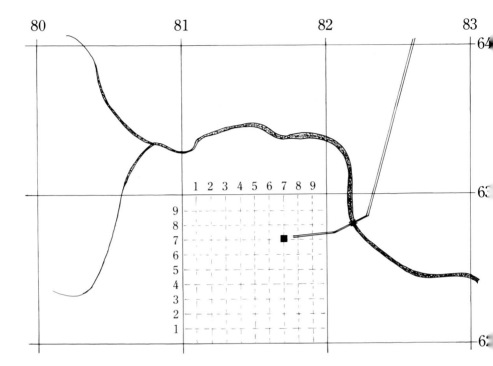

Figure 7.7

(5) The full grid reference is expressed 817 627. Similarly the grid reference of the ford across the creek would be 822 628.

Technically, all grid references should be prefixed by initials denoting the 100 000 grid square identification (refer to a topographic map for explanation), but for purposes of conciseness this practice is not followed in this book.

The eastings reference is always stated first - it may be useful to remember that the references are stated alphabetically i.e. eastings before northings. Note also that grid references must contain an even number of figures, usually six. However four figure grid references can be used for describing approximate locations, or for especially large features such as lakes or towns which might occupy a whole square.

All official topographic maps in the scale range 1:10 000 to 1:100 000 employ the same grid system. This means that a grid reference calculated from a map of 1:25 000 scale will describe exactly the same position on the 1:10 000, 1:50 000 and 1:100 000 sheets covering the same area.

Other Uses of Grid Systems: Grid squares provide a convenient linear scale across the map. Each grid square represents an area on the ground 1km by 1km, with 1.41km (just less than a mile) across the diagonal. Such an area is about 100 hectares (250 acres).

The map's grid system also provides a convenient directional frame of reference when measuring bearings, which is a great advantage if accurate navigation is required. This procedure is described later in this chapter.

Magnetic Grids: Some state forest and national park maps, as well as those produced by orienteering clubs, use magnetic grids - i.e. the eastings run from magnetic north to magnetic south rather than true north to true south. This makes it easier to measure magnetic bearings. If you encounter such a map when bushwalking, there are several points to note. One is that grid references calculated from these maps (if in fact the grid lines are numbered) cannot be used with other maps. Another is that no conversion for magnetic variation is necessary when using bearings measured from such maps in field navigation.

COMPASSES AND DIRECTIONS

ELEMENTS OF A COMPASS

Information on choosing compasses has been given in Chapter 5 (page 41). It is necessary to know the terminology used to describe the various features of a compass. This terminology is illustrated with reference to the diagram of a typical bushwalking compass in Figure 7.8

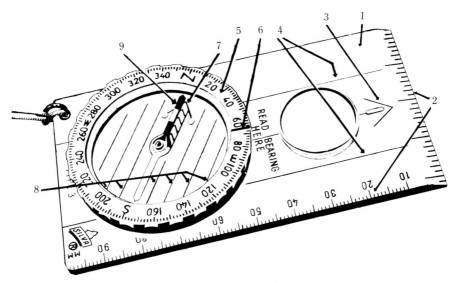

Figure 7.8: *A typical bushwalking compass*

1. Base plate;   2. Edge of base plate, usually possessing a short ruler and scale; 3. Travel Arrow; 4. Aid lines; 5. Dial (rotating), graduated from 0° to 360°; 6. Index marker, located over the dial in line with the travel arrow; 7. Orienting arrow, which points to 0° on the dial; 8. Orienting lines, which run parallel to the orienting arrow; 9. Magnetic compass needle, the red end of which points to magnetic north.

65

MEASURING DIRECTIONS

Directions can be indicated descriptively or numerically. Most of us are familiar with the descriptive method which makes use of the four main points of the compass rose - north, south, east and west. With this method intermediate directions can be indicated by various levels of hyphenation e.g. north-east, north-north-west etc. However, the procedure is wordy and approximate, so the numeric method is necessary for accurate navigation.

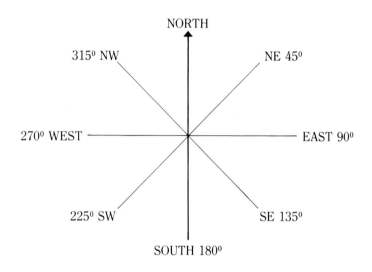

Figure 7.9

With the numeric method, angles are measured off from north in a clockwise manner to indicate particular directions (refer Figure 7.9). East is 90°, south is 180°, and west is 270°. North-east is 45°, south-east is 135°, south-west is 225° and north-west is 315°.North is arbitrarily either 0° or 360°. Opposite directions differ by exactly 180°.

The procedure for measuring a direction, or bearing, on a map using a bushwalking compass is described below. Precision is important at each step.

(1) Lay the map on a flat surface for easiest working, and clearly identify the direction or bearing you wish to measure.

(2) Place the compass flat on the map with the edge located precisely along the line of the bearing, and the travel arrow in the direction of the target feature.

(3) Without moving the base plate, rotate the dial unit so that the orienting arrow points to the map's north, and the orienting lines are parallel with the grid lines. Take no notice of the magnetic needle.

(4) The reading of the dial at the index marker gives you the bearing based on grid north. However, before use in field navigation, this bearing should normally be adjusted for magnetic variation. This subject is discussed below.

MAGNETIC VARIATION

Magnetic variation is often a source of great confusion, although once properly understood, it is neither complex nor difficult. Magnetic variation is simply the difference in direction between true north (or grid north, which for bushwalking purposes is usually identical) and magnetic north. True north is the position of the north pole, which is a stable geographic point on the earth's surface, and for this reason is the directional basis of most maps. However, the magnetic north pole, to which your compass needle will point, is located about 2000km closer to North America. Its position also moves very slightly each year.

In south-east Queensland, magnetic variation is always about 11° to the east of true north, as shown in Figure 7.10. In other parts of Australia there are different amounts of magnetic variation.

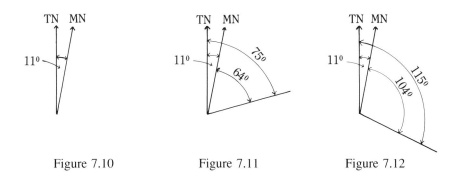

Figure 7.10   Figure 7.11   Figure 7.12

By reference to Figures 7.11 and 7.12, one can see that, in this region, the value of a bearing measured from magnetic north is always about 11° less than the same bearing measured from true north. Conversely, the value of a bearing measured off true north is always about 11° greater than the same bearing measured from magnetic north. Accordingly, when adjusting for magnetic variation in south-east Queensland, use the following simple rules. **N.B. These conversion rules do not necessarily apply in other parts of Australia.**

(i) If converting a bearing measured off a map (true north) for use in field navigation (magnetic north), subtract 11° - i.e. rotate the compass dial so that it reads 11° less.

(ii) If converting a bearing measured in the field (magnetic north) for use on a map (true north), add 11° - i.e. rotate the compass dial so that it reads 11° greater.

Note that these conversion rules assume that you are not using a magnetic grid (refer page 65). The type of grid, and more details about the map's magnetic variation, can be found by reference to the magnetic variation diagram at the bottom of the map.

Many people question if it is necessary to adjust for magnetic variation, since 11° appears to be a very small angle. In cases when only an approximate direction is required, the procedure can be avoided. However, it is best not to adopt such practice too widely, especially when descending ridges. Two ridges running down from a knoll in directions within 30° of each other can easily be mistaken unless precise bearings are followed.

USING BEARINGS IN THE FIELD

In south-east Queensland, bushwalkers most commonly use bearings when descending ridges. In this situation, the bearing down the ridge would be measured on a map, and then, after adjustment for magnetic variation, it would be followed in descent. To follow a bearing in the field:

(1) Ensure the dial is set correctly and that you are holding the compass level.
(2) Rotate the whole compass (not the dial) until the north end of the magnetic needle coincides with the arrow end of the orienting arrow.
(3) Your direction of travel is now indicated by the travel arrow. However, don't simply start off in a rough direction. Far greater accuracy is achieved if you sight along the travel arrow, and select a clear target. Once you reach this target, repeat the exercise until you have travelled the relevant distance.

To measure a field bearing, sight along the travel arrow towards the target feature, and while keeping the compass level, rotate the dial until the north end of the magnetic needle coincides exactly with the orienting arrow. Field bearings are commonly employed on maps to either identify landmarks or find your position from landmarks. Readers should refer to a good navigation text to acquire information on these topics, and on the host of other ways that bearings can be used.

ORIENTING A MAP

A simple method for identifying landmarks is to orientate your map. This can be done with a compass as follows:

(1) Lay the map flat on the ground.
(2) Set the compass dial so that index marker reads "0" (the orienting and travel arrows should coincide).
(3) Position the compass on the magnetic variation diagram, with the edge of the compass precisely along the magnetic variation line and the travel arrow pointing towards the map's magnetic north. Take no notice of the magnetic needle at this stage.
(4) Carefully keeping the compass in this position on the map, rotate the map and compass together until the magnetic needle and the orienting arrow coincide.

If a map is orientated correctly, you should be able to run a straight line from your position on the map to a feature visible in the field, precisely crossing the feature's map position.

It is also possible to orientate your map without a compass. Carefully run a line from your position on the map to a feature in the field, then rotate the map so that this line crosses over the map position of the feature. Sometimes this technique can be used for identifying directions without a compass.

COMMON ERRORS

Beginners in particular often make simple but drastic errors when using compasses. Common examples include aligning the wrong end of the magnetic needle with the incorrect end of the orienting arrow, or similarly, having the travel or orienting arrows pointing in the wrong directions when measuring bearings on maps. In both cases your bearings will be in error by 180°. Lack of precision is another common fault.

Many south-east Queensland peaks have a significant magnetic content, which can

sway compass needles dramatically. The high iron content of the basalt is responsible for this phenomenon, which is common on the peaks of the Main Range (the razorback at the end of the graded track at Mt Mitchell is an excellent place to demonstrate the phenomenon). However, despite the great influence on the needle, it mainly only occurs on the actual summits, and accordingly is rarely of major concern.

NAVIGATIONAL EMERGENCIES

The navigation information presented in this and earlier chapters, although only brief, should be sufficient to prevent you becoming seriously lost. However, there will probably be occasions when you become disorientated by vegetation. The best strategy in these situations is to either retrace your steps a short distance before searching for a track, or to sit down and calmly and logically work out your route. It may be useful to climb up to a major landmark, either to obtain views, or simply because a prominent feature should be easier to locate on the map.

An estimate of north can be found without a compass by pointing the "12" of your watch at the sun, and dissecting the angle between the 12 and the hour hand. If you have a digital watch, you'll have to imagine the position of the hour hand. However, this method is only approximate.

If you do become seriously lost, the most important action initially is to sit down and think out your situation. Examine the map in intricate detail to try to work out your previous route. You will probably have three alternative courses of action.

• Travel back the way you came
• Travel by the shortest route to civilisation or safety
• Travel towards some landmark or clearing which will help you regain your bearings, or at which searchers will be able to find you.

Following creeks downstream will lead to civilisation within about a day for virtually all areas covered in this book (the lower Boonoo Boonoo River may be an exception). While some creeks in Lamington are exceptionally rugged, waterfalls can generally be bypassed along ridges. A few creeks in or near the graded track regions of Lamington may be blocked off by major waterfalls or gorges, but graded tracks nearly always lie a short distance upstream of these obstacles. Nevertheless, it is important to remember if lost in rugged terrain that you should never cut off your means of retreat.

Always travel on major ridges, creeks or tracks if lost. Not only will these ease travel, but in rugged regions these are the only areas feasible to search. Leave written notes or markers to direct searchers, and be prepared to signal searching aircraft with coloured items, movement, mirrors or smoky fires. Whistles may attract ground searchers. Searches are generally organised in south-east Queensland if a party is overdue by 24 hours, but this delay time (necessary to prevent false alarms) will vary with the area and circumstances. Naturally a search can only be organised if you have left information with a responsible person about the duration and location of your trip.

If lost, you should adopt a calm logical plan, and only change plans if clearly necessary. Chopping and changing is likely to confuse both you and searchers. Once overdue by 24 hours, it is generally advisable to stay on a major ridge, track or creek and wait for searchers to find you, unless you are sure of your route to safety.

7

MINIMUM IMPACT BUSHWALKING

There have been three major changes to bushwalking in Australia during the last twenty years. Most evident are the great increases in the numbers of participants and the huge technological advances in the quality and range of equipment. The third major change is the development of the minimum impact bushwalking philosophy. To some extent, this has evolved in response to the increase in the number of bushwalkers.

Quite simply, minimum impact bushwalking is a code aimed at preserving both the ecological values and the wilderness values of bushwalking areas. To preserve ecological values, it is necessary to minimise physical damage such as erosion, vegetation trampling and disturbance of fauna. To preserve wilderness values, it is necessary to protect the opportunities that these areas provide for solitude, peace and pristine surroundings.

Sadly, the last twenty years have seen a marked decline in the environmental quality of Australian bushwalking regions, despite the upsurge in minimum impact practices. This has largely been due to the high proportion of inexperienced bushwalkers who are uncaring or ignorant of ways to preserve the environment. Consequently, many bushwalking regions are now suffering major degradation. The problems are diverse, ranging from litter, track erosion, campsite degradation and pollution of waterways to vegetation damage caused by firewood collection. What many people fail to understand is that with today's heavy visitation rates, much of this damage is irreparable, so that each year the environmental quality deteriorates further.

When novice bushwalkers first hear of minimum impact bushwalking practices, they sometimes consider the code extremist. However, all practices have been formulated for good reasons and purposes. The code itself is summarised in Chapter 1, but so that readers can obtain a more comprehensive understanding, this chapter explains the reasons for the various practices and expands on particular points.

THE PHILOSOPHY OF MINIMUM IMPACT BUSHWALKING

When books discuss bushwalking ethics, it is common to provide readers with a list of "rules". While a code of ethics has been summarised in Chapter 1, minimum impact bushwalking is more of a general bushwalking philosophy than a set of rules.

HISTORY

Before about 1970, bushwalking environmental practices were relatively basic. Litter was considered offensive, but otherwise there were few stringent guidelines. Indeed many bushwalkers shared the common view of Australians that bushwalking was mainly a challenge against nature. Nature was there to be "conquered" and it was acceptable to modify the environment to suit human needs. Many bushwalking books of the era told how to build shelters and various utilities using felled trees and other living vegetation.

Because there were relatively low numbers of bushwalkers, the areas were usually able to recover from this disturbance. However, with the increase in population, upsurge in outdoor recreation and decrease in bush localities to visit, all that has now changed. Where twenty people may have visited a site during all of 1960, there now might come five hundred. A place which annually received a few hundred people in the 1960s may now have to cope with ten thousand or more. In the seventies in particular, it soon became evident that the environment could not withstand many thousands of people using the same camping and bushwalking practices used by a mere handful in the past.

Experienced bushwalkers were quick to recognise the decline and soon began to develop a code to help preserve the environment. Later this became known as minimum impact bushwalking.

Unfortunately, a large proportion of bushwalkers are novices or only casual bush visitors, and the problem continues that one or two reckless visitors can have more impact than fifty who practice minimum impact bushwalking. Sadly, many Australians continue to associate bushwalking with the pioneering spirit and the "taming of nature", and there is little doubt that most environmental degradation in bushwalking areas nowadays is caused by people ignorant or uncaring of proper conservation practices. As one might imagine, this situation often angers experienced bushwalkers.

PRINCIPLES OF MINIMUM IMPACT BUSHWALKING

Several fundamental principles underlie the philosophy of minimum impact bushwalking. One is the recognition of the need to preserve the ecological integrity and the wilderness values of our bushwalking areas, both for our own enjoyment and future generations. Not only are the ecological values important, but the mind and spirit receive their greatest fulfilment if we can enjoy the bush in pristine condition, free from the marks of human intrusion. It is also recognised that to achieve these aims, some controls and precautions are required because of the great visitation pressures that currently exist.

However, just as important is a subtle change of philosophical approach - that the bush should not be modified to meet human needs, but that human behaviour should be modified to suit the needs of the environment. This can be done by sacrificing only a small part of the traditional freedoms and pleasures of a visit to the bush. What is required mostly is simple care and commonsense.

The aims of minimum impact bushwalking include control of environmental degradation in popular bushwalking areas and maintenance of the pristine qualities of more remote regions. To achieve this, bushwalkers must try to leave the areas they visit unmarked and unaltered, as close as possible to their natural condition. This aim is broadly achievable if all walkers practise the code. In fact, it is often possible to visit a bushwalking area and leave virtually no sign of your visit.

KEEPING WILDERNESS WILD

To understand the philosophies behind minimum impact bushwalking, it is valuable to identify the qualities which people seek from this rewarding but sometimes demanding form of recreation. Some of these qualities are obvious e.g. beautiful natural scenery, challenge, adventure, relaxation and exercise. In addition, there is a variety of subtle and often subconscious factors which conceive much of the enjoyment and fulfilment that bushwalkers experience.

Probably the most common motivation for regular bushwalkers (even if it is subconscious) is that bushwalking allows people to divorce themselves from the rigours and stresses of human society. There is a variety of related emotions - feelings of affinity with nature, enjoyment of peaceful surroundings, enjoyment of opportunities for solitude, and increased feelings of freedom, independence and self-reliance. The capacity of an area to facilitate these types of emotions is largely dependent on what is commonly called its "wilderness value".

An area's wilderness value depends on two basic factors - pristinity values (absence of evidence of human impact) and solitude/remoteness values (the region's size and remoteness, and the opportunity available to enjoy the area in reasonable solitude). Any impact which reduces these values, whether it be damage of vegetation around a campsite or invasion of an area with an excessively large group of people, will reduce the wilderness value to a greater or lesser extent. Consequently, many minimum impact practices are specifically aimed at maintaining the pristine qualities of bushwalking areas and preventing visitation levels becoming excessive.

RUBBISH DISPOSAL AND LITTER

The reasons for controlling rubbish and litter in bushwalking areas seem obvious, since rubbish, whether in a city street or on a mountain summit, is universally considered ugly and repugnant. However, the unsightliness is far more pronounced in bush areas. Contrasting starkly with the natural beauty, the ugliness of rubbish is an affront to the pure and pristine nature of the environment, which bushwalkers value highly. Experienced walkers try to keep the bush free from any signs of human intrusion, taking great care to avoid leaving any form of rubbish.

Carry Out What You Carry In: The general rule is to carry out what you carry in, so always keep a plastic bag handy in which to take your rubbish back to civilisation. This includes small items such as cigarette butts, match ends, orange peel, lolly wrappers and any twist ties used to seal plastic bags. While some people may consider these too small to worry about, others will find them objectionable.

Tins and Glass: Among the misconceptions held by the general public about rubbish disposal in the bush, the old "burn, bash and bury" rule for disposal of tin cans is probably still the most common. This practice has long been discredited since the environment around campsites cannot cope with people burying numerous tins. In any event, the long time taken for rusting almost guarantees that the tins will become litter well before they break down. An additional objection in this era is that many cans nowadays are made of aluminium, which doesn't rust or corrode (nor, for that matter, do they burn - see below for more details). Therefore, cans should always be carried out. Similarly, glass should never be left in the bush since it is totally non-degradable. Glass has the additional unpleasant consequence of being dangerous to anyone walking around a campsite with bare feet.

What You Can Burn and What You Can't: Another common misconception relates to the burning of rubbish. If you have a wood fire, there may be little harm in burning rubbish that is entirely non-toxic and combustible. However, often apparently burnable rubbish is not entirely combustible, so that popular fireplaces accumulate considerable quantities of non-decaying litter. This may not be evident when you leave the camp in the morning, but becomes visible after the first heavy rains wash the white ash from the fireplace. The greatest offenders in this regard are food packages and aluminium products (see below).

Unburnt rubbish shouldn't be left in fireplaces for the next party to destroy. You will find that other bushwalkers value highly the natural appearance of campsites and object to rubbish being left around them or in their fireplaces. If you are unable to burn litter at the time, put it in your rubbish bag and take it with you.

Food Packages, Aluminium Foil and Aluminium Cans: The majority of food packages apparently made from paper actually have thin aluminium foil linings. Burning does not destroy aluminium, even when it is in foil form. While aluminium foil may appear to break down in a fire, in fact it simply breaks up, creating an ugly white residue in the coals after rain washes away the surface layer of white ash.

Some people have a mistaken belief that aluminium cans will burn. As with foil, attempts to burn aluminium cans will always leave ugly remains in the fireplace, even though the deformed white metal may not be evident initially.

If you are on a long trip and have accumulated a great number of old food packages, it may be possible to carefully burn the paper off the foil at the side of the fire to reduce their volume, and later transfer the foil to your rubbish bag. However, the packages or foil should never be simply discarded in the fire.

Plastic: As a general rule, plastic shouldn't be burnt since the fumes are noxious and the unpleasant smell will linger for a considerable time. One sure way to anger your campsite companions is to burn a plastic item or plastic-coated food packet while food is being cooked or people are standing around a fire.

Tampons and Sanitary Pads: As a general rule, tampons and sanitary pads should not be left in the bush, even if they are well buried. See page 79 for more details.

What You Can Bury and What You Can't: Whether you should bury rubbish will depend on its biodegradability and the remoteness of the area. Most heavily used bushwalking areas cannot cope with visitors continually burying rubbish under rocks and the like, even if it is readily biodegradable. Buried rubbish is simply likely to be unearthed by the next bushwalker, or by the scavenging animals which become tame around popular campsites. A good guideline is to carry out all rubbish if you are in a popular area, or on a trip of two days or less. On longer trips in more remote areas, there may be little harm in burying scraps such as orange peel, but care should be taken to ensure that all such rubbish is fully biodegradable and well covered. While the visitor numbers and consequent pressures may not be as great in remote areas as in popular localities, the pristine qualities of these regions are more readily devalued by minor disturbances.

CAMPING AND DOMESTIC PRACTICES

Camping ethics are possibly the most important of minimum impact bushwalking practices, since it is around campsites that the greatest amount of unnecessary environmental degradation is occurring. While problems such as erosion on popular tracks can never be eradicated completely, it is often quite possible to camp in an area and leave the site virtually as you found it. Despite this, each year the environment around recognised campsites deteriorates further. The pristine qualities of campsites are highly valued by bushwalkers, for it is often at the camp, or in the light of the setting sun or early morning, that the mind and spirit receive their greatest fulfilment. The joys and rigours of the walk are reflected upon, and the full atmosphere of the trip is experienced. Such satisfaction can be quickly shattered if the campsite is degraded and ruined. We need to adopt every reasonable means of preserving the pristine qualities and environmental integrity of campsites.

GENERAL PRACTICES

In terms of erosion and vegetation damage, the basic principle of caring for campsites is embodied in the main philosophical principle of minimum impact bushwalking i.e. don't mould the environment to suit your requirements, but mould your behaviour so as not to disturb your surroundings.

The following measures do more than simply maintain the natural appearance of bush environments. They also help to reduce the profusion of sprawling, untidy, eroded campsites which often result from continuous camping in one area.

Popular Campsites: In popular campsites, there will always be some sign of previous presence, but you can help to maintain their natural appearance by a variety of simple measures. Camp on previously used tent sites and use existing fireplaces, instead of creating new sites. Don't build fireplaces on live vegetation or tent sites. Carry out any existing rubbish from fireplaces and the campsite surrounds. Don't leave any of your own rubbish.

Pristine Campsites: In campsites showing little or no sign of previous usage, leave them in this condition. It is usually possible to conceal virtually all evidence of your visit. In pristine areas especially, search for a site where you can sleep or pitch your tent without moving rocks or branches, or damaging any vegetation. If rocks or fallen branches must be moved to provide a comfortable sleep, replace them the next morning to maintain the area's natural appearance. Just before leaving, ruffle up any grass or other compacted vegetation to help its recovery, and to disguise the site so that it won't be chosen by other campers in the near future. Preferably don't use wood fires, but if you do, scatter the ashes (after ensuring they are well doused with water) so there are no remnants of a fireplace. Don't modify the environment by leaving circular rings of logs and rocks around old fireplaces.

Tents: In all areas, use aluminium tent poles and pegs. Poles and pegs should never be cut from the bush. Don't dig trenches around tents, and don't construct tent platforms or bed sites or otherwise mark or alter the environment.

Vegetation Vandalism: Great care should be taken not to damage the vegetation around campsites. One practice to be condemned is that of hacking wantonly at trees and logs with axes and machetes. This creates a badly degraded appearance. Sometimes this type of damage is caused by family groups with uncontrolled children, so if you take your children in the bush, educate them early. Even better, leave your axes and machetes at home so they aren't available for the children (or adults) to misuse (see pages 82 and 83).

CAMPFIRES AND FIREWOOD

One of the most alarming impacts on bushwalking areas today is the damage caused by the collection of wood for campfires. This can cause severe long term destruction in localised areas. Unfortunately the issue is frequently overlooked, partly since the damage is often not immediately evident, and partly because wood fires have long been considered a traditional camping pleasure. Many novice bushwalkers continue to use campfires in places where fires should be avoided.

The Pattern of Destruction: There are many ways by which fires and firewood collection contribute to the environmental deterioration around campsites. Sometimes the damage is caused by simple vandalism or recklessness e.g. irresponsible campers breaking live branches off standing vegetation. However, less obvious effects can be just as serious, sometimes more so. Damage caused by firewood collection is insidious, worsening gradually over time, so that its effects are not immediately apparent.

The pattern is similar in most popular areas. Firstly the ground is scoured and cleared of fallen branches around the campsite. Then, as firewood becomes more scarce, campers progressively venture further afield to collect wood. This usually results in carrying large bundles of branches and dragging logs back through the scrub, actions which inevitably bash and damage vegetation on the way. Eventually irresponsible campers begin breaking both dead and live branches from standing vegetation. As the vegetation is thinned out, the campsite grows larger, and the pattern of destruction begins spiralling.

Common Misconceptions: There is a common belief that regrowth can overcome damage of this type, but this is erroneous. In many natural areas, vegetation growth is very slow, being controlled by seasonal temperatures and soil infertility. In any event, the immense usage pressures nowadays rarely give the areas any chance of regeneration. The firewood foraging process is so intense that even apparently minor actions often contribute significantly to the long term thinning of vegetation around campsites.

Another erroneous belief that it is acceptable to break dead wood from live vegetation. However, even dead twigs and branches have an ecological value. The larger dead branches provide habitats for animals and birds, while the smaller branches and twigs help protect green shoots from the abrasion damage that would otherwise be caused by people continuously brushing against vegetation and dragging bundles of sticks through the scrub.

General Guidelines: The first and possibly most important guideline regarding the use of wood fires is that you should always be prepared to cook with a stove (or do without a fire). Never depend on wood fires for either comfort or survival, since not

By using a stove ...

. . . you can help prevent campsite destruction such as this.

only are there increasing environmental disadvantages, but there are also many circumstances when it is difficult or impossible to light a fire. In south-east Queensland, this includes most rainforest areas.

The main environmental problems with wood fires occur around established camp-sites and places where firewood is scarce. In south-east Queensland, use of wood fires is rarely a problem if you are camping in a site showing few previous signs of visitation, with fallen wood readily available and no bushfire safety problems. Therefore, **a good general guideline is to avoid wood fires at any site where firewood cannot be readily collected from the ground nearby.**

Different Vegetation Types: Heath areas usually suffer most from firewood collection, since the thick vegetation is inevitably damaged by people scouring the ground and dragging out branches. Heath areas in south-east Queensland which are particularly susceptible include the peaks of Mt Barney and some sites in the coastal sandmasses. In contrast, most open eucalypt areas are relatively hardy, provided that only fallen branches are collected. The fragility of rainforest areas depends on the thickness and type of vegetation.

If Fires Are Used, ensure that they are not located on fragile vegetation such as mosses or lichen, which are very slow growing. Preferably locate fires on bare earth or previous campfire sites, but if necessary build them on less fragile vegetation such as grass (after taking appropriate action to ensure fire safety).

Campsite Rehabilitation: In areas showing no sign of previous visitation, it is important to scatter the ashes of campfires before you leave camp. Thoroughly extinguish the ashes with water, then scatter the dead coals where they won't be easily seen. This not only assists to keep the area pristine by disguising the fire site, but it also helps the surrounding vegetation grow over the scorched ground.

FIRE SAFETY

Bushfires are among the most destructive and feared phenomena in the Australian bush, so all bushwalkers should take extreme care with fires. While most practices are commonsense, all people are not as careful as they should be. Certain practices, mistakenly considered by some people to be traditional and safe, can sometimes be quite hazardous.

General Rules of Fire Safety dictate that you don't light fires in any area or time of severe fire danger, or in a place where wind could scatter live embers. There should be a reasonable area clear of vegetation surrounding the fireplace, and tents should be at least 4m away. You should never leave a fire unattended. This means that you don't leave smouldering ashes after you leave camp, or leave a fire burning after you go to bed at night or while you are away at the creek collecting water. Preferably all fires should be doused after use with ample quantities of water, although if fire danger isn't high, it may suffice to crush and stamp on the coals or cover them with wet earth. If you intend to scatter the ashes after you leave camp, firstly ensure they are thoroughly extinguished (preferably wait some time after dousing before you scatter them). Keep your campfires small. Small fires are not only safer, but help to conserve firewood.

Burning Toilet Paper: It is common bushwalking advice to burn toilet paper, but this should only be done if there is no fire risk.

Sand Regions: While not widely realised, it is probable that some of the disastrous fires which have occurred in recent decades at places such as Moreton Island have actually been caused by a common "fire safety" practice used by campers i.e. the practice of covering the fire with earth after you leave camp. While usually effective in terrains with normal soil, in sand areas this practice often substantially increases the fire danger. When buried under dry sand, burning coals can smoulder for days or even weeks (if a camp fire was large), since the sand insulates the heat while allowing seepage of oxygen. During this time the fire can be easily rekindled and spread by a strong wind blowing off the surface sand, and there is even the possibility of the fire spreading via dead tree roots. Consequently, **do not attempt to extinguish camp-fires by covering with sand unless the sand is very wet.**

SANITATION, HYGIENE AND WATER SUPPLIES

When bushwalking, it is important to observe proper sanitation and hygiene practices, and to keep water supplies free from pollutants. Camping sanitation practices originate from normal standards of hygiene and decency.

Bush Sanitation: It is important to ensure that all faecal matter and toilet paper are properly buried, well away from tracks, campsites, water courses and drainage channels (whether running or dry). Of course, if the ground is hard it is not always possible to follow this practice to the letter of the law, but some satisfactory solution can usually be found e.g. it might be feasible to unearth a large rock, or use loose soil and humus to assist with burial. Bushwalking shops now sell special lightweight trowels made of hard plastic which can help solve these delicate problems on throughwalks. On base camps, a spade or garden trowel can be used.

Burning Toilet Paper: It is common bushwalking advice to burn toilet paper, since this is usually the last material to decompose. Experienced bushwalkers often carry a set of matches in their toilet kit specifically for this reason. However, the practice should only be followed if there is no possible fire risk.

Mosses and Urine Don't Mix: In all sanitation practices, care should be taken not to harm fragile vegetation. In particular, mosses and lichens are particularly sensitive to urine and hot water, and to a less extent, soapy water (patches of dead moss are often seen around well used campsites, from these causes). Mosses and lichen are also very slow growing and take a long time to recover.

Tampons and Sanitary Pads: As a general rule, tampons and sanitary pads should not be left in the bush, even if they are well buried. This is particularly important around popular campsites, where scavenging animals can dig them up. The best solution seems to be to transfer used tampons and pads to small brown paper bags (available in supermarkets), which are carried in a plastic bag. They can then be either carried out with the rest of the rubbish, or - if the circumstances are appropriate - disposed of by burning on a hot fire.

Water Purity: The purity of water supplies is sacred in the bush. Water supplies should be kept free of all pollutants, including detergents, soap, hair shampoo and food scraps. Actually, there is rarely any need for dish washing agents in the bush, since boiling and scraping will clean most dishes. However, on long trips walkers may desire the comfort of soap and shampoo. The main restrictions on these compounds are to ensure they are used well away from water courses, and are not used in excessive quantities. Washing water should either be disposed of on the fire site, or drained off in porous soil, away from creeks and fragile vegetation such as mosses and lichens. As a general rule, don't rinse dishes or utensils in creeks as this normally releases grease and food scraps.

TRACK MARKING AND WALKING PRACTICES

With the high levels of visitation to bushwalking areas, it is important to limit erosion and vegetation damage as much as possible. In this respect, some minimum impact ethics are self-explanatory e.g. by using formed tracks where they exist, you can help avoid making new parallel tracks. However, two subjects which often cause contention are track marking and party size limitations.

TRACK MARKING

As discussed in Chapter 4, bush tracks vary in quality and definition, and to assist with navigation some walkers mark the routes with coloured tape or by other means. However, modern bushwalking ethics disapprove of track marking on unofficial bushwalking routes (i.e. tracks that are not maintained by management authorities), except in special circumstances. In some cases there are direct ecological detriments, but it is usually the indirect disadvantages which are most serious in the long term.

Arguments For Track Marking are usually quite simple - track marking is intended to make navigation easier. Track marking supporters also usually claim that this makes bushwalking safer, especially for inexperienced walkers. A third argument sometimes put forward is that track marking opens up rugged areas to more people, and to people with less skill and experience. This is claimed as a benefit by some people, but is also used by others as an argument against track marking.

Arguments Against Track Marking: The disadvantages of track marking are more subtle and long term, but nevertheless quite serious. There are many interrelated arguments, including:

• Track marking decreases the range of bushwalking recreation experiences available, especially more challenging experiences. People have just as much right for challenging bushwalking experiences as other types, yet the opportunities available for challenging bushwalks are being diminished while other opportunities are often being increased.

• Track marking decreases the wilderness value of bushwalking areas. Not only does it introduce foreign marking tape and decrease the challenge, but it also makes the areas more accessible and increases the level of general visitation.

• Track marking encourages less experienced bushwalkers to visit more pristine bushwalking regions, increasing environmental damage (it is an established fact that less experienced walkers cause by far the greatest amount of environmental damage in bushwalking regions).

• Track marking encourages less experienced bushwalkers to visit more rugged bushwalking regions, increasing safety problems.

• In the long term, track marking doesn't decrease the chance of people becoming lost, but substantially increases the risk. This is because people become accustomed to relying on track marking and don't develop appropriate navigation skills. In addition, the proportion of inexperienced walkers using the areas increases. Unless the track marking is rigorously maintained, it is inevitable that the marking system will deteriorate at some time and that inexperienced walkers will become lost (this can be demonstrated with historical cases).

• Track marking contributes to spiralling usage of bushwalking areas, which eventually leads to management authorities limiting visitor numbers by direct controls.

If possible it is preferable to prevent overusage by indirect controls (e.g. the ruggedness of the terrain).

- Track marking continues the tradition of people modifying the environment to suit their own needs and purposes, instead of bushwalking in an area on its own terms. The question is then asked, "Where does it stop?" The same principles used to support track marking can be used to support arguments that graded track systems or even roads be provided throughout all national park areas.
- Track marking subverts national park management planning, both with respect to the provision of a range of recreational experiences and with regard to management of the area's conservation values.
- National park and other relevant management authorities invariably oppose track marking, so the activity is almost certainly illegal.

Recommended Guidelines: It is probably too extreme to say that there is no place for track marking at all, but it certainly should be limited to particular localities and circumstances. There should be no need for track marking on routes which follow obvious physical features such as ridges or creeks, but track marking could be considered acceptable in circumstances such as:

- A situation where a major route travels through navigationally difficult terrain but does not follow physical terrain features (only a few routes in south Queensland meet this criterion, since most follow terrain features).
- Low key marking (e.g. a rock cairn) for a route junction which might otherwise be missed, such as an ascent point from a creek.
- Localised track marking to show a route to negotiate a dangerous feature, or to prevent erosion or some other environmental damage.

If track marking is undertaken, ensure that you know the route well and that it is marked correctly. Only use methods which don't involve vegetation damage, such as plastic tape or rock cairns. Machete blazing should never be used, and even the nailing of markers to trees should be avoided (see below).

"De-marking" Tracks: Many bushwalkers are so opposed to track marking that they remove any track marking tape they find.

Blazing Destruction: Whatever else you think about track marking, one practice that is now universally condemned is the old practice of marking tracks with machete blazes. Not only are the blazes unsightly, but they also harm the trees by rendering them susceptible to termites and fungi. In the higher wetter rainforest areas especially, machete blazes promote fungal infection which may result in major amounts of tree death in the long term. In the 1970s, a section of the border route in Lamington National Park provided clear evidence of this damage, with numerous dead and fallen trees invariably marked by machete blazes (the route on this section has since been altered). The clear message from this case is that machetes have no place in modern bushwalking (see also page 82 and 83).

PARTY SIZE

While the desirable minimum size for a bushwalking party depends on safety factors, the desirable maximum size depends on environmental factors and the rights of other bushwalkers to an harmonious social atmosphere. In the bush, an "harmonious social atmosphere" includes the right to peace and reasonable solitude values. People visit the bush for its tranquillity and natural attributes, not to be overrun by hordes of others or drowned out by noisy or boisterous behaviour. If you are organising a group trip, you should consider whether the sheer size of the group is likely to damage the environment or mar the enjoyment of others.

This is not an issue in which clear guidelines are possible, particularly considering the great range of user groups and the variety of bushwalking terrains and experiences. However, here are some general principles.

Management Perspectives: Management authorities consider the party size issue from two perspectives. The first are the ecological implications. Some questions which might be asked include: What size of bushwalking party can be accommodated in a region's campsites without causing environmental damage? What levels of usage can be permitted without causing erosion and vegetation trampling damage? Are any rare or sensitive species of fauna or flora under threat?

The secondary considerations are the types of social experiences desired by visitors. These not only vary with the type of visitor, but also (and just as importantly) with the type of area e.g. the same individuals will be more tolerant of crowds at a place such as Mt Edwards than on the high peaks of the Main Range, partly because people's expectations are different and partly because of the intrinsic nature of the areas themselves.

Throughwalk Guidelines: The principle agreed for most circumstances is that party size be limited by the size and frequency of campsites, so it is possible to set specific limits for different trips. Desirable party sizes for throughwalking in most areas are from 4 to 10, although occasionally groups of 12 can be accommodated if you are prepared to plan your itinerary around specific large campsites. Larger groups should normally only be considered if using developed camp grounds. On all trips remember that yours may not be the only party intending to camp at a particular site, and that significant environmental damage may be caused if a campsite is filled beyond capacity. N.B. Currently the Queensland National Parks and Wildlife Service is incorporating throughwalk party size limits in its management plans. Limits could be as low as six in some places.

Day Walk Guidelines: It is much harder to make clear guidelines for day walks. In south-east Queensland, it would probably be appropriate to limit day walk parties to about 20 to 25, perhaps splitting the group and visiting separate localities if the party numbers are excessive. However, this is only an approximate guideline. In fragile areas, party sizes should have much lower limits.

GENERAL ISSUES

THE PHILOSOPHY OF NON-DISTURBANCE

It should be obvious by now that the general philosophy of bushwalking conservation is one of non-disturbance. Rocks, vegetation, animals and archeological sites should be left undisturbed unless quite unavoidable, and naturally nothing should be purposely damaged or defaced. However, no "list of rules" is comprehensive. If you are uncertain whether a particular action is environmentally sound, the general guideline of non-disturbance will often indicate the best solution.

MACHETES AND AXES

With the exception of the occasional use of an axe to split wood at developed camp grounds, machetes and axes have no place in modern bushwalking. Not only are they undesirable, they are also unnecessary and often illegal. The following summarises the issues involved:

General Objections: As previously mentioned, the old practice of marking tracks with machete blazes is now universally condemned. Similarly, the use of machetes to hack away thick or thorny scrub is undesirable, since rarely is the damage restricted to the truly offensive plants. Machetes are actually a very inefficient means of clearing away offensive undergrowth - garden gloves, gaiters and perhaps a stout stick (for patches of nettles and the like) are usually much quicker.

Safety Aspects: If you are not fully competent with a machete, there is always a significant danger involved. Tired sweaty hands can easily cause a blow to glance off harder wood, rebounding onto the user. In the bush, such an accident could become a major medical emergency.

Legalities: Machetes are actually illegal in Queensland national parks, with a $500 fine for contravention of the regulation. While rangers may apply this regulation with some discretion, it is almost impossible from a management viewpoint to assess whether the implements would be used responsibly or irresponsibly by particular individuals. There are also cases of unintentional misuse e.g. sometimes trees around camp grounds are hacked by the uncontrolled children of otherwise responsible campers. The aftermath of one person's reckless machete work can last 30 years or even longer. The only practical management approach is to ban machetes completely.

Use of Axes at Developed Camp Grounds: Axes are sometimes required for splitting firewood supplied by rangers, although in these circumstances there is usually an axe supplied.

FIREARMS AND DOMESTIC ANIMALS

Firearms and domestic animals are illegal in national parks. Even in those state forests and crown lands where some domestic animals are permitted, it is desirable that they not be taken. Not only might they disturb wildlife and other visitors, but cats can stray and go feral, and the animals themselves are at risk e.g. in the past many dogs taken to Fraser Island have been killed by dingoes. It is better to leave them in the safety of a boarding kennel for everyone's benefit.

SOUND POLLUTION AND OTHER IMPACTS

An impact that many people underestimate when they visit the bush is that of sheer presence. While there may not be major ecological consequences, other visitors will certainly object if a group is excessively large, unruly or inconsiderate. People visit the bush for its tranquillity and natural attributes, not to be overrun by hordes of others, be drowned out by noisy or boisterous behaviour, or have their peace of mind intruded upon by radios and generators. Even shouting from lookouts and mountain tops can be offensive to other visitors. In the bush, let the sounds of the natural inhabitants predominate. Behave responsibly, respect the rights of others and don't take radios, sound systems or generators. Naturally party size is a major consideration.

A final word on this aspect is to be self-reliant. People may not mind loaning an item of equipment to a walker who has genuinely forgotten something, but never make a practice of borrowing to make up for lack of preparation or unwillingness to carry a full kit.

PART TWO
REGIONAL DESCRIPTIONS

South-east Queensland bushwalkers are favoured in having a choice of terrain types for their recreation, from high rocky peaks to extensive graded track systems, from rainforest creeks to coastal sandmasses. Although the heavy hand of western civilisation has had extensive impact on the region, Brisbane has a greater variety of bushwalking terrain in its environs than most of Australia's principal cities.

It is commonly thought that the majority of south-east Queensland's bushwalking opportunities are contained in the Scenic Rim - the name given to that continuous sweeping crescent of mountains stretching over 200km from Laidley to the Gold Coast. While this area certainly provides the most classic bushwalking experiences, it accounts for only six of the regions discussed in the following chapters.

CONTENTS OF PART TWO

8

ONE HUNDRED SUGGESTED WALKS

This chapter lists a range of suggestions for bushwalking trips, grouped into eight categories. These can be used in several ways:

- Thirty-five day walks in Sections 1 and 2 have been especially chosen to help people starting bushwalking choose their first trips. These walks are intended to develop fitness, experience and familiarity with bushwalking conditions, without the need (in most cases) for navigation and scrambling skills. The main difference between the two sections is the level of fitness required. N.B. The fact that the trips are suitable for beginners doesn't mean that they are any less interesting than the trips listed later. Experienced bushwalkers will also find them inspiring.

- Trip suggestions in other sections are arranged with a graduated scale of difficulty to help bushwalkers of varying levels of experience choose walks appropriate to their skill and fitness, thereby enabling them to develop their knowledge and ability safely.

- Bushwalks in Section 3 have been especially chosen to help people develop navigation skills, although they also provide enjoyable bushwalks in their own right.

- Bushwalks in Section 4 are mainly easy throughwalks, intended to help non-throughwalkers overcome the barriers of tackling their first trips carrying a full pack. The trips will develop fitness and experience, without the demands of rugged terrains and serious obstacles. Experienced throughwalkers will also find these trips interesting.

- In addition, all the trip suggestions can be used by experienced bushwalkers who are unfamiliar with south-east Queensland conditions as a means of short-listing notable walks in the region (e.g. people who are visiting the region or have recently moved here). N.B. In these circumstances it is suggested that you also refer to the information in Chapter 4.

It is generally recommended that less experienced bushwalkers complete at least four walks from a particular section before progressing to the next section higher. Thoroughly read the explanation of the route grading system, given in Chapter 2, before attempting any trips. In the schedules, references are given to pages where the walks are described in more detail.

SECTION 1:
TWENTY OUTSTANDING TRACK WALKS

The day walks listed in this section will provide enjoyment to bushwalkers of all levels of experience, although they are especially recommended to beginners who lack fitness (this includes most people taking up bushwalking who do not exercise on a regular basis). The tracks provide the opportunity to develop basic walking fitness while sharing the delights of some of the most beautiful natural scenery in southern Queensland. Most are on graded tracks, which are constructed so as to eliminate steep hill climbs, and little navigation skill is required since all the tracks are signposted. Provided you undertake some basic safety preparations, you can set out on most of these trips with a small group of friends without needing much previous knowledge of the areas. N.B. Unless otherwise indicated, assume that these trips need a full day.

It is recommended that all beginners try several graded track walks when they first start bushwalking, even if they are fit. It is important to realise that a graded track leading to a feature doesn't mean that the trip is less interesting or spectacular than an off-track walk. The Coomera and Lightning Falls circuits, for example, are considered by many people to be the most beautiful waterfall areas in southern Queensland (see Walks 3 and 8).

Gradings: Most of the trips listed here would be rated between grade 1 and 2 on the grading scale used in this book (the equation for flat track walking is approximately half a grading unit per 5km of distance). However, some people who are very unfit may still find that their first few walks are quite demanding. While fairly flat, the tracks cover long distances, and this type of walking can cause blisters and sore feet in some situations. If you are very unfit, try a few shorter walks first (e.g. the Daves Creek Circuit, or some of the shorter walks at Binna Burra and Green Mountains, outlined on pages 127 to 132). Don't be disheartened if you find your first few track walks tiring. Your fitness will build quickly after you complete two or three trips.

N.B. Take careful note of the information on page 127 regarding preparation and time requirements for track walking.

SPRINGBROOK: Although there is only one graded track at Springbrook of sufficient length for a full day trip, it provides an outstanding walk, especially when the waterfalls are flowing well. There is also a range of shorter track walks available.

(1) Warrie Circuit (superb waterfalls, rainforest and creek scenery; 17km, but slightly harder than might be envisaged on the basis of its length due to a considerable elevation change around the circuit; page 115).

LAMINGTON - BINNA BURRA: Brisbane people can undertake the following graded track walks equally conveniently by either driving to Binna Burra for the day or camping overnight at the Binna Burra camp ground.

(2) Daves Creek Circuit (lookouts and unusual wildflower displays; 12km; 2/3 day; page 128).

(3) Coomera Circuit (brilliant waterfall circuit & rainforest; 18km; page 128).

(4) Ship Stern Circuit and Lower Ballanjui Falls (wide variety of attractions - rainforest, waterfalls, open forest and lookouts; 19km; page 128).

(5) Border Lookouts (rainforest, antarctic beech trees & views towards Numinbah

Valley and Mt Warning; various walks from 18km to 22km; page 129).

(6) Illinbah Circuit (attractive creek circuit; 17km; page 129).

LAMINGTON - GREEN MOUNTAINS: The various graded track walks in this beautiful area are especially popular with campers and visitors at O'Reillys Guest House. However, with an early start, the trips can also be conveniently undertaken from Brisbane by driving to Green Mountains for the day.

(7) Morans Falls and Western Lookouts (differing in character from most walks in the Green Mountains region, with outstanding views to the west; various options available; 5km to 12km, depending on the route; 2/3 day; page 130).

(8) Lightning Falls Circuit (brilliant waterfall circuit, with rainforest, antarctic beech trees and views of Mt Warning; 21km; page 132).

(9) Toolona Circuit and Mt Wanungra (brilliant waterfall circuit, with rainforest, antarctic beech trees and views of Mt Warning; 19km; page 132).

(10) Blue Pool, Stairway Falls and the Box Forest (creek scenery, waterfalls, rainforest and superb box trees; several options from 10km to 14km; page 132).

BORDER RANGES REGION: These walks are usually undertaken by camping overnight, although with an early start the trips can also be undertaken by driving from Brisbane for the day.

(11) Brindle Creek Track (truly outstanding rainforest and creek scenery, with antarctic beech trees growing beside the creeks; 12km return; 2/3 day; page 160).

(12) Sheepstation Creek to Forest Top (rainforest and creek scenery; various options from 9km to 22km; 1/2 day to full day; page 160).

(13) Mt Warning (rainforest and good views from a memorable summit; page 163).

MAIN RANGE (CUNNINGHAMS GAP): The graded track walks at Cunninghams Gap have a notably different character to others along the Scenic Rim, with drier types of vegetation and superb views along the Main Range. There are four walks available, although the following are considered to be the "classics". Cunninghams Gap makes a convenient day outing from Brisbane.

(14) Mt Mitchell (including grasstrees and open forest; 10km; 1/2 day; page 201).

(15) Mt Cordeaux and Bare Rock (rainforest and lookouts; 12km; 2/3 day; page 201).

GIRRAWEEN AND BALD ROCK NATIONAL PARKS: Girraween and Bald Rock are excellent base camping localities, with the track systems providing a range of day walks. The open eucalypt terrain makes the areas especially recommended in spring and autumn, with spring having the advantage of brilliant wildflower displays. Some of the best walks are listed below. All exhibit striking granite scenery.

(16) First Pyramid and/or The Junction (about half a day; page 245).

(17) Sphinx Rock and/or Castle Rock and/or Mt Norman (without the final climb) (a long day would be necessary to visit all these features, but half day trips are possible if you only wish to visit Castle or Sphinx Rocks; page 245).

(18) Bald Rock (normally a half day, but with an option for a longer walk; page 247).

NORTHERN COOLOOLA (RAINBOW BEACH): The coastal scenery in northern Cooloola provides these walks with a notably different character to other track walks in southern Queensland. N.B. Walking in sandy terrain is usually slower than other types of track walking.

(19) Bymien Picnic Area to Lake Freshwater (magnificent coastal rainforest of special interest to bird watchers; 12km return; page 283).

(20) Rainbow Beach to Burwilla Lookout (scribbly gum forest with excellent views over Rainbow Beach and Double Island Point; some steep hills; 16km return or 21km circuit; page 282).

SECTION 2:
FIFTEEN EASY-INTERMEDIATE WALKS

The following day trips follow reasonably well-worn tracks, although all are cross-country routes which are usually much steeper than the walks in Section 1. The suggestions are intended to help inexperienced bushwalkers choose interesting bushwalks which will develop hill climbing fitness and familiarity with bushwalking conditions. Experienced walkers will also find many of the walks quite inspiring.

Most of these walks are on unofficial tracks without signposting. Generally only very basic navigation skills are required, although some care and planning is still necessary since there may be occasional places where the routes are confusing. With the exception of Mt Beerwah, there is little scrambling necessary on the first ten walks listed, although many are rough underfoot. Some scrambling may be necessary on the latter walks, especially Walks 34 and 35. Unless indicated otherwise, assume that all trips can be done as day trips from Brisbane and require a full day.

The walks are listed in approximate order of difficulty (based on a balance of physical fitness required and any navigation or scrambling difficulties). N.B. If you lack bushwalking experience and don't get regular exercise, it is recommended that you try several walks from Section 1 before tackling the trips here.

(21) Spicers Gap: Mt Mathieson Circuit (an official track but with some short steep hills; interesting forest and views; most suited to cooler months; 1/2 day; grade 11/2; page 201 and 202).

(22) Boonah Region: Mt Edwards (not as good as some walks but interesting forest and views; most suited to cooler months; 1/2 day; grade 11/2; page 234).

(23) Goomburra State Forest: Ridge and Cascades Tracks (official tracks but with some short steep hills; interesting forest and creek scenery; usually done from a base camp but day trips from Brisbane are possible with an early start; flexible length; grade 1 to 11/2; page 222).

(24) Lamington: Westrays Grave (historical interest; attractive creek scenery; swimming; rainforest; suited to warmer weather but not extreme heat; grade 11/2 to 2; page 146).

(25) Glass House Mountains: Mt Ngungun (delightful small mountain with interesting views and wildflowers; 1/2 day; grade 11/2; page 268).

(26) Conondale Ranges: Mt Allan from Booloumba Creek (not as inspiring as some walks but interesting views; quite steep; usually done from a base camp but a day trip from Brisbane is possible with an early start; 1/2 day; grade 2; page 257).

(27) Glass House Mountains: Mt Tibberoowuccum (an interesting small mountain with an unusual but easy razorback near the summit; 1/2 day; grade 11/2 to 2; page 269).

(28) Glass House Mountains: Mt Beerwah (highest of the Glass House Mountains; some care required; scrambling necessary; 1/2 day; grade 21/2 to 3; page 269).

(29) Glass House Mountains: Mt Tunbubudla East Peak (perhaps the most under-rated Glass House peak; 1/2 to 2/3 day; grade 2; page 269). N.B. The west peak is lower than the east peak but considerably harder. It should not be attempted by inexperienced bushwalkers.

(30) Brisbane Forest Park: Middle Kobble Creek Circuit (interesting waterfalls and open forest; an unusual walk best suited to late autumn and winter; basic map reading skill required; grade 2 to 3; page 107).

(31) Lamington: Wagawn from Numinbah Valley (rainforest, a large cave and views over Numinbah and northern NSW; some navigation care required and a little easy scrambling involved; a short day; grade 2 to 21/2; page 132).

(32) Sundown National Park: Ooline Creek (creek features in an unusually arid landscape; not suited to warmer months; visited from a base camp at the national park camp ground; grade 2 to 3, with the difficulty increasing as you go higher up the creek; scrambling in the higher sections; pages 248 and 251).

(33) Sundown National Park: McAllisters Creek (red cliffs in a relatively arid landscape; not suited to warmer months; visited from a base camp at the national park camp ground; some scrambling and rock fall danger on the bypass around Split Rock Falls; grade 2 to 31/2, depending on the distance travelled up the creek; pages 248 to 249).

(34) Barney/Ballow Region: Mt Clunie from White Swamp (extremely steep and quite an arduous climb, but not technically difficult; follows border fence so no navigational problems; awkward slippery slopes; grade 31/2 to 4; page 175).

(35) Springbrook: Mt Cougal via East Ridge (the distinctive twin summit west of Coolangatta; good views; some scrambling involved and some navigation care required; grade 3; page 116).

SECTION 3:
FIFTEEN NAVIGATION WALKS

From the point of view of physical fitness, the trips in this section are (on average) only marginally harder than those in Section 2. However, all involve some naviga-tion difficulty. The navigation problems vary from quite minor situations which mainly require basic map reading abilities, to very confusing terrains which need advanced compass skills. The suggestions are intended to help bushwalkers of intermediate experience choose interesting walks which will develop navigation abilities, as well as hill climbing fitness and familiarity with bushwalking conditions. All the suggestions make interesting trips in their own right, so experienced walkers will also find them enjoyable. Unless indicated otherwise, assume that all trips can be done as day trips from Brisbane and require a full day.

The trips are listed in approximate order of difficulty (based on a balance of the physical fitness required and navigation and scrambling difficulties). Unless specific mention is made that the navigation problems are easy, it is generally best to assume that all trips require reasonable map reading skills and at least a basic idea of compasses and directions. Trips requiring advanced compass skills or which involve especially rugged terrain are indicated, and these should only be tackled after you have navigated successfully on several less difficult walks.

(36) Ipswich Region: White Rock (reasonably easy terrain needing only basic navigation skills; open vegetation; ideal for beginners' navigation exercises; interesting cliffs and sandstone caves; 2/3 day; grade 11/2; page 238).

(37) Isolated Areas: Crows Nest/Perseverance Circuit (creek scenery with rockhopping; open vegetation; moderate terrain needing relatively basic navigation skills; grade 21/2 to 3; page 296).

(38) Boonah Region: Mt Greville: South-East Ridge/Palm Gorge Circuit (very interesting mountain; some scrambling and rockhopping; potentially rugged terrain if the route is lost but needing relatively basic navigation skills; open vegetation on the ridges; grade 21/2 to 3; page 235).

(39) Boonoo Boonoo: Mt Prentice (day trip from base camp at Boonoo Boonoo Falls; open vegetation; moderate terrain needing relatively basic navigation skills; 2/3 day; grade 2 to 21/2; page 252).

(40) Boonoo Boonoo: Hairy Mans Rock (day trip from base camp at Boonoo Boonoo Falls; open vegetation; moderate terrain needing relatively basic navigation skills; 2/3 day; grade 2 to 21/2; page 252).

(41) Border Ranges: Gradys Creek Circuit (beautiful rainforest creek scenery with antarctic beech trees along the vague remnants of an old track; potentially difficult to follow but the road can be easily regained if the route is lost; usually done from a base camp but a day trip from Brisbane is possible with an early start; 2/3 day; grade 3; page 161).

(42) Brisbane Forest Park: Piper Comanche Wreck (good navigation exercise, although navigation difficulty very variable; rainforest and logging regrowth; compass bearings required; 1/2 to 2/3 day; grade 21/2; page 101).

(43) Goomburra State Forest: Laidley Falls from Sylvesters Lookout (interesting views of Mt Castle; navigation difficulty variable but usually relatively easy; normally done from a base camp but a day trip from Brisbane is possible with an early start; 2/3 day; grade 21/2; page 222). N.B. The terrain beyond Laidley Falls is much more rugged than the route to the falls.

(44) Main Range: Wilsons Creek Circuit (interesting combination of steep rainforest terrain and waterfalls in open forest; moderate navigation difficulty; grade 31/2; page 216).

(45) Brisbane Forest Park: Love Creek Falls from Mt Glorious (compass skills required; rainforest potentially very confusing; allow plenty of time; some steep hills which can become very muddy in wet weather; grade 3; pages 104 to 107).

(46) Barney/Ballow Region: Upper Portals Circuit (enjoyable walk with swimming and excellent views; navigation easy if done anticlockwise but somewhat harder if done clockwise; road access steep and rough and not suited to wet weather; grade 21/2 to 31/2, page 185).

(47) Lamington: Laheys Tabletop (unusual walk with views of Pyramid Rock; some sections very scrubby; compass bearings required; landowner liaison required; grade 3; page 133).

(48) Barney/Ballow Region: Minnages Mountain (relatively little known walk with good views of the Main Range and Mt Ballow; some thick rainforest; compass bearings required; landowner liaison possibly required; grade 3$1/2$; pages 187 to 188).

(49) Brisbane Forest Park: Mt Samson via Piper Comanche Wreck (a long day; rainforest and logging regrowth potentially very confusing, so allow plenty of time; some steep hills; advanced compass skills required; only for experienced bush navigators; grade 3$1/2$ to 4; page 103).

(50) Main Range: Teviot Falls and Mt Bell (hard walk with potentially very difficult navigation, and very rugged if the route is lost; thick rainforest and logging regrowth but with some unusual views; advanced compass skills required; only for experienced bush navigators; grade 3$1/2$ to 4; pages 212 to 213).

SECTION 4:
TEN INTRODUCTORY THROUGHWALKS

Some people who take up bushwalking are perpetual day walkers, never believing that they can develop sufficient strength and fitness to carry a pack. The following suggestions are designed to help overcome this obstacle. Most of these trips do not involve steep hill climbs, for walks in flatter terrain are generally better for bridging the gap from day walking to throughwalking. Even more importantly, most of the trips have easy and/or flexible itineraries, allowing time for relaxation and rests along the way. It is always advisable to give yourself an easy timetable on your first half dozen or so throughwalks.

When tackling your first throughwalk, early impressions are important. If you select a trip beyond your abilities, you may well be put off the activity for life. Like day walking, you will usually find that your first few throughwalks are the hardest. After that, your fitness will quickly develop if you persevere.

The following trips are listed approximately in their order of suitability for novice throughwalkers, with the most highly recommended trips listed first. On some walks, reasonable water supplies need to be carried for use during the day. However, with the exception of the Richmond Gap to Collins Gap route (Walk 59), water is available at all campsites. N.B. Walks 57 to 60 require more fitness and leadership skills than the others and they may not be suitable for people who are totally without throughwalking experience.

(51) Cooloola: Cooloola Wilderness Trail, Harrys Hut to Mt Mullen segment (car shuttle required; interesting waterholes, forests and wildflowers; 2 days; grade 3; page 279).

(52) Sundown National Park: Severn River (lazy walks up and down the river with plenty of swimming, but not suitable for peak summer heat; flexible length - 2 or 3 days; about grade 2$1/2$ in normal conditions but more difficult if the rock is wet; page 248).

(53) Fraser Island: Southern Lakes Circuit (marvellous scenery; flexible from 3 to 7 days, depending on how much time you want for lazing about; official tracks and camp sites with facilities; grade 3; page 278).

(54) Moreton Island: Southern Sandhills Circuit (an unusual walk with excellent coastal scenery and vegetation; 2 days; grade 3; page 286).

(55) Cooloola: Rainbow Beach/Freshwater Circuit (energetic walk but splendid

Bushwalkers on the shore of Lake Birrabeen, Fraser Island.

scenery; scribbly gum forest and coastal rainforest; excellent views over Rainbow Beach and Double Island Point; a few steep hills; 3 days preferred; grade 3 to 31/2, depending on the exact itinerary; page 283).

(56) Boonoo Boonoo: Undercliffe Falls to Boonoo Boonoo Falls (car shuttle required; lazy river walk with plenty of swimming; 3 to 4 days; grade 3 to 31/2; page 252).

(57) Lamington: Morans Creek/Commando Track Circuit (a good creek trip when the rocks are dry; some difficult rockhopping; basic navigation skills required, but easily completed in 2 days; grade 3 to 31/2; page 138).

(58) Mt Barney: Mt Barney Creek from Lower Portals to Upper Portals, then returning via the ridge route (a good creek trip when the rocks are dry; lots of rockhopping and scrambling but not too difficult in dry conditions; some navigation skills required; grade 31/2; 2 days; pages 178 and 186).

(59) Border Ranges: Collins Gap to Richmond Gap (inspiring views; no navigation difficulty since it follows the border fence, but many steep hills; an excellent training walk but reasonably good prior fitness is essential; water must be carried in some quantity since the camp sites are rarely near water; normally 3 days but it can be done in longer or shorter times; grade 31/2 to 4; page 164).

(60) Girraween: Circuit via Underground River, Aztec Temple, Bald Rock, South Bald Rock, Mt Norman (navigation skill definitely required; 2 energetic days; reasonable fitness and good leadership necessary; grade 31/2 to 4; page 247).

SECTION 5:
TEN INTERMEDIATE DAY WALKS

All of the following walks make enjoyable trips. Many require basic navigation and scrambling skills, although you shouldn't experience too much difficulty if you have undertaken an appropriate number of trips from earlier sections. The walks are listed approximately in order of difficulty and all are full day trips.

(61) Lamington: Nixon Creek (attractive rainforest and creek scenery; lots of rockhopping, so best avoided after rain; grade 21/2; page 133).

(62) Lamington: Turtle Rock (interesting caves and scrambles on a well known Numinbah Valley landmark; grade 3; page 134).

(63) Ipswich Region: Flinders Peak (good views around the Scenic Rim from the most prominent peak near Ipswich; landowner liaison required; grade 3; page 237).

(64) Barney/Ballow Region: Knapps Peak (outstanding views of the Scenic Rim in clear weather; ideal in late autumn or early winter; landowner liaison required; grade 3; page 192).

(65) Little Liverpool Range: Mt Beau Brummel (delightful twin peak near Laidley; magnificent grasstrees; some steep terrain; best suited to late winter or early spring; landowner liaison required; grade 21/2; page 225).

(66) Main Range: Wilsons Peak from White Swamp Border Gate (the most attractive route to Wilsons Peak; open eucalypt forest then steep rainforest slopes; follows border fence so no navigation difficulty; grade 31/2; page 216).

(67) Lamington: Running Creek Falls (excellent waterfall trip in southern Lamington; usually on a rough track although its clarity varies with seasons; a reasonably long day; grade 31/2; page 143).

(68) Main Range: Mt Bangalore via northern ridge (good views and attractive open forest; heath wildflowers on rocky sections; grade 3; pages 214 to 215).

(69) Barney/Ballow Region: Mt May (brilliant views; various options available, some making a reasonably long day; some scrambling and navigation skill necessary; grade 21/2 to 31/2; page 190).

(70) Cooloola: Cooloola Sandpatch from Harrys Hut (superb coastal scenery includes the Noosa River, Sandpatch, heath wildflowers and open forests; official track, so no navigation difficulty; 26km of sand walking so it makes for a long and very tiring day; usually undertaken from a base camp on the Noosa River, with a canoe or dinghy normally used for crossings; grade 31/2; page 282).

SECTION 6:
TEN ADVANCED-INTERMEDIATE THROUGHWALKS

All of the following walks make enjoyable trips, although most require reasonable navigation and scrambling skills. Considerable bushwalking fitness and experience are essential prerequisites for most trips. The walks are listed in approximate order of difficulty. N.B. Water must be carried in quantity on most itineraries.

(71) Mistake Mountains Region: Goomburra Valley to Cunninghams Gap (car shuttle required; an intermediate throughwalk requiring some navigation skills; considerable rainforest, but good views at Bare Rock and Sylvesters Lookout; 11/2 to 2 days; grade 31/2; pages 222 and 224).

(72) Barney/Ballow Region: Circuit via Mt May, Paddys Peak and Mt Barney Creek (excellent views; creek rockhopping; good swimming in Mt Barney Creek; road access steep and rough and not suited to wet weather; 2 days; grade 3 1/2; pages 190 and 192).

(73) Sundown: Mt Lofty/Red Rock Falls Circuit (good introductory throughwalk in northern Sundown; ideal in late winter when the wattles make a dazzling display; not suitable for warmer months; 2 days; grade 3 1/2; page 249).

(74) Sundown: McAllisters Creek/Mt Donaldson Circuit (impressive red cliffs and gorges and the best views in the Sundown region; best in early winter; not suitable for warmer months; 2 days; grade 4; page 249).

(75) Main Range: Emu Creek, Steamer Range, Mt Steamer, Davies Ridge (superb perspectives of the Steamer Range; 2 days, but a reasonably short second day; grade 4 to 4 1/2; pages 209, 206 and 207).

(76) Lamington: O'Reillys to Binna Burra via Middle Ridge Traverse and return via graded track (a classic Lamington circuit with rainforest and brilliant waterfalls; either 2 or 3 days; grade 4 1/2; pages 140, 136 and 129).

(77) Border Ranges: Levers Plateau, ascending via Bald Knob ridge or the Queensland Spur, and descending via Long Creek (less visited than other areas; some logging regrowth; Long Creek Falls impressive; 2 to 3 days; grade 4 to 4 1/2; page 166).

(78) Barney/Ballow Region: Ballow Range Circuit, ascending either Mowburra Peak or Montserrat Lookout, then to Double and Junction Peaks and descending via Big Lonely to the Upper Portals (good views and antarctic beech forest; usually 3 days but can be done in 2 days; grade 4 1/2; page 187 and 186).

(79) Main Range: Hell Hole Gorge, Mt Doubletop via west ridge, Mt Huntley, Western Huntley Saddle, then return to Swan Creek. Optional side trips to Sentinel and Panorama Points depending on the time available (classic Main Range scenery; 2 to 3 days depending on exact itinerary; grade 4 1/2; pages 207, 208 and 205).

(80) Main Range: Emu Creek, Lincoln Wreck, Mt Superbus, Lizard Point, Mt Steamer, Steamer Range, Emu Creek (classic Main Range scenery; 2 long days; grade 4 1/2; pages 209, 211 and 207).

SECTION 7:
TEN CLASSIC HARD DAY WALKS

Most of the following walks require advanced navigation and scrambling skills, so good bushwalking fitness and experience are essential prerequisites. The first few walks are only slightly harder than intermediate difficulty, but the latter routes are much tougher. In particular, Walks 88, 89 and 90 should only be tackled by very fit and experienced bushwalkers. All walks require a long day.

(81) Springbrook: Mt Cougal via Boyds Butte (ideally done with a car shuttle; good views; rainforest; some logging regrowth; grade 3 1/2; page 116).

(82) Brisbane Forest Park: Circuit via Love Creek Falls, Cedar Creek and Greenes Falls (extends Walk 45 into a circuit; excellent waterfalls and creek scenery; rainforest; considerable scrambling; not suitable if conditions are wet; grade 4 to 4 1/2; pages 104 to 107).

(83) Lamington: Black Snake Ridge/Mt Gipps Circuit (unusual circuit in southern

Lamington; grade 4 to 4½; page 145 and 162).

(84) Little Liverpool Range: Traverse from Mt Beau Brummel to Kangaroo Mountain (open terrain suitable for fast travelling, but still a long day; grasstrees; landowner liaison essential; grade 4 to 4½; page 224 to 225).

(85) Conondale Ranges: Frog Falls/Booloumba Gorge Circuit (superb waterfalls with a swim through the gorge; plenty of scrambling; ideal in warm weather but should be avoided after rain; grade 3½ to 4½, depending on conditions; pages 258 to 263).

(86) Lamington: Binna Burra to O'Reillys and return (42km of graded track; an extremely long day or an easy throughwalk; grade 4 to 4½; page 129). N.B. Long distances of graded track are very hard on the feet; you should undertake several warm-up walks around 30km in the weeks prior to attempting this route.

(87) Beechmont: Back Creek (waterfalls, scrambling, swimming and interesting basalt caves and columns; abseiling usually required although it may be possible to find bypass routes; preferable in warmer weather but not in very hot conditions; grade 4 to 5; page 294).

(88) Barney/Ballow Region: North Ridge/Rocky Creek Circuit (great views on a less travelled part of Mt Barney; good route finding and scrambling skills required; some scrub; avoid Rocky Creek after rain; grade 4 to 5; pages 182 to 183).

(89) Barney/Ballow Region: Mt Barney Traverse, ascending by either South-East Ridge or Logans Ridge, and descending by Savages Ridge (one of the longest and best day trips in south Queensland, with outstanding views; considerable scrambling; ropes may be necessary; an extremely long day - grade 6; also can be done as a 2 day throughwalk - grade 5+; page 179 and 183).

(90) Barney/Ballow Region: Eagles Ridge (one of the longest and best day trips in south Queensland, with outstanding views; considerable scrambling; a full length belay rope is usually necessary; an extremely long day, or it can be done as a 2 day throughwalk; grade 6; page 181 to 182).

SECTION 8:
TEN CLASSIC HARD THROUGHWALKS

All of the following walks require very good fitness, and usually good navigation and/or scrambling skills. The walks are listed in approximate order of difficulty. N.B. All these trips are better suited to cooler weather, and only the Lamington trips are considered suitable for warm conditions. Water must be carried in quantity on many itineraries.

(91) Lamington: Running Creek, Running Creek Falls, Stretcher Track, Stinson Wreck, Tweed Trig, then returning to Running Creek via either Black Snake Ridge or Richmond Gap (a classic Lamington circuit, with a spectacular waterfall, rainforest and awkward navigation in scrubby conditions; ideal in mid-seasons; 3 days; grade 4½; different parts of the route are covered on pages 143, 144, 147, 142, 162, 163 and 145).

(92) Moreton Island: Traverse from south to north (sandy coastal terrain but quite long and tiring; several very long days; different route options, some of which are exploratory and may involve difficult scrubby conditions; preferable in winter; 5 to 7 days; grade 4; page 289).

(93) Lamington: Richmond Gap to O'Reillys via Tweed Trig and Pt Lookout (a classic Lamington throughwalk, with rainforest and awkward navigation in scrubby conditions; ideal in mid-seasons; 3 days; grade 41/2; different parts of the route are covered on pages 162, 163, 142 and 143).

(94) Cooloola: Grand Cooloola Circuit (sandy coastal terrain but very long and tiring; several very long days; different route options, some of which may involve scrubby conditions; preferable in late winter; 7 to 10 days, depending on the route chosen and the fitness of the party; grade 4 to 5; page 284).

(95) Mistake Mountains: North-West Ranges to Goomburra (the classic through-walk in the Mistake Mountains; arduous climbs; large quantities of water must be carried on first 2 days; some scrambling; long car shuttle; landowner liaison required; preferable in early winter; 3 days; grade 5; pages 228, 229 and 227).

(96) Main Range: Emu Creek, Mt Guymer, Sentinel Point, Mt Huntley, Panorama Point, Davies Ridge (classic Main Range circuit; arduous climbs carrying considerable water supplies; preferable in winter; 2 long days; grade 5; pages 209 and 206).

(97) Main Range: Traverse from Spicers Gap to Teviot Gap (the classic Main Range traverse; arduous climbs carrying considerable water supplies; superb views and rugged mountain scenery; considerable scrambling; preferable in winter; 2 to 4 days; grade 41/2 to 51/2; pages 202 and 204 to 207).

(98) Barney/Ballow Region: Barney/Ballow Circuit; ascend by Barney Gorge or Midget Ridge, follow the Barney Spur to the border, then west to Junction Peak and north along the Ballow Range (classic rugged Barney/Ballow scenery; arduous climbs, sometimes carrying considerable water supplies; superb views and rugged mountain scenery; some scrambling; very scrubby in parts; preferable in winter; 4 days; grade 5; different parts of the route are covered on pages 180, 179, 175 and 187).

(99) Barney/Ballow Region: Barrabool Ridge and Midget Ridge Circuit (classic Barney circuit; arduous climbs carrying considerable water supplies; superb views and rugged mountain scenery; considerable scrambling; very scrubby in parts; preferable in winter; 2 or 3 days; grade 5; page 180).

(100) Sundown: Grand Sundown Circuit, including Blue Gorge (the classic Sundown circuit, visiting McAllisters Creek, Mt Donaldson, Blue Gorge and Ooline Creek; Blue Gorge route is exploratory and may require climbing and belaying skills; only suited to winter and should not be tackled unless there has been reasonable autumn rains; 4 days; grade 51/2 to 6; pages 249 to 252).

9

BRISBANE FOREST PARK
AND ENVIRONS

Starting in the foothills immediately west of Brisbane, Brisbane Forest Park is a multi-use, multi-tenure land management region which is intended to ensure a permanent green belt at the city's back doorstep. It is largely comprised of state forest, but also includes four national parks and a variety of other crown and city council lands. It is managed to provide for forestry, conservation, water catchment and various types of outdoor recreation, including sightseeing, picnicking, bushwalking and horse riding (the latter in non-national park areas).

Perhaps surprisingly, many Brisbane people aren't aware of the park's existence or don't realise how close it is to the city. The park covers much of the D'Aguilar Ranges, extending from Mt Coot-tha and Enoggera Reservoir to within a few kilometres of Wivenhoe Dam. In some places at The Gap, the park extends almost to the edge of suburban backyards. It has a range of facilities and is extremely popular with day trippers, tourists, picnickers and sightseers. A recently completed tourist road called the Northbrook Parkway connects Mt Glorious with Wivenhoe Dam, providing a sightseeing through route from Brisbane. The park also has excellent birdwatching opportunities, particularly if you visit midweek when you can avoid the crowds.

Brisbane Forest Park offers a variety of bushwalking opportunities, from short graded track walks to quite challenging ventures in rugged localities. This chapter also describes some nearby areas just to the north.

The Brisbane Forest Park headquarters and visitor information centre is located at The Gap, just beyond Enoggera Reservoir, and is open 7 days a week (see Directory).

N.B. Brisbane Forest Park staff have provided considerable information to help complete this chapter. In particular, *Bushpeople Publications* would like to thank Martin Fingland who has almost singlehandedly explored the Park's bushwalking routes and established its bushwalking reputation.

SPECIAL NOTES

BUSHWALKING CONDITIONS AND HAZARDS

General Terrain: Brisbane Forest Park provides a large range of day walk ventures, as well as good learning opportunities for novice bushwalkers wishing to push themselves into harder walks. Novice walkers are encouraged to consider several off-track walks in the park prior to tackling difficult trips in areas such as the Scenic Rim.

While the region is not as extensive, rugged or environmentally fragile as most of the areas around the Scenic Rim, many localities are still quite challenging. The region definitely requires caution. It is particularly important to appreciate the peculiar vegetation difficulties (see below) prior to embarking on any off-track bushwalking ventures. There are also various precipitous areas, so care needs to be taken when planning trips and navigating.

Vegetation and Navigation: The nature of the vegetation is the most significant bushwalking difficulty in the park. While the region tends to be either rainforest or eucalypt forest, many areas (including national park land) have considerable under-story regrowth as a result of past forestry operations. This logging regrowth is often very thick and extensive, with large amounts of lawyer and lantana in some localities. Take considerable care with navigation planning if venturing off the graded tracks, and ensure you have ample time since trips can take longer than expected due to the scratchy scrub. Gloves and long gaiters are desirable. Navigation can also be difficult in the rainforest areas, especially around Mt D'Aguilar where there are many indistinct ridges. N.B. Accurate information on proposed walks can be obtained by contacting staff at the Brisbane Forest Park Information Centre.

Carrying Water: It is best to carry a good supply of water unless you know the area well. While there are quite a few major creeks in this region, side trips to obtain water can sometimes be quite lengthy due to the extent of regrowth scrub in the region. In addition, many of the smaller creeks are dry except after rain.

Wetness: As with other rainforest areas, you need to be prepared for wet conditions, especially in the autumn months. Take a parka in case of rain, a groundsheet to have lunch on and plenty of rub-on insect repellent to apply to your boots to repel leeches.

Rockhopping: Many of the rainforest creeks are quite rugged and rockhopping trips can be very slow, especially in the wetter months.

ACCESS

Water Catchments: All the walking routes described in this chapter are open to the public, although access to the water catchment areas above Enoggera Reservoir, Gold Creek and Lake Manchester is not permitted.

FACILITIES AND CAMPING

Information Centre: The Brisbane Forest Park headquarters and visitor information centre is located at The Gap, just beyond Enoggera Reservoir, and is open seven days a week (see Directory).

Base Camping: Manorina National Park has a developed camp ground which is popular for short stays, with plenty of nocturnal wildlife to enthuse visitors. There are

Photo by *Martin Fingland*

no shower facilities. Permits are required and can be obtained at the Park Information Centre. There are also commercial camping facilities at Mt Glorious.

Throughwalk Camping: Throughwalking is not a popular activity at Brisbane Forest Park since all areas can be visited on day trips, but bush camping permits can be issued in specific circumstances. Some restrictions apply (depending on location, group size, etc), due to the need to control the immense people pressures on the park.

THE "GO BUSH" PROGRAM

"Go Bush" is the Brisbane Forest Park's official education and recreation program. It includes activities ranging from films, lectures and safari tours to possum spotlighting, star gazing, bird watching, photography and bushwalking. Possibly the greatest advantage from the bushwalking perspective is that beginners, who might otherwise be hampered by lack of skills, equipment or walking companions, are able to tackle trips of various levels of difficulty with an experienced guide. Enquire regarding the program at the Brisbane Forest Park's Information Centre at The Gap (see Directory).

MAPS

Brisbane Forest Park has a topographic vegetation map which is suitable for bush navigation, except that information on roads is outdated and often very inaccurate (the main road past Mt Glorious is marked as a rough track and erroneous information is given on the locations and standards of some forestry tracks). You also need to take care that the unusual scale of 1:32 000 doesn't mislead you. The sheet covers all the areas discussed in this chapter except for Mt Mee and Dianas Bath.

The SUNMAP 1:25 000 topographic maps for this region are also of reasonably good quality, but once again information on roads is grossly inaccurate. The relevant sheets are *Samsonvale, Lake Manchester, Kipper Creek, Laceys Creek* and *Mt Byron*. The *Samford* 1:50 000 sheet is useful in combination with some of these maps.

ROAD ACCESS

There are two roads to Mt Glorious from Brisbane - the route via The Gap and Mt Nebo (47km) and the road via Ferny Grove and Samford (41km). Although slightly longer, the Mt Nebo road gives access to more of the park's interest features, including various picnic grounds and lookouts. The park's information centre is located at The Gap, on the left of the road just past Enoggera Reservoir. The other major road in the area is the Northbrook Parkway, which provides a scenic drive from Mt Glorious to Wivenhoe Dam. All these roads are evident on any good road map and are well signposted.

Other road directions are given with the various walk descriptions in the following pages.

OFFICIAL TRACK WALKS

Although the track walks in Brisbane Forest Park are relatively short (the longest is only a few hours), they are worth mention since they often visit unusual and interesting attractions.

MT GLORIOUS

Maiala National Park: The walk to Greenes Falls is probably the best graded track walk in Brisbane Forest Park. It leaves from the bottom of the Maiala picnic ground and passes through a section of superb rainforest, before arriving at the falls. At 5km return, it can be completed easily in a couple of hours. N.B. The location of Greenes Falls shown on the maps is slightly incorrect, although this is not of any significance unless you are undertaking off-track walks.

There is also a graded track on the west of the main road, between Maiala picnic ground and Lawton Road (about 2km one way).

MT NEBO AREA

Jollys Lookout and Boombana National Parks are located approximately 2km east of Mt Nebo. A graded track connects the two national park picnic areas and is about 4km in length.

Manorina National Park: There is also a track leading from Manorina camp ground to Mt Nebo Lookout, which gives good views over the Samford valley. The track passes through eucalypt forest and rainforest (6km return).

MT COOT-THA

Many people are unaware that Mt Coot-tha has a substantial number of bushwalking tracks, ranging from easy strolls to half day ventures. There are also many old fire trails and unofficial paths which can be used when exploring the mountain. These pass through dry sclerophyll forest with a range of interesting and attractive eucalypt species.

The paths are not graded tracks and many are quite steep, so do not underestimate the terrain. At the time of writing, some of the junctions on the official tracks are not signposted, especially where they meet old paths and fire trails. However, this is not a major problem, provided you carry a map and give yourself plenty of time. If you do become disorientated, walking downhill will always lead to a major road within about an hour.

A free track map is available at the Mt Coot-tha Botanic Gardens. It is understood that additional signs are proposed in the near future.

JC Slaughter Falls Area: A track leads from JC Slaughter Falls picnic ground to the kiosk at the top of Mt Coot-tha (2km one way). Branching off this is the hoop pine circuit (3km return from JC Slaughter Falls).

Simpsons Falls Area: There is a 1km circuit track leading from Peters Pound, which is the major picnic ground at the end of the road at Simpsons Falls. Branching off this is the Eugenia Circuit (3km to 4km return from Peters Pound), which leads up the creek with offshoot paths to several television towers.

Gold Mine Track: This is a short track located near the Channel 9 television tower (about 1km one way).

Mt Coot-tha Botanic Gardens: The trails through the botanic gardens should not be overlooked when considering the bushwalking opportunities at Mt Coot-tha, since they have many interesting features. The botanic gardens is Brisbane's most popular tourist attraction.

MT D'AGUILAR REGION

The region around Mt D'Aguilar, comprising a broad triangle between Mt Glorious, Tenison Woods Mountain and Mt Samson, is one of the most popular off-track bushwalking areas of Brisbane Forest Park. It is also one of the most difficult areas for navigation, with much rainforest, wet sclerophyll forest and logging regrowth, as well as several rugged features. The area is covered by the *Samsonvale* 1:25 000 map.

THE PIPER COMANCHE WRECK

Purist bushwalkers don't regard plane wrecks as legitimate bushwalking attractions. *(Walk* Despite this, plane wrecks in bush areas often hold a peculiar interest for the public, *42)* either for historical reasons or simple curiosity about the aftermath of some newsworthy event. This twin-engined light aircraft crashed in March 1977 due to navigational difficulties in bad weather and poor visibility. The pilot lost his life in the crash. All items of value in the plane were subsequently removed by salvage agents. Since then, the wreck has been depleted by souvenir hunters.

The wreck can be visited on a half day trip (grade 2 1/2), although more time is recommended since the route requires some navigation skill. At least one person has spent an unscheduled and uncomfortable night in the bush due to underestimating the terrain in this region. After the crash, it took several days of intense searching by air and ground parties to discover the wreckage, which gives some idea of the thickness

of the vegetation. Many bushwalkers use the trip as a navigation exercise, although the navigation difficulty is highly variable.

To find the start of the walk (755 804), drive to a Y-junction 5.5km north of Maiala National Park picnic ground. The main road is the left hand fork of the Y-junction, while the right hand fork is blocked by a locked gate about 100m up the road. There is ample space for parking. From here, follow the directions below:

(1) Walk up the minor road until about 50m or so past the gate, then turn off to the right on an old firebreak track (756 806) and follow the easterly ridge. This track is sometimes overgrown and occasionally has some confusing turn-offs, but the main route is usually clear. After some 1.4km (about 20 minutes), you should reach a point where the main track descends to the left and a foot trail leads uphill on the right. Follow the latter, which leads up steeply to a knoll (769 807).

(2) On reaching the knoll, proceed south by south-east along the top of a ridge, which is flat except for a few small undulations. A rough track is usually present on this section. After about 600m, stop where the ridge suddenly starts to rise (771 801).

(3) There are two options here. One route is to proceed up the hill in front of you and find the plane by following a compass bearing down the slope. The wreck lies at about 775 801. However, good navigation is required since the wreck is very difficult to detect, even when only 50m away.

(4) An alternative and probably preferable route is to descend on a course of 50 degrees magnetic from the start of the steep rise (772 801). A small creek is reached after a short but steep descent. From here, the wreck is located by contouring around the slope to the south-east (right) for about 300m. On the way you will cross several small gullies and ridges not marked on the maps. The gullies in this area often have attractive palm groves but seldom contain water.

(5) When contouring, try hard to stay on the same level. The distance to contour may seem short, but it is best paced out since distances are very difficult to estimate in hilly terrain. The wreck is located just beyond the crest of a ridge, half way down the southern slope. Depending on your exact elevation when contouring, it will be on either the third or fourth ridge crossed (often the fourth). Search up and down each spur if you are unable to find it. A useful indicator is that it lies close to the boundary of two forest types. If you are walking through lantana or with grass underfoot, you are probably too low on the slope. The predominant close ground cover at the wreck site is small ferns.

The route out is the reverse of the above directions. An alternative exit route is to ascend to the knoll at 772 798, then take a northerly course back to the original track. The latter has patches of very thick scrub.

MT D'AGUILAR AND MT SAMSON

Both these peaks can be visited on a long return day trip starting from the same Y-junction as the Piper Comanche walk. Rainforest around Mt D'Aguilar obscures all views, although the Mt Samson area is eucalypt forest and offers some outlooks. Good navigation is required, especially when trying to descend the indistinct winding ridges around Mt D'Aguilar. This route would be about grade 3 1/2 to 4. *(Walk 49)*

Mt Samson can also be climbed via its long north-eastern ridge extending out to Mt

Left: Cascades above Love Creek Falls

Kobble, although access to this ridge from the Kobble Creek valley is now becoming difficult due to subdivision in the region. However, if access is feasible, this route is straightforward (grade 21/2). The various north-western ridges (783 807, 787 813 and 795 813) leading up from the South Kobble Creek valley can also be used to ascend the peak, although once again you would normally need to obtain permission to cross private lands. An alternative itinerary is to ascend one of the north-western ridges after descending South Kobble Creek from Tenison Woods Mountain (see page 108). This could be done as either a moderate overnight walk (grade 31/2), camping at the junction at 784 817, or an extremely long day circuit (grade 4 to 41/2).

The tributary descending from Mt D'Aguilar to South Kobble Creek (785 800) is best avoided due to the prevalence of large loose rocks in the gully.

Several of the smaller creek valleys around Mt D'Aguilar contain patches of superb rainforest and are worth exploration. It is also possible to walk to the top of Love Creek Falls (767 785) from the Mt D'Aguilar region by descending south-west and then south from the knoll at 773 798 (refer later descriptions). Alternatively, Mt D'Aguilar can be approached from Cedar and Love Creeks, starting out from either Mt Glorious or the Cedar Creek Cascades (refer descriptions below).

LOVE CREEK FALLS REGION

Cedar and Love Creeks have a variety of superb creek scenery, including several major waterfalls. Considerable care is necessary, since the creeks are rugged and often very slow to travel. Some areas also have mazes of old forestry tracks which cause navigational confusion.

A large number of walking options are available as there are four possible starting points for exploring this region. These are:

- The Y-junction at the start of the Piper Comanche walk (755 805).
- Cedar Creek Cascades (782 776).
- The graded track from Maiala picnic area to Greenes Falls (764 776; see also page 100).
- The end of Alex Road (754 783; see description below).

Many trips in this area aim at visiting Love Creek Falls (767 785), although the rainforest creeks also have many smaller but equally impressive cascades.

From the Piper Comanche Wreck: To walk to the top of Love Creek Falls (767 785), descend south-west and then south from the knoll at 773 798, travelling along the obvious ridge (refer topographic map). Provided you navigate carefully, this ridge should provide an easy and quick route all the way to the falls (grade 21/2 to 3). Alternatively, the ridge can be used for ascent from the falls to the knoll, although some navigational care may be required after the knoll is reached.

It is also possible to make a day walk circuit by rockhopping either up or down Love Creek between the falls and the start of the Piper Comanche walk. However, while the creek is very pretty, there is much scrambling around waterfalls and the trip should only be attempted by small agile groups. Progress could be very slow if there has been recent wet weather. Depending on conditions, this trip would be about grade 31/2 to 4.

Cedar Creek Cascades (782 776) is a popular swimming spot in the Samford Valley. The turn-off is well signposted on the Samford-Dayboro road, about 6km north of

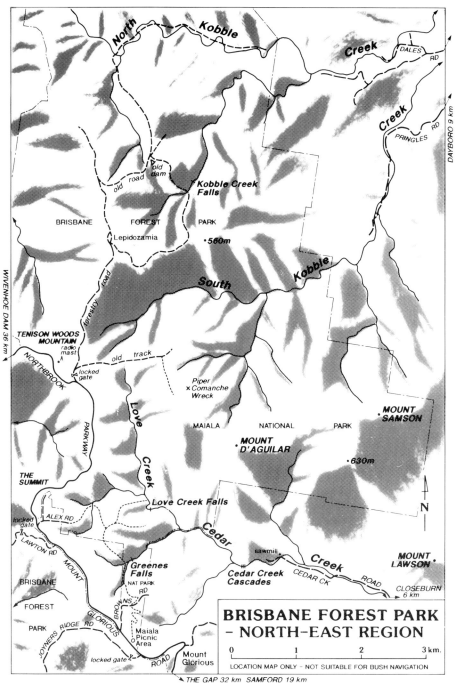

North Kobble Creek

DALES RD

Creek

PRINGLES RD

DAYBORO 9 km

old dam

old road

old

Kobble Creek Falls

BRISBANE   FOREST   PARK

Lepidozamia

•560m

South   Kobble

WIVENHOE DAM 36 km

forestry road

TENISON WOODS MOUNTAIN
radio mast

NORTHBROOK

old   track

locked gate

Piper
×Comanche
Wreck

MOUNT
SAMSON

PARKWAY

Love

MAIALA   NATIONAL   PARK

MOUNT
D'AGUILAR

•630m

Creek

THE
SUMMIT

Love Creek Falls

N

locked gate

ALEX RD

Cedar

LAWTON RD

MOUNT

sawmill

Creek

MOUNT
LAWSON

BRISBANE

Greenes
Falls

NAT PARK
RD

Cedar Creek
Cascades

CEDAR CK

ROAD

CLOSEBURN
6 km

FOREST

PARK

RIDGE RD

BROWNS

GLORIOUS

Maiala
Picnic
Area

JOYNERS

locked gate

ROAD

Mount
Glorious

BRISBANE FOREST PARK
– NORTH-EAST REGION

0   1   2   3 km.

LOCATION MAP ONLY – NOT SUITABLE FOR BUSH NAVIGATION

THE GAP 32 km   SAMFORD 19 km

Samford. While the cascades are on private land, access is freely available during the day, the owner operating a small kiosk to satisfy the crowds who visit on hot summer weekends. Since the access route is immediately beside the owner's residence, don't arrive out of normal daylight hours.

From the cascades, Love Creek Falls is usually an easy day trip (grade 2 to 2½ in normal conditions). The only point of possible navigation confusion is at the junction of Cedar and Love Creeks (771 781). Here it is important to take the right hand fork (Love Creek), although it is usual to negotiate a waterfall at this junction by firstly ascending a few metres up Cedar Creek (the left hand branch). The remainder of the trip should be straightforward. Occasional scrambling obstacles would require care if the rocks are slippery.

The Greenes Falls and Alex Road Routes are difficult to describe, since both cross the hill at 760 781 which has a maze of old logging tracks. With a car shuttle between Maiala picnic ground and Alex Road, it is possible to organise a walk starting at one access point and finishing at the other.

(Walks 45/82 **Greenes Falls:** From Maiala picnic ground, Greenes Falls is an easy walk on a graded track (see page 100). However, to proceed further, it is important to note that the location of the falls shown on the maps is slightly incorrect. The falls are actually located about a hundred metres further downstream, between the two creek junctions shown at 764 777, not above them as is shown on the maps. At the top of Greenes Falls, a footworn track can be found ascending the ridge to the north-west (762 778), eventually reaching the knoll at 760 781. Here it joins the route from Alex Road.

Alex Road is a short residential street which can be found by turning off on the right about 2½km north of Maiala picnic ground, then turning right again at a junction a few hundred metres later. There is a small parking area at the end of the street. From here, an old forestry road descends down the ridge to the east. This gradually narrows into a walking track, which crosses the small creek at 758 784 (the crossing is a short distance south of the creek junction shown on the map). It then ascends the ridge to the south-east (759 784) to the top of the knoll (760 781), where it joins the route from Greenes Falls (junction marked by a forked box tree).

From the top of this knoll, the route to Love Creek Falls proceeds along old logging roads and foot tracks, down the steep ridge at 765 786, to eventually reach the creek just upstream of the falls. The route is difficult to follow in descent without prior knowledge of it. There are several old road junctions, some of which are quite indistinct. One of these old logging roads leads towards Love Creek in much more precipitous terrain downstream of the falls, while another leads to the creek further upstream. Considerable exploration may be required to find the correct route.

The ascent route from Love Creek Falls to the knoll begins at a bend in the creek (767 786), a few hundred metres upstream of the falls. The route is easy to navigate in ascent, although good navigation skill is required once on top of the knoll in order to clearly identify the tracks to Greenes Falls and Alex Road.

Other possible bushwalking routes in this area include the scramble down Cedar Creek between Greenes Falls and the Love Creek junction, and the rockhop down the creek below Alex Road to Love Creek Falls. Both creeks have numerous waterfalls and are quite difficult to descend (possibly around grade 4 or 4½). For both safety reasons and to prevent erosion damage, the trips should only be attempted by small agile experienced parties.

Negotiating Love Creek Falls: The falls can be ascended and descended by a loose eroded route on the north-east bank (i.e. on the right when facing upstream and on the left when facing downstream). They have a total height over 60m, although it is difficult to find a vantage point where the entire feature can be seen at a glance. The waterfall is possibly more accurately described as a set of cascades and waterfalls than a single feature. The bypass track has much loose rock and is only suitable for small agile parties.

KOBBLE CREEK

The Kobble Creek region lies in the north of Brisbane Forest Park and north of Mt D'Aguilar. There are three branches of the creek - south branch, middle branch and north branch. The middle branch (unnamed on maps) provides the easiest walking since there are a number of old logging roads in this vicinity.

Trips around the north and middle branches of Kobble Creek are best planned for the cooler months since the area can be very hot in summer. The upper section of the south branch is mainly rainforest and wet eucalypt forest, but much of the rest of this region is dry sclerophyll forest.

Start of Walks: Walks to this area usually start at the Y-junction at the beginning of the Piper Comanche walk (see page 101). For the middle and north branch walks described in this section, follow the road north from the Y-junction for about 1 1/2km to the knoll at 761 823. This knoll is named Lepidozamia on the Brisbane Forest Park map and can be distinguished from others by the presence of a short loop road in a clearing. The name is derived from the numerous cycad plants which grow around the knoll (these plants superficially resemble tree ferns).

MIDDLE KOBBLE CREEK

Middle Kobble Creek has two waterfalls located close together at 773 833. These falls can be readily visited from a circuit forestry road. The circuit walk has little navigation difficulty although some care is required at the various junctions. It is also important to note that the topographic and Brisbane Forest Park maps do not show the correct locations of the forestry roads in this area. Some roads shown do not exist and other roads exist which aren't shown. *(Walk 30)*

The walk would be about grade 2 1/2 and would normally be a relatively easy day trip. The main difficulty is the very steep descents and ascents along the old logging tracks. From Lepidozamia to the waterfalls, there is a total elevation loss of some 350m, which must be regained on the return journey.

The southern turn-off to the circuit can be found by walking south from the loop road at Lepidozamia (usually retracing your steps) for about 100m. The vehicle track should be clearly apparent turning off east. The road can be followed all the way down to a large open grassy flat just upstream from the first waterfall (the road descends the ridge at 773 830; it does not pass over the spot height 560m, as is shown on the maps).

If the walk is done clockwise, the sharp northern turn-off will be found about 900m north of the Lepidozamia loop road. At one point on this northern ridge, there is an old dam (767 838). Here you can avoid a zigzag in the road by walking overland for about 100m along the ridge. The road descends down to the waterfalls via the ridge at 771 834.

Both waterfalls are about 20m high and are best viewed from below. The top falls can be bypassed on either the northern bank or by an easier but longer route on the southern bank. The lower falls are bypassed by the northern bank. Care is required since the banks are steep and have many loose rocks. The falls flow well after rains but slow to a trickle for much of the year.

Alternative Itinerary: It is possible to modify this circuit to approach the waterfalls from downstream, providing a more interesting route with better views of the falls. This is about grade 3 and includes some steep cross country walking. The usual route is anticlockwise and passes over the knolls at 776 825 (spot height 560m) and 778 828, then descends one of the ridges to the north-west to meet the creek below the falls.

SOUTH KOBBLE CREEK

The upper section of South Kobble Creek has numerous small to medium sized waterfalls set amid rainforest and wet eucalypt forest. It provides enjoyable walking opportunities although requires more fitness and agility than the other branches of Kobble Creek.

From the knoll at 769 807 (see the directions given for the Piper Comanche walk on page 101), a ridge leading east-north-east can be followed down to the junction at 784 817. Initially there is very thick lantana when descending from this knoll, but later this eases to provide reasonable travelling amid open eucalypt forest. Care is required with navigation. From the junction, simply rockhop up the main branch of the creek (on your left facing downstream and on your right facing upstream). With good navigation, it is possible to follow the creek almost all the way to the saddle at 766 807, just east of Tenison Woods Mountain. This circuit would be about grade 31/2 to 4, depending on conditions.

The walking routes between South Kobble Creek and the D'Aguilar/Samson area have already been described (see page 104).

NORTH KOBBLE CREEK

North Kobble Creek is usually visited on a long circuit day walk which also visits the waterfalls in Middle Kobble Creek. The region is mainly open eucalypt forest. From Lepidozamia, follow the old forestry trails to the saddle at 767 840, where four tracks intersect. Here you can either take the north-western track down a spur into Kobble Creek, or ascend the knoll at 768 844 (spot height 499m) and then descend to the creek (via one of the north-west spurs). Rockhop down the creek, carefully monitoring your progress so that you can clearly identify the tight bend at 784 852. From here, cross over the saddle to the south into Middle Kobble Creek, which is followed upstream to the waterfalls and route previously described. Due to its length, this circuit would be about grade 31/2, although the terrain is not as difficult as that in South Kobble Creek.

THE WESTERN CATCHMENTS

The western valleys of Brisbane Forest Park provide a number of exploratory bushwalking opportunities. The main features of interest are Northbrook Creek, Northbrook Mountain and the various branches of England Creek. These areas are shown on the *Kipper Creek* 1:25 000 map.

NORTHBROOK CREEK

Northbrook Creek is an attractive small creek with palm tree groves in its higher sections and two gorges lower down. It is ideally suited to day walks in the warmer months. Trips to the area normally start from the car park at the third crossing of Northbrook Creek, approximately 5km west of Wivenhoe Outlook (i.e. about 8km past the Y-junction at the start of the Piper Comanche walk). From here, walk and rockhop up the creek for approximately 3.5km to reach the lower gorge (717 788), which has good swimming holes.

To get to the upstream gorge, it is usually necessary to swim through the lower gorge, although it can be bypassed high up on the south-western bank (care is required due to loose rocks). The upstream gorge (723 787) is longer and higher and even more difficult to bypass. Don't dive into the pools without exploring the water since at least one of these pools has a rather nasty submerged log.

Northbrook Gorge is a very special place. Please behave responsibly and don't damage the environment or leave rubbish.

NORTHBROOK MOUNTAIN

Located in the western part of the park between the Northbrook and England Creek catchments, Northbrook Mountain has a number of interesting cliffs and vegetation features. The upper slopes of the mountain can be reached by walking along an old forestry road (Lawton Road), which diverges left from the main road about 1 1/2km north of Maiala picnic ground. It is blocked to vehicular traffic by a locked gate just after the start.

It is possible to walk between Northbrook Mountain and Northbrook Creek by several ridges on the northern slopes.

ENGLAND CREEK

This area mainly provides exploratory opportunities for experienced walkers. It is possible to descend into the north branch of England Creek via the south-east ridge of Northbrook Mountain, although there is severe lantana in this area. Alternatively, you can descend to the creek from the eastern end of Lawton Road. Once in the creek, you can travel downstream by rockhopping and scrambling, with occasional small waterfalls. Once you reach the crossing of the England Creek road (marked on the vegetation map), either walk back up the road to Northbrook Mountain, or take a ridge route up to Joyners Ridge Road in the south.

NEARBY AREAS

MT MEE AND DIANAS BATH

Dianas Bath is the name of a swimming spot just west of Mt Mee. With good prior rains, it is an exceptionally pleasant swimming hole only a half kilometre walk from the cars. It is marked on the *Laceys Creek* map at 680 993. The only difficult part is road access.

Approach is via Somerset Dam and a good road map is useful. However, a map alone is not sufficient because there is a profusion of minor roads in the area. Directions are as follows:

Odometer	Feature/Directions	Distance Between Features
0	Fernvale turn-off south of Dam	
2.9	Turn left at crossroads into "Mt Byron Road"	2.9
7.9	Keep left	5.0
11.3	Keep right (640 980)	3.4
12.7	Turn left after grid	1.4
13.0	Concrete causeway (655 978 - the next section crosses a steep hill)	0.3
14.8	Keep left	1.8
15.4	Turn left (676 978)	0.6
16.2	Keep right - leave cars here just before a creek crossing and locked gate (680 986).	0.8

From the cars cross over the creek and the locked gate. After the gate, turn immediately left and walk 200m back down to the creek where a sign will be found, advising the access conditions over the private lands and marking the start of the short trail to Dianas Bath. You approach the swimming hole from an upstream direction; downstream is out of bounds. Please take note of the sign and respect the area.

You can also walk to Dianas Bath from the Mt Mee area. For this you will need the Mt Byron 1:25 000 map and possibly a permit from the Forestry Department. The walk is about grade 2 1/2 to 3. Several routes are possible but remember to ensure that you approach the area from upstream.

A number of other walks in the Mt Mee region, including Mt Byron, provide exploratory bushwalking opportunities.

DIRECTORY

BRISBANE FOREST PARK
Office and Information Centre: 60 Mt Nebo Road, The Gap. Q. 4061.
Telephone: (07) 300 4855.

MT COOT-THA
Mt Coot-tha Botanic Gardens: Mt Coot-tha Road, Toowong. Q. 4066.
Telephone: (07) 377 8893.

10

SPRINGBROOK AND THE COUGALS

Springbrook is a plateau located in the Gold Coast hinterland at the eastern end of the Scenic Rim. It is an area well known for its greenness and peacefulness and, being close to the Gold Coast and Brisbane, is popular with tourists. Most of the top of the plateau is either residential or farming land, but the steep eastern escarpment is largely national park. The escarpment is an area of rugged cliffs and rainforest, with a number of easy and enjoyable walking opportunities provided by several excellent graded tracks. Further east lies the twin summit of Mt Cougal (often simply called the Cougals), a landmark of some distinction which offers interesting off-track bushwalking ventures.

From the bushwalking perspective, Springbrook is possibly best thought of as a place of waterfalls. The plateau is the wettest place recorded in southern Queensland (annual precipitation - 3070mm), and in the wetter months it produces some truly amazing waterfall displays. Two unusual amphitheatres of cliffs provide the most spectacular areas. The best known is Purling Brook Falls (106m), which is located in the north. There is also a second less obvious amphitheatre of cliffs further south, near the Goomoolahra picnic ground. While seemingly unremarkable in the dry season, after heavy rains this amphitheatre can be an amazing sight from the various vantage points.

Originally there were three national parks at Springbrook - Gwongorella, Warrie and Mt Cougal. These are all now known simply as Springbrook National Park.

SPECIAL NOTES

BUSHWALKING CONDITIONS AND HAZARDS

General Walking Conditions are similar throughout the eastern Scenic Rim, so to save repetition, comprehensive information which can be applied to this entire region is provided in Chapter 11 (Lamington National Park). The following notes emphasise the most important points as well as features of special significance to

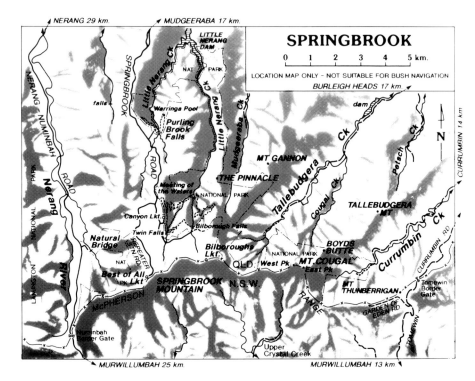

LITTLE NERANG DAM

SPRINGBROOK

0   1   2   3   4   5 km.

LOCATION MAP ONLY - NOT SUITABLE FOR BUSH NAVIGATION

BURLEIGH HEADS 17 km.

N

CURRUMBIN 14 km

falls

Warringa Pool

Purling Brook Falls

MT GANNON

THE PINNACLE

TALLEBUDGERA MT

Canyon Lkt.

Twin Falls

Bilborough Falls

Natural Bridge

Bilborough Lkt.

BOYDS BUTTE

QLD. West Pk MT COUGAL East Pk

NAT

Best of All Lkt.

SPRINGBROOK MOUNTAIN

QLD. N.S.W.

MT THUNDERRIGAN

Tomewin Border Gate

nbah er Gate

Upper Crystal Creek

Springbrook, but it is recommended that anyone considering off-track walking in this area also refer to the *Special Notes* for Lamington.

Graded Tracks and Off-Track Terrain: Many bushwalkers concentrate on graded track walks in this region, since these provide access to many of the area's most outstanding attractions. Various off-track bushwalks are also available, although considerable care is required due to the numerous cliffs in the area. The combination of frequent cliffs and thick scrub presents particularly hazardous conditions for inexperienced walkers. Even on the graded track system, some care is required. The QNPWS simply cannot fence off every place where a track goes close to a cliff or waterfall, so accidents are possible unless you stay alert.

Vegetation in this area is predominately either subtropical rainforest or wet eucalypt forest. Consequently, expect the usual variety of stinging and thorny plants typical of rainforest areas, especially along creeks and in disturbed localities. There is also considerable regrowth scrub in many localities around Tallebudgera and Currumbin Creeks, including extensive areas of lawyer and lantana, a legacy of past clearing and logging operations. This can be extremely obstructive so garden gloves and long gaiters are advisable in these areas, and considerable care is necessary when planning trips.

Navigation: As in all rainforest areas, navigation can be very difficult once you leave the official tracks.

Wetness: In autumn and other wet seasons, it may seem that the rainforest never dries out, but even in drier seasons you often need to be prepared for wet conditions e.g. carry a parka in case of rain, a groundsheet on which to have lunch and a rub-on insect repellent to apply to your boots to repel leeches.

FACILITIES AND CAMPING

The Queensland National Parks and Wildlife Service operates a small camping ground near Purling Brook Falls in the north. Facilities include composting toilets suitable for wheelchairs but do not include showers. There is also a national park information centre and various picnic facilities on Springbrook Plateau, as well as picnic areas at the head of the Currumbin Valley and at Natural Arch in the Numinbah Valley.

MAPS

There are two main maps available, the SUNMAP 1:25 000 topographic sheet titled *Springbrook* and the QNPWS 1:15 000 map. The latter does not possess contours and is mainly suited to graded track walking. The topographic map should be carried for most off-track walking, especially at Mt Cougal, although the ideal is to carry both maps. For bushwalkers travelling the Scenic Rim, the *Currumbin* 1:25 000 topo-graphic sheet shows most of the border route between the Tomewin border gate and the coast, while both the *Beechmont* and *Springbrook* 1:25 000 topographic sheets are required to show the route between Numinbah Valley and Springbrook Plateau.

ROAD ACCESS

Springbrook: Access is via either Mudgeeraba or Numinbah Valley - these roads are evident on any road map. The turn-off to Purling Brook Falls is the first access point and is clearly signposted. The Warrie circuit is accessible from various lookouts and picnic areas further south.

Mt Cougal (Border Route): This is reached by driving west from Currumbin for about 9km, where you take the turn-off to the Tomewin border gate. About 1.3km south of the border gate, take the Garden of Eden Road which branches off on the right. Proceed along this road until the border fence is reached after about 2½km (approximately 359 753, on the very edge of the Springbrook topographic sheet). Parking space is limited.

Mt Cougal (Currumbin Valley Route): This is reached by turning off at Currumbin and driving to the head of the Currumbin Valley (ignoring the Tomewin border gate turn-off). The QNPWS has provided day facilities at the edge of the national park at the very end of the valley road (approximately 348 764). In summer this is an extremely popular swimming area.

Tallebudgera Creek Valley: This access route is mainly suitable for experienced walkers who are seeking exploratory ventures in the Mt Cougal area. Simply follow the road up the valley (refer topographic map).

Natural Arch: This is more a destination for tourists than bushwalkers, but is also used by bushwalkers wishing to explore the part of the Scenic Rim route between Numinbah Valley and Springbrook Plateau. The turn-off to Natural Arch is clearly signposted near the head of Numinbah Valley.

SPRINGBROOK

GRADED TRACK WALKS

Purling Brook Falls: Purling Brook Falls (106m high) is the major attraction in the north of Springbrook. A circuit graded track visits both the top and bottom of the falls, with various vantage points. The path actually leads behind the bottom of the waterfall. The circuit takes about an hour and is 4km long, although it can be easily extended to 6km by taking an offshoot track which leads to Warringa Pool.

Warrie Circuit: The longest and possibly the most scenic track at Springbrook is *(Walk* the 17km circuit to the Meeting-of-the-Waters (grade 11/2 to 2). This outstanding *1)* walk provides an excellent insight into the area's varying terrain and vegetation. It has plenty of waterfalls and attractive rainforest, as well as some unusual features such as split boulders. It traverses along the southern cliffs and amphitheatres, both above and below many of the waterfalls, then descends through a variety of forest types to the junction of Boy-ull and Mundora Creeks. The track passes behind three waterfalls (Twin Falls, Blackfellow Falls and Rainbow Falls), giving walkers an outlook through the cascading droplets. The lower section of track also provides good swimming opportunities.

The circuit is especially recommended following rain when the waterfalls are at their best (although not in flood conditions, since you have to cross several creeks at the tops of the waterfalls, which would be dangerous if the water level was particularly high). The Goomoolahra Falls amphitheatre, downstream from Goomoolahra picnic ground, is particularly impressive after heavy rain when there are at least ten waterfalls plunging down the cliffs. The falls are at their best in the morning sunlight. A lookout on the track a short distance to the east of this amphitheatre (perhaps 500m past Goomoolahra Falls when walking anticlockwise) gives one of the best views of the amphitheatre.

The circuit can be accessed at various places along the Springbrook road, but one of the best places to start and finish the walk is from Canyon Lookout. If you wish, a shorter circuit can be done visiting Twin Falls and Blackfellow Falls and omitting the descent to the Meeting-of-the-Waters.

Other Walks: A number of other short track walks on the Springbrook Plateau lead to various features, including the plateau's outstanding southern lookouts.

OFF-TRACK WALKS

The Pinnacle, located at 290 801, provides a short side trip from the Warrie circuit (perhaps 1 to 11/2 hours return to the track; grade 2 to 21/2). Care is needed for the final scramble up the rocks. Care is also required with navigation, since an obscure division in the ridge at 287 794 (not obvious on the map) can mislead walkers on the return journey.

Exploratory possibilities at Springbrook include walks down the branches of Little Nerang Creek from the Purling Brook Falls track and the Warrie Circuit. Enquire with the QNPWS regarding these trips, since much of the land near Little Nerang Dam is water catchment reserve to which entry is restricted. There are also rough tracks to Natural Arch and Tallebudgera Creek (see page 117).

Left: Goomoolahra Falls, Warrie Cicuit

MT COUGAL

(Walk 35) **Mt Cougal:** This twin summit is a distinctive landmark west of Coolangatta, and provides the best off-track bushwalking in the Springbrook region. The easiest route to the summit is from the east near the Tomewin border gate (grade 3; 3/4 day). If you wish you can walk directly from the border gate over the hill at 362 755 (called Mt Thunberrigan on recent maps and Mt Tomewin on old maps). Alternatively, take the Garden of Eden Road (see page 113), bypassing Mt Thunberrigan and rejoining the border fence just east of Mt Cougal (approximately 359 753, on the very edge of the Springbrook topographic sheet). From here, follow the border fence through areas of attractive forest, then up some steep slopes to the cliff line. Contour north (right) to an obvious cliff break. The first summit provides the main views although the western summit also has a number of interesting features. Ascent of the western summit is slightly harder than the eastern summit and involves some scrambling, although nowadays there is a good track which bypasses nearly all places of potential exposure (grade 31/2).

(Walk 81) **Boyds Butte,** which lies just north-east from Mt Cougal, features a number of pinnacles which provide considerable interest. The Butte can be visited either on a return side trip from Mt Cougal, or by ascending Mt Cougal from the Currumbin Valley (grade 3 to 31/2; full day). In the latter case, take the graded track from the car park (348 764) up to the old saw mill ruins (on the south bank at approximately 343 762), then continue beyond the saw mill to the sharp bend in the creek at 341 761. Climb the ridge to the north (340 764) from anywhere in this vicinity. An old forestry road will be found on the lower section of this ridge but for the most part the regrowth scrub is relatively mild. The ridge leads directly to Boyds Butte, although near the top it steepens considerably and presents some difficulties. Good compass work would be required to find the ridge in descent.

Considerable care is necessary when scrambling around the pinnacles on Boyds Butte. The section of ridge from the Butte to Mt Cougal has some scrub but should not present major difficulties.

THE BORDER ROUTE :
NUMINBAH VALLEY TO COOLANGATTA

The Springbrook cliffs are major obstacles to bushwalkers travelling between Numinbah Valley and Mt Cougal, and consequently the Scenic Rim walking route is forced to divert from the main crest on this section. The recognised routes are described here, although experienced walkers may be interested to know that a number of other routes have been explored by bushwalking parties in the area e.g. around the base of Springbrook's southern cliffs, or descending to the base of the southern cliffs via the power lines near Best-of-All Lookout. However, walkers exploring these routes have often encountered thick lawyer entanglements and precipitous terrain, so the routes should not be attempted by inexperienced parties. Nevertheless, with further exploration, it may be that they will ultimately provide more direct routes than those described here.

Numinbah Valley to Springbrook: From the Numinbah border gate, the usual route is to walk down the road to Natural Arch (238 771), approximately 4km north of the border gate. Follow the graded track anticlockwise to the upper crossing of Cave Creek, then locate a rough track which diverges off on the right about 20m beyond the creek crossing. This ascends the ridge to the east, leading to Repeater Station Road on Springbrook Plateau (255 776). If descending this route, the start of the track can be located behind the national park boundary sign on Repeater Station Road, about 2km north of the Best-of-All Lookout car park.

Best-of-All Lookout to Bilbrough Lookout: A thin strip of national park land provides a walking route along this section.

Springbrook to Mt Cougal: It is necessary to detour away from the border route to avoid Springbrook's massive eastern cliffs. The usual route follows the remains of an old road, nicknamed the "Cream Track", down to Tallebudgera Creek. This nickname originates from the days when the route was used to transport cream from the Springbrook dairy farms to Murwillumbah. The route is marked by cadastral lines on the topographic map.

Walk to the grassy knoll at 284 776, either by following the old road from the parking area at the end of Springbrook Road, or by descending from the radio tower near Bilbrough Lookout. From the knoll, the Cream Track can be located by descending north-east down the ridge crest. It soon enters rainforest and begins to descend steeply. Initially it is a narrow foot track, but later, where it descends beside the edge of an old banana plantation, it broadens into a vehicular track.

At 305 775, a junction is reached (marked on the topographic map) where you should turn sharp left. About a hundred metres or so further on, a second junction is reached (not marked on the maps). Ignore the sharp right hand turn here and continue straight ahead. Shortly after this, there is yet another road junction (marked on the topographic map at 305 777), where you should turn right and follow the ridge crest to Tallebudgera Creek (310 780).

Mt Cougal can be reached by walking up any of the ridges which ascend to the south-east from this region, but be prepared for thick patches of lawyer vine and logging regrowth. Once at the base of the summit cliffs, it is normal to contour around on the north of the mountain and then ascend via the east peak route, although the contouring section is slow due to large boulders. Refer to page 116 for further information on Mt Cougal.

Tomewin Border Gate to Coolangatta: This section of the Scenic Rim route is of considerable distance (almost 20km), but can be walked in one long day. It is entirely along border fence and is easy travelling, although many walkers find it rather tedious.

DIRECTORY

QUEENSLAND NATIONAL PARKS AND WILDLIFE SERVICE

Springbrook: via Mudgeeraba. Q. 4215. Telephone: (075) 33 5147.

Natural Arch: via Nerang. Q. 4211. Telephone: (075) 33 6156.

Tamborine: Knoll Road, North Tamborine. Q. 4272. Telephone: (075) 451171

Burleigh Heads Information Centre: Gold Coast Highway, Burleigh Heads. Q. 4220. Telephone: (075) 35 3032

11

LAMINGTON NATIONAL PARK

Exceeding 20,000 hectares in area, Lamington is by far the largest national park in the Eastern Scenic Rim, a region which contains the most extensive areas of rainforest in southern Queensland. The region is distinct in character, even on an Australia wide basis, being typified by rain and rainforest, rocky mountain creeks, moss, ferns, deep gorges, large waterfalls and an extremely rugged topography.

Lamington is one of Queensland's best known national parks, not only because of its superb natural wonders, but also due to its unique place in the history of the state's national park system, its scientific values and its visitor facilities. The campaign to preserve the region started in the nineteenth century and was the first such campaign in the state. Later the region was to become immortalised in two inspiring books, Arthur Groom's *One Mountain After Another* and Bernard O'Reilly's *Green Mountains*.

The Eastern Scenic Rim and the Tweed Range section of New South Wales' Border Ranges are the remnants of an old shield volcano, the plug of which remains at Mt Warning. The area's lushness not only derives from its high rainfall, but also from the rich soils, most of which are formed from basalt. The region has an enormous diversity of plant and animal life, the types and origins of plant species making the area an important key to Australia's biogeography.

Today Lamington offers a wide range of bushwalking activities. The rugged topography provides many off-track bushwalking experiences, while an extensive system of graded tracks unparalleled in Australia provides numerous opportunities for those who wish for less challenging ventures. There are also two major camping grounds and several guest house accommodation centres.

Left: Running Creek Falls

SPECIAL NOTES

BUSHWALKING CONDITIONS AND HAZARDS

Lamington National Park is an enchanting place with plenty of bushwalking attractions. However, it is important that visitors are prepared for the discomforts and dangers of the region.

Graded Tracks and Off-Track Terrain: Although the entire region is very rugged, an extensive system of excellently constructed graded tracks covers much of the northern section of the park. The total length of the tracks is approximately 150km and they visit many of the park's most outstanding features. The tracks are constructed to specific gradient standards which eliminate the need for steep climbs and scrambles (hence the word "graded"), and allow day walks ranging from easy strolls to arduous epics. However, despite these tracks being signposted and well maintained, you still need to take care and stay reasonably alert. Even here there are occasional serious accidents, since the Queensland National Parks and Wildlife Service (QNPWS) simply cannot fence off every place a track goes close to a cliff or waterfall.

A wide range of more challenging bushwalking opportunities are also available, both in the southern "wilderness" section and in the northern graded track section. Some of these follow rough footworn tracks, some are creek rockhopping ventures, and some involve difficult navigation without assistance from any track or natural feature. While these off-track bushwalks often provide exciting and immensely rewarding experiences, it is always important to prepare well and never underestimate the potential difficulties. The region is one of the most rugged in southern Queensland, and numerous cliffs, gorges and waterfalls lie amid the rainforest covered mountains. The region can be very hazardous if inexperienced parties lose the way or tackle trips beyond their abilities, a fact clearly evident from the park's substantial record of serious search and rescue incidents.

Although not essential on all routes, good scrambling abilities are necessary on many off-track itineraries.

Vegetation in the region is predominately subtropical rainforest or wet sclerophyll forest. This can cause substantial navigation difficulties for off-track bushwalkers (see below). In addition, the rainforest has a considerable number of stinging and thorny plants, especially along creeks and in disturbed localities. It helps to be able to recognise the more potent of these, such as stinging trees and lawyer vine, before setting out on a bushwalk (see the national park information displays and Chapter 4 for more information). Garden gloves and gaiters are useful for many trips in the more scrubby areas.

Navigation: The vegetation blankets out views from large areas of Lamington, ensuring that off-track bushwalking navigation is thwart with traps and problems. If you become confused about your location, it is often extremely difficult to work out your position again, and trips in these circumstances can sometimes become exhausting and anxious affairs. In the past many inexperienced bushwalkers have become disorientated and overdue on bushwalks because they underestimated the navigation difficulties. It is essential to constantly and meticulously monitor your progress and position on all off-track ventures. Don't go bushwalking without good maps and compasses, and knowledge of how to use them. In addition, beware that the sheer thickness of some vegetation doesn't cause your party to become overdue, since in many less-travelled areas progress can be tediously slow.

The clarity of footworn tracks varies substantially with the season and recent usage, so finding a clear track on one occasion does not necessarily mean that it will be easy to follow on a future occasion. Usually footworn routes are easiest to follow in late winter, and most difficult between late spring and late autumn.

While navigation on the graded tracks is reasonably straightforward, it is always necessary to monitor time and ensure you have sufficient daylight. Inexperienced walkers often underestimate the time needed on track walks.

Wetness: There is no season which is reliably dry, although winter and spring are usually much drier and more stable than the mid summer to autumn period. When conditions do become wet, it may seem that the wetness is perpetual, so good tents and tent floors are advisable on overnight trips to keep out water and leeches.

Even in drier seasons, you need to be prepared for wet conditions. Always carry a parka in case of rain, and apply plenty of rub-on insect repellant to your boots to repel leeches. A groundsheet can often be used on day trips to provide a dry spot for lunch.

Rockhopping: The creeks in these regions are typically very slippery, particularly in autumn and winter. Rockhopping can be hazardous and tediously slow when conditions are wet. Many of the lesser travelled creeks are also very rugged, with numerous waterfall hazards. Inexperienced walkers should avoid exploratory creek trips for this reason. Some of the most rugged creeks lie in southern Lamington in the vicinity of the Stinson wreck, so it is important to navigate carefully in this area so that you don't descend the creeks in error.

Climate Considerations: The region is suitable for bushwalking at all times of year. While autumn is often wet, it can be among the most pleasant of walking times if you are adequately prepared and get reasonable weather. Spring and early summer are preferable for rockhopping trips.

Water Availability: Creeks are common at Lamington, but the availability of water varies from place to place. Don't assume that water can be obtained everywhere. It may even be necessary to carry reasonable quantities of water on a few throughwalking routes in southern Lamington, depending on the exact itinerary.

FACILITIES AND CAMPING

Base Camping and Guest House Accommodation: In the northern section of the park, there are two camping grounds located close to two major accommodation centres. In the north-east of the park, Binna Burra Mountain Lodge operates both the resort and a private camping ground. O'Reillys Guest House is located at Green Mountains in the north-west of the park, and here the camping ground is operated by the Queensland National Parks and Wildlife Service (QNPWS).

There are camping areas at Stinson Park in the Christmas Creek valley and Darlington Park in the Albert River valley, both only a few kilometres west of the southern wilderness section of the national park. There are also several small accommodation centres run by local landowners in these south-western valleys (see Directory), while Andrew Drynan Park offers camping beside the Lions Road (refer to the road directions for more details). However, there are no track walks in this southern part of the national park and it is only suitable for experienced bushwalkers.

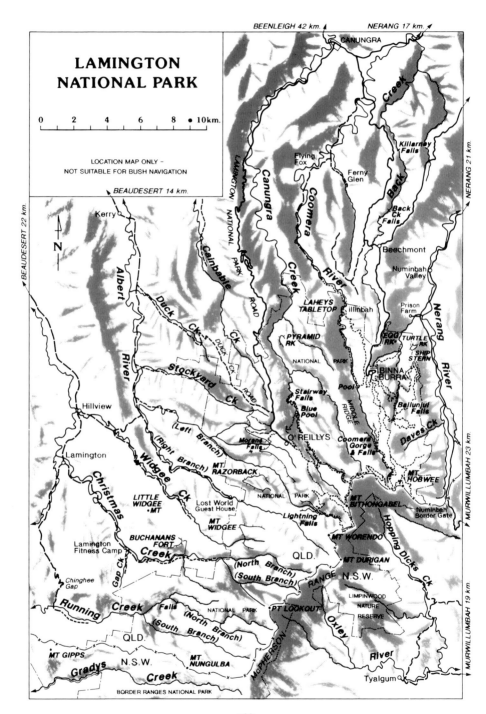

Bush Camping is allowed in most areas away from the guest houses but there may be restrictions in some seasons and localities. Limits are placed on the maximum size of throughwalking parties. Enquire with the local rangers to obtain permits and the latest information on camping conditions.

MAPS

For graded track walks, simple but satisfactory track maps are available from O'Reillys Guest House and Binna Burra Lodge.

For off-track walks, a number of standard SUNMAP 1:25 000 topographic maps are available, the most relevant sheets being *Lamington* (covering the south-west), *Tyalgum* (the south-east), *Hillview* (north-west) and *Beechmont* (north-east). The *Cougal* sheet is also required if walking near Mt Gipps in the far south-west. However, these sheets don't accurately show all aspects of the graded track system, so if undertaking walks in the northern region, they should be used in combination with either the relevant track maps or the QNPWS sheet (see below).

The QNPWS also sells a reasonably good 1:25 000 map of Lamington National Park. It is suitable for off-track bushwalking and, since the one map covers the whole park, it is much cheaper than purchasing all the above five sheets. It also shows the graded track system reasonably well. However, it fails to map an adequate area beyond the park boundaries, so you need to ensure that it covers your access route and any routes you could possibly need to use in an emergency. It also lacks a proper grid. Interestingly, its general relief presentation is not as accurate as the standard SUNMAP topographic sheets, although it is superior in showing minor creeks and gullies. For these reasons, some bushwalkers use a combination of the QNPWS and standard topographic sheets.

N.B. Both the standard topographic sheets and the QNPWS map only show approximate locations for the various unofficial tracks in the south of the park.

ROAD ACCESS

Numinbah Border Gate: Simply drive via Nerang to the far end of Numinbah Valley. The road is evident on any road map.

Egg Rock: The usual access is via the prison farm in Numinbah Valley. Permission from the prison farm authorities is required (refer to the Gold Coast telephone book under the Government listing "Queensland Corrective Services Commission - Numinbah Correctional Centre").

Turtle Rock: The usual access is across private lands just south of the Numinbah Prison Farm, on the grazing property titled "Yowgurrabah". It may be possible to leave cars at the farmhouse. Permission from the landowners is required (the landowners also operate commercial horse riding trips to Turtle Rock and other nearby features; for more details, refer to the Directory and route description).

Binna Burra: Drive via either Canungra (28km) or Nerang (35km). The road is evident on any road map.

Illinbah and Laheys Tabletop: This road turns off the Canungra-Beechmont road about 5km south of Canungra. Refer to the route description for more details. Permission from the landowners is required.

Green Mountains (O'Reillys Guest House): Drive via Canungra - the road is evident on any road map. Green Mountains is 36km from Canungra and parts of the road are very bendy.

The Duck Creek Road: This rough road provides an alternative route to Green Mountains via Beaudesert and Kerry. The turn-off is obviously signposted at the O'Reillys end of the road about 2 1/2km from the guest house. At the Kerry end it is signposted less obviously on the road to Lost World about 20km south of Beaudesert (it is marked on the RACQ road map of the Gold Coast and Northern Rivers). The road, which has several steep hills and many rough patches, is officially considered a four wheel drive route, although many high clearance two wheel drive cars are able to negotiate it in dry conditions. N.B. Some of the steep sections become extremely dangerous with just a sprinkle of rain, even for four wheel drive vehicles.

Albert River (Lost World): Drive south-east from Beaudesert, through Kerry. The road terminates near the national park boundary approximately 35km from Beaudesert. The Lost World Guest House is located near the end of the road (see Directory).

Christmas Creek: Turn left off the Mt Lindesay Highway at Laravale 14km south of Beaudesert, and drive 26km to the camping ground at Stinson Park (at 035 707, just after the Christmas Creek Recreation Camp). The road continues most of the way to the national park boundary, but vehicular progress is usually stopped by a locked gate at 047 702, about a kilometre beyond Stinson Park and a good hour's walk from the national park boundary. Vehicular access was blocked after a tragic bus accident on this road in the 1970s, in which several school children were killed.

Running Creek: Take the Christmas Creek turn-off at Laravale, 14km south of Beaudesert. After 19km (3.4km beyond Hillview), the Running Creek road branches off on the right. It climbs steeply over Chinghee Gap before descending to the Running Creek valley. Leave cars between the bridge (989 672) and the farmhouse at the end of the road. Permission to cross the private lands is required from the occupants of this farmhouse (see Rimfall Cottage in the Directory).

Richmond Gap (Mt Gipps): Drive via the Lions Road, which branches off the Mt Lindesay Highway 27km south of Beaudesert, just before a railway bridge. From the turn-off, drive 26km along the lower Running Creek valley to Richmond Gap. N.B. There is no road connecting the Lions Road to the upper Running Creek area.

HISTORICAL PERSPECTIVES

Lamington National Park has a rich history, which is recorded in detail in a number of major books. However, it is worth briefly recounting a few of the main episodes here, because even today they continue to have a profound effect on the way the public views and uses the national park. Readers can obtain many more details about Binna Burra and the start of the national park in Arthur Groom's book *One Mountain after Another* (out of print but probably available in libraries), and Keith Jarrott's recently published *History of Lamington National Park*. The full remarkable story of the Stinson and the early beginnings of O'Reillys Guest House is told in Bernard O'Reilly's book *Green Mountains*.

The Creation of Lamington National Park: The campaign which led to the proclamation of Lamington National Park may well mark the birth of conservation in Queensland. The saga begins in the latter half of the nineteenth century, when Robert Martin Collins grew up near the Albert River within sight of the McPherson Ranges. He became successful in various ventures and visited America during a world trip in 1878. By coincidence, America was creating the world's first national parks at this time, and Collins brought the national park concept back to Queensland.

He was elected a Member of Parliament in 1896 and campaigned with letters and speeches towards the creation of a national park in the McPherson Ranges. Unfortunately, with so much land undeveloped in Australia, few people at the time could understand the reasons for preserving large natural areas. Nevertheless, in 1908 Collins' efforts saw the creation of Queensland's first national park, albeit a relatively tiny area at Witches Falls on Mt Tamborine. This was quickly followed by a much more substantial park in the Bunya Mountains.

When he died aged 70 in 1913, Collins' work was continued by Romeo Lahey, a Canungra timber miller who adopted more militant lobbying methods such as petitions and door-knocking. The park was finally proclaimed on July 31st, 1915, and at the time encompassed 18,800 hectares. Interestingly, few nowadays would argue the wisdom of the creation of Lamington National Park, and there is surely a lesson here for those who oppose conservation efforts today.

Binna Burra and the Graded Track System: Much of this early history is recorded in detailed and inspiring accounts in Arthur Groom's book *One Mountain after Another*. Arthur Groom was a driving force behind the establishment of Binna Burra and was primarily responsible for the development of the Scenic Rim concept.

Binna Burra was started by a huge co-operative effort from people who had a vision of a facility which would help people share the wilderness. Initially people visited on organised camps and stayed in tents, then gradually the first buildings were constructed. For many years there was no road access for the final steep 2km, and visitors had to scramble up this section. A wheel-winch turned by a draught horse was used to drive a flying fox that hoisted the visitors' luggage to the mountain top. The lodge has gone through many changes since those days.

The desire to share the wilderness resulted in other initiatives. One of its greatest legacies is the system of graded tracks which now exist in Lamington National Park. Their construction with pick, shovel and barrow started in 1937 and remained a major project until the early war years, when military needs for finance predominated. Today there are some 150km of excellently constructed tracks, the style, standard and extent of which are probably without parallel in Australia.

Green Mountains: In 1911, five O'Reilly brothers and three cousins had ascended a steep western ridge of what is now Lamington National Park, and taken up occupancy of eight blocks of land selected in the high rainforest covered ranges. They established small farms, but only after years of struggle. Their diet consisted largely of corned beef and potatoes, and to obtain provisions they had to walk 25km to Kerry and then back again. They backpacked their goods because in those early years there was no fodder for pack-horses in the mountains.

More of the family joined them, but the creation of Lamington National Park caused much uncertainty. For many years they had envisaged a road to ensure the future of their dairies, but at that time the national park deemed a road unlikely, effectively isolating their lands.

It was from this predicament that the idea of a guest house was born. The guest house project was well under way when the first great track building operations began in 1937, and so O'Reillys became an integral part of this track system. The legacy remains today.

The Stinson Crash: The event which brought the national park greatest publicity in its first half century of existence was the crash of the Stinson airliner. On February 19th, 1937, the plane with two pilots and five passengers disappeared en route from Brisbane to Sydney. The story of the discovery of this plane crash and the rescue of the survivors is a genuine epic, and at the time brought the area worldwide attention. The story is still an inspiration to anyone who has ever questioned overwhelming public and official opinion.

When it disappeared, many people reported seeing the plane supposedly flying down the coast, and even near Sydney, so a major search operation was concentrated on the last part of its flight path. It had not been reported at Lismore, but officials simply assumed that it had taken a course out to sea to avoid a severe storm that had struck the McPherson Ranges. There was no way of knowing about in-flight variations to its course because radio communications then were very basic. As days went by, it seemed evident that the plane had crashed in the sea somewhere near Sydney. Hopes began to fade and the search began to scale down.

Interestingly, the people at Kerry and O'Reillys had known that the Stinson had not taken a course out to sea, because on that day they had seen it flying on its usual path, over their roof tops. But these reports were discounted among the flood of sightings further south. Nor did the people around Lamington realise the significance of their sightings. Busy with the clean-up after the storm, it was not until a week after the disappearance that Bernard O'Reilly managed to catch up on the week's newspaper reading, which was full of theories about the Stinson. He then learned how the plane had failed to arrive at Lismore. His reasoning was simple - despite the number of contrary reports, the plane must have crashed somewhere on a direct line between O'Reillys and Lismore.

He set out to search this flight path. Early in his search, he noted a dead tree way to the south, on a rainforest hillside which lay on his course. This is where he later found the wreck, the tree having been killed by the plane's burning fuel. Two survivors greeted him with elation. Both were in a desperate state, and one had a broken leg crawling with maggots, but within minutes they asked him for a cup of tea and the latest cricket score.

There had been a third survivor, Jim Westray, who had set out to find help. Sadly, O'Reilly later found Westray's body beside one of the branches of Christmas Creek, his death caused by a fall down a waterfall. However, the other survivors were rescued, the operation accomplished with a massive co-operative effort from the local rural community. O'Reilly himself had no sleep for forty hours and travelled much of the most rugged terrain at night, an amazing feat considering the nature of the country.

The full remarkable story of the Stinson crash is told in Bernard O'Reilly's book *Green Mountains.* Today visitors to the crash site will see little of the original plane, most having been destroyed in the fire and subsequent years of decay. But there are many memorials and features in the region which bear the Stinson name.

NORTHERN LAMINGTON: GRADED TRACKS

Many visitors underestimate the scope and the quality of bushwalking opportunities on the graded tracks in northern Lamington. This is unfortunate since the tracks offer walks ranging from easy strolls to lengthy epics, and visit many of the most beautiful and spectacular features in the national park. They provide an excellent opportunity for inexperienced walkers to develop basic walking fitness while sharing some of south Queensland's most outstanding bushwalking sights. There are very few difficulties involved, since graded tracks eliminate the need for steep climbs and scrambles and require only basic navigation skills.

Preparation: Graded track walking requires reasonably comfortable footwear. While fairly flat, the tracks cover long distances, and this type of walking can cause blisters if your footwear is too small or unsuited to your feet. It is best to start out on a few shorter walks, although it doesn't take long to work up to the 20km circuits. You should also carry a few basic essentials regardless of season - track map, watch, torch, first aid kit, parka, pullover and a little extra food (e.g. chocolates or sweets which have a high energy value).

Time Requirements: Keep careful note of the time you have available on all walks. While a few superfit people can walk the graded tracks at speeds of 7km per hour or more, most people find that their walking speed is between 41/2km per hour and 51/2km per hour. If you have not bushwalked before and don't exercise regularly, you may start out at around 31/2km per hour. These walking speeds can be used to estimate the times you will need for the various trips, but remember to add an allowance for rest stops, lunches etc.

Most graded track walks would be between grade 1 to 2 on the scale used in this book to indicate route difficulty (i.e. about half a unit on the grading scale per 5km of distance). N.B. The word "graded" in the term "graded track" refers to the maximum gradient standard used when the tracks were constructed, and has nothing to do with the route grading scale used in this book. The maximum gradient standard is 1 in 10 and the average is 1 in 33.

BINNA BURRA REGION

The Binna Burra section of the national park has a greater range of vegetation and topography than the rest of Lamington, and it is this variation which is responsible for much of its appeal. The graded tracks allow you to choose between rainforest terrain with its coolness, creeks, waterfalls and gorges, and walks partly in open sclerophyll country with high lookouts and heath wildflowers. There are many track walks available. Some can be combined to provide longer circuits.

Track Starting Points: There are five starting points for the track walks:

- The Main Entrance starts above the camp ground near the national park information boards (there are two tracks which start here, but these later link up). Various track systems divide off at signposted junctions between 2km and 3km out.

- The Lower Entrance, used for Bell Bird Lookout, Lower Ballanjui and Ships Stern, starts below the camp ground on the east of the road (just above the road junction between the camp ground and the lodge).

- The Upper Caves Track Entrance starts just west of the road junction between the camp ground and the lodge.

- The Information Centre Entrances start from the national park information centre, situated about 11/2km below the guest house, at the bottom of the final steep climb in the road (there are two track entrances close together at this location).
- The Paddock Entrance receives less use than the others, being constructed mainly to provide access to the graded track system from a future national park camping ground. Walk north along the road from the Information Centre for about 400m and locate an old vehicle track which leads down through the paddocks to the east. A graded track, connecting with the Ships Stern circuit, starts from near the bottom of these paddocks.

Bell Bird Lookout Circuit (2km): This short walk is located on private land owned by the lodge. It starts from the Lower Entrance and visits a popular lookout with excellent views of Ships Stern and the Numinbah Valley. Koalas are sometimes seen in this area. The track differs in character to others in the region, being rougher and steeper. It returns via an old four wheel drive track.

Caves Circuit (5km; 2 hours): This is an easy stroll through attractive forest, visiting two sets of caves. The caves track is actually about 31/2km long, running between the Upper Caves Track Entrance and the Information Centre Entrance. The remainder of the circuit involves 11/2km of road walking between the Information Centre and the lodge. The track is probably best appreciated by completing the road walk first, leaving cars at the Information Centre and walking anticlockwise. Koalas are sometimes observed around the eucalypt areas of the track.

Gwongoorool Pool (6km return; 1/2 day): Known simply as "The Swimming Pool" by many Binna Burrians, this is a particularly popular walk in warmer weather. It starts from the Information Centre Entrance and makes a zigzag descent down steep rainforest slopes to the Coomera River. Koalas are sometimes seen on the upper section. The walk can also be done as part of the Illinbah circuit.

(Walk 3) **Coomera Falls Circuit** (171/2km; full day): This is one of the most famous graded track walks in Lamington, with superb rainforest waterfalls and serenely beautiful creeks. The most spectacular sight is the Coomera Gorge, which has sheer walls over 150m high, split at the top end by the Coomera Crevice (a narrow 100m deep chasm), with Coomera Falls plummeting down 64m from the crevice to the gorge floor. If you wish, you can choose to walk to the gorge lookout and back by the same route (11km return). However, despite the magnificence of the main gorge, many people believe that the most beautiful scenery lies upstream, so there are plenty of reasons for completing the full circuit. You can also choose to include Mt Hobwee in this walk, lengthening it by several kilometres (see the later description of the Border Lookouts). N.B. Do not attempt the full circuit if heavy rains have swollen the creeks, since there are many creek crossings which could become dangerous.

(Walk 4) **Ships Stern Circuit** (19km; full day): Another classic Lamington track walk, combining rainforest and palm groves with open eucalypt forest, wildflower vegetation and excellent lookouts over the Numinbah Valley. Most people prefer to do the walk clockwise, starting at the Lower Entrance and finishing at the Main Entrance. The circuit can be lengthened to include many nearby attractions, the most obvious being Lower Ballanjui Falls, which adds only a kilometre or two to the trip. It is also possible to combine the walk with the Daves Creek circuit (add another 5km) and, if you're really energetic, the steep Upper Ballanjui Falls track (add another 3km).

(Walk 2) **Daves Creek Circuit** (12km; 2/3 day): A very unusual walk for Lamington, and one of the most popular. You start by walking through rainforest from the Main Entrance.

However, the vegetation changes dramatically soon after the circuit splits, near the old Nagarigoon forester's hut about 4km out. The rainforest gives way to beautiful smooth barked mountain mallees, which in turn give way to low wildflower heath. The heath is famed for its profuse large bright yellow *Banksia spinulosa* blooms, and the striking deep red flowers of the mountain callistemon. It is one of the few areas In Lamington where the vegetation is low enough to allow almost continuous views. The track can be readily combined with Upper Ballanjui Falls to make a full day trip.

Ballanjui Falls (12km return; 2/3 day): Ballanjui Falls have several drops totalling over 150m in height. There are two quite separate walks to the falls, both 12km in length (although they are both often combined with other circuits - see previous descriptions). The Lower Ballanjui Falls walk starts at the Lower Entrance and gives a single spectacular view looking directly up at the main falls. The Upper Ballanjui Falls walk starts at the Main Entrance and visits a variety of cascades before stopping at the top of the main falls. N.B. There is no direct route between Upper and Lower Ballanjui Falls - this has been the site of a fatal accident in the past. Also, take extreme care around Upper Ballanjui Falls if the rocks are wet or the creek is swollen.

Tullawallal (5km return) is a small hilltop grove of beech trees. It can be be readily visited as a side trip from any of the walks which leave from the Main Entrance, lying only 500m off the other tracks. These are the closest beech trees to Binna Burra.

The Border Lookouts (various full day walks, all between 18km and 22km): No *(Walk* inventory of the walks at Binna Burra would be complete without mention of the *5)* Border lookouts, which provide panoramas over Numinbah Valley and towards Mt Warning. Mt Hobwee, Wagawn and Mt Merino are all spectacular lookouts located on the state border, while Orchid Bower and Araucaria Lookout are just north of the border and give similarly outstanding views. All are attractive walks although some of the bush near Mt Merino was severely damaged in a tornado in September 1983. There are also many areas of enchanting beech forests around these high border regions. It is possible to visit more than one feature in a day by extending the length of the walk, or to combine some of the trips with the Coomera Falls circuit.

Illinbah Circuit (17km; full day): The Illinbah track leaves from the Information *(Walk* Centre Entrance and splits to provide two quite different walks to Illinbah clearing, *6)* which is located downstream on the Coomera River at the edge of the national park. The high track passes through attractive wet sclerophyll forest where bell birds are often heard. The low track travels through rainforest, following the creek on a route known as "the old cedar track" (once used to extract timber). The circuit also includes most of the track to Gwongoorool Pool. It is possibly best appreciated when done anticlockwise. Since there are many creek crossings, it should not be attempted if the river is swollen.

To O'Reillys (42km return; 21km one way): This is the ultimate day trip for all those *(Walk* who pride themselves on being able to walk long distances on the graded tracks. It *86)* is the same length as a marathon road race but, of course, the scenery is far more attractive. Most people need a 6am start and at least a 10 hour day to do the return itinerary. It is strongly recommended that you complete at least two track walks of around 30km in the fortnight beforehand, and only attempt the longer walk if these 30km trips are easily within your abilities. Only then can you be confident that your feet aren't going to pack it in half way through the return journey, when you are still 10km from a warm bed. Even with an appropriate build-up, many people find that their feet become very sore in the final few kilometres.

Alternatively, the trip can be done one way by organising a long car shuttle, or by arranging for two groups to walk in opposite directions and swap car keys. Another possibility is an overnight trip. In the latter case, you may wish to include parts of the Coomera and Toolona circuits for variety, or to walk via the Fountain Falls and Middle Ridge Traverse routes on one of the days (see later descriptions).

GREEN MOUNTAINS REGION

The Green Mountains region of the national park is renowned for its extensive rainforest, profuse bird life, dazzling western panoramas and its sense of coolness and greenness. The area has the best assortment of rainforest graded tracks in southern Queensland, and possibly Australia. In many of the high misty border areas, the tracks twist between 1,000 year old beech trees. These ancient moss-covered trunks, lit by dappled sunlight amid open rainforest, have an especially mystic appeal.

The western panoramas from the Green Mountains area are also renowned. They feature the rugged profiles of Mts Barney and Lindesay, which are frequently silhouetted at dusk by brilliant sunsets.

N.B. All the following walks are popular itineraries and have general public access, although some of the shorter walks described are on private lands owned by the O'Reilly family. The latter are often slightly steeper than the national park graded tracks.

Track Starting Points: Most tracks at Green Mountains start near the top of the road adjacent to the guest house, but walks to the western lookouts and Morans Falls start on the main road about half a kilometre north-west of the camping ground (see later directions).

Tree Top Walk (20 minutes or longer): Although not actually a track walk, this superb feature warrants mention. It is a system of suspended walkways which allow a unique insight into the world at the top of the rainforest trees. It lies on the Botanical Gardens track only a short distance up from the guest house.

(Walk 7) **Morans Falls** (5km return): Morans Falls can be approached by two tracks, the main one starting along the main road about a kilometre from the guest house, and a steeper route descending by the "Red Road" below the campsite. They can both be used for an easy 11/2 hour circuit. A lookout on the former track provides a dramatic view of the spectacular 80m falls, which is one of this area's "trademarks". The top of the falls was the site of the original O'Reilly home, built in 1912. The Morans Falls walk can be extended by combination with trips to the western lookouts and/or the Castle Crag area.

(Walk 7) **The Western Lookouts** (5 to 8km, depending on route): This track starts on the main road just over a kilometre from the guest house, adjacent to the start of the Morans Falls track. The walk visits Python Rock and the top of the massive cliffs on Pats Bluff, an area which is another famous Green Mountains trademark. The views are particularly good in the early morning and late afternoon. The vegetation on the western cliffs is mainly eucalypt forest, providing a different character to most of the other walks in this region. It is possible to walk to Pats Bluff and return by the same route, or complete a circuit by taking a rough track to Lukes Bluff. Alternatively, you can combine this circuit with a trip to Morans Falls. If you intend to start at Lukes Bluff, ask for directions from the Guest House or QNPWS office since this end of the circuit is a little confusing.

Balancing Rock/Castle Crag (6km; 1/2 day): Castle Crag is a spectacular razorback bluff about 21/2km west of the guest house. The track starts at the Red Road below the camping ground, descends to cross the top of Morans Creek, then zigzags up the hill to the west (refer O'Reillys track map). The walk provides excellent views over the Albert River to the Lost World razorback, as well as panoramas of Mts Lindesay and Barney.

There are several options in this area. The razorback on Castle Crag itself is not a standard track walk, being very narrow and extremely precipitous. There are no actual climbing difficulties, but the route requires good balance and constant care and alertness. A fatal accident has occurred here in the past.

If you wish you can choose to walk only as far as Balancing Rock, which stands just before the razorback section. This walk can be readily combined with trips to Moonlight Crag and Lyre Bird Lookout (see below), which offer similar views.

Lyre Bird Lookout and the Old Forestry Camp Circuit (about 8km; 1/2 day): From near Balancing Rock on Castle Crag, a rough path leads south-east along the top of the cliffs to several interesting features and lookouts, including Moonlight Crag and Lyre Bird Lookout. The latter provides excellent views up the north Albert River valley to the rugged border regions of southern Lamington. A circuit can then be completed, returning to O'Reillys by a track which leads past the site of an old forestry camp and then via the botanic gardens. Refer to the O'Reillys track map for details of the route.

(Walk 8) **Lightning Falls Circuit** (21km; full day): Many people regard this as the most beautiful track walk in the Green Mountains area. It features a variety of serenely beautiful cascades set amid tranquil forest groves, with a glimpse into the mysterious depths of Black Canyon from the top of Lightning Falls. Higher on the circuit, the track passes through a number of areas of superb beech forest, while Echo Point provides good views of Mt Warning. It starts from the main track entrance and proceeds out along the Border Track.

(Walk 9) **Toolona Circuit and Mt Wanungra** (19km; full day): The Toolona circuit is another excellent creek walk. The vegetation around some of the best waterfalls was destroyed in a tornado in September 1983, but the walk still retains much of its enchanting appeal. There is also attractive beech forest on the top part of the track, while Mt Wanungra lies only a few hundred metres off the circuit and offers good views of Mt Warning. The circuit can be extended to include parts of Canungra Creek further downstream as well as the box forest area.

The Box Forest: Nobody visiting Green Mountains should miss seeing the superb trees in this area. The forest can be visited on any of several trips to Canungra Creek. A particularly massive specimen, metres in diameter, grows just to the right of the junction of the Elabana Falls track and the Box Forest track (149 759).

(Walk 10) **Blue Pool and Stairway Falls:** You can choose to visit only Blue Pool (10km return or a 14km circuit via either the Box Forest or Elabana Falls), or you can extend the walk to include Stairway Falls. The falls lie 1.8km downstream from Blue Pool (3.5km return). Blue Pool is a popular swimming spot in warmer weather. Blue Pool can also be reached by the Bull Ant Spur route (see page 137).

Mt Merino (24km return): Mt Merino lies midway between O'Reillys and Binna Burra. The walk passes through attractive beech forest and offers excellent views of the Mt Warning region.

To Binna Burra: Either one way or return; refer to the description on page 129.

NORTHERN LAMINGTON: OFF-TRACK WALKS

As well as graded track walks, northern Lamington offers a variety of off-track trips which range from quite easy to very hard. The following describe most of the more popular routes. Many can be done as day trips, although there are also several good throughwalking opportunities.

BINNA BURRA REGION

(Walk 31) **Wagawn and Bushrangers Cave** (3/4 day, grade 2 to 21/2): While Wagawn is normally reached from Binna Burra via the graded track system, it can also be visited from Numinbah Valley using a rough track which climbs up from the border gate. It is an interesting option with lots of opportunities for bird watching and nature studies as well as bushwalking. Bushrangers Cave is a large overhang which is visited along the way.

Leaving cars at the border gate (parking space may be restrictive for large groups), the route starts simply following up the border fence to the west. This section is easy going, although you need to avoid several false trails at the start which lead away from the fence line. The fence eventually terminates at the bottom of a cliff, where you should turn right (northwards) to enter Bushrangers Cave. A long wispy waterfall is usually found at the far end of the cave.

To find the trail to Wagawn, simply continue past the waterfall until the cliffs diminish, and soon a steep track will be evident climbing up the slope. It meets several other bands of cliffs on ascent, all of which are bypassed by veering left. Eventually it regains the ridge crest and leads up to the lookout at Wagawn. When descending back from Wagawn to the caves, you need to be observant because false trails lead off in several places.

The route between Wagawn and Numinbah Valley travels along the state border and is part of the Scenic Rim walking route. If walking westwards along the Scenic Rim route, follow the graded track system from Wagawn to Echo Point.

Nixon Creek (1 day, grade 21/2 to 3): This is an attractive rockhopping trip when the creek is flowing well, but is probably best avoided if there has been recent rain which could make the rockhopping hazardous. *(Walk 61)*

From the national park information centre at Binna Burra (situated just before the road takes the final steep climb up to the guest house), walk north along the road for about 400m and locate an old vehicle track which leads down through the paddocks to the east. Ignore the graded track which starts at the bottom of these paddocks, and instead find a path through the lantana and continue to follow the overgrown vehicle track down the ridge to the junction of Nixon and Egg Rock Creeks (201 824). Once in the valley, follow up Nixon Creek through a pleasant mixture of rainforest and box forest, passing Bohgaban Falls (about 12m) on the east bank. The falls make a pleasant lunch spot.

Some 30 minutes to an hour above Bohgaban Falls, a graded track (the Ships Stern circuit) crosses the creek. Watch keenly for this crossing since it can be easily missed. Follow the track on the right hand (western) side of the creek. This leads further up the creek to a junction, where there is a side track to Lower Ballanjui Falls. Continuing up the main track, there is a second junction only a short distance further on. Here take the right hand turn, which leads via Bell Bird Falls to the paddocks at the start of the walk.

Split Rock (1/2 day, grade 21/2): This is a rough and often vague track, requiring astute observation and good navigation skills. The main attractions at Split Rock are the views of the Coomera Valley and its unusual heath vegetation. The route is scrubby so gloves and gaiters are useful. The track starts near the Binna Burra camping ground.

The beginning of the track is difficult to detect. It can sometimes be found behind a large eucalypt about 50m down from the kiosk, on the other side of the road. However, if you cannot locate the track, simply cross the road from the kiosk and descend through the scrub for a short distance. It should be found about 50m from the road, crossing the slope. It contours southwards through rainforest for about 40 minutes, before descending to Split Rock (179 797). The end of the track is often difficult to follow and a compass may be necessary to locate the Rock. Care is also required when returning to choose the right place to start contouring back along the slopes. However, if the return route cannot be located, a direct ascent up the ridge from anywhere in this vicinity will eventually lead to the graded track near Tullawallal.

Laheys Tabletop (1 day, grade 3): This feature is located in the far north of the park. The main attractions are two lookouts, one of which gives an unusual view of Pyramid Rock. There are two route options, the longer one being more interesting. *(Walk 47)*

Both require permission to cross private lands. Enquire with the QNPWS Ranger at Binna Burra for details about how to contact the landowners rather than turn up at the doorstep unannounced. Part of the walk is rather scrubby, so gloves and gaiters may be handy.

Take the Illinbah road which turns off on the west 5km south of Canungra. To do the normal route (the longer option), proceed to the end of the valley road and leave cars near the farmhouse at 153 867. From here ascend the steep ridge to the south, leading to Bimboolba Lookout (157 859), which provides good views. Then walk along the boundary of the national park, firstly south to the sharp boundary corner at 154 839, then westwards to the boundary corner at 143 842. From here some rather scrubby navigation will lead you to a lookout at 138 845, which provides unusual views of Pyramid Rock.

The easier option to this walk is to drive to the top of the Darlington Range, omitting the first steep climb to Bimboolba Lookout. The turn-off to this road is is about 4km before the farmhouse at the end of the valley road.

(Walk 62) **Turtle Rock** (1 day, grade 2 1/2 to 4, depending on the route): This is marked as "Ship Stern" on the topographic map, but is traditionally known as Turtle Rock by bushwalkers and most others who visit the feature. Other place names in use in this area of Numinbah Valley can also cause confusion. This book follows bushwalking tradition, defining the place names as follows:

- "Turtle Rock" is the broad expanse of low rocky bluff at 208 827, which has some resemblance to the shape of a turtle when viewed from Binna Burra.
- "Ship Stern Range" is the long ridge which extends some 4km from Turtle Rock to just east of Ballanjui Falls.
- "Ship Stern" is a synonym for Kooloobano Point, which is the rocky lookout at the northern limit of the Ships Stern Range graded track south of Turtle Rock.
- "Yowgurrabah" is the name of the grazing property which covers most of Turtle Rock, extending out to the north-east. In particular the name is used to refer to the farm house at 213 838 where cars are left when visiting the Rock (see below). N.B. The local landowners also often use the term Yowgurrabah to refer to Turtle Rock.

Turtle Rock is a small plateau banded on most sides by interesting cliffs with dramatic vertical cracks. Perhaps the highlight is a system of caves at the north of the summit. They are probably the most extensive caves in any bushwalking area in south-east Queensland, and a torch is required to explore the various passages. At several places the caves open out onto the sheer cliff face, giving window views of the valley below.

The usual route to Turtle Rock is to ascend along the northern ridge from the Yowgurrabah farm house. Permission for access is required (the landowners also operate commercial horse riding day trips to Turtle Rock and other nearby features - see the Directory for more details). This ridge leads to the base of the cliffs where you will find the first cave. To reach the top of the Rock, contour around below the cliffs on the western side, then ascend the saddle on the south of the Rock. From here a good track leads to the north-western point where the main caves can be found. Care is required in a couple of places when exploring around this area. Some parties finish this walk with an abseil off Turtle Rock.

N.B. It is also possible to approach Turtle Rock from Nixon Creek in the west or by descending from the Ship Stern graded track (see page 136). However, the Rock is

The finest range of outdoor equipment

Specialist Equipment for Bushwalking, Lightweight Camping & Travelling.

- Day packs, Travel packs & Backpacks
- Tents & Sleeping Bags
- Boots & Outdoor Clothing
- Books, Maps & Compasses
- Ropes & Climbing Gear
- Inflatable Boats
- Thermal Underwear
- Lightweight Food
- Stoves

Mail Orders Welcome
Bankcard. Mastercard
& Visa Accepted.

SCOUT OUTDOOR CENTRE

132 Wickham Street, Fortitude Valley
P.O. Box 50, Broadway Qld. 4006
Suppliers to Schools, Churches and other Youth Groups.
Come and browse in our showroom. Fax: 252 2406

252 4744

mostly on private property and permission for access must be obtained regardless of the route used. Take great care not to litter or damage the vegetation in the area, and do not use wood fires in the area unless you have the specific permission from the landowners. As on all private lands, any irresponsible actions by even small groups of visitors can destroy access privileges for future bushwalkers.

Egg Rock (1/2 day plus the walk to the base, grade 4 to 41/2): Egg Rock is a distinctive sharp pinnacle in Numinbah Valley. In good conditions it is a scramble of moderate difficulty, but it becomes much more hazardous if the rock is wet. Prior scrambling experience is recommended.

The Rock is usually approached from the Numinbah Prison Farm (permission to cross the lands is necessary), although it can also be reached from either the Nixon Creek route previously described or by descending from Turtle Rock. In all cases, follow the old four wheel drive track, which wanders beside Nixon Creek, to the creek crossing at 201 830. From here follow the creek downstream for about 50m and turn up a lantana choked tributary on the left.

This tributary takes you up beside the rock to a steep slab about 20m high, which is the start of the climb. This slab is awkward in dry conditions and may be extremely difficult if wet. Less experienced scramblers will probably require ropes to negotiate the slab, especially for the descent. From the top of the slab, a track proceeds up through the scrub to the saddle between Egg Rock and Little Egg Rock, from where the route is obvious.

Ship Stern Descent (grade 31/2 to 4): It is possible to approach Turtle Rock and other features in Numinbah Valley by descending directly down the ridge from Kooloobano Point lookout at the end of Ship Stern. This is not as difficult as it may initially appear, although some care and scrambling skills are obviously required. Near the bottom of the descent, there are two pitches which are often negotiated by abseiling, although competent scramblers may find abseiling unnecessary.

To return to Binna Burra, it would be necessary either to have previously arranged a car shuttle from Yowgurrabah (see description for Turtle Rock) or the prison farm, or to walk back via the ridge at 197 820 or via Nixon Creek. The latter option would require a long day.

Fountain Falls (1 day, grade 4): These falls are among the most enchanting of Lamington's attractions. They can be reached from O'Reillys in a long return day trip using the Middle Ridge Traverse (see later description), although the route from Binna Burra (outlined here) is easier to describe and follow and probably slightly shorter. The falls can also be visited on various throughwalk itineraries.

The falls lie on East Canungra Creek on the west side of the Darlington Range. The route is difficult and requires a long day and an experienced leader. There are a number of route variations and the vegetation is thick and scratchy.

Start by taking the graded track down towards Gwongoorool Pool on the Coomera River (174 803). There are at least two possible routes to the top of the Darlington Range. The most reliable route for most walkers is rather scratchy, but there is no precipitous terrain. Just before you reach Gwongoorool Pool, take the right hand graded track (the lower turn-off to the Illinbah Circuit) which leads to the Coomera River several hundred metres downstream. Descend another hundred metres along the creek, then ascend the slopes on the west to the top of the Range. Once on the crest, walk south to the saddle at 163 801 (marked by a rock cairn), then south-east over several small knolls and saddles until you reach Noowongbill Lookout (located at

166 797, not in the strange position shown on the *Beechmont* topographic map). The lookout can be recognised by an opening in the trees on the left, allowing a view from a small rocky ledge. A very old sign still carries the lookout's name from the days when it was part of an old track system.

The other route to the top of the Darlington Range climbs the ridge which starts across the creek and a few metres upstream from Gwongoorool Pool. This has remnants of an old graded track zigzagging up the slope and is blocked by cliffs near the top. At the cliffs, it is necessary to contour left to a cliff break (the exact difficulty of this cliff break is unknown). To find Noowongbill Lookout, you would probably have to turn right once on top of the cliffs.

To descend to the falls, walk north-west from the lookout for 200m (possibly retracing your steps), then begin descending in a west-south-westerly direction. This is very steep. If in doubt at any time, veer to the right to ensure you meet the creek downstream from the falls (and thereby avoid any precipitous terrain). You will probably hear the falls before you see the creek. Eventually you will meet an old overgrown graded track which you should follow to the left, and then down several obscure zigzags, to the falls.

The return trip is the reverse of the previous directions. However, when ascending from Fountain Falls to the Darlington Range, it is preferable to follow the old graded track system several hundred metres downstream and begin the ascent at the nose of a spur (because of zigzags in the track, you initially follow the track upstream, on your right). Once on the Darlington Range, follow it north-westwards for several hundred metres before searching for a suitable place to descend to the Coomera River. Near the bottom, you may cross an overgrown graded track which can be followed to the right, leading to the river just upstream of Gwongoorool Pool.

Pyramid Rock (1 very long day, grade 5+, or part of a weekend throughwalk): Ascend the Darlington Range as outlined in the description for Fountain Falls, then follow the rather bendy ridge out to Pyramid Rock at 129 834. This is very scrubby and requires good navigation skills.

Mallawa Track (1 hour, grade 2): This is not actually a bushwalking trip as such but is a short cut between the border track and the Daves Creek circuit, linking the points 195 777 and 200 780 via the obvious ridge. It is difficult to describe how to find the turn-off from the Border Track. The lower end joins the southern section of the Daves Creek circuit near the boundary of the heath and rainforest.

GREEN MOUNTAINS REGION

Most of the following routes are marked on the O'Reillys track map, which is adequate for the first two walks described. A topographic map should be used for all the other walks.

Bull Ant Spur (grade 2): This is the name of the ridge which runs between Blue Pool (Yerralahla Pool) and the O'Reillys road. It was originally a short cut route from the guest house to the pool, but nowadays it is simply considered to be an interesting off-track variation (the graded track is now quicker). The route is easily followed in ascent. Simply head uphill from the starting point, which can be found about 50m upstream from Blue Pool, above the graded track on the western bank. In descent, the route is slightly more difficult to follow, since several sections may be vague in particular seasons. The start is on the east side of the road about 2km from the guest house, 450m north of the base of the hill marked by the road sign "Steep Ascent".

Alternatively, walk towards the guest house along the bitumen road from the Duck Creek road turn-off. After about 150m, there is a tree with a distinctive curved buttress on the east side of the road. The start of the track is about 30m beyond this on a low rise.

Valley of Pines Lookout (several hours; grade 11/2): This is an interesting walk to a lookout which overlooks the Canungra Creek valley. Driving from O'Reillys, the walk starts from a small open area used for car parking about 3km from the guest house (about 500m north of the Duck Creek Road junction, just before the road enters rainforest again after passing through a short section of eucalypt forest). The track to the lookout proceeds down the grassy ridge to the north-east for 1.6km, the main lookout being located at about 129 807. There are good views of Pyramid Rock. Hundreds of hoop pines can be seen emerging from the forest canopy on the ridge slopes around the valley.

(Walk 57) **Commando Track/Morans Creek Circuit:** This circuit makes an excellent long day walk (grade 31/2), provided rockhopping conditions are suitable. Alternatively, it can be done as an easy two day throughwalk (grade 3). The circuit involves a ridge descent to the farmland valleys west of the guest house, followed by a pleasant rockhop up Morans Creek to the base of Morans Falls. It is normally done anticlockwise, leaving the more interesting creek section until last. Campsites are small, so throughwalking parties should be restricted to about 3 hike tents.

Before setting out, it is advisable to check the condition of the old graded track which leads to the bottom of Morans Falls. This track, used for the ascent from the creek at the end of the trip, is officially closed due to its dangerous condition. Many of the old fence rails have been severely damaged by falling boulders and several cliff edges beside the track are concealed by long grass and loose rocks. It is likely to deteriorate further as time goes by. Despite this, it has been used frequently by club bushwalkers up until 1990, most of whom do not regard it as particularly difficult provided care is taken. Given a spare hour or so beforehand, you can walk down and check the condition of the track prior to starting out on the circuit. Alternatively, you can choose to walk the circuit in reverse so that you tackle this doubtful section first (if the track is left to the end of the circuit and doesn't prove suitable, there are no other routes of comparable difficulty for returning to O'Reillys, other than turning around and going back).

To start the circuit, walk along the road from O'Reillys for 11/2km and take the road turning off on the left, a short distance past the Western Lookouts track (the turn-off road is marked by the well known but frequently inconspicuous "green letter box"). This takes you through farmlands (Lukes clearing) to Lukes Bluff, at the northern end of the western lookouts track. On the right (north) of the Bluff, search for a track which zigzags steeply down the western slope. This is the start of the Commando track, which shortly leads out onto a ridge.

Follow this ridge west, ignoring all diversions. At one point a heavily worn track should be seen veering off right (the Stockyard Creek track, described later), but this should be ignored when walking to Morans Creek. The route follows the crest for almost 2km. At one point the ridge flattens notably and then descends again to a small saddle. Just after this, at about 093 784, there is a small hill. Here you need to branch off the main ridge and take a steep spur to the south to reach the valley. Be sure not to turn off the ridge too early.

There are three creeks in the valley in this vicinity - Morans Creek, Rocky Creek and

You can
lose yourself

in the vast beauty of
Queensland, but you
will always know
where you are with a
**Sunmap
Topographic Map**

Topo maps are easy to read and they
highlight features such as forests,
roads, mountains, railways,
bridges and built-up areas

They also show contours of the land,
which help you to plot the easiest path
from A to B and are available in scales
from 1:2 500 up to 1:250 000

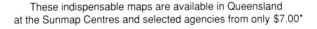

the north branch of the Albert River. Ensure that you clearly identify Morans Creek. While it is unlikely that you would continue for long on the wrong creek, a navigation error here could result in many wasted hours. If undertaking the trip in reverse, care is also required at this point to ensure that you ascend to the north of Rocky Creek.

On day trips, aim to commence the creek section well before lunch to give yourself time to complete the trip. Morans Creek is easier rockhopping than most Lamington creeks. It has many interesting features, including several falls and an impressive water race. If camping, it is best to stop amid the open eucalypt forest just inside the national park boundary, in the lower reaches of the creek. Campsites are virtually nonexistent in the steeper rockier terrain higher up.

The final stretch of rock hopping just before the main falls is often quite slow because of an abundance of very large rocks, but this section is brief. Soon the falls will be heard, making a magnificent sight as you approach from below. The old graded track back to O'Reillys starts on your right at the base of the falls.

Stockyard Creek Track (3/4 day; grade 2 1/2): This is the original pack horse track to O'Reillys from the Kerry valley. The trip has historical and curiosity interest, although there are few particularly notable features. The track turns off the Commando Track part way down the ridge (see previous description). It descends through open eucalypt forest to the Stockyard Creek valley, where there is a patch of attractive open rainforest just before the national park boundary. To return to the Commando Track and O'Reillys, either ascend one of the spurs to the south or retrace your steps.

(Walk 76) **Middle Ridge Traverse** (1 day each way, grade 4): Many experienced parties could use this route to walk to Fountain Falls on day trips from O'Reillys, but it is normally considered a throughwalk route. Various itineraries are possible, one of the most popular being a two day circuit, camping overnight at Fountain Falls and returning to O'Reillys via East Canungra Creek (see next description). In addition, the traverse can be used on trips between O'Reillys and Binna Burra e.g. a circuit, walking to Binna Burra via Fountain Falls (a long day), then returning to O'Reillys by the graded track. It would also be possible to extend this itinerary to three days by including Pyramid Rock, camping the first night at Fountain Falls and the second night at Binna Burra.

Since the route does not always follow major terrain features, it is difficult to describe and at times could be difficult to locate. It is often marked by tapes but this marking isn't reliable. Consequently it is advisable to undertake the trip with somebody who knows the route. Only summary directions are given here.

From O'Reillys, take either the graded track or the Bull Ant Spur route to Blue Pool (Yarralahla Pool), then continue downstream 250m to Purragulli Creek. The route branches off right about 200m beyond this creek. Follow the track uphill to the ridge crest, then ascend south-easterly along the crest to a point at about 153 787, where the route leaves the ridge and begins to descend to Fountain Falls. It is important to follow the track carefully on this section, since the route does not follow terrain features but traverses the slopes and in and out of gullies. If you lose the track, it may be feasible to descend directly to the creek, although the creek is very rugged in this region. In the last few hundred metres, the route approaches the falls from an upstream direction.

At the end, there is a short cliff which blocks the descent to a small palm valley beside the falls, but a cliff break can be found by walking west for a few metres and descending a gully. There are some impressive basalt columns near here. These mark the ascent route if undertaking the trip in the reverse direction.

The palm valley beside the falls provides an attractive campsite for small parties, but great care must be taken to preserve its pristine condition. Refer to the earlier description of Fountain Falls regarding the route from the falls to Binna Burra. The Canungra Creek route back to O'Reillys is outlined below.

East Canungra Creek (grade 3 1/2 to 4 1/2): After taking the Middle Ridge Traverse to Fountain Falls (see description above), the rockhop down East Canungra Creek to the junction of West Canungra Creek would normally take about two-thirds of a day. There are several notable obstacles, but in normal conditions these are not particularly serious provided care is taken.

Initially the old graded track on the east side of Fountain Falls is followed downstream, but after a very short distance it is necessary to descend into the creek. This will probably involve either a short awkward scramble or a section of wading, depending on the route chosen. Further downstream the way appears to be blocked by Toombinya Falls, but these can be bypassed by the remnants of the graded track on the west of the creek. The next major obstacle is Kareeba Falls, which lie just after a series of small cascades called The Giants Stairway. Initially Kareeba Falls may appear impassable, but the old graded track can be found only a few metres up the east bank and again provides a bypass route. However, care is required in several places when bypassing both waterfalls.

In the last section before the junction of the two Canungra Creeks, it is best to keep mainly to the west bank. From the junction, it takes only an hour or so to rockhop up West Canungra Creek to the graded track system at Stairway Falls.

Castle Crag to Albert River (grade 4 to 5): This route is mainly used by through-walkers undertaking overnight circuit walks in the region, since it provides a quick means of travelling between O'Reillys and the two Albert River valleys. It should not be used by inexperienced walkers. While the correct route is not particularly dangerous, it is difficult to find and follow without previous experience of its location. If the correct route is not followed, there is considerable potential to err into very precipitous terrain.

The section of the route which bypasses the Castle Crag cliffs does much traversing on very steep grass slopes and up and down small awkward gullies and rock ledges. Many people find that the steepness of these slopes is unnerving, and there are in fact places where a slip could mean a slide or a fall of several metres. However, while there is often the impression of exposure, a critical examination will show that the correct route has no locations where a slip would lead to a substantial fall. Any dangerously precipitous terrain is probably a sign that you have gone the wrong way.

The ascent route is easier to find. Ascend the ridge from near the junction of Morans Creek and the north branch of the Albert River, until the cliffs are met underneath Castle Crag. Then contour around on the north side of the Crag for several hundred metres. It may be necessary to keep a little below the base of the cliffs on this contouring section, and there are frequent small scrambles. The route doesn't receive much usage so there won't necessarily be much footworn erosion to help mark the way. Contour around until you can locate the route up through the cliffs to the top of the ridge.

The descent route is basically the reverse of the ascent, but the start is difficult to locate. Some marks on a tree several hundred metres from the end of Castle Crag may provide some assistance in its location.

SOUTHERN LAMINGTON

The classic throughwalks in the eastern Scenic Rim mostly lie in southern Lamington, which is that section of the national park extending from Mt Gipps to the graded track system near Echo Point. This area is mountainous and many localities are exceptionally rugged.

Numerous circuit throughwalks are possible in southern Lamington. Some walks are suitable for beginners provided they have good fitness and experienced leadership (some suggestions have been given in Chapter 8). However, although the tracks are much more used and worn than in the past, most still have parts where the route can be easily lost. If the tracks are lost, navigation can become extremely difficult. Some areas are also very precipitous (see Special Notes).

For convenience, the area is described in this chapter using the following regions:
• The Border Route
• Running Creek Region
• Christmas Creek Region
• Albert River Region.

THE BORDER ROUTE

The Border Route via Mt Gipps, Tweed Trig, Point Lookout and Echo Point would normally take about three days to complete. With a long car shuffle between Richmond Gap and O'Reillys, it makes an interesting long weekend walk (about grade 4). Alternatively, segments can be traversed on shorter circuit walks originating from either the western valleys or O'Reillys.

The directions given here can also be followed by bushwalkers travelling the Scenic Rim route. However, note that:
• The section from Mt Gipps to Tweed Trig is described in Chapter 12.
• No description is given on the route from Echo Point to Wagawn, since this is entirely graded track.
• The descent from Wagawn to Numinbah Valley has already been described on page 132.

TWEED TRIG TO POINT LOOKOUT

This section has seen some track variations in recent years. While much of the route is reasonably easy to follow, a few sections can be very confusing. It normally takes about two-thirds of a day to travel.

The route junction on Tweed Trig is actually on the west of the knoll (105 631), not on the east as is shown on the maps. The track which leads to Point Lookout initially takes an eastwards course for several hundred metres before turning north. The track does not follow the exact course shown on the maps, and there will probably be occasions when you take false offshoot trails. Several knolls midway along the route (near Cockscomb Point) may be particularly confusing, with false trails that often lead too far east. There is another place where an easterly route could be followed by mistake about a kilometre south of Point Lookout. In this vicinity, a track leads off down the scarp to Tyalgum.

Experienced bushwalkers may wish to make a side trip to Cockscomb Point (121 648), a ridge which is similar in shape to Tweed Pinnacle. It provides good views but navigation can be awkward.

Water can be obtained by dropping west from various saddles along this route, including the saddle south of Cockscomb Point (112 642).

POINT LOOKOUT TO ECHO POINT

The route from Point Lookout to the graded track near Echo Point is heavily trodden and usually easy to follow. It has many "ups and downs" and crosses a number of major summits, including a long climb up Mt Throakban. With throughwalking packs, it takes about a day to travel. Once again, the course of the track often varies somewhat from that shown on the map.

Along this section there are several saddles where water can be obtained by dropping westward. There is also a very well known campsite at Rat-a-tat (at approximately 161 703, and slightly further off the main track than is indicated on the maps), which can be reached by dropping westwards for about 5 minutes from a track junction on the western slopes of Mt Durigan. This campsite is quite spacious and has water, but is in a disgustingly degraded condition. Walkers should not rely on the derelict hut for shelter (there are proposals to remove the hut and clean up the campsite).

The graded track is reached just west of Echo Point. Turn right and walk via Echo Point if doing either the Scenic Rim walk or if wanting to take the shortest route to O'Reillys.

If walking south on this route, you may be confused by the turn-off from the graded track, which is a few hundred metres west of Echo Point. Follow the track which leads south directly up the hill, not the false trail which leads off to the right.

RUNNING CREEK REGION

Of the three major catchments in southern Lamington, the Running Creek catchment is the furthest south. It has two substantial tributaries, North Branch and South Branch, and between them lies the true Lamington Plateau. The best known feature in this area is Running Creek Falls.

RUNNING CREEK FALLS

Running Creek Falls are about 100m high and are among the most spectacular sights *(Walk* in southern Lamington. The falls lie on the north branch at 065 675. They can be *67)* visited on a day walk from the farmhouse at the end of the Running Creek road, although most parties would require a reasonably long day for the return trip. As a day trip, the walk would normally be rated about grade 3½, but the difficulty could vary significantly with the state of the track and the rockhopping conditions. The trip could be questionable in very hot conditions since there is a 5km stretch of open farmlands between the end of the road and the national park boundary. The falls can also be visited on a wide variety of throughwalk itineraries.

Permission should normally be obtained to cross the grazing lands on the outskirts of the national park (refer to Rimfall Cottage in the Directory). In particular, don't turn up at the farmhouse at the end of the road out of normal daylight hours, and be careful to leave the various gates on the route as you find them. Car camping is no longer allowed near the end of the Running Creek road. The nearest car camping area is Stinson Park at Christmas Creek.

The start of the walk follows up the valley on old cattle trails. After 2 1/2 km, the route veers left to cross an unnamed tributary of Running Creek (021 664). Ensure that you don't walk up this right hand tributary by mistake. About a kilometre after this tributary, try to locate a track high up on the bank at the end of a long open flat (028 669). Some old yellow markers on trees may help to locate the track, although they are easy to miss. If you miss the track, simply continue walking on the old cattle trails near the creek until progress is obstructed by a steep gully, then locate the correct track (perhaps 80m in elevation above the creek) by ascending directly up to the south.

The track contours high on the slopes and, once located, is fairly clear until it descends back to the creek a few hundred metres below the junction of the north and south branches. At this point, cross the creek and pick up the trail which leads into rainforest on the north bank. This rainforest track follows up the north bank to the junction of England and North Running Creeks. It can be difficult to follow at times, often changing direction quickly and meandering up and down slopes well above the creek. If you lose the track, it is usually preferable to persevere in relocating it, since otherwise travel is likely to be slow. From the England Creek junction, there is a 600m rockhop up Running Creek to the falls.

Campsites on Running Creek: Although some searching may be necessary to find them, there are several pleasant campsites for small parties on the banks of Running Creek, along the rainforest section of the route downstream from the England Creek junction. There is also a campsite on the south bank above the junction of the north and south branches, several hundred metres upstream from where the main track crosses the creek. It may also be possible to negotiate with the landowners about camping in the upper paddocks of their property (walk-in access only; refer to Rimfall Cottage in the Directory).

ROUTES TO THE STRETCHER TRACK

Saddle Track: There are two routes to the Stretcher Track from Running Creek. The easiest is by following a horse path up the spur at 027 673 (opposite the foot of Black Snake Ridge) to the main western saddle (029 680). However, ensure you clearly locate the correct starting point for this spur, since the spurs either side do not lead to the saddle. The sharp bend in the creek in this vicinity should enable you to locate the route. The horse track may be a little faint at the very start of the spur but is quite evident a short distance higher up. If descending by this track, note that there are two small knolls close together at the eastern end of this saddle, not one as is shown on the map. The horse track descends south from the more western of these two knolls.

England Creek Track: The second route is the England Creek "track", which ascends from an indistinct turn-off at the junction of England and Running Creeks to a point on the Stretcher Track at about 058 687. Nowadays there is rarely much sign of an actual track, but the route can be followed by ascending to the north from junction of the two creeks. Descent on this route is not recommended unless you have travelled it previously, since the turn-off on the Stretcher Track is now very difficult to locate.

BLACK SNAKE RIDGE

Black Snake Ridge is the major humped summit evident when you look eastwards from the farmhouse at the end of the Running Creek road. It provides a steep but very direct route between the upper Running Creek valley and the border. It is especially useful if doing circuit throughwalks in this area, since it meets the border midway between Mt Gipps and Tweed Trig. The ridge provides good views and has a spacious campsite in eucalypt forest just east of the summit (043 660). Water can be readily obtained by descending a short distance south-west from the saddle that lies between the campsite and the border (046 657).

The ridge starts at about 024 668 on the Running Creek Falls track, about a kilometre west of the national park boundary. The exact commencement point isn't critical, since any of the spurs which start just east of the major unnamed tributary at 021 664 will take you up the ridge. The route climbs very steeply but has no serious difficulties. The vegetation here is open eucalypt forest.

If descending Black Snake Ridge, the turn-off can be found at a sharp turn in the border fence on a knoll at 050 648, about 800 metres east of a derelict hut (042 649) and 700 metres west of the eastern end of the fence (057 647). Refer to Chapter 12 for more details of the border route in this vicinity. The rainforest vegetation at the top of Black Snake Ridge is initially very scrubby but soon opens out.

It is possible to visit both Black Snake Ridge and Mt Gipps on a long circuit day walk *(Walk* from the Running Creek valley. If done anticlockwise, climb Mt Gipps either by its *83)* very steep northern slopes (not recommended in wet conditions) or by firstly walking overland to Richmond Gap. Then walk along the border route and descend by Black Snake Ridge. If the circuit is done clockwise, descent on the north side of Mt Gipps is not recommended unless you know the route. Further details of routes on Mt Gipps and the border are given in Chapter 12 (page 162).

OTHER ROUTES

Various other routes are possible in the Running Creek catchment, although these should only be tackled by experienced bushwalkers. The true Lamington Plateau lies in the upper reaches of Running Creek, and it is possible to combine a traverse of the plateau with full traverses of the north and south branch tributaries. This would be a difficult walk (grade 5+) and would need at least three days. Various waterfalls and at least one gorge are present on the south branch. Running Creek Falls on the north branch are bypassed via the scrubby ridge to the north which leads down to the England Creek junction.

CHRISTMAS CREEK REGION

The catchment of Christmas Creek is bounded by Mt Widgee in the north and the long western ridge of Point Lookout in the south. This is a popular but rugged bushwalking area. However, its popularity is due more to the presence and fame of the Stinson wreck than the area's natural attractions.

The story of the Stinson has been outlined earlier in this chapter. There is actually very little left of the wreck today. Fire destroyed much at the time of the crash, and the remnants have largely been destroyed by decay, removed by souvenir hunters or covered in undergrowth. A cross commemorating those who died is one memorial of the tragedy. Westrays Grave is marked in a rainforest glade beside Christmas Creek, downstream from where he died.

While the epic events and deeds pertaining to the plane crash have deservedly received wide acclaim, the resulting bushwalking popularity has had many detrimental consequences for this area of the national park. The sheer number and concentration of visitors has brought bad erosion to the tracks, while severe campsite degradation continues to be caused by visitors who are ignorant or uncaring about bushwalking conservation practices. There have even been cases of trees being killed by people lighting camp fires beside them. In addition, a number of serious safety problems have resulted, with inexperienced bushwalkers underestimating the navigation problems and losing their way. For these reasons, visitors need to take special care to conserve the environment and to ensure they are adequately skilled and prepared for the conditions. Always carry and use a fuel stove for both environmental and safety reasons.

Aside from the border track, there are only two recognised bushwalking routes in this region - the Christmas Creek (Westrays Grave) track and the Stretcher Track. The former follows up the south branch of Christmas Creek to the site where Jim Westray was buried, and from near here climbs a steep spur to the Stinson campsite. The latter, originally cut in the rescue operation for the Stinson survivors, traverses the west ridge of Point Lookout.

CHRISTMAS CREEK TRACK

(Walk 24) **Westrays Grave:** The trip to Westrays Grave makes an easy return day walk from the end of the Christmas Creek road (grade 11/2 to 2). From the locked gate at 047 702, simply walk up the valley road for 5km to the park boundary. At the end of the road, a rough but well-used footworn track leads up the south branch of Christmas Creek for approximately 3km to the grave site. There are good swimming holes along this part of the creek, and platypus have also been sighted here.

Silent and mossy in the middle of the wilderness, the grave lies near the creek in a serenely peaceful rainforest glade. No city cemetery garden can compare with the beauty of its natural garden of greenery.

The Stinson Route: About 300m downstream from Westrays Grave, a very steep eroded track leads up the slopes to the south. After a diversion around a cliff part way up, it climbs the nose of the spur to the Stinson campsite (115 676; see below), and then to Point Lookout. The ascent to Point Lookout from Westrays Grave normally takes from 2 to 4 hours and is about grade 31/2.

The Stretcher Track turns off on the south several hundred metres before Point Lookout. In the past this junction has sometimes causes confusion, although the Christmas Creek track is easily identified at this point because it leads straight up and down the slope. If time allows, bushwalkers on throughwalks are encouraged to use the Stretcher Track instead of the Christmas Creek route, due to the severe erosion problem on the slopes leading out of Christmas Creek. The Stretcher Track is described below.

When descending from Point Lookout on the Christmas Creek route, considerable alertness is required at a place about half way down. This location has a small campsite in open forest, with the ridge becoming sharp and rocky. The track appears to go straight ahead at this point, but the correct track turns sharp left (the route ahead is blocked by cliffs). A little lower down, be sure to veer around to the right again and follow the bottom of the cliffs back to the ridge crest. Losing the track in this area leads to very rugged terrain (see pages 121 and 147 to 148).

The Stinson Campsite is large and degraded. From the campsite, one track leads north off the ridge crest to the remains of the wreck, while another leads south to a creek and water. Both are steep and eroded. There is another smaller campsite at Point Lookout but this doesn't have water.

THE STRETCHER TRACK

The Stretcher Track was originally cut in the rescue operation for the Stinson survivors. It traverses the west ridge of Point Lookout and is longer and rougher than the Christmas Creek track (about grade 31/2 to 4). A full day is normally required to reach Point Lookout by this route. While much of the path is clear, there are several sections where the route can be easily lost.

To find the Stretcher Track from Christmas Creek, walk up the valley from the Christmas Creek Recreation Camp for about 100m, then take the steep road which turns off on the south (right). This road (034 707) leads up to the saddle to the south (028 680), from where the Stretcher Track is evident proceeding east along the ridge. This is normally a general access route but if there is any doubt you should enquire with the Recreation Camp or the Green Mountains national park office.

From Point Lookout, the Stretcher Track can be found turning off south, a few hundred metres down to the west from Point Lookout (refer to the previous description of the Stinson Route on page 146). Care is required since the multitude of tracks in this region often causes confusion.

Along the Stretcher Track, there are many places where the track winds through patches of thick vines and old storm damage. Care must be taken not to lose the track in these areas. A few old turn-off tracks may also be evident, possibly denoted by red or yellow markers. One old route leads to Lamington Falls (071 690). Another leads to Running Creek (see comments below).

It is also possible to ascend to the Stretcher Track from the Christmas Creek road, by taking a steep ridge on the south about a kilometre beyond the Recreation Camp. This route is not generally recommended since it is very steep and requires considerable care in a number of places. It is also on private land. Its only advantage is a small water soak near the top, at a point where you must veer right under some cliffs (approximately 044 687).

Although the turn-off to this latter ridge may be marked on the Stretcher Track by a metal plate on a tree near 044 682, it is not recommended as a descent route unless you have travelled it before.

Routes to Running Creek: There are two routes between the Stretcher Track and Running Creek - a horse track south from the western saddle and the England Creek track. The latter is almost indiscernible these days but meets the Stretcher Track at about 058 687. See page 144 for full details of both routes.

OTHER ROUTES

Occasionally bushwalkers who lose the route in the vicinity of the Stinson mistakenly descend the tributaries in the upper Christmas Creek region. However, the creeks are not recommended if they can be avoided, since they are very rugged and most have frequent waterfall hazards. Progress can be tediously slow, as the routes which bypass the various waterfalls usually require considerable care. Nevertheless, if by chance you do become disorientated in this area, you can be confident that all the major creeks will ultimately lead out of the national park to the west, with no obstacles impossible to bypass (virtually all the Christmas Creek tributaries were explored by search parties during a spate of major search and rescue incidents in southern Lamington in the late 1970s).

ALBERT RIVER REGION

This section of the national park has many well known bushwalking features, including Lost World, Black Canyon and Mt Widgee. It offers a choice of either creek and waterfall trips, or ridge walks with good lookouts on the western bluffs. However, all routes should be regarded with respect, even though some may not be technically difficult. It is a very rugged area with considerable potential for serious accidents, the precipitous western ridges having been responsible for several fatalities. In particular, Mt Widgee is regarded by some bushwalkers as one of the most dangerous mountains in southern Queensland, while the spectacular and awesome nature of the sharp western razorback of Lost World can prompt some visitors to overlook the hazards.

Note that this book refers to the Albert River branches with the terms "North Branch" and "South Branch", instead of the highly confusing terms "left branch" and "right branch" used on the maps (some people consider that the use of the terms "left branch" and "right branch", as reflected on the maps, is actually incorrect, there being a belief that the left and right banks of a watercourse should be named when facing downstream).

LOST WORLD MASSIF

Lost World is the name of the cliff-ringed massif which lies between the two branches of the Albert River, north of Mt Widgee. Located on the north-west ridge of Mt Worendo, it is a rainforest plateau surrounded by a seemingly impregnable parapet of cliffs. On some maps the massif is called Mt Razorback, since two spectacular razorback ridges leading to the west and east provide the only routes on and off the mountain. The western end of the mountain is frequently visited by day trippers using the western ridge near the Lost World Guest House, although unfortunately many embark on the outing unaware of the potential danger of the mountain. It is also a popular route on throughwalks.

Western Ascent: Lost World is readily accessible from the south branch of the Albert River, although this western route is very sheer. The standard of climbing skill necessary is not great, but considerable care is required. In several places you walk above cliffs which aren't immediately evident, so it is important to remain alert even when the track seems relatively easy. There have been two fatal accidents on this western part of the mountain.

The ascent of the western razorback starts from the road approximately 2km downstream from the Lost World Guest House, and about 400m east of the Albert River's "Lost World Crossing" (signposted at 079 751, but difficult to locate on the topographic maps since it is on the edge of two sheets). A spur leading north to a saddle on the main ridge can be identified by a large solitary fig tree (084 751) in the otherwise cleared grazing lands. The route passes through private property and the road here is likely to be fenced in the near future. All access enquiries should be directed to the proprietors of the Lost World Guest House (see the Directory; enquiries should preferably be made by telephone).

Once the saddle is reached, the track simply follows up the ridge, keeping close to the crest in most places. The ridge quickly sharpens and there are several places which require particular care. The first lies just beyond a small bluff which appears to block the way. The bluff itself can be easily bypassed by contouring a short distance to an easy ascent point on the north slope. After this, the ridge becomes a true razorback, sheer on both sides and sometimes as little as half a metre wide. The razorback is not difficult to scramble along, although great care is necessary.

The route continues up the ridge, contouring north occasionally where cliffs block the way. Near the top, a false trail leads up to a bluff on the crest. At this point it is important to locate the final ascent path, which zigzags up between cliffs on the north of the ridge. It can be found by contouring across the slopes below the bluff for a short distance (possibly about a hundred metres). Care is required at the top of the zigzag ascent track, since it sidles above a drop which is not readily obvious. There is a memorial here to Heather Easton, who was sadly killed in a fall on this section in 1974.

There is a small creek and camping area about 300m down from this top end of the track, in a north-easterly direction. There is also a good lookout with excellent views of Mounts Lindesay and Barney at the top of the hill on the southern crest of the mountain. Although the main Lost World plateau is further on, there are no views further east.

Western Descent: To locate the western descent route if traversing Lost World from the east, cross the creek near the campsite and proceed south-west up the hill. After about 300m, a track veers off right across the northern flanks of the hill. Proceed cautiously along this track since it sidles above high cliffs which aren't immediately evident. Refer to the description above when descending down the ridge.

Lost World Traverse: If traversing Lost World from west to east (normally a throughwalk), it is usual to ascend from the campsite, rather than take the ridge which forms the actual southern backbone of Lost World. As you ascend, you gradually pass from eucalypt forest into rainforest. Some navigation skill is required when descending from the summit to the eastern razorback (see below). The Worendo-Lost World saddle has a reasonably spacious campsite, but the nearest water is the north branch of the Albert River.

Various sections of the ridge between Mt Worendo and Lost World can be combined with stretches of the Albert River to form interesting circuit throughwalks e.g. it would be possible to walk via Lost World, Mt Worendo and Rat-a-tat, and descend via the south branch of the Albert River, in a long weekend or perhaps even two long days.

Many experienced bushwalkers would be able to complete a full traverse of Lost World as a day trip, by ascending the mountain from the west, descending via the eastern razorback to the saddle, then rockhopping down the south branch of the Albert River to return to the Lost World Guest House. However, this trip is only suitable for fast fit parties. The creek rockhop takes about 2 to 3 hours.

The Eastern Razorback: Compass navigation is recommended when descending from Lost World to the start of the eastern razorback, since the top section of this ridge is very confusing. If in doubt, stay close to the northern escarpment. The eastern

149

razorback is much less sheer than the western razorback, although care is still required in some places. Several hoop pines along here have spectacular displays of hanging lichens. There are no navigation problems on ascent.

Lost World to Mt Worendo: The route from the Worendo-Lost World saddle to Mt Worendo is relatively straightforward in ascent, although careful navigation may be necessary in descent since the track is vague in the top rainforest section. The lower part of the ridge is a relatively easy razorback.

ALBERT RIVER NORTH BRANCH

Black Canyon: The most spectacular feature on the north branch of the Albert River is Black Canyon, which is considered one of the gems of Lamington. It is a box canyon which becomes narrower and darker as you travel up the creek. At the head of the gorge, the walls become very high and there is a superb set of twin falls.

Black Canyon can be visited in a circuit throughwalk from O'Reillys, walking via Mt Worendo and returning via either the Commando track, Morans Creek or Castle Crag. This full trip would be about grade 41/2 to 5. In good conditions experienced parties could complete the trip in two long days, but a very early start would be necessary on the first day. Less experienced parties would probably require three days. The canyon is a fragile area, so it is important to keep the party size small.

This route proceeds via the graded track to Echo Point, then via the border route to Mt Worendo (refer to the description of the Border Route). At Worendo, leave the border route and proceed to the Worendo-Lost World saddle. You will need to navigate carefully since the track here is often vague. From the saddle, drop north to the creek.

The usual campsites on the trip lie along the Albert River near the point of descent from the saddle. On a two day trip, Black Canyon must be visited on a half day side trip on the first afternoon. It is necessary to reach the creek by about lunch to give yourself time for the return journey to the Canyon. Keep careful note of the available time if entering the canyon without overnight gear and carry a good torch. Ensure you leave your packs somewhere where they can be clearly seen on your return.

Red Rock Cutting lies about 30 minutes upstream after you reach the creek. It is a short gorge blocked by a pool. It can be bypassed by a rough track high up on the north bank, which links points several hundred metres upstream and downstream of the cutting. However, this bypass track is not always easy to locate, so it is best to carry either lilos or large plastic bags to float your gear in case you have to swim through the few metres of water which block the way. Upstream from the cutting you pass over the Red Slab from which Red Rock Cutting acquires its name. About 300m further on, there is a small creek entering on the left (Shooting Creek). This marks an exit route which can be used on other itineraries (see later description).

Proceeding up the Canyon from Red Rock Cutting, rockhopping is usually slow. About half way up, a gorge is bypassed via a track high up on the south bank. Eventually you arrive at the head of the canyon, where Lightning Falls drop in a long wispy streak, while the more voluminous Thunder Falls tumble from a narrow crevice into the same pool. Another feature of interest, the "Rock of Hidden Faces", is located nearby on the southern wall. In certain lighting, faces seem to be engraved in the rock's peculiar sculpting.

Cascades on the Lightning Falls graded track circuit,
Green Mountains, Lamington National Park (Walk 8)

Mt Barney from Montserrat Lookout.

Mt Lindesay from Bald Knob, near Levers Plateau (Walk 77)

Fungi, Mt Mitchell (Walk 14).

Typical Main Range grasstrees in afternoon light.

Unamed waterfall on the south branch of Kobble Creek,
Brisbane Forest Park.

England Creek Falls, Brisbane Forest Park.

Mt Barney at sunset, from near Lovers Plateau (Walks 50 and 77)

Typical Main Range sunrise.

Western cascade of Twin Falls, Back Creek (Walk 87).

Pristine rainforest creek, Mt Glorious/Mt D'Aguilar region, Brisbane Forest Park.

Red Rock Falls, Sundown National Park (Walk 73).

Granite boulder, Girraween National Park.

An unusual view of the Pyramids from north-east, Girraween National Park.

Fungi, Lake McKenzie, Fraser Island (Walk 53).

Burwilla Lookout, with Double Island Point in the background, Rainbow Beach, northern Cooloola (Walks 20 and 55).

Lake Boomanjin, Fraser Island (Walk 53).

Walking Moreton Island's picturesque north-west beach

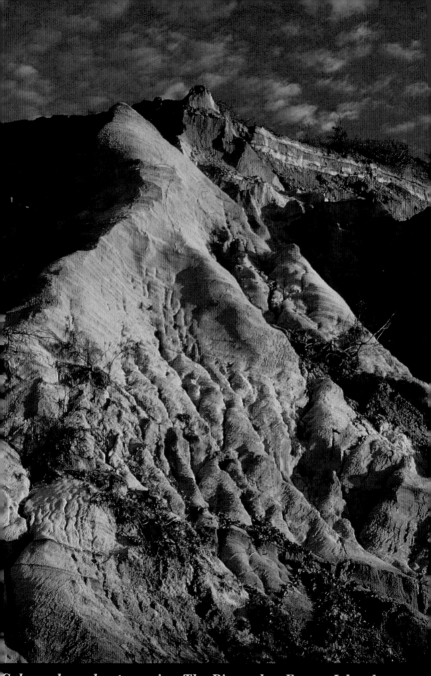

Coloured sands at sunrise, The Pinnacles, Fraser Island

Stars emerging through fading sunset glow, Noosa River

The second day of this trip involves rockhopping down the Albert River to the Morans Creek junction, then ascending to Green Mountains via either of three routes - the Commando track (the easiest route), Morans Creek or Castle Crag (the latter is potentially hazardous). All are described separately in this chapter.

Lower Reaches: There are no notable obstacles on the north branch of the Albert River downstream from Red Rock Cutting, although it is frequently slow and slippery. With throughwalk packs and dry rocks, allow a long half day to rockhop to the Morans Creek junction. More time would be required if the rocks were wet.

Shooting Creek Route: It is possible to visit Black Canyon on a shorter trip from O'Reillys than that just described, but the alternative route is only suitable for small experienced parties. It involves a very steep haul up out of Black Canyon via a track just east of Shooting Creek. Nowadays this track is eroded and landslipped and has a considerable rock fall danger. The route is best avoided after heavy rains or very wet seasons due to the danger of major landslides.

On this itinerary, Black Canyon is visited on the second day, the first day being relatively short. Proceed as on the first itinerary until the Albert River is reached - camp is made at this point or just upstream. During the second day, rockhop with packs to a point about 300m upstream from Red Rock Cutting, where Shooting Creek enters on the left (at the time of writing this point can be identified by a massive double log jam deposited by recent floods). Leave packs here and visit the top of the Canyon, returning to the packs by lunch.

The exit route is only suitable for small parties. The first section climbs an eroded gully on the east of Shooting Creek, and it is here that the rockfall danger is greatest. Near the head of the gully it is possible to do a short side trip to the left to view Silver Falls. Later the route proceeds very steeply up the side of the Canyon, with considerable scrambling although no obvious exposure. However, there is a large drop concealed by fragile vegetation in one section near an old landslide, so care is required. Once at the top of the steep canyon sides, a vague track can be followed uphill to the graded track system. Turn left at the graded track for the shortest route back to O'Reillys.

It is possible to use this route in descent but it is essential that the leader knows the route well, since otherwise the top section is almost impossible to follow. With an experienced leader and a small agile fast party, it is also possible to use this route to visit Black Canyon on a long day trip.

ALBERT RIVER SOUTH BRANCH

The south branch is not frequently travelled by bushwalkers, so would mainly be suited to exploratory ventures. There are no major obstacles on the lower section below the descent from the Worendo-Lost World saddle, although it is frequently slow and slippery. Some obstacles should be expected higher up. It would be advisable to allow at least one long day to travel the full distance from Rat-a-tat campsite to the Lost World Guest House, even in good conditions. If the rocks were slippery or the party wasn't adept at scrambling and rockhopping, progress could be substantially slower.

MT WIDGEE

Mt Widgee lies at the end of the long western ridge of Mt Throakban, the two mountains being basically opposite extremities of the same massif. There are only two routes normally used to access Mt Widgee, these being an unstable climb up precipitous grassy slopes to the north of the mountain's western cliffs, and a long tedious scrub-push from Mt Throakban (although see later comments about a possible third route). It is primarily visited by throughwalkers doing circuit walks in the Albert River region, who may ascend by the western route and then travel along to Mt Throakban, or vice versa. The main attractions of the mountain are the views from above its western cliffs and the simple satisfaction of exploratory curiosity. The mountain is not a popular bushwalking feature, which is probably just as well. The western ascent is potentially one of the most dangerous routes in southern Queensland, and its condition would rapidly deteriorate if it received any substantial usage.

The western ascent starts from the Albert River, initially climbing the ridge just south-east of the Lost World Guest House (099 735). Near the top of the ridge is a memorial to Desmond Dickie, who was sadly killed in a fall on this route in May 1969. Some distance above the memorial, the route contours left (east) along the base of the cliffs, before commencing a treacherous ascent.

The danger of the climb is not so much because of any notable technical climbing difficulty, but rather due to a combination of its precipitous nature and the instability of the footholds. The route zigzags up between cliffs on steep grassy slopes, and any slip in these circumstances could easily lead to a fatal fall. Sometimes the exposure is quite evident, but in a few places the route does not appear as exposed as it actually is, the drop below being disguised by grass and other fragile vegetation. This can lead to overconfidence.

In many of the most exposed places there are no substantial footholds and handholds, other than those that have been kicked into the earth. In dry conditions these may appear quite safe, but after rain or heavy usage by other walkers, the holds can be quite slippery and unstable. Some bushwalkers have experienced frightening occasions when, climbing at the tail of a party when the soil was very wet, whole mounds of earth have begun to move beneath their feet and hands. Consequently, it is recommended that the route only be tackled by small experienced parties when the soil is dry.

The descent path is difficult to locate without prior experience of the route, but lies a short distance north of the western bluff. Ropes are recommended for descent, at least for the top section.

From Mt Widgee to Mt Throakban, the route is scratchy and time-consuming (perhaps 4 to 5 hours) and is unlikely to have any track.

There is also the possibility of a third access route on this massif, using the ridge north-east of the peak at 130 712 (midway between Mts Widgee and Throakban), leading down to the Albert River. Visual inspection from the Worendo-Lost World saddle suggests that this route would be feasible, although the national park map indicates a cliff line on the ridge which may need to be negotiated via a gully on the west.

NEARBY PEAKS

Buchanans Fort, a spectacular bluff north-east of Stinson Park in the Christmas Creek valley, offers interesting views of the national park. It is a steep but straightforward ascent via the western ridge (grade 2 to 2$1/2$), although permission is required to traverse the private lands. From Stinson Park, the route proceeds up the slopes to the north, then turns eastwards along the crest of the ridge. The Christmas Creek Recreation Camp or the Green Mountains national park office are possibly the best places to enquire about how to contact the landowner.

Mt Chinghee National Park lies west of Chinghee Gap on the Running Creek road. The peak can be readily ascended by following up the fence line from the gap, although the mountain offers no views. Permission would be required to cross the private lands near the gap.

Mt Misery is another peak which gives interesting views of the national park. It lies on private land 2km west of Canungra. Permission must be obtained from land owners to access the mountain.

DIRECTORY

QUEENSLAND NATIONAL PARKS AND WILDLIFE SERVICE

Binna Burra: Beechmont, via Nerang. Q. 4211. Telephone: (075) 33 3584.

Green Mountains: via Canungra. Q. 4275. Telephone: (075) 44 0634 (between 2pm and 4pm).

PRIVATE ACCOMMODATION CENTRES AND CAMP GROUNDS

O'Reillys Guest House: Green Mountains, via Canungra. Q. 4275. Telephone (075) 44 0644. See advertisement on page 131.

Binna Burra (Lodge and Campsite): Beechmont, via Nerang. Q. 4211. Telephone: (075) 33 3536.

Rimfall Cottage (Upper Running Creek Valley): Jan and Ken Drynan, Mt Gipps, Mail Service 98, via Beaudesert. 4285. Telephone: (075) 44 8235.

Lost World Guest House (Albert River): Mail Service 413, Darlington, via Beaudesert. Q. 4285. Telephone: (075) 44 8141. (Enquiries preferred by phone).

Christmas Creek Recreation Camp: Christmas Creek, via Beaudesert. Q. 4285. Telephone: (075) 44 8100.

OTHER USEFUL ADDRESSES

Yowgurrabah/Numinbah Valley Adventure Trails: Numinbah Valley, via Nerang. Q. 4211. Telephone: (075) 33 4137. (For enquiries regarding access to Turtle Rock, horse riding day trips and possibly future camping accommodation).

Note: Since the first printing of this book, wood fires have been completely prohibited in all bush camping areas in Scenic Rim national parks. Machetes and similar brush cutting implements are also banned in national parks.

12

THE BORDER RANGES
AND ENVIRONS

While the areas discussed in this chapter are located in New South Wales, most lie along the Queensland border and within the Scenic Rim. These areas are now known as the Border Ranges National Park, although previously they were the subjects of one of the longest running conservation battles in New South Wales.

For descriptive purposes the region can be readily considered as two major subregions - the eastern Tweed Range area (formerly called Wiangaree) and the western Levers Plateau area. A brief description of Mt Warning is also included in this chapter, although this peak lies some kilometres south-west of Murwillumbah and well to the east of the Border Ranges.

The Tweed Range area has been developed with a scenic drive, graded tracks and picnic and camping areas. It is mainly suited to base camping and track walks, although a couple of good off-track walks are possible. In contrast, Levers Plateau is undeveloped and mainly provides throughwalking opportunities. Levers Plateau has not received the intensive bushwalking exploration that has occurred over many years in other parts of the Scenic Rim, so it is likely that more bushwalking opportunities will be discovered here in future years.

SPECIAL NOTES

BUSHWALKING CONDITIONS AND HAZARDS

General Walking Conditions are similar throughout the eastern Scenic Rim, so to save repetition, comprehensive information which can be applied to this entire region is provided in Chapter 11 (Lamington National Park). The following notes emphasise the most important points as well as features of special significance to the Border Ranges, but it is recommended that anyone considering off-track walking in

Left: Selva Falls, Brindle Creek

this area also refer to the "Special Notes" for Lamington. N.B. The Tweed Range region is identical in geological origin to Lamington, but for historical reasons the former is called the Tweed Range while the latter is considered part of the McPherson Ranges. This is rather anomalous scientifically since the McPherson Ranges also extend west to the Mt Barney region, which is of quite different geological origin.

Major Tracks: The Tweed Range area has a variety of facilities, including several impressive track walks. In addition, the route between Collins Gap and Richmond Gap follows border fence maintenance tracks for virtually the entire distance. It is an interesting 3 day throughwalk suitable for inexperienced parties, provided the members have adequate fitness to handle the numerous steep hills.

Off-Track Terrain: All off-track areas in the Border Ranges should be considered very rugged, with frequent cliffs and thick scrub, so this is not the place for inexperienced walkers to undertake off-track exploratory ventures. Despite this, most of the popular off-track routes avoid precipitous areas, so climbing and scrambling skills are not normally essential if you are competent at navigation and trip planning (except for the climb up Mt Lindesay - see later comments).

Rockhopping: The creeks in this region are typically very slippery, particularly in autumn and winter. Rockhopping can be a tedious, tiring and hazardous activity in wet conditions.

Vegetation in this area is predominately subtropical rainforest or wet eucalypt forest. Consequently, expect the usual variety of stinging and thorny plants typical of rainforest areas, especially along creeks and in disturbed localities. There is also considerable regrowth scrub in both the eastern and western regions, including extensive areas of lantana, a legacy of past clearing and logging operations. This regrowth scrub can be quite thick in some areas, so garden gloves and long gaiters are often advisable and care is required when planning trips.

Navigation: As in all rainforest areas, good navigation skills are essential once you leave the official tracks. Views are very limited in most areas (except along the Tweed Range escarpment and on the border crest west of Mt Gipps), and the thickness of some regrowth vegetation can also cause navigational difficulties.

Wetness: In autumn and other wet seasons, it may seem that the rainforest never dries out, but you often need to be prepared for wet conditions even in drier seasons. Carry a parka in case of rain and a rub-on insect repellent to apply to your boots to repel leeches. If conditions are wet, a groundsheet is useful even on day trips e.g. to provide a dry site for lunch.

Other Climate Considerations: The Border Ranges suit bushwalking at all times of year. Winter and spring are usually much drier and more stable than the mid summer to autumn period, although autumn is one of the best seasons for general walking if the weather is fine. Creek trips are usually best in spring and early summer.

Mt Lindesay, described at the end of this chapter, is recommended only for experienced rockclimbers.

FACILITIES AND CAMPING

In the Tweed Range, the NSW National Parks and Wildlife Service operates camping areas with basic facilities at Sheepstation Creek (located in the western foothills at 024 570) and at Forest Top (higher up on the Tweed Range Scenic Drive at 061 597). There are also a number of picnic areas on the Tweed Range Scenic Drive. No

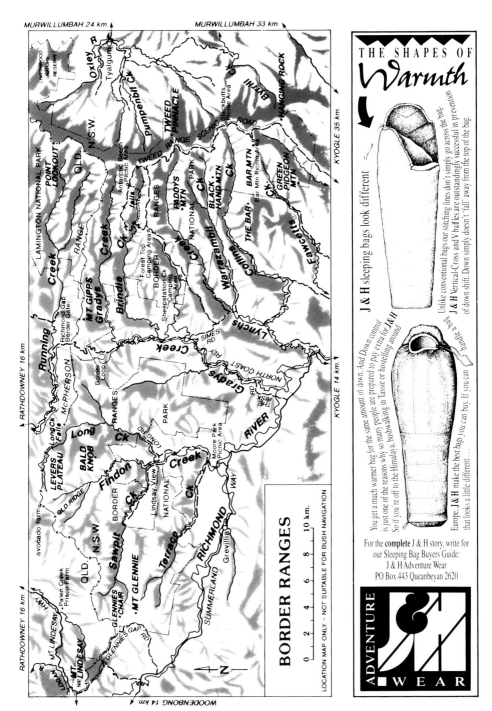

facilities have been provided in the western section although there is a picnic area at Moore Park Nature Reserve, on the Lindesay View road a kilometre from the junction with the Summerland Way (refer to road directions). This has basic facilities and may be useful for Friday night bivouacs.

MAPS

Excellent 1:25 000 topographic maps cover the entire region, although those published by Queensland SUNMAP differ in style and coverage from those published by the NSW Central Mapping Authority. The SUNMAP sheets cover the border regions, while the NSW sheets cover the adjoining areas to the south. The most useful maps are:

Queensland Issue:

Palen Creek, Cougal, Lamington, Tyalgum and *Mt Lindesay.*

NSW Issue (each twice the size and coverage of the Queensland maps):

Brays Creek and *Grevillea.*

Because of their large coverage, the *Woodenbong, Grevillea* and *Tyalgum* 1:50 000 sheets are also useful for secondary reference purposes, although the maps are now out-of-date and some information is grossly inaccurate.

ROAD ACCESS

Three major roads which form a triangle around the broad Levers Plateau region are the basis of most vehicular access to the Border Ranges. These are:

• The Richmond Gap road, which crosses the border between the Levers Plateau region and the Tweed Range/Lamington region.

• The Mt Lindesay Highway, which crosses the border at Collins Gap in the west.

• The Summerland Way, which runs between Kyogle and Woodenbong, meeting the Mt Lindesay Highway 9km south of the Collins Gap border gate.

It is also possible to access the Tweed Range from near Nimbin in the south.

Richmond Gap: This provides access to the border route just west of Mt Gipps. If driving from Queensland, turn left off the Mt Lindesay Highway 27km south of Beaudesert, just before a railway bridge. The road proceeds along the Running Creek valley for 26km before crossing into New South Wales at the Richmond Gap border gate.

Driving from Kyogle, take the road up the Gradys Creek Valley, which turns north off the Summerland Way at a well signposted junction 19km from Kyogle. The distance from the junction to the border gate is 25km. The top section is known as the Lions Road since it was developed by the Lions Club.

Tweed Range Scenic Drive (via Richmond Gap): About 14km south of the Richmond Gap border gate, a left hand turn (Simes Road) leads to the Tweed Range Scenic Drive. This set of roads is well signposted and trafficable by two wheel drive vehicles in normal conditions. Formerly called the Wiangaree Forest Drive, it forms a loop in the headwaters of Gradys and Brindle Creeks, with an offshoot running south along the Tweed Range to join the Kyogle-Murwillumbah road. This road system gives access to all the Tweed Range graded tracks and to Tweed Pinnacle. The northern part of the loop road is one-way traffic (clockwise).

Tweed Range Scenic Drive (from Summerland Way): Simes Road can be found turning off the Gradys Creek road (see previous descriptions), 11km north of the Summerland Way junction. Alternatively, take the Lynchs Creek Road which turns north off the Summerland Way 14km west of Kyogle.

Tweed Range Scenic Drive (Southern Access): The Tweed Range Scenic Drive can also be approached from the Kyogle-Murwillumbah road by turning off west at Lillian Rock north-west of Nimbin. However, this approach road is very steep. Car engines should be in good condition to ascend the road and good brakes are required in descent.

Mt Warning: This well known peak lies east of the Tweed Range. The road is evident on any road map, turning off the Murwillumbah-Kyogle road 10km south-west of Murwillumbah.

Lindesay View: Access to the Levers Plateau region is mainly through the roads around Lindesay View, a small community of scattered farm houses just north of Old Grevillea. The turn north off the Summerland Way at Old Grevillea is signposted "Findon Creek" and lies 28km east of the junction with the Mt Lindesay Highway, and 8km west of the Gradys Creek road junction (i.e. the turn-off to Richmond Gap). There are four different access points from this road system - Terrace Creek, Long Creek, Sawpit Creek and Findon Creek. Driving north from the Summerland Way junction, a picnic area will be found after 1km (the Moore Park Nature Reserve), on the right just before a bridge (880 542). This may be useful for Friday night bivouacs. A junction is reached after a further 1.2km (884 550). The left hand road here goes to Terrace Creek; for the other access points you should follow the right hand fork. After another 5.3km, a T-junction is reached where the Long Creek road turns right. Taking the left road, the junction to Sawpit Creek (on the left) and Findon Creek (on the right) is reached after another 1.2km (882 596).

Permission from the landowner is essential to use the Terrace Creek route. The Findon Creek route also requires travel over private lands, although at the time of writing access conditions here are good. However, it is one of those places where the road goes right to the farmhouse door, so respect the occupants' privacy and don't arrive out of daylight hours. Enquire with the NSW National Parks and Wildlife Service at Kyogle about how to contact the landholders. The Long Creek and Sawpit Creek roads terminate at the boundaries of the national park (signposted).

Glennie Gap Road: This road travels along the border ridge for some kilometres between Mt Lindesay and Mt Glennie. In dry conditions it is normally trafficable by two wheel drive vehicles, although vehicular access is banned in wet conditions since it deteriorates very quickly. The road gives quick access to the border. It is most easily found from the direction of the Mt Lindesay Highway - turn sharp left off the Summerland Way after 7.9km, just before Hixons Creek Bridge at Dairy Flat (723 602). The turn-off and start of the road may be confusing, since there are two apparent junctions within a few metres and the correct road is often concealed by thick grass. Keep left at both "junctions" (the offshoot road is actually a driveway to a house), then follow the road all the way to Glennie Gap. There are several old offshoot tracks but the main route is generally evident. A national park sign is reached

4.1km from Dairy Flat, near a side road (used for fence maintenance) which turns off on the left. Glennie Gap lies 400m further on.

The road makes a circuit and returns to the highway 1km east of the Hixons Creek bridge. The full circuit is about 14km. Although much of the forest is badly logged, other parts are very picturesque. The road follows the border for some kilometres.

If driving down from Glennie Gap via the western part of the circuit, beware of the final unmarked left turn just before Dairy Flat. Missing this turn would result in crashing down a sheer bank onto the Summerland Way.

Collins Gap: This is on the Mt Lindesay Highway 61km south of Beaudesert.

TWEED RANGE REGION

The Tweed Range region is mainly suited to easy day walks, base camps and forest drives due to the extent of road systems and previous logging activities. The region is well worth visiting. It is one of the few places in northern Australia where beech trees can be seen growing on creek banks, and the beauty of the rainforest and creek scenery is truly outstanding. The area offers both graded track walks and off-track walks. Picnic areas abound in the park and there are two attractive camping areas with basic facilities.

OFFICIAL TRACK WALKS

(Walk 12) **Sheepstation Creek:** As you approach from the west on the Tweed Range Scenic Drive, the first camping ground is at Sheepstation Creek on the national park border. There are several track walk options from this site. The longest walk is the Booyong Track, which leads up to the Forest Tops camping area (11km one way). This walk passes through brush box, bangalow palms and rainforest, with various cascades and creek scenery. About midway along the Booyong Track, there is a 1 1/2km loop track which visits an enormous rosewood tree (*Dysoxylum fraserianum*). The Rosewood Circuit makes a convenient 1/2 day walk from Sheepstation Creek camp ground (about 9 1/2km return).

For people only looking for short forest strolls, there is swimming hole and waterfall (Lophostemon Falls) about 1 1/2km from the camp ground, as well as an historic rock bearing the names of bullockies from yesteryear.

(Walk 11) **Brindle Creek:** This track connects the Brindle Creek picnic area (066 607) with the Antarctic Beech picnic area (093 612), a distance of about 5.5km one way. It offers some outstanding creek scenery, with beech trees seemingly growing with "their feet in the water" beside peaceful pools and banks decked in *Helmholtzia* lilies. Long silent pools amid the rainforest are particularly notable. These features provide a quite different character to most of the Lamington creeks, which tend to have a continuous steep gradient at this altitude. Numerous small waterfalls complement the serene and enchanting setting. The scenery is probably best appreciated by walking upstream from the Brindle Creek Picnic Area.

Bar Mountain Area: This circuit track is a short walk from the Bar Mountain picnic area in the south and is well worth a visit. It gives unusual views of many well known border peaks, with Mt Lindesay being particularly notable. For unusual views of Mt Warning, the nearby Blackbutts lookout is also spectacular.

TWEED PINNACLE

Another significant bushwalking feature in this region is Tweed Pinnacle, named on the *Brays Creek* map as Pinnacle Hill (132 579). A good track leads to the feature from the Pinnacle car park, 4.3km south of the junction of the Tweed Range road and the Loop Road. The track descends steeply before a final short ascent. The route is not particularly difficult by bushwalking standards, although the razorback has precipitous sides and care is needed in several places.

It is apparently possible to climb Tweed Pinnacle from South Pumpenbill Creek in the east. This would be a difficult walk (probably at least grade 5) for experienced walkers only, since the top section could be dangerous. At the top of the ridge, the route contours around on the north of the Pinnacle, then up through a cliff break to the saddle. Ropes are recommended and a car shuffle would normally be necessary.

GRADYS CREEK

Gradys Creek is similar in character to Brindle Creek, with long pools and beech *(Walk* trees. This area is now managed as a wilderness area, although the remnants of an old *41)* graded track (once called the Gradys Creek circuit) still meander along the creek. While this track is now officially closed, experienced bushwalkers with astute observation skills can still follow the route. It is rated about grade 3, more for its navigational difficulty than for the physical effort required.

The full circuit is about 8km long (including 2km of road), but you should allow yourself at least 4 hours since considerable time may be required for route finding. It is probably best to walk the circuit in a clockwise direction, possibly starting from the Antarctic beech picnic area (093 612) which is situated on the road about midway between the two track entrances. The track starts about a kilometre west of the picnic area at about 083 613, and descends down the ridge to the north to Upper Gradys Creek Falls (089 625). It then meanders up the creek before returning to the loop road at about 104 610. This eastern track entrance is about a kilometre east of the Antarctic beech picnic area and 800m north of the Tweed Valley Lookout.

You need to be especially alert not to lose the track, particularly along the flatter sections of the creek where the route meanders about and sometimes fades out. In other places the route climbs awkwardly up steep slopes well away from the creek banks. If by chance you do become disorientated, the loop road can be gained from any point by ascending to the south.

At the eastern end of the circuit, do not become confused by an old turn-off which leads north to Lamington National Park. This is usually marked by an old sign. The location is on the north side of the creek at about 104 623, approximately 45 minutes from the eastern entrance. The side track leads to Tweed Trig (105 631). Refer to descriptions of the Lamington border route (pages 142 and 162) for further information on this route, which should only be attempted by experienced bushwalkers.

EXPLORATORY FEATURES

With a long car shuffle, experienced bushwalkers can rockhop the full length of Gradys Creek to where it meets the Lions Road at 972 621. Alternatively, some bushwalkers prefer to rockhop up from the Lions Road to Lower Gradys Creek Falls, which lie on a tributary at 036 637. However, the lower part of Gradys Creek runs through private property. Gaining permission to cross this land may be difficult.

Other features in the Tweed Range area include Paddys Mountain, Black Hand Mountain and Green Pigeon Mountain. Apparently all can be climbed from both the east and west, although Black Hand Mountain is very precipitous from the west (possibly about grade 5). The other features are reportedly around grade 3, but this grading is only approximate. Green Pigeon Mountain, Bar Mountain and the Bar could be done as a circuit if an acceptable access route can be found. There may be scrub in some of these areas.

THE BORDER ROUTE: RICHMOND GAP TO TWEED TRIG

General: From Richmond Gap, the Border route runs east over Mt Gipps and Mt Nungulba to Tweed Trig (105 631). Tweed Trig is the junction of the McPherson and Tweed Ranges, and also the site of a major change of direction in the state border. The route normally represents about 11/2 days walking (grade 4), although the time required will vary with the party and conditions. Nowadays there is little trace of a track east of Mt Nungulba, and progress can become tediously slow in this section. In the western section, parts of the track are becoming overgrown where the border fence is no longer maintained.

Route Description: The border fence is followed up steeply from Richmond Gap, providing a straightforward ascent of Mt Gipps. The summit is forested, although good views can be obtained on the ascent as well as from several places on the surrounding slopes. Just east of Mt Gipps, at 995 650, there is an old hut nicknamed "the birdcage". At this point there is a division in the fence, with a new fence departing from the border and descending to the south-east. It is important not to follow this in error. The older and relatively dilapidated border fence branches to the left.

For several kilometres east of the birdcage, parts of the track may be overgrown where the fence is no longer maintained. Several patches of lantana could become particularly severe in future years. Travel becomes easier further east, and the track reforms completely when you enter the rainforest at 030 650.

Another old hut is found at 042 649. About 700m east of this latter hut, at approximately 049 648, water can be found by descending to the north. A further hundred metres east, at 050 648, there is a sharp turn in the border fence on top of a knoll. This is the junction of the Black Snake Ridge route which leads down to Running Creek. It is an excellent route if undertaking circuit walks in the Running Creek region, and can be used to access the border instead of the Mt Gipps route. It has good campsites with water available south-west of the main saddle (refer to page 145 for a full description).

The fence terminates 700 metres further east at 057 647. From here to Tweed Trig, the route is entirely through rainforest and rarely has any trace of a track. Progress can be tediously slow in places, especially east of Mt Nungulba. Water can be found by descending southwards from the saddle east of Mt Nungulba. The point is marked by an old "W" blazed on a tree.

It is worth noting that the cairn on Tweed Trig, as well as the junction with the track from Gradys Creek, is actually on the western end of the knoll (105 631), not on the eastern end (107 631) as is marked on the topographic map. The track which leads north into Lamington National Park from the Trig actually starts off on an easterly course for the first couple of hundred metres.

Other Routes in this area include the northern ridge of Mt Gipps. This gives a direct ascent from Running Creek but is extremely steep. Several minor ridges on the north slopes between Mt Gipps and Black Snake Ridge also appear to be feasible ascent routes from Running Creek to the border, although none are recommended for descent due to the danger of encountering precipitous terrain. Yet another route on Mt Gipps is via the south-west ridge (968 647). This crosses the true summit.

MT WARNING

Mt Warning National Park lies just south-west of Murwillumbah in northern New South Wales, the peak being the first place on mainland Australia to receive the morning sun. The mountain is very popular with visitors for both scenic and historical reasons. It has a superbly picturesque shape, complemented perfectly by the typically green countryside. Its Aboriginal name is "Wollumbin", which means "cloud catcher" or "weather-maker". No name could be more appropriate, for the region is often wet, and mist and cloud frequently envelopes the pinnacle even when the rest of the sky is clear. *(Walk 13)*

The route up the mountain is mainly graded track, although many people find that the track is somewhat more tiring than comparable tracks in nearby areas such as Lamington. The last few hundred metres involves a scramble up a deeply eroded gully, with a chain providing some assistance. **Camping on the peak is definitely not permitted**. The walk is rated about grade 2.

LEVERS PLATEAU REGION

Specifically, Levers Plateau is the area of ranges which lies roughly around the point 880 670, but the name is also popularly used to refer to the broad sweep of the Border Ranges from Mt Glennie to Richmond Gap. This is the region referred to in this section.

Much of the region has been logged, although the high areas around Levers Plateau itself are untouched. The upper section of Long Creek is a particularly notable highlight. The area provides good opportunities for circuit throughwalks, most including at least a short section of the border route.

THE BORDER ROUTE: COLLINS GAP TO RICHMOND GAP

General: This section describes the border route from Collins Gap to Richmond Gap, including Mt Glennie, but excluding the extremely difficult climb up Mt Lindesay. The latter climb is described separately at the end of this chapter.

(Walk 59) This part of the border route follows the border fence, except for around Mt Lindesay which is bypassed via a fence maintenance road high up on the southern side. While there is a considerable distance involved (over 30km), progress is fast and fit parties are often able to complete the trip in 2 days (grade 31/2). There are many steep hills on the route but no navigational or scrambling difficulties.

For much of the trip the lands to the north of the fence are cleared, so it won't necessarily appeal to the wilderness enthusiast. However, compensation is found in the views of Lamington and Mts Barney, Lindesay and Maroon, especially from the area near the "avocado farm" (851 681; see later comments). There are also many sections of attractive eucalypt forest.

Water: The most reliable water supply is Long Creek, which runs close to the border for some kilometres above Long Creek Falls (894 674). However, water can probably also be obtained by descending down the southern slopes at a number of other places. Two suggested sites are 813 645 and 830 664. The old fencers' tanks which were once located along this route are now mostly too dilapidated and holed to contain water.

Alternative Access Routes: Some parties prefer to leave cars at either Glennie Gap or the Palen Creek Prison Farm, rather than at Collins Gap. Descent to the prison farm can be made from near 747 627, via an old road to the north (permission would probably need to be sought from the prison farm authorities to leave cars). In addition, the border can be reached from one of the southern access routes, which are described later in this section.

Route Description: Most of the route between Collins Gap and Richmond Gap is easily followed regardless of your direction of travel. The fence maintenance road which bypasses Mt Lindesay on the south is shown on the topographic maps and is easily found from the west. If walking from the east, follow the Glennie Gap road until it starts to descend to the south. The bypass road turns off on the right several hundred metres after the road leaves the western end of the Gap.

Just east of Glennie Gap, at 762 623, there is a division in the border fence amid open rainforest. If walking eastwards, the fence division can be located just after a very steep rainforest ascent - the left hand branch leads towards Richmond Gap. If walking westwards, the main fence to Glennie and Collins Gaps is the right hand branch - it takes a course down a very steep rainforest slope almost immediately after the fence division. The uphill fence at this division leads to Glennies Chair and Mt Glennie (see later description).

Mt Tanna is the name of the mountain at 812 637 (spot height 795m). At the bottom of the slope on the north-east of Mt Tanna, a track leads off sharply to a clearing and a hut at 805 640. From here an old road leads down to the Palen Creek Forest Station

and Back Creek. At a point further east, an avocado farm has been established close to the border fence (851 681), and you pass within fifty metres of several houses.

You may be tempted to skirt around some of the hills in this region on their north-west flanks, but it is generally preferable to stay on the crest. Access is restricted to some of the lands to the north.

Long Creek Falls, situated at 894 674, are visible from the border fence and make an impressive spectacle. The falls drop well over a hundred metres in several sets of cascades. The upper section of Long Creek runs close to the border for several kilometres and is an easy side trip. Refer to the description later in this chapter for more information on Long Creek.

Glennies Chair and Mt Glennie: The fence leading uphill from the fence division at 762 623, east of Glennie Gap (refer previous description), leads to Glennies Chair. This rocky pinnacle on the north of Mt Glennie actually resembles a chair when viewed from the Mt Lindesay region. It lies only a short distance off the main walking route, although rainforest obscures most of the views in this vicinity and so it is not possible to get much of a perspective of the Chair close up. There is no route suitable for bushwalkers for ascending the Chair.

From Glennies Chair, the fence line continues to lead uphill, although much of the fence has now fallen down. It terminates at the base of the north-western cliffs of Mt Glennie. The mountain can be climbed by contouring right for a short distance along the base of the cliffs, and then ascending through scrub between the cliffs. However, there are no views from the summit and the scrub is very thick. Great care must also be taken to remember the route, since it can be very difficult to locate when descending from the summit. N.B. Some plant communities around Mt Glennie have not experienced fire for many decades and have accumulated large depths of fuel. These areas are very valuable for scientific purposes. It is important that walkers help safeguard these areas by not using fires in this vicinity.

SOUTHERN ROUTES

A variety of routes can be used to ascend to Levers Plateau from the Lindesay View region just to the south. Many pass through logging regrowth, although this generally reduces as you get closer to the border. The routes provide a number of opportunities for excellent circuit throughwalks, most including at least a short section of the border route.

While numerous exploratory routes are possible around Sawpit, Findon and Long Creeks, four recognised ridge routes are:

- The Queensland Spur (860 650), which is found by walking up Findon Creek to the Middle Creek junction.

(Walk 77) • The Bald Knob ridge (887 638). To find this ridge, follow an old road which starts near a farmhouse on the right, 400m up the Findon Creek road from the Sawpit Creek road junction (882 596). It goes over bare paddocks at first (permission from the landowner is required), with little evidence of a track, and then proceeds across the flanks of a hill. It climbs the ridge at 890 600 and then proceeds north-north-west to Bald Knob and the headwaters of Surveyors Creek. Despite the presence of the old road for much of the way, the ridge has much attractive forest and provides a good route to Levers Plateau and Long Creek. The area around Bald Knob provides an excellent view of Mt Lindesay.
- The steep spur at 914 654 between the border and Long Creek.
- The longer ridge at 918 639 between the border and Long Creek. This has some scratchy regrowth due to the presence of an old logging road, although the scrub is not obstructive.

All the above routes are about grade 3 1/2 to 4.

LEVERS PLATEAU AND LONG CREEK

Numerous exploratory trips can be done in the Levers Plateau area to view the towering hoop pines, as well as the rainforest in the headwaters of Plateau and Long Creeks. There aren't any routes which are particularly recommended, since the whole area is worth exploring. There are good campsites in the plateau region above Long Creek Falls (894 674), Long Creek itself being relatively easy travelling in this area.

Long Creek Falls can be descended for a considerable distance by carefully zigzagging between the cascades. The falls have a total drop exceeding a hundred metres, although there are a number of cascades and it is difficult to find a vantage point where the entire set of waterfalls can be observed at once. To reach the falls from the border route, cross the fence and descend just upstream of the top cascades.

Downstream from the falls, Long Creek becomes more difficult to travel with only occasional small campsites.

MT LINDESAY

This peak is very difficult and exposed and should only be attempted by people with rope and rockclimbing skills (about grade 6 1/2 to 7). One if not two full length rockclimbing ropes are required for belaying, fixed ropes being handy if the party is any more than three or four people. Somebody who has climbed the peak previously should preferably be in the party.

There are various locations to start the ascent. The only place to climb the final summit cliffs is via a route on the eastern side of the mountain, so all ascent routes meet at this point.

The most commonly used ascent route, and possibly the most scenic, is from the Collins Gap border gate. Follow the border ridge up to the summit cliffs, then contour right along the base of the southern cliffs to the start of the climb.

Glennie Gap provides the highest starting elevation but the ridge is very steep. Ascent is started from the south-east along the new border fence, but after a short distance it is necessary to branch off right, following the vague remnants of the old fence all the way to the summit cliffs. There is a steep bluff on this ridge at 732 639. An alternative route from near Glennie Gap is via the ridge at 730 635. This is found by ascending from the eastern end of the fence maintenance road that runs just south of the mountain between Glennie and Collins Gaps. This ridge is not as steep as the direct ascent from Glennie Gap.

The northern ridge provides yet another ascent route for the mountain. This is longer than the other routes, but was once very popular. It starts along the Mt Lindesay Highway roughly 23km south of Rathdowney (almost any point along the section of road between 736 665 and 722 660 can be used). Ascend the steep grassy ridge to the base of the first cliff, then veer right and climb to the base of the summit cliffs. From here drop leftwards into the rainforest and contour around below the cliffs for a considerable distance. At times when contouring you may drop somewhat below the cliff line, since there is no definite track. Eventually you will arrive at the vague remnants of the old border fence at the east of the mountain. This is followed up to the summit cliffs again.

Just near where you first enter the rainforest on the above traverse, there is a chimney in the cliffs. This is Vidlers chimney, named after Lyle Vidler, an experienced walker who was sadly killed here on Boxing Day, 1928, while soloing to find a new route to the summit. His body was discovered at the base some days later.

From near the top of the eastern border fence, the route up the cliffs should be evident by the footworn marks of previous climbers. The first cliff is particularly exposed and ropes are required. From the top of this cliff, follow the ridge up to the second cliff, which can be ascended directly or via a route further around on the left. Some parties may prefer to abseil when descending these summit cliffs.

In the early 1970s a large patch of the rainforest which covers the summit was cleared by a surveyor who became marooned on the mountain. Apparently he tried to clear a helicopter pad. After word was received a day or so later he was rescued by Federation Mountain Rescue personnel (the Queensland Federation of Bushwalking Clubs' search and rescue division) and taken down the cliffs by ropes. There is still much evidence of the clearing but the views that it afforded to the south-east for several years are largely obscured by regrowth.

DIRECTORY

NSW NATIONAL PARKS AND WILDLIFE SERVICE

Border Ranges: P.O. Box 174, Kyogle. NSW. 2474. (63 Summerland Way, Kyogle). Telephone: (066) 32 2068.

Mt Warning: P.O. Box 91, Alstonville. NSW. 2477. Telephone: (066) 28 1177.

Enquiries can also be directed to the Kyogle Office (see above).

PRIVATE CAMPING GROUNDS

Mt Warning: Wollumbin Wildlife Refuge Caravan Park, Mt Warning Road, via Murwillumbah. NSW. 2484. Telephone: (066) 79 5120.

13

THE BARNEY/BALLOW REGION

The central Scenic Rim includes many of south-east Queensland's best known and most spectacular mountains - Mt Lindesay, whose "wedding cake" shape is discernable even from the buildings of Brisbane in clear weather; Mts Barney, Ernest, May and Maroon, which offer spectacular and rugged bushwalking opportunities; and the large rainforest covered massifs of Mts Ballow and Clunie. These seven peaks form the core of the central Scenic Rim.

For descriptive purposes, this book divides the central Scenic Rim into the Barney/Ballow region (which includes Mts Clunie and Maroon) and the Border Ranges (including Mt Lindesay). This chapter describes the former region.

SPECIAL NOTES

BUSHWALKING CONDITIONS AND HAZARDS

General Terrain: This region is mainly undeveloped and contains some of the most rugged bushwalking areas in southern Queensland. Few routes can be considered suitable for beginners. This is unfortunate since the region has become very popular with tourists and novice bushwalkers in recent years, due to the development of camping areas at places such as Yellowpinch and Mt May. This popularity has inadvertently led to an undesirable situation, with hundreds of people tackling trips beyond their abilities every year. Inexperienced bushwalkers need to realise that even the so-called "easy" routes in this region, such as South Ridge (the "tourist" route up Mt Barney), require a reasonable level of fitness and competence (refer to page 176).

There are several localities in the central Scenic Rim which should be considered extremely difficult and potentially dangerous, even for experienced bushwalkers. A few routes are rated at grade 7, and even very experienced parties normally require belay ropes in such localities.

Left: Mts Lindesay and Ernest from the summit of Mt Barney

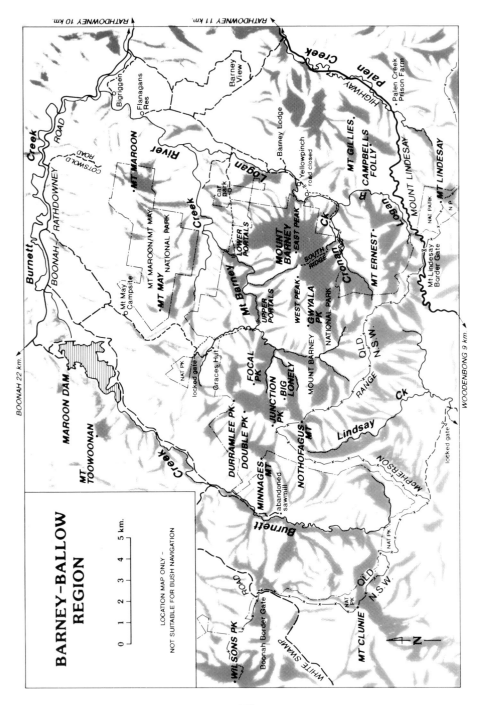

BARNEY-BALLOW REGION

0 1 2 3 4 5 km.

LOCATION MAP ONLY –
NOT SUITABLE FOR BUSH NAVIGATION

Navigation: The amount of navigation skill required varies with each particular area. From the navigation viewpoint, many of the ridges in this region are reasonably easy on ascent but are much more difficult on descent. Such routes are recommended for ascent only unless you have travelled them several times. In the Barney area, careful navigation is sometimes also required to find the start of ascent routes, the way being confused by thick scrub and lack of views. Frequent cliffs, both large and small, are another common navigation hazard in the region.

In general, a reasonably good level of navigation skill is required to walk in the extensive rainforest and scrub areas of the western Barney and Ballow regions. In particular, descents along ridges require good compass skills in these western areas.

Climatic Hazards and Water Availability are variable in this region. While the northern ridges of Barney are definitely not recommended in summer due to their open and unforested nature, a few creeks, rainforest areas and southern ridges do offer enjoyable summer walking opportunities. The ridge routes are invariably dry throughout the entire region, so water must be carried in quantity. However, there are water points in several obscure localities in the western areas. In winter expect the region to be very cold at night, frosts being particularly severe in the open farmlands surrounding the peaks. Watch out for thunderstorms in late spring and early summer. These can bring lightning and unseasonally cold weather.

Rockhopping on Mt Barney Creek downstream of the Upper Portals is much easier and faster than is typical for south-east Queensland, especially in spring and early summer when this section of creek can be an idyllic delight. In autumn when the weather is wet and in winter when many rocks are in perpetual shade, the creek becomes harder to negotiate, especially upstream of the Barrabool Creek junction. Upstream from Upper Portals the creek rapidly changes in nature, the slabs giving way to intermittent rocks and making travel slow and difficult.

Vegetation: Expect some difficulties with the vegetation on most of the less travelled routes, since very thick heath understories are typical of the region. To a great extent, vegetation density in the heath areas is influenced by recent bushfire activity, so the nature of some routes may change in time (note comments on page 179).

CONSERVATION PRACTICES

Particular note is required regarding environmental problems in this area, since the East Peak and saddle regions of Mt Barney have become very degraded in recent years due to abuse and overuse. Most of the problems are caused by people ignorant or uncaring of accepted bushwalking conservation practices, resulting in a great deal of unnecessary damage, especially around campsites. Rubbish and faecal pollution are only part of the problem. Many trees and smaller plants are badly damaged by people making shelters, campfires or bedding, to compensate for lack of suitable tents, stoves, sleeping bags and other standard equipment. Much of this damage will never repair unless visitor habits and numbers are controlled through management. At Mt Barney there is a considerable argument for the QNPWS to restrict camping to bona-fide bushwalkers who carry proper and adequate equipment. Strict number limits are also required, since severe damage is often caused by excessively large groups congregating in the saddle.

It would be beneficial for wood fires to be totally banned at the East Peak/saddle area. At popular campsites, wood has to be collected from considerable distances and carried or dragged back through the scrub. In thick heath areas such as at Mt Barney, much damage is caused to the living vegetation by this practice. If done frequently, the shrubs will actually be killed. The banning of wood fires from the East Peak-saddle area would also impress upon tourists and novice bushwalkers the seriousness of the situation, and the importance other national park users place on a responsible attitude towards camping practices.

FACILITIES AND CAMPING

Base Camping: There are no national park camp grounds in this region, although there is a variety of official camping reserves and private camp grounds. The main sites are camping reserves at Yellowpinch and Flanagans Reserve (basic facilities), a camping reserve at Mt May (no facilities), and private camp grounds with full facilities at Bigriggen and Barney Lodge (see the Directory and advertisements later in this chapter). Refer to the road directions for details about the locations of these areas.

Throughwalk Camping: Most bush camp sites in the higher regions tend to be quite small, although there are occasional sites along the creeks which are of moderate size. As in other regions of the Scenic Rim, the Queensland National Parks and Wildlife Service places number limits on the sizes of throughwalking parties in this region. At the time of writing the management plan policies are being reviewed, but it is quite likely that maximum party size limits of around six to eight people will be applied. It is also hoped that special management efforts will be made to control the camping impacts in the East Peak/saddle area, and along Mt Barney Creek between Upper Portals and Lower Portals.

MAPS

The 1:25 000 topographic maps published by SUNMAP are recommended for most bushwalking purposes. The most relevant sheets are *Mt Clunie*, *Mt Lindesay*, *Teviot*, *Maroon* and *Palen Creek*. There is also a good 1:25 000 forestry/national park map of the Barney/Ballow region, available through SUNMAP and other outlets. However, this doesn't extend much beyond the park boundaries or clearly show all road access. It also doesn't cover Mts May or Maroon. Consequently, check that your intended route is fully covered by the map before your trip.

ROAD ACCESS

The principal access points in this region are as follows:

Yellowpinch (from Mt Lindesay Highway): The camping reserve at Yellowpinch can be reached by turning right onto the Barney View road, 10.5km south of Rathdowney. Drive 6.7km, ignoring all turn-off roads (including the road marked "Barney View" 3km from the highway), then turn left at a T-junction (767 764). Drive a further 6.6km, ignoring all turn-offs. The camping ground lies at 737 714, just beyond a causeway on the Logan River. The road beyond the camping reserve has now been closed, although it may still be trafficable by four wheel drive vehicles (see topographic map for route).

Yellowpinch (from Boonah-Rathdowney Road): Turn south 39km from Boonah or 10km from Rathdowney, onto the road marked "Barney View". Drive 3km and turn right onto a dirt road, then drive a further kilometre and turn left at a T-junction (the right hand road at this point goes to Flanagans Reserve, a picnic and camping area). After a further 1.2km you will reach the intersection described above (767 764), with the road from the Mt Lindesay Highway joining on the left. Drive straight ahead at this intersection for 6.6km, as outlined above.

Mt Barney Lodge is being developed at the time of writing. It is intended to be a low key camping and accommodation centre, with the camping area due to open in early 1991. It is located on the left just before Yellowpinch (see Directory and advertisement).

Lower Portals: Follow the Yellowpinch directions until 2.6km south of the intersection at 767 764. At this point (approximately 753 746), take a signposted right hand turn. Drive a further 600m, passing through a gate, and turn left. The car park and the start of the Lower Portals track lies about 1.7km further on, at about 733 746.

Those familiar with the old access track via Drynans Hut should note that the old route is now closed and trespassers may be prosecuted. Therefore, avoid the entire Drynans Hut region which extends from just downstream of Lower Portals to Drynans Hut at 727 761.

Flanagans Reserve: Refer to the road directions given above for locating Yellowpinch from the Boonah-Rathdowney road.

Bigriggen Park: This commercial camping ground leased from the Beaudesert Shire Council lies adjacent to the Logan River and is readily accessible from the Boonah-Rathdowney road. Turn south 39km from Boonah or 10km from Rathdowney into the road marked "Barney View", then drive 700m and turn right. From this junction, it is only a few kilometres to Bigriggen (see Directory and advertisement).

Burnett Creek: Drive south from Boonah for about 26km ignoring all turn-off roads. Three kilometres past the Maroon Dam turn-off, the Burnett Creek road turns off right. Mt Ballow can be climbed (by crossing private property) from various points along the latter half of this road. The far end of the road is not recommended in wet conditions.

Mt May and Graces Hut: Take the Burnett Creek road, then turn left after 2.5km into Newmans Road. Follow this for almost 2km until you find a junction near some houses. Take the right hand fork, which passes through a gate after about 500m before leading to the Mt May campsite (674 798; no facilities). Beyond the campsite the quality of the road varies considerably - sometimes it is in good condition and sometimes it is almost untrafficable due to deep water ruts. One fact is certain - it should be used only in dry weather. In wet weather the steep sections become very dangerous on descent, even for four wheel drive vehicles. The first steep pinch lies just after the Mt May campsite and later there is a much longer climb. While maps show the road continuing to Graces Hut (659 757), nowadays vehicular progress is stopped a kilometre beforehand by a locked gate on the top of the ridge (655 765). Signs mark the start of the walking track to Upper Portals, the ridge in this vicinity being open and grassy and providing brilliant views of the surrounding mountains. N.B. Newmans Road can also be followed from Maroon township.

Mt Maroon (Cotswold): This road turns south off the Boonah-Rathdowney road 2.7km east of Maroon township (start odometer at school). From the turn-off it is 3.5km to the small lagoon where the normal ascent route begins.

Knapps Peak is reached by turning off the Boonah-Rathdowney road about a kilometre east of Maroon township, into a side road signposted "Cannon Creek". Refer to page 192 for more details.

White Swamp (Boonah Border Gate): This is used when climbing Mt Clunie. Drive south from Boonah towards Maroon, but after 16km take the right hand road marked "Carneys Creek". Drive 26km along the this road, ignoring turn-offs, to the Boonah Border Gate.

Collins Gap Border Gate: This is the border gate on the Mt Lindesay Highway 27km south of Rathdowney. This access point is sometimes used when visiting the Mt Ernest region.

Access from New South Wales: It is possible to access the border route between Mt Ballow and Mt Clunie via the Lindesay Creek road which lies north of Woodenbong (do not confuse this with Lindesay View). Driving from Queensland, the turn-off lies on the right a few hundred metres beyond the centre of Woodenbong. Turn left after 4.7km and follow the road for 1.4km to a locked gate (622 643). From here it is approximately a 5km walk to the border, the road being managed by the NSW Rabbit Board.

THE BORDER ROUTE

The most popular bushwalking areas in the Central Scenic Rim are around Mts Barney, Ballow and Maroon, which are described later in this chapter. The actual Scenic Rim route, which in this region extends along the border from the Boonah border gate to Collins Gap, lacks the spectacular views and features of these nearby mountains. There are also several detractions along the route. These include the rabbit fence, which destroys the pristinity along much of this part of the border, and a section of severe logging regrowth south of Nothofagus Mountain.

However, there are still many features to attract walkers. The summit of Mt Clunie provides views and is well worth visiting. The route also forms a significant portion of the Scenic Rim route and there are many sections of attractive forest. In addition, the area between White Swamp and Collins Gap represents a vast and seemingly unexplored area on the map, and the fact that only a minority of people visit the area is sufficient to stimulate the exploratory instincts.

The region is described below in two stages. The full trip from White Swamp to Collins Gap would take about three days and be rated about grade 4$_{1/2}$.

MT CLUNIE TO MT BALLOW

Mt Clunie provides interesting views and has attractive eucalypt forest on its western approaches. It can be ascended as a day trip from the Boonah border gate (grade 3$_{1/2}$ to 4), or it can be traversed as part of a longer trip. *(Walk 34)*

Leave your cars about 700m south of the Boonah border gate and simply follow the border fence south. The fence crosses over the summit of Mt Clunie, so there is no navigational difficulty. However, on both sides of Mt Clunie the fence takes an incredibly steep course directly up the slope. There are many steep and slippery sections of border and rabbit fence in south-east Queensland, at localities such as Wilsons Peak, Mt Superbus and Mt Cougal, but none compare with Mt Clunie.

The Border Fence can be followed for many kilometres along the winding ridge east of Mt Clunie, finishing about 4km south of Mt Ballow. If walking in the reverse direction, careful compass work is required when descending from Mt Ballow until the border fence is reached. Possible water points (reliability unknown) are 549 675, 563 671, 574 667 and 575 665.

Other Routes: The route from the Boonah border gate to Mt Ballow is actually a huge horseshoe. Inspection of the map shows that walking between the two points could also be done via two ridges - one running east from the border gate and the other west from Mt Ballow over Minnages Mountain. These could provide the basis of an interesting 2 or 3 day circuit walk which would probably be about grade 4. The route on Minnages Ridge is described on page 187.

MT BALLOW TO COLLINS GAP

This section of the border is largely devoid of fence line and takes about 1$_{1/2}$ days to walk with packs. It is mainly rainforest except for some areas near the east. Considerable navigation competence is required, compass work being necessary on most descents.

For several kilometres between the points 628 700 and 640 687, an old logging road is followed along the border crest. This is badly overgrown in most seasons and slows progress to a tediously irritating rate. Progress is good for most of the remainder of the trip, although careful navigation is required for several kilometres before the fence resumes west of Collins Gap.

There is a known water point at 659 682, although a number of other creeks just off the crest should also provide reliable water (especially those that drain southern slopes, such as at 640 688).

MT BARNEY

Possibly the best known mountain in southern Queensland, Mt Barney can be climbed by over twenty different routes. While most routes are either precipitous or very scrubby, they also provide excellent views. It is for its views that Mt Barney is renowned.

The severe environmental problems caused by overcamping and abuse at East Peak and the Barney saddle have already been mentioned in this chapter. Please be extremely responsible in your camping practices - avoid wood fires on or near the peaks, don't damage the vegetation in any way and don't take axes or machetes into the national park. Be careful not to litter or pollute the water supplies. For further details, see pages 171 and 76.

None of the routes in the Barney region except South Ridge and Gwyala Peak are rated below grade 4, and even South Ridge is rated at grade 3 to 31/2. Many of the ridges on the northern aspect of East Peak are particularly precipitous and difficult.

Unless otherwise noted in the following pages, assume that all routes discussed take at least one long day to complete, in addition to the time taken to walk to and from the base of the route.

SOUTH RIDGE (grade 3 to 31/2)

South Ridge is the easiest route on Mt Barney and leads to the Barney Saddle, located between East and West Peaks. The ridge has a good track along its entire length. However, despite it being nicknamed Peasants Ridge and being regarded as the "tourist route" to the summit, it requires reasonably good fitness. If you are not an experienced bushwalker, you should exercise or play sport regularly in order to consider yourself adequately fit to climb Mt Barney. Even by the "tourist route", there is simply no easy way to climb a 1300m high mountain. Parts of the ridge are very steep and it may seem never-ending if you are not used to bushwalking. There are many stories of experienced walkers, descending South Ridge late in the afternoon, meeting evidently unfit and tired walkers about a third of the way up asking, "How much further to the top? Can't be far now, ah?" Remember to always carry emergency items even on day trips e.g. torch, map, compass, watch, parka, pullover, first aid kit, water bottle and a little extra food.

The ridge also has several climbing difficulties. While these are not hard by bushwalking standards, many of the novices who travel the route find them very tough. Furthermore, the top of the slab section (the most awkward pitch) lies above a small cliff, the danger of which is easily overlooked. Loose earth and twigs make the path slippery above this cliff. There have been a number of serious accidents on the ridge, and sadly these have included a fatality.

To reach South Ridge, follow the road from the Yellowpinch camping reserve, crossing the ridge and descending to a floodway on the Logan River (728 698). Continue on the road for about 2km beyond the floodway, to a point where the road divides (715 697). Here a large national park sign blocks the road climbing the hill straight ahead, while the main road swings left down through a gate (this left hand road soon leads to a creek crossing). Take the right hand fork up the hill. This actually starts ascending Mezzanine Ridge, but the track later contours left and crosses a creek onto South Ridge. The track is heavily trodden virtually all the way to the Barney saddle, although there are some false offshoot tracks at the very top. The

PERSPECTIVES FOR THOUGHT

Between the late 1940s and the late 1960s, Mt Barney's abundance of ridges and creeks prompted feverish bushwalking exploration and discovery of numerous different routes to the summit. Early bushwalkers were particularly enthusiastic about the mountain's precipitous northern aspect, where there are routes as hard as any in Australia. South Ridge was one of the last routes to become known, mainly because it doesn't extend all the way to the valley. In comparison to the northern routes, those early walkers considered that the new route was so straightforward that they nicknamed it Peasants Ridge. This is how the ridge obtained its "easy" reputation. Unfortunately, this is misleading for novice bushwalkers today, many of whom have quite different perceptions of the word "easy" and would marvel at the toughness of those early walkers.

Sadly, the discovery of South Ridge has also had a dramatic detrimental effect on the mountain; allowing large numbers of inexperienced bushwalkers to travel into the heart of a rugged wild area. The situation has continued to worsen over the years, with an increasing proportion of visitors having little idea of environmental and safety practices. Vegetation continues to be destroyed to provide shelters, bedding and firewood, due to the failure of visitors to carry stoves, tents, warm clothing and quality sleeping gear.

During the 1960s, Mt Barney was regarded as the "Mecca" of bushwalking in south Queensland, being given a level of respect which could be considered the bushwalking equivalent of strong religious zeal. Often it was also a meeting place for bushwalkers of different origins, and the ultimate bush-walking communion was sharing thoughts when camped in the saddle at the end of a hard day's walk.

Nowadays the saddle/summit area caters for more backpack campers than ever, but experienced bushwalkers are rarely found among them. In recent years experienced walkers have all but surrendered the saddle/summit area as a genuine overnight bushwalking location, and many - especially those who remember the mountain in its pristine condition - regret that South Ridge was ever discovered.

ridge is reasonably well shaded but dry, so water should be carried.

Most people on day trips take between 2 and 3 hours to climb to the Barney Saddle from the start of South Ridge, but this depends greatly on fitness. There have been instances of people taking one hour and others taking eight hours. In addition the walk from Yellowpinch to the start of South Ridge takes about an hour.

On descent from the Barney Saddle, the track to South Ridge can be found to the south-east of the Rum Jungle campsite. It initially climbs over a knoll (697 713) before taking its descent course. Care is needed in the first few hundred metres to avoid taking a couple of false offshoot tracks.

THE SADDLE-SUMMIT REGION

There are two campsites in the Saddle region. The first is at Rum Jungle, located in the Saddle proper. The second lies at the old hut site 150m down to the north. Both are in a badly degraded condition. Water is available in most seasons from the small creek near the old hut site, although it is advisable to obtain water supplies from well upstream.

Permits must be obtained from the QNPWS in order to camp either on the summit or in the saddle of Mt Barney. Please do not litter or damage the vegetation and please use fuel stoves instead of wood campfires (see pages 171 and 176 regarding camping practices here).

To reach East Peak from the saddle, pick up the track leading up from the old hut site. You still have 250m in elevation to climb and the route involves some scrambling, but there is no major technical difficulty. This final climb takes between 30 minutes and an hour. There are some small degraded campsites just to the east side of the summit.

The route to East Peak is fairly distinct despite the multitude of scrubby tracks. In descent, keep to the left hand tracks when you get close to the old hut site.

West Peak is slightly higher than East Peak but the views are not so sweeping. It is ascended from Rum Jungle, starting at the mossy slabs just to the west. The route is less distinct than that up East Peak and also involves some climbing difficulties. Depending on the exact route taken, some of these difficulties may be moderately hard. There are no campsites on the summit.

LOWER PORTALS AND MT BARNEY CREEK

Lower Portals is one of the most popular areas at Mt Barney. Following the road directions given previously, this gorge on Mt Barney Creek can be reached in an hour's walk from the car park via a good track. Along the western section, the track is located just inside the national park boundary (refer topographic map).

When returning from the Portals to the car park, care is needed not to miss the point where the track crosses the creek. Walking downstream on the left bank, look for a slab after about 400 metres. This marks the creek crossing, which lies just inside the national park boundary. Lands downstream of the boundary are private property and are strictly out-of-bounds (see page 173).

To travel further upstream, it is necessary to bypass the Portals by a track across the ridge to the north, crossing the small saddle at 700 744. To locate the track from the campsite, walk westwards for a hundred metres or so before ascending. In descent the track can be found in the gully on the left of the bend at 700 743. It is also possible to swim through the Lower Portals, although the entry and exit at the top end is difficult.

(Walk 58) Mt Barney Waterfall, which lies on a tributary of Mt Barney Creek at 697 735, is a popular destination of day trippers venturing above the Portals. A popular overnight trip is the rockhop between Lower and Upper Portals, Mt Barney Creek being noted for its wide easy slabs. The trip is relatively easy in drier seasons and normally takes about a day (one way), although several sections higher up may be difficult in winter and after rain. Another route between the Lower and Upper Portals is the ridge system north of Mt Barney Creek, leading between the Lower Portals bypass track and the knoll at 675 743. It also gives access to various parts of Barney Creek. Information on routes near the Upper Portals is given on pages 184 to 186.

THE SOUTHERN AND WESTERN ROUTES

Normally most routes on the western side of Mt Barney are very scrubby, but in 1989 severe bushfires cleared out undergrowth from large areas. At the time of writing it is uncertain what further changes will result. In places where the canopy trees have survived, easier walking conditions can be expected for some years. However, in places where canopy trees have been killed, regrowth is likely to grow quickly and be thick and weedy, hindering walking considerably. The exact extent of the fires is also unclear, so parts of the original thick scrub may still be encountered.

Moving in a clockwise direction around the mountain from South Ridge, the recognised routes are described below:

Egan Creek (grade 4; descent about 3 to 4 hours): Also called Eden Creek, this is mainly used as a descent route since it is navigationally easier in this direction. Simply walk south from the Barney Saddle at Rum Jungle and begin the descent. The creek is set among open rainforest and is very pretty. There is some steep country and at least one large waterfall to negotiate, so it requires reasonable fitness and considerable scrambling agility. Allow yourself about double the time that you would take to descend South Ridge. At the bottom, you cross an overgrown road just before Cronans Creek. Follow this to the left (down the Cronans Creek valley) until it joins up with the road at the start of the South Ridge track. N.B. Due to several diverging tributaries, ascent of Egan Creek is not recommended unless you know the route.

Savages Ridge (grade 5 to 6; full day): Normally very scrubby, this is one of the major areas affected by the 1989 fires (see previous comments). It can be used for either ascent or descent. In the former case start just west of Egan Creek at about 706 694 and travel up to Savages Point, the knoll located at 688 712. In descent keep to the east of the ridge when travelling down from Savages Point. Savages Point gives a rather unusual view of the twin peaks of Barney.

There are several variations for negotiating west peak. If ascending from Savages Point, keep close to the ridge initially and aim towards the chimney gullies which break the peak's western cliffs. These provide the shortest route to the summit, although in wet weather they may be very difficult to climb (there are possibly a couple of gullies in this vicinity, some harder than others). If this route doesn't prove feasible, simply contour north around the base of the cliffs to the West Peak/ Barrabool saddle.

A 30m abseil or belay rope is recommended to negotiate the gullies in descent, especially in wet conditions. From the summit, strike straight through the scrub towards Savages Point until you find one of the gullies, where you will probably need to abseil about 10m under awkward scrubby conditions (but note the previous comments about the possible existence of several routes of varying difficulty). Less experienced parties are advised to descend via the West Peak-Barrabool Saddle and then to contour back through the scrub below the cliff line.

Savages Ridge forms part of the Barney Traverse, a grade 6 route traversing both the *(Walk* East and West Peaks of Barney which ascends via Logans or South-East Ridges and *89)* descends via Savages. This weekend or extremely long day trip gives an excellent and compact appreciation of Mt Barney.

The Barney Spur (grade 5 to 6; throughwalk) is the name given to the long ridge running from West Peak via Savages Point and Burrajum Peak, out to the border at

673 680. In terms of sheer effort and thickness of vegetation, this is normally one of the most difficult ridges on Barney, although the extremely thick heath scrub around Burrajum Peak is now likely to have been cleared out by the 1989 fires. Good navigation skills are required to follow the vague ridge crests after the route enters rainforest south-west of Burrajum Peak. Water can often be found at a gully just off the route at 674 697.

Apparently it is also possible to ascend Burrajum Peak directly from Cronans Creek, but no information is available about the nature of this route.

Note the comments regarding the ascent and descent of West Peak given in the description of Savages Ridge if using the Barney Spur.

Gwyala Peak makes an interesting return day trip from Upper Portals (grade 3 to 31/2; perhaps 4 to 5 hours return from the campsite), or it can be used to access the Barney Spur (see comments and grading above). From Upper Portals, simply ascend the ridge which lies directly south of the campsite. The ascent route is straightforward although some navigational care may be needed on descent. The peak is rainforest covered, but near the summit on the north-west side there is a large rock slab which gives good views towards Mt Ballow, while just east of the summit there are places where you may be able to obtain limited views through trees towards Mt Barney. A much underrated peak.

(Walk 99) **Long and Short Barrabool Ridges** (grade 5; throughwalk): To access the Barrabool Ridges, start by rockhopping up Barrabool Creek. Short Barrabool Ridge (the quicker route) starts at the first creek junction (679 730), while Long Barrabool Ridge starts at the second junction (677 726). This is another area which is normally very scrubby but was burnt out by the 1989 fires. Barrabool Peak has space for camping and offers unusual views of Mt Barney. The ridges are better suited to ascent but can be used for descent with careful navigation. There are several scrambling difficulties.

(Walk 99) **Midget Ridge** (grade 41/2; throughwalk) starts at the large bend on Barney Creek at 686 739 and can be used for ascent or descent. This is another area which is normally very scrubby but was burnt out by the 1989 fires. Keep west of any cliffs and you should not encounter any climbing difficulties. There are no campsites on the ridge except for a couple of small sites in the Midget Peak/West Peak saddle. View spots are rare but Midget Peak (also called Bippoh Peak) offers unusual perspectives of Mt Barney and its northern ridges, especially Leaning Peak. N.B. Before discovery of South Ridge, Midget Ridge was apparently the "easy" ascent route for Mt Barney.

THE NORTHERN AND EASTERN ROUTES

The northern and eastern routes are typified by cliffs and rocky terrain, although there are also many areas of thick scrub. Some routes are extremely precipitous.

Barney Gorge (grade 4 to 51/2; 2 to 5 hours one way, plus the walk on Barney Creek): The gorge is a very popular route, especially in spring and early summer when the dry rocks provide easier travelling. There is a lot of rockhopping, and some scrambling around cliffs and waterfalls, so the exact difficulty will depend on the season and wetness of the rocks. When rockhopping along Mt Barney Creek, the start of the gorge is easy to miss, but can be located by the large camping site on the opposite bank. In ascent it leads directly to the old hut site, while in descent the gorge creek is easily found by descending straight down to the north from the saddle. Two waterfalls require care, the lower one normally being passed by a long detour on the

west, and the upper one by a scrubby route on the east. In dry conditions it may be possible to bypass these waterfalls by shorter routes.

Long and Short Leaning Ridges (grade 7; full day): Both these ridges are extremely airy, requiring careful scrambling and climbing near precipitous drops. They join near Leaning Peak. Short Leaning Ridge starts at 696 735. It is best accessed by firstly rockhopping to the top of Barney waterfall at 697 735, bypassing the falls themselves on the eastern side. Long Leaning Ridge starts near the junction of Mt Barney and Barney Gorge Creeks at 690 738.

A belay rope is strongly recommended on these ridges. In any event a 50m abseil rope is required to descend off Leaning Peak towards North Peak.

Moonlight Slabs (grade 6; this grading is based on the northern part of Eagles Ridge): This is the name given to the route which follows Barney Waterfall Creek (697 735) up to the Isolated Peak-North Peak saddle (703 727). However, since the first bushwalking party ascended and named the route, the location (and existence) of the moonlight slabs themselves has become something of a mystery. Apparently the lower part of the route is not too difficult, the waterfall itself being bypassed on the eastern side. To ascend further from the saddle, follow the Eagles Ridge route (see below). Note that the most exposed section of Eagles Ridge lies between the saddle and North Peak, which is the reason for this route's high grading.

Eagles Ridge (grade 6 to 6½; at least one full day): By many regarded as the premier ridge on Mt Barney, Eagles Ridge is a long arduous route with many ups and downs and just as many outstanding view spots. It ascends and descends quite a few of the "minor" peaks of Barney, including Toms Tum (704 734), Isolated Peak (also called North-East Rock) and North Peak. All offer excellent views, the changing nature of the views being the major attraction of the ridge. However, it is a very long route. *(Walk 90)*

181

A 50m abseil and belay rope is strongly recommended. The ascent of North Peak is via some exposed slabs and anyone not competent and experienced at scrambling in exposed situations will require a belay rope at this point. In addition many parties abseil from several of the minor peaks. Although there are scrambles to bypass all the abseils, the alternative routes are sometimes difficult to locate.

Start just before the Lower Portals track meets Barney Creek (703 747). Any of the ridges running south along this section will lead onto the ridge. The first high point is an unnamed knoll, from which Toms Tum is easily climbed. The abseil off Toms Tum can be avoided by descending east along a rocky spur which leads off just back from the summit. Descend a short distance down this spur, then look for a route to the right which leads into a ferny gully back towards the main ridge.

Vague tracks usually lead through the ferns, initially ascending towards the ridge crest, but then leaving the crest again to bypass a large rock pinnacle on the eastern side. After the pinnacle, ascent back to the main ridge is done via a tight scrubby gully. Isolated Peak is climbed after this point. Fit parties would take between 3 and 5 hours to reach Isolated Peak from the Lower Portals car park, depending whether overnight gear is carried.

There are several route options to descend from Isolated Peak to the saddle. The easiest route has little technical difficulty except for a short section of down climbing, although an abseil rope may be necessary if this route cannot be found.

There are probably also a number of route options for ascending from the saddle to North Peak. On the normal route, the ridge is followed up from the saddle, around to the left of some short rock obstacles, then up three pitches of slabby rock. The climbing becomes more exposed and slightly harder as you ascend, although it is not of extreme difficulty. It may also be possible to avoid any climbing and exposure by undertaking a long traverse to a sloping scrubby ledge on the left, although the viability of this route is unknown.

After the top of the climbing pitches, the summit of North Peak is easily attained. To travel from North Peak to East Peak, you will initially have to divert around a short chasm close to the summit of North Peak. After this it is best to keep as close to the main ridge line as possible in order to avoid thick scrub lower down the slope.

North-East Ridge (grade 6; full day): The start of this ridge is found by walking along the Lower Portals track for about ten minutes to the crossing of Rocky Creek (726 747), then following Rocky Creek upstream for about ten minutes to a major junction (727 745). The ridge starts between the two tributaries and leads up to Isolated (North-East) Peak, from where the Eagles Ridge route is followed. N.B. Rocky Creek can also be followed downstream to the Rocky Creek Portals (about 20 minutes one way), although private land must be crossed.

(Walk 88) **North Ridge** (grade 4 1/2; ascent about 5 hours): An underrated ascent route, the ridge running directly east from North Peak. There are patches of thick scrub, and several rocky sections need to be bypassed low on the south side, but there are also good views in the upper section.

To find the beginning of North Ridge, start by ascending Logans ridge from just north of the gate at 742 720. After about 2km you will reach the national park boundary fence just beyond a knoll (724 719). Continue a further 600m along the ridge, then contour right to cross Rocky Creek at about 715 722. Once Rocky Creek is crossed, you are on North Ridge.

To travel from North Peak to East Peak, you will initially have to divert around a short chasm close to the summit of North Peak. After this it is best to keep as close to the main ridge line as possible, in order to avoid thick scrub lower down the slope.

Rocky Creek (grade 41/2 to 51/2; 3 to 5 hours down): A good descent route in dry weather - simply descend east from the North Peak-East Peak saddle. It is popularly combined with either Logans or North Ridges to make a long day trip for a fit party. There is much scrambling on steep ground and a few difficult sections, but in normal conditions (i.e. when the creek and rocks are virtually dry) these are not severe. However, avoid this route in or after wet weather. *(Walk 88)*

At about 715 722, the right hand bank opens up, and it is possible to travel directly east over the lower parts of Logans Ridge to the Yellowpinch road. This is open going and very easy - follow the reverse of the directions given above for the start of North Ridge. Alternatively, you may choose to follow Rocky Creek down to the Lower Portals track, which crosses the creek about ten minutes from the Lower Portals car park. Rocky Creek can also be followed downstream from the Lower Portals track to the Rocky Creek Portals (about 20 minutes one way), although private land must be crossed.

Logans Ridge (grade 51/2 to 6; 6 hours one way): This is the original 1828 ascent route of Mt Barney by Captain Logan, the first European to climb the summit (his expedition was originally intended to search for Mt Warning). The ridge can be reached by following up any of the spurs west of the road just before the first Yellowpinch ford (739 715). However, the northern spur, which starts just north of the gate at 742 720, is more open and slightly easier. Logans Ridge involves a considerable amount of scrambling but there are only two very exposed sections. The first is unavoidable, and involves scrambling in a short chimney and up a tree. The second section is just before the summit. A direct ascent here can be difficult and dangerous, but it can be avoided by traversing right into a gully. Follow the gully up until cliffs obstruct progress, then traverse back left along the base of the cliffs to regain the ridge. From here an easy scramble up a short chimney gully will take you to the summit. Parts of the upper section of Logans Ridge provide excellent views of Mt Barney's east face. *(Walk 89)*

South-East Ridge (grade 4; 4 to 5 hours one way): A direct route to the summit of East Peak, starting just west of the second Yellowpinch ford at 728 698. From the ford ascend the hill to the west, then descend on the other side to a small saddle. From here on it is uphill all the way. The slopes are invariably steep but there are only a few difficulties, none of which are very severe. The first, about halfway, is a razorback which is easy but requires care. Later there are a number of short scrambles, although none are exposed. Just before the final summit climb, the ridge levels off for a short distance (about 706 712). By carefully descending from this point for a short distance through the scrub to the north, a view can be obtained of Mt Barney's massive east face.

The last major climb of the ridge lies just beyond this level section. One chimney looks difficult and exposed when viewed from a distance, but turns out to be quite straightforward. However, between the chimney and the summit, care is required in one brief section where you scramble upwards for perhaps four or five steps immediately above the east face. Although the section is so easy and quick that few people even notice the drop below, care is required. There is little scrub between you and the cliff edge at this point and any mistake could lead to a fall of some 300m.

South-East Ridge is recommended for ascent only unless you know the route well, since there are many diverging ridges not shown on the maps which confuse the descent. Some lead into thick lantana patches on the lower slopes, another onto a cliff buttress.

Mezzanine Ridge (grade 5 1/2 to 6; 5 hours one way): This ridge is so named because it lies seemingly inferior between the more prominent South and South-East Ridges. However, it is considerably harder than both, with an awkward and exposed razorback about halfway and some hard scrub-pushing and route-finding in the upper sections. Start off on the South Ridge track, but instead of following the old road when it turns left across the slope towards the creek crossing and South Ridge (see description on page 176), stay on the ridge and head straight up. A rope is recommended. Suggested for ascents only.

Other Routes: Apparently it is possible to ascend and descend via the creek between North-East and North Ridges, which is supposedly easier and prettier than Rocky Creek. The creek between South and Mezzanine Ridges is also feasible, but is extremely difficult to enter and exit at its upper end. No doubt numerous other exploratory possibilities exist.

MT BALLOW MASSIF

The Mt Ballow Massif is usually regarded as including Mt Ballow itself (Junction Peak - 621 727), the peaks of the Ballow Range (Double Peak, Durramlee Peak and Mowburra Peak), and the various other peaks nearby - Montserrat Lookout, Focal Peak, Mt Philip, Big Lonely, Minnages Mountain and Nothofagus Mountain. This is the general area described here.

Virtually the entire region is covered in rainforest, although views are obtainable from Montserrat Lookout, Double Peak, Mowburra Peak, Minnages Mountain and from parts of Durramlee Peak. Some of these views are outstanding, with the first three mentioned locations giving particularly good and unusual views of Mt Barney's western aspect. From parts of Minnages Mountain there are also good views of the Main Range and Teviot Gap.

Junction Peak and Nothofagus Peak are covered in antarctic beech (*Nothofagus moorei*). These trees provide much of the enchanting appeal for trips in this region.

UPPER PORTALS, MT BARNEY CREEK AND MT BALLOW CREEK

Upper Portals: From the start of the walking track on the ridge above Graces Hut (see road directions on page 174), the Upper Portals can be reached in about an hour (4km one way; grade 2). The old access route via the hut is now closed, but a walking route has been provided along the ridge to the south-east. The start is clearly signposted. The new track follows a disused vehicle road and the way is well defined. It proceeds along the ridge top for about a kilometre, then at about 664 758 it branches off to the right on another old road which descends steeply to Yamahra Creek just downstream of Graces Hut (662 755). The old route is then followed, crisscrossing Yamahra Creek, to the Upper Portals. There is a campsite at the junction of Yamahra and Mt Barney Creeks although it is sometimes crowded. The Upper Portals lie several hundred metres downstream.

If the water is low, agile people may be able to scramble and swim down through the

Portals gorge, although a rope may need to be left in place at several locations to aid the return journey. In high water the Upper Portals are extremely dangerous. Normally they are bypassed by a track high on the northern bank. This starts a few metres upstream from the gorge and is a clear track despite an indefinite start.

Upper Portals Ridge: In this general area there are four good vantage points to view the surrounding peaks. The first is the start of the walking route, already described. Others are Montserrat Lookout (page 186), Gwyala Peak (page 180) and the ridge north of the Portals.

This latter ridge can be used to make an excellent circuit day walk to the Upper *(Walk* Portals (anticlockwise grade 2½; clockwise grade 3 to 3½). It is especially *46)* recommended as an exit route from the Portals - simply head upwards from the highest point on the track which bypasses the gorge on its north side (see above). Navigation is straightforward in this direction, although the steep ascent passes through a patch of thick heath vegetation. Once the top of the ridge is reached, progress is unimpeded and the ridge crest can be followed first northerly and then north-westerly back to the official access route. There is much attractive open forest and some brilliant close-up panoramas of the Barney/Ballow massif.

The ridge is less suitable as a descent (walk in) route due to navigation difficulties at the southern end. However, several options are available for experienced navigators. By taking the spur running south-south-west from the knoll at 671 736, you will meet the track which bypasses the Upper Portals high on the northern bank. This track can then be followed to either the upstream or downstream end of the Portals. Alternatively, the spur at 674 735 leads further down Mt Barney Creek. However, the ridge further east (680 737) is not recommended since a number of cliffs cause very slow progress.

(Walk 58) There are several other useful routes in this vicinity. The ridge leading north-north-east off the knoll at 675 743 (spot height 762m) can be used as a quick walking route to the Lower Portals, or to give access to various parts of Barney Creek (see page 178). Another fast route to the Lower Portals area is via an old road which descends north off the ridge at 673 750, then follows the valley down to meet Mt Barney Creek about a kilometre downstream of Lower Portals.

Mt Barney and Ballow Creeks: Mt Barney Creek changes dramatically in character upstream from the Upper Portals, the wide easy slabs of the lower reaches giving way to intermittent rocks and becoming more slippery and difficult. Campsites are very rare, although there are good sites at the sharp bend at 661 730.

It is possible to rockhop via Ballow Creek all the way to Cedar Pass north of Focal Peak, and via Barney Creek at least as far as the T-Junction at 654 704. However, unless conditions are dry (e.g. late spring), the going would be rather slow and unrewarding.

MONTSERRAT LOOKOUT, FOCAL PEAK AND MOWBURRA PEAK

Montserrat Lookout provides rewarding and spectacular views of Mt Barney, with Mt Warning visible in the far distance. The lookout is less than an hour from Graces Hut (1 1/2 hours with throughwalk gear). From the point where the official access track descends to meet Yamahra Creek (662 755), simply walk upstream towards the hut for a short distance before ascending to the south just before some stock yards. If walking from Graces Hut, ascend the ridge which starts beyond the stock yards on the other side of the small tributary of Yamahra Creek 70m to the south. The ridge is covered in open eucalypt forest and is easy going.

Mowburra Peak also provides good views of Mt Barney. It can be done as a day trip although takes longer to climb than Montserrat Lookout. Ascend via either of the ridges to the south-west of Graces Hut. If you intend descending from Mowburra Peak to Graces Hut, study the maps carefully since it is easy to take an incorrect ridge (added confusion is caused by the area lying near the junction of four maps).

It would be possible to do both Mowburra Peak and Montserrat Lookout as a very long day trip from Graces Hut (grade 41/2), by walking via Focal Peak and Cedar Pass. If this is done it would probably be easier to climb Mowburra Peak first. Ascend to the shoulder of Durramlee Peak (634 746), then carefully follow a compass bearing down the veering ridge to Cedar Pass. Water is available at a soak just to the west of the Pass. Ascend Focal Peak and follow the ridge to Montserrat Lookout. It is also possible to contour around Focal Peak, but due to thick scrub and rough terrain it is often quicker to walk over the summit.

Montserrat Lookout can also be climbed via its south-eastern ridge which leads up from the Upper Portals campsite. The ascent is straightforward - simply cross to the north-western bank of Mt Barney Creek upstream of the Yamahra Creek junction, then walk uphill. On descent, start 50m south of Montserrat Lookout and maintain a course towards the east summit of Mt Barney.

Another variation is to use Montserrat Lookout and Focal Peak as an ascent route to the Ballow Range. There are small campsites at most of the saddles between Montserrat Lookout and Cedar Pass.

THE BALLOW RANGE

The Ballow Range from Mowburra Peak to Junction Peak is less than five hours walking for a fit party. It is entirely rainforest and has some minor navigational difficulties, but travel is rarely impeded. Good campsites are not plentiful, but with care small sites can be picked out at most of the saddles if necessary. There is a large campsite amid the beech trees on Junction Peak (Mt Ballow) and more sites on its northern shoulder. Small parties have been known to bivouac on the rock shelves of Double Peak. The nearest recognised water point on the range is just to the south-west of Cedar Pass, although it would probably also be possible to obtain water by descending east from some of the saddles between Double Peak and Junction Peak. For environmental reasons, wood fires should not be used in this area.

On the south side of Double Peak, there is a cliff which may require a belay rope. If ascending Double Peak from the south, the cliff break lies just to the right (east) of the ridge. Descent is slightly more awkward but some searching will find the correct path just to the left of the ridge. The cliff is not large but is typically wet and slippery and has a further drop to the east. A 25m belay rope would be adequate.

The Ballow Range is usually done as a 2 or 3 day throughwalk on a circuit from either *(Walk* Graces Hut or Burnett Creek. In the former case ascent can be made via either *78)* Montserrat Lookout or direct to Mowburra Peak, and descent via either Big Lonely or Snake Ridge on the east of Nothofagus Mountain. From Burnett Creek, Minnages Mountain and Mt Philip are common routes. All are described in this section.

BIG LONELY AND NOTHOFAGUS MOUNTAIN

Both of these peaks are heavily forested with few views. Attractions include the beech forest on the summit of Nothofagus Mountain and some marvellous box and New England ash trees on the eastern ridge of Big Lonely.

Big Lonely is reached via a ridge off the northern shoulder of Nothofagus Mountain. This veers in a semicircle and requires careful compass work. After crossing over Big Lonely, descent to the junction of the two Ballow Creeks is made via its eastern ridge.

Alternatively, Nothofagus Mountain can be crossed to its south-eastern shoulder, where a long scrubby ridge leads off to the east to the junction of Mt Barney and Ballow Creeks. This has been nicknamed Snake Ridge because of the many subtle direction changes along its length, and it requires even more accurate compass work than the Big Lonely route. There are some cliffs near 638 707 but these are readily bypassed.

If doing either of these routes on a 2½ day trip, you could camp for one night on the Ballow Range and another night at the campsite on Mt Barney Creek at 661 730 (page 186). This would be about a grade 4½ throughwalk.

MINNAGES MOUNTAIN AND THE WESTERN RIDGES

Minnages Ridge and Mt Philip are the two major western approach routes to Mt Ballow, although several other routes may also be possible. All ridges take considerably longer than the ascent routes from Graces Hut since the starting elevation at Burnett Creek is almost 350m lower.

Minnages Mountain can be approached via either its northern or western ridges, and *(Walk* in fact the two routes provide an excellent circuit day walk (grade 3½). The views *48)* from the summit are somewhat limited, but the north ridge has a number of good vantage points with unusual views of the Main Range. Minnages Ridge can be followed further east to Junction Peak.

Mt Philip can be climbed from the ridge which leads up from the west and meets the crest just down from and south-east of the summit. This route leads straight to Durramlee Peak and has no major difficulties.

Other Routes: The saddle west of Yamahra Creek is easily approached via its western ridges. It may also be possible for experienced parties to ascend via two ridges which run north-west off Double Peak and its southern shoulder, although no information on the routes is available. One has a cliff line evident on visual inspection from the valley and the starting points of all ridges would be awkward to find among the gullies and farmland below.

MT ERNEST REGION

East and south-east of Mt Barney are a number of peaks and outcrops which provide good bushwalking opportunities not appreciated by many walkers. These include Mt Ernest, Campbells Folly and Mt Gillies.

MT ERNEST

This peak is normally climbed from the east. The ascent is a fairly straightforward ridge walk (grade 3 to 3 1/2), although there is a good deal of loose rock. Permission must be obtained from the landholders east of the peak. The turn-off to their property is on the Mt Lindesay Highway 21km south of Rathdowney and is marked by a very distinctive letter box. Enquire with the QNPWS ranger at Boonah regarding the landholder's name and phone number rather than turn up at the doorstep unannounced.

Ascent Routes: The eastern ridge (730 681) is the main ascent route. Other feasible routes include the two ridges directly west of the homestead (728 678 or 728 674) and the south-eastern ridge (724 670), although if using the latter you need to take great care that you don't end up on the precipitous south ridge (720 666) by mistake. It would probably also be possible to climb the north-east ridge, which leads down to the Logan River just upstream from the Cronans Creek junction. On all these ridges it is necessary to take careful note of the return route, since there are several ridge divisions which may cause navigational confusion on descent, and many of the gullies in this area are blocked by large cliffs.

Mt Ernest Traverse: This follows the crest of the ridge out to the border at 679 673, and is possibly the most spectacular trip in this area (grade 4 1/2). With an early start, it can be done as a long day walk by fast fit experienced parties with good scrambling and navigation skills. An idea of the traverse can be obtained when Mount Ernest is viewed from the south ridge of Mount Barney. From this angle, Mount Ernest presents a spectacularly jagged skyline, with a series of sloping organ-pipe cliffs directly facing you. The traverse route proceeds along the very crest of these organ pipes, with spectacular sweeping views. There is a good deal of loose rock and scrambling although there are only a few exposed sections. You need to reach the summit for an early lunch to have time to complete the traverse in a day.

To descend from the summit to the traverse route, walk back a few metres, then head downwards directly towards the top of the organ pipes. This appears very steep but there are no cliffs. From here until the end of the organ pipes, stay on or near the crest of the ridge. This takes several hours. Provided you stay on the correct route, the scrambling should only be of moderate difficulty, although care is required in a number of razorback sections. People afraid of heights may prefer a belay in a few places.

The ridge makes a slight twist to the left (not clear on some maps) at the end of the organ pipes, before resuming its west-south-west direction. Good navigation is required from here until the border fence is met at about 679 671. The last few hundred metres of navigation south from the knoll at 679 674 is particularly confusing. Once the fence is met it is simply followed to Collins Gap.

If you wish to avoid the border fence, a number of creeks and side ridges leading down from near the western end of the organ pipes would provide alternatives for completing the Mt Ernest Traverse e.g. the ridge at 700 668 which leads down to the south, or the ridges and creeks in the vicinity of 695 682 which lead down to Cronans Creek. However, these routes would be exploratory and it would be unwise to include them on a day trip itinerary. Some old bushwalking guide books also mention the old forestry road which starts at 711 654 as a means of accessing Mt Ernest.

There are several possible campsites for small parties on the top of the ridges. There are no regular water pick-ups but water could probably be obtained by descending to the south from saddles in the main ridge.

CAMPBELLS FOLLY

This peak lies east of Mt Ernest at 754 678 and provides excellent views of Mt Lindesay. The eastern face is very sheer, making a spectacular sight from the Mt Lindesay Highway. It is usually climbed from the south-west, from near the quarry at 742 670 (about grade 21/2). Access is via the property already described (see the description of Mt Ernest) and permission should be obtained. It is also possible to ascend and descend the mountain from the north, although this route is considerably harder. Cliffs block most of the western approaches. There is no water in this area.

MT GILLIES AND STONEHENGE

Mt Gillies (765 717) lies amongst the indistinct sprawl of ridges and rocky terrain north of Campbells Folly and east of Yellowpinch. The area has many outcrops of boulders and spires which provide a great deal of interest. Some of these are quite large and spectacular, while others form small but intriguing mazes. Dry eucalypt woodland covers most of the ridges and the heath understory produces excellent spring wildflower displays.

The area can be explored from a variety of directions, being bounded by the Mt Lindesay Highway, the Barney View road and the Yellowpinch road. Most access requires permission to traverse private lands. Two of the best access routes are ridges near Mt Barney Lodge - one ascending from the small dam at 752 720 and the other from 750 715. Another possible route is the ridge east of Yellowpinch, ascending to the knoll marked 422m (745 707), then east to the main crest and north along the crest to the summit. It would also be possible to ascend from Stonehenge (see below). However, care is needed when descending the peak since the gullies have many cliffs and much loose rock. Allow yourself plenty of time for exploration and route finding. Additional navigational confusion may be caused due to the area lying on the junction of two topographic maps (Mt Lindesay and Palen Creek). The region is usually waterless.

Stonehenge (785 724) is a jumble of large boulders about a kilometre south from the Barney View road. Several hours can be spent exploring and scrambling around this feature.

MT MAY AND MT MAROON

Mts May and Maroon are two semi-isolated peaks lying north of Mt Barney, connected to each other and to the Barney-Ballow massif by a loose pattern of low sprawling ridges. This whole region is dry eucalypt woodland and heath, excellent for spring wildflowers, with Mt Maroon in particular presenting a glorious array. There is little or no water in the area, except possibly for the creeks in Paddys Gully and in the valley south of Mt May. For this reason the region is mainly visited on day trips, although various circuit throughwalks can be organised if you camp on Mt Barney Creek.

MT MAY (grade 2 1/2 to 3)

(Walk 69) The main peak of Mt May has excellent and unusual views of Mt Barney.

About 3km beyond the Mt May campsite, the Graces Hut road suddenly turns right onto flat ground after a long steep ascent (670 776). From this point, the peak can be climbed in under an hour by a good track up the obvious south-western ridge (grade 2 1/2). There is little difficulty except for an easy climb up a short rock face.

Traversing between north and south peaks is slightly more difficult due to some scree and rock ledges, but presents no major problems.

The other main ascent route used for Mt May is via the ridge which starts adjacent to the Mt May campsite (674 798). The heavily eroded track which ascends this northern ridge is easy to follow in ascent, although there are occasional sections of loose rock and scrambling. The track can be quickly found by ascending the obvious steep slope immediately east of the Mt May campsite. Allow 2 to 3 hours for the ascent (grade 2 1/2 to 3). If used for descent, care is needed when navigating in the vicinity of 677 789, since the turn-off down the ridge from the main crest is not always obvious. Descending parties may also experience occasional difficulties navigating around small cliffs and scree slopes.

Many parties use both routes described above for an excellent circuit day walk from the Mt May campsite. It is best done in a clockwise direction, ascending via the northern ridge, then descending via the south-west ridge and back along the road to the campsite.

Another northern ridge that starts just downstream from the Mt May campsite can also be used to ascend the peak. This ridge runs on a similar course to the ridge already described, but it receives less usage and has no track. It is not quite as steep as the former ridge and gives a better overall appreciation of the region, although several sections would require careful navigation if the ridge was used for descent. Walkers are encouraged to ascend by this route to ease the erosion on the former ridge. At the bottom, the start of the ridge can be found by crossing the gully just north-east of the camping area before ascending (676 800).

MT MAROON

Another excellent day trip, with superb wildflower displays on the summit plateau and unparalleled close-up views of the central Scenic Rim and Mt Barney's craggy profile. The usual ascent route takes about 3/4 day for the return trip (grade 3). Follow the road directions previously given for Cotswold and leave cars near the old dam at the end of the road, or in the clearing just beforehand.

The main ascent route starts on the high open hill just to the south-west of the dam. It initially ascends the mountain's steep north-east ridge (743 805) before veering right into the major gully. Nowadays a heavily worn track leads up the ridge, then veers off across the ridge's western side to the gully. However, if you miss this track, simply ascend the ridge until cliffs appear to block the route. With the cliffs in sight but at a point some distance below them, traverse right into the gully. Care will be required if you don't know the route, for there are several places to traverse. One is reasonably easy, but the others are more difficult and could be dangerous to inexperienced walkers.

The gully has a great deal of scree and great care must be taken not to dislodge rocks. The danger is greatest in the lower section. At the top of the gully there is a small waterless camping area next to a small dry creek - this is the start of the summit plateau. Cross the camping area and dry creek and wind your way up to the summit through the slabs and wildflowers. The vista of Mount Barney unfolds on the final crest.

It is possible to climb around to the left of the cliffs at the top of the north-east ridge, although care is required. If you camp on Mt Maroon, please avoid the use of wood fires.

Mt Maroon can also be readily ascended from the west, climbing either the ridge just north-east of Paddys Plain (710 783) or the main watershed ridge from Mt May. The latter is difficult to trace on the map but passes over the knolls marked 445m (707 804) and 512m (713 800), before joining the ridge from Paddys Plain higher up the slope. It is also possible to ascend from the south, by a long scrubby ridge starting from the road at 734 772. This latter route crosses private property.

A gorge starting on the summit plateau of Mt Maroon provides an excellent descent route to Paddys Plain, although the route may be difficult to recognise without prior experience. There are at least two gorges close together on the west of the summit plateau. The correct route is the more northerly gorge - marks of previous usage and possibly a vague track should soon become evident. The gorge provides the opportunity for an energetic circuit day trip, climbing the peak via the north-east ridge then descending to Paddys Plain. It is then possible to return to the cars by the mountain's north-west "shelf", which extends broadly between the knolls at 713 800 (512m) and 724 806. This shelf, visible from the Boonah road, is fairly flat walking for the most part, although some of the sides are very steep. Care is required at the north-eastern end (726 806) where you will need to search around for the best place to negotiate a steep descent into a small creek. Cross to the creek's eastern bank to descend to the paddocks below.

While reasonably easy to descend, Mt Maroon's western gorge is not recommended for ascent without prior experience of the route, since it has at least one obscure division which confuses the way.

OTHER TRIPS AND FEATURES

Paddys Peak is the unofficial name given to a small peak at 700 773, just south-west of Paddys Plain. Seemingly unremarkable, this sprawl of spurs and ridges gives some excellent views of the north aspect of Mt Barney. The best view spots may be hard to find but lie on its south-eastern ridge around 704 768. Keep to the south of this ridge as you traverse it and the views should appear through gaps in the trees.

There is also a small waterfall downstream from Paddys Plain which is worth a visit, but note that access to all private lands in this area is restricted.

(Walk 72) Several circuit throughwalks are possible in the May/Maroon region, traversing various mountains and ridges and camping on Mt Barney Creek. For example, if leaving cars on the Graces Hut road, the trip over Mt May and Paddys Peak, then returning via Mt Barney Creek, can be done comfortably in a weekend (grade 3 1/2).

The watershed ridge between Mts May and Maroon also provides an interesting route. It can be followed in its entirety, although it is difficult to trace on the map and careful navigation is required in several places to identify the exact route. It makes an obscure divergence from a more prominent ridge system at 688 787, then passes over the knolls marked 445m (707 804) and 512m (713 800).

NEARBY PEAKS

KNAPPS PEAK (grade 2 1/2 to 3; 3/4 day)

(Walk 64) Although this peak is separated from Mt Maroon by 9km of cleared grazing lands, it is probably better associated with the Barney area than with any other region. Located to the north of Maroon and approximately midway between the Main Range and Lamington, it provides sweeping panoramas of the three main arms of the Scenic Rim crescent - Lamington National Park (eastern Scenic Rim), the Barney/Ballow region (central Scenic Rim) and the Main Range (western Scenic Rim). The peak is especially recommended in late autumn and early winter, when the atmosphere is often very clear. At this time of year, it is frequently possible to pick out the glistening white waters of Lamington's Morans Falls far away in the east, as well as the sharp western ridges of Castle Crag, Lost World and Mount Widgee. To the south, the massive rock buttresses of Mt Maroon loom quite close, neatly framed on either side by Mts Lindesay and Barney. In the west lie the peaks and ridges of the Main Range from Wilsons Peak to Cunninghams Gap. Brush-tailed rock wallabies and wildflowers, including the small cerise blooms of *Bossiaea rupicola*, are other attractions of the area.

Knapps Peak is not in national park. For this peak particularly, bushwalkers should make great efforts to respect the rights and privacy of local landowners and to maintain good relations with them. The usual access is via a property named *Green Hills*, but enquire with the QNPWS ranger at Boonah regarding the landholder's name and phone number rather than turn up at the doorstep unannounced. *Green Hills* is reached by turning off the Boonah-Rathdowney road about a kilometre east of Maroon township, onto a side road signposted "Cannon Creek". After about 4km, the turn-off to the property is found on the right, marked by a large wooden letter box. Follow this road for another kilometre to the farm house. Please treat the property with the greatest respect. Don't use campfires and be very careful not to drop litter.

The peak is shown in the corner of the Maroon 1:25 000 topographic map (752 884), while the farm house at *Green Hills* is marked just west of the peak (733 883).

Possibly the best ascent route is the southern ridge, reached by walking down Knapp Creek. After several kilometres of easy walking on cattle tracks, you will reach a gate on the southern bank (751 869; on the topographic map, caves are marked at this point, but these are actually about 700 metres further downstream). Start the ascent at any convenient location across the creek from the gate. There are a few steep sections and some loose rock, but the climb is only of moderate difficulty. The peak has a large cliff immediately east of the summit.

Another approach route to the mountain is via the north-west ridge, extending from a small peak called Ben Lomond which has a number of interesting features. However, at the time of writing access to Ben Lomond is totally restricted by landowners.

MT TOOWOONAN (3/4 day, grade 2 to 21/2)

This mountain is located just west of Maroon Dam, overlooking the lake shores. However, while it is a notable peak of the district, it is entirely on private property and obtaining the landholder's consent to traverse the land is currently extremely difficult if not impossible. It is included here simply as a matter of record in case access conditions ease in the future. While not as inspiring as many mountains in the region, it gives views of the Main Range and parts of its southern and eastern flanks should provide interesting perspectives on the Barney/Ballow area.

The Maroon Dam Outdoor Education Centre may be a good place to start enquiries about how and where to approach the landholder in hope of obtaining permission. Apparently it can be climbed by virtually any of its numerous ridges, although some are obviously much steeper than others. Reportedly there is also a considerable loose rock danger in some places and the steeper ridges should be avoided by large groups for this reason. The relevant map is the Teviot 1:25 000 sheet.

DIRECTORY

QUEENSLAND NATIONAL PARKS AND WILDLIFE SERVICE
Boonah: P.O. Box 121, Boonah. Q. 4310. Telephone: (074) 63 5041.

PRIVATE CAMPING AREAS
Bigriggen Park: MS 768, Rathdowney. Q. 4287. Telephone: (074) 63 6190.
                     See road directions and advertisement on page 173.
Mt Barney Lodge: MS 768, Rathdowney. Q. 4287. Telephone: (075) 44 3233.
                     See road directions on page 173 and advertisement on page 181.

Note: Since the first printing of this book, wood fires have been completely prohibited in all bush camping areas in Scenic Rim national parks. Machetes and similar brush cutting implements are also banned in national parks.

14

THE MAIN RANGE: CUNNINGHAMS GAP TO WILSONS PEAK

The section of the Great Divide which lies east and north-east of Warwick is referred to as "the Main Range". This is a very rugged bushwalking region, with high steep mountains providing arduous ascents and descents as well as superb views. The region can be divided into two main subregions:

- The southern segment between Cunninghams Gap and Wilsons Peak, which is often regarded as the classic section of the Main Range and is the subject of this chapter.

- The segment north of Cunninghams Gap, which is described in Chapter 15 along with the Mistake Mountains and the Little Liverpool Range.

The terrain between Cunninghams Gap and Wilsons Peak provides some of the best bushwalking in south-east Queensland. While not possessing the vastness of wilderness areas elsewhere in Australia, and being relatively small in national park area even compared with Lamington, it nevertheless has a classic appeal. The crest, being linear in nature, provides an excellent opportunity for traversing from end to end, and the frequent views back over the peaks one has traversed promote feelings of progression and achievement while climbing each mountain. There are numerous peaks over 1000m in this region, and the high sharp nature of the peaks and the steep eastern scarp together provide a great sense of elevation for bushwalkers on the crest. It is to the Main Range that the impression provoked by the book title *One Mountain After Another* * most accurately applies. It was the Main Range which prompted the major part of the Scenic Rim conservation movement in the late 1970s.

* by Arthur Groom; see Appendix 1, "Further Reading"

Left: View north from Spicers Peak, with Mts Mitchell and Castle.

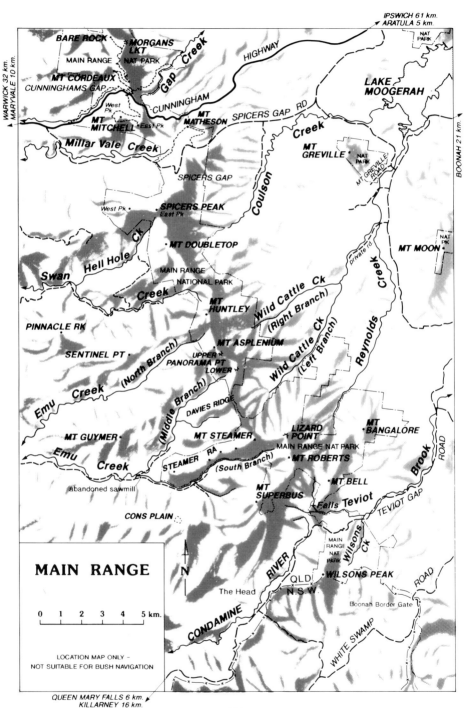

SPECIAL NOTES

BUSHWALKING CONDITIONS AND HAZARDS

General Terrain: The Main Range has distinct topographic and vegetation patterns. The main crest runs north-south with a very steep eastern scarp. To the west are a series of east-west running ridges and valleys, the ridges providing many access routes to the crest. The ridges gradually become drier as they run westwards. Near the crest, there tends to be rainforest on the southern slopes and open eucalypt forest on the northern slopes, and the northern slopes usually have some cliffs. There is apparently an ecological relationship here - the northern slopes, being sunnier and drier, have a more open vegetation, and in turn have been eroded more readily by rain and are now steeper. This does not mean, however, that the only cliffs you will find will be on northern slopes.

Official Tracks: Most of the region is undeveloped, although there are several excellent graded track walks at Cunninghams Gap, while Spicers Gap has a half day track circuit and a number of shorter strolls. There is also an interesting track circuit in the national park at Queen Mary Falls, which lies near the Main Range to the south-west.

Off-Track Terrain: The region is primarily regarded as a throughwalking area, although some undeveloped localities offer enjoyable base camps and day walks.

Good hill-climbing fitness is absolutely essential if venturing off the graded tracks. The terrain is very mountainous and rugged, and off-track walking usually involves repetitive steep ascents and descents. Associated difficulties include frequent scrambles, slippery grass on the northern slopes and heavy packs due to the infrequency of water points.

Cliffs: Many areas are precipitous and most routes have some form of cliff to negotiate. While sometimes these are only small, or are easily bypassed if you know the route, a number are potentially dangerous. The Main Range is not an area for people who fear heights or don't have basic rock scrambling capabilities. Despite this, only a few routes are of extreme difficulty, and most of the region can be considered suitable for bushwalkers of moderate experience provided the party members are fit and there is an experienced sensible leader.

Most of the higher cliffs in this region tend to be on the northern slopes. Therefore, if walking north to south, most cliffs are encountered on ascent, and the general rule is to contour right (westwards) to find the relevant cliff break. Some of these cliff breaks are much more difficult to find on descent if walking south to north.

In order to negotiate the various cliff breaks, most parties should carry at least a pack hauling rope. A full length belay rope is recommended on some routes, such as Lizard Ridge and the northern ascent and descent of Mt Huntley.

Heat and Cold: With the exception of areas around Cunninghams Gap and possibly Teviot Gap, the region is not recommended in hot weather. Due to the steep slopes and extensive areas of open forest, most localities are likely to be far hotter than average in hot conditions. Very few creeks are deep enough for swimming.

Winter is the recommended walking season, although the area is often extremely cold at night. The valleys around the Main Range tend to be enclosed basins which act as "cold sinks", trapping the colder heavier air and becoming extremely frosty on still winter nights. In windless conditions the peaks are often warmer than the valleys, although they can be extremely cold in windy conditions. Very occasionally, snow falls on the high peaks.

Water: Large water bottles (from 2 to 4 litres per person) are always essential if camping on the crests. Sometimes you must drop down the western gullies considerable distances to obtain water from the creeks, and typically there is only one water point each day. A cup should be carried when collecting water as the pools are often very shallow. However, unless the summer and autumn have been particularly dry, water can usually be obtained by these methods during the whole of the main walking season (April to August) regardless of any lack of rain in winter. Some water points dry up quickly in spring

Vegetation and Navigation: The vegetation is reasonably trafficable on most of the range. There is no lawyer vine, and only a few main bushwalking routes pass through bad scrub. Where there is scrub it is almost always because of previous logging activities, the worst areas being the Emu Creek valley and the Teviot Brook region.

There is a good deal of open vegetation on the crests and northern slopes between Lizard Point and Mt Mitchell, and most of the ridges are clear and distinct. These characteristics ease the navigational difficulties, although reasonable navigation skills are still required.

Camping Hazards: The majority of camping areas on the Main Range are in tall eucalypt forest and there are often dead limbs overhead. Always choose your tent site carefully to minimise the danger of falling branches.

FACILITIES AND CAMPING

Base Camping: There are two national park camping grounds, one at Cunninghams Gap and the other at Spicers Gap. The former is beside a busy highway and is not highly recommended for weekend camping, but is suitable for overnight stops while travelling. The only other official camping ground in the vicinity is a private camping park at Queen Mary Falls, which is situated about 20km west of Teviot Gap and about 10km east of Killarney. In addition, the state forest lands in the Swan Creek and Emu Creek valleys west of the range can be used for base camping, although road access is very rough and there are no facilities.

Throughwalk Camping: There are numerous throughwalking campsites on the Main Range. Those on or near the high peaks are often quite small, but there are also some extremely spacious areas on the western ridges and in a couple of the saddles. **Wood fires should be avoided in some places, especially Panorama Point, Lizard Point and Mt Doubletop.** As in other areas of the Scenic Rim, the Queensland National Parks and Wildlife Service places number limits on the size of throughwalking parties in this region. These are still being finalised at the time of writing, but it is likely that some sites will be restricted to party sizes of 6 or less.

MAPS

The entire area is covered by excellent 1:25 000 and 1:50 000 topographic maps. The main 1:25 000 sheets are *Cunninghams Gap* and *Mt Superbus*, with the *Wilsons Peak*, *Teviot*, *Mt Clunie* and *Mt Alford* sheets necessary for certain trips on the eastern ridges and in the south. The *Cunninghams Gap* 1:50 000 sheet covers the main region and is also an excellent map, although the adjoining southern and eastern sheets are not of comparable quality.

The Forestry maps are also suitable for much off-track navigation, the relevant sheets being titled *Main Range*, *Emu Vale State Forest* and *Teviot Falls*. Interestingly, they are superior to the standard topographic maps in showing drainage features, cliffs, forestry roads and walking tracks. However, their general relief representation is not as good and, from a bushwalking perspective, their coverage of the region is rather piecemeal i.e. the forestry regions do not conform to patterns of bushwalking usage, so that often major walking routes occur on the extreme edges of the maps.

ROAD ACCESS

There are a large number of back roads in the Main Range region, although most are evident if you combine a good road map with the relevant topographic maps. Here are the main access points:

Cunninghams Gap lies on the main highway between Ipswich and Warwick and can be easily found on any road map.

Spicers Gap (Eastern Route): This road is only accessible in dry weather, being closed by a locked gate in wet conditions. Take the road marked "Lake Moogerah" which turns off the highway 5km south-west of Aratula. Follow this for 6km and turn right at a marked junction. Avoid any further turns. This leads to a QNPWS camping ground near the Pioneer Graves area.

Spicers Gap (Western Route): This four wheel drive road approaches Spicers Gap from the west, but is strictly a dry weather route only. The signposted turn-off is on the south of the main highway, just after a small rise 1km west of the Cunninghams Gap roadhouse. In dry weather this road is trafficable by high clearance two wheel drive vehicles as far as the State Forest boundary.

Swan Creek: Turn left towards Freestone 26km west of Cunninghams Gap, then drive to Yangan. The various road junctions along this section are well marked on most maps and are signposted either "Yangan" or "Killarney Falls". Take the Swanfels road, which is on the left at a junction 2km beyond Yangan. About 16km after Yangan (9km beyond Swanfels), the road crosses a series of small ridges and starts to become rough. This section is often slow to travel and can be very awkward in wet conditions. About 6km further on (approximately 22km from Yangan), it reaches the state forest boundary. There are various camping areas in the upper section of the valley although some are on private property.

Emu Creek: Once again, these access routes are difficult in wet conditions. Proceed through Yangan to Emuvale, then turn left just after the school into the village centre. Proceed through the tiny township, turning right to follow the bitumen at the end of the town (ignore the dirt track straight ahead at this point). Follow this main road as described below:

Odometer	Feature/Directions	Distance Between Features
0	Emuvale	
1.6	Low causeway	1.6
3.2	Bitumen ceases	1.6
4.1	Keep left, ignore right hand road	0.9
6.3 - 8.0	Four creek crossings in 1.7km, possibly deep and rough	2.2 - 1.7

8.6	Gate	0.6
9.7	Ignore road coming in at angle on right	1.1
13.4 - 14.6	Two gates	3.7 - 1.2
16.9	Ignore "Private Road" sign and very old road on left	2.3
17.2	Road intersection	0.3

The left hand fork at this intersection proceeds down to the old sawmill site (407 792), which is often used for camping but is actually on private property. This road then continues up Emu Creek (middle branch) and Reedy Creek, and is in reasonable condition for some kilometres.

The right hand fork proceeds up the south branch of Emu Creek. It is a public road, although it may not be readily trafficable by two wheel drive vehicles due to rough patches and several bad creek crossings. After 3km, another intersection is reached (434 786). The left hand branch here makes two more rough creek crossings before leading to a good campsite in the state forest. The right hand branch is the start of the old forestry road up to Mt Superbus. It is now a walking route only, with vehicular access being blocked a hundred metres or so up from the second junction.

White Swamp (Boonah Border Gate): This route is mainly used when climbing Wilsons Peak from the east. Drive south from Boonah towards Maroon, but take the right hand road marked "Carneys Creek" 16km from Boonah township. Follow this road all the way to the border gate. It can also be used to reach Teviot Gap in wet conditions (see below).

Teviot Gap: Take the "Carneys Creek" turn-off 16km south of Boonah (as described in the directions for White Swamp), then drive 15km and turn right just after a bridge. The Teviot road is rough and steep and is rarely trafficable in wet weather. In wet conditions the worst part of the road can sometimes be bypassed by taking the White Swamp road until 7km south of the Boonah border gate, then turning right and following an old dirt road back to The Head via the Condamine border gate.

Queen Mary Falls: This national park is actually some 20km west of the Main Range, but is sometimes visited by base campers. It lies on the road between Killarney and Teviot Gap, about 10km east of Killarney.

Wild Cattle Creek: On the east of the Main Range, roads follow up both branches of Wild Cattle Creek from a turn-off 2.6km south of the intersection of the Coulson and Croftby-Moogerah roads. The actual turn-off is at 528 910 (there are several turn-offs here but all are shown on the *Mt Alford* 1:25 000 topographic map). **All lands around Wild Cattle Creek and the foothills of Panorama and Lizard Ridges are private property and permission to traverse MUST be obtained beforehand.**

CUNNINGHAMS GAP

Cunninghams Gap is mainly a day trip area, although there is a national park camp ground opposite the roadhouse a few kilometres to the west. There are two major graded track walks, one to Bare Rock near Mt Cordeaux in the north, and one to Mt Mitchell in the south. These tracks present an appeal which is typically "Main Range" in character - a sense of elevation, clean air and mountain grandeur. These qualities are strongly evident despite the close proximity of the highway and its obtrusive heavy vehicle noises, which sometimes carry for a considerable distance. In addition, there are also several other shorter track walks.

Mt Cordeaux and Bare Rock: A graded track zigzags up the slopes of Mt Cordeaux *(Walk* north of Cunninghams Gap, passing through rainforest with some superb brush box *15)* trees. It then contours around to the north of the mountain to Morgans Lookout, before terminating about 20 minutes further on at Bare Rock. The latter is an unusual rocky knoll with interesting views. It makes a good half day walk from Cunninghams Gap (about 12½km return, grade 1½), or a very easy day walk. Because the climb up the slopes of Mt Cordeaux is rainforest, this walk is relatively cool in warm weather.

The graded track does not actually reach the summit of Mt Cordeaux, but skirts around its western flanks. There is little to see from the summit, although if they wish competent scramblers can climb the peak from near the saddle to the north (402 980). A belay rope is recommended, and it is necessary to take care not to dislodge rocks, since the cliffs are located directly above the graded track. For these reasons it should only be attempted by small groups of competent scramblers.

Mt Mitchell: Much of this track passes through eucalypt forest with attractive *(Walk* grasstrees - a typical vegetation type on a northern slope of the Main Range. The track *14)* then circles around to the west and south of the mountain, before ascending to the saddle and finally the east peak. The saddle provides excellent views north towards Mt Castle, especially in the early morning. At the east peak, there is a short but spectacular razorback which provides inspiring views to the south. However, great care should be taken around this razorback, since there is a massive cliff to the east which has previously been responsible for a fatal accident (if you have small children, you would need to take care to control them both near the razorback and at one or two other places up from the saddle). This walk is only about 10km return, but in warm weather it is slightly hotter than the Bare Rock walk (½ day, grade 1½).

An interesting feature of the razorback is the high iron content of the basalt, particularly in the fissures. If you hold a compass close to the ground and slowly move it over the rocks, the needle will rotate wildly.

Other Track Walks at Cunninghams Gap include Gap Creek Falls (9½ km return) and the Box Forest Track. The latter leads between Cunninghams Gap and the national park camp ground to the west, a distance of 4km one way.

SPICERS GAP

Spicers Gap is becoming popular for base camps and day walks due to the development of the national park camp ground just east of the Gap. The walks are best suited to winter conditions, despite the camp ground being extremely cold when the westerlies are blowing. There are several inspiring walking possibilities, although there is only one major track walk and the main off-track walks are quite hard and long. In addition, the Governors Chair Lookout is a popular picnic area close to the road. N.B. The Spicers Gap road is usually closed by a locked gate in wet conditions.

MT MATHIESON TRACK

This is the only official track walk of any length that has been developed at Spicers *(Walk* Gap to the date of writing. It is not actually a graded track, being somewhat steeper *21)* and rougher, but is well marked and provides a relatively easy half day circuit (grade 1 1/2). An old timber jinker on the track provides historical interest.

SPICERS PEAK

Spicers Peak can be visited on either day walks from the camp ground or as part of a throughwalk itinerary. The two main routes are the north-east and north-west ridges. The steep north-east ridge provides the quickest route to the eastern summit, but requires considerable care (3/4 day return; grade 3 1/2 to 4). Alternatively, both ridges can be combined to make an excellent circuit requiring a full day (grade 4). An early start is recommended on the longer walk since a number of difficulties often take longer than expected. The circuit includes about 4km of road walking on the Spicers Gap road.

* **North-East Ridge** (grade 3 1/2 to 4): This route is steep and very loose in places. Although it is not as exposed as it appears from a distance, it is not suitable for people nervous of heights and would require particular care if carrying throughwalk packs. It should not be tackled by inexperienced walkers, since there are several areas where you need to scramble amid loose rocks, and where you could venture into precipitous terrain if you lost the route.

The ridge can be found by simply walking towards the mountain from the Governors Chair lookout in the Gap, taking care to stay on the crest (avoid an old road which leads down to the east just past the Governors Chair). The route quickly steepens and at one point climbs a band of cliffs. These cliffs are not difficult and if you stay on the correct route there should only be a few brief sections which are exposed. However, there are a number of large loose rocks which require great care (these have caused a fatal accident in the past). Near the top of the ridge, the route contours west below the summit cliff line into a rainforest gully. This contouring section also requires care since there is a small cliff below.

Descent on this ridge is not recommended unless you know the route. However, if descent is attempted, the rainforest gully lies only a hundred metres or so west of the eastern lookout. After dropping down a short way, search for a route on the right which contours on a scrubby ledge below the summit cliffs.

Summit to Summit: Allow several hours for the journey between east and west peaks, this often taking much longer than expected. It is largely rainforest but a number of small grassy sections provide good views. Several rocky obstacles present minor difficulties, the main one being negotiated on the northern side. Considerable navigational care is necessary around the west peak, especially if travelling westwards. There are two major ridges and several lesser spurs diverging westwards off the west summit, and the rainforest can cause considerable confusion.

It is possible to descend north from the saddle on Spicers Peak (410 916). Descend to a rainforest gully from the western side of the saddle, then once below the steepest slopes near the bottom of the rainforest, contour back east to the main north ridge.

North-West Ridge (grade 3): For throughwalkers who are nervous of heights, this route provides an alternative to the north-east ridge, although it is much longer due to the time consuming traverse between the two peaks. It provides good winter views out onto the Darling Downs.

In ascent the route is straightforward, with a couple of minor rocky obstacles being easily bypassed on the south. However, it is usually necessary to access the ridge

* see changes on
    page 309.
202

across private lands just west of the state forest boundary (cars are probably best parked just inside the state forest). The ascent is started just west of a small creek (389 939), which crosses the road about 200m west of the gate at the state forest boundary (signposted).

If descending this ridge, you need to navigate carefully when descending through the rainforest in the top section, since several other spurs lead off the west peak. It may be best to err a little to the north. Some care is also required to find the start of the spur at 390 930 when descending off the main ridge to the road, although the spurs which lie further west can be used if necessary.

MT MITCHELL

Mt Mitchell can be visited from Spicers Gap on an adventurous full day circuit, ascending the south-east ridge and descending the south-west ridge (the circuit includes about 4km of road walking on the Spicers Gap road). However, the south-east ridge route is only suitable for experienced walkers. Less experienced walkers are advised to ascend and descend by the relatively easy south-west ridge.

South-East Ridge (grade 4 to 41/2): To ascend this ridge, take the Mt Mathieson track and locate a bend in the path at 426 947, on the main crest just inside the eastern boundary of the rainforest. From here, follow the ridge north-west for a considerable distance, initially passing through old logging regrowth on a very gradual ascent. Later the ridge steepens dramatically, and the vegetation changes to an attractive mixture of rainforest, eucalypt forest and grasstrees.

After a while you will encounter the first band of cliffs. This band, as well as one or two others higher up, can be negotiated by contouring westwards. The scrambles gradually become more difficult. Some care is required on the second last band of cliffs, where you usually climb up at an angle for a few metres on a scrubby crumbly ledge above a short drop. A belay rope may be useful if any party members are not competent scramblers.

The summit cliffs are best negotiated at the eastern razorback. This is a surprisingly easy scramble with no initial exposure, although once on top of the razorback there is an extremely airy traverse for about 50m until the graded track is reached. Great care is needed on this razorback (refer to previous comments on page 201). There are one or two other routes up the final summit cliffs. However, the routes become harder and probably more dangerous as you go westwards, not easier (an unusual feature on the Main Range).

It is also possible to avoid all scrambling and exposure on this route, by contouring for a considerable distance west of the bottom cliff line, then ascending to the graded track just west of the saddle.

The south-east ridge is not recommended for descent unless you have travelled it previously. The route down the summit cliffs at the end of the razorback is relatively easy to locate, but the cliff breaks lower down may be much more difficult to find. In descent, it may be useful to carry an abseil rope as a safeguard against becoming cliff bound.

South-West Ridge (grade 21/2): To descend this ridge, find the sharp turn on the graded track at 398 957. A clear footworn track should be evident leading down the ridge through eucalypt forest. Later this crosses into private land and becomes an old and very steep road. Stay on the ridge crest until it flattens and reaches a small knoll at 388 948, then descend the spur to the south to Millar Vale Creek. Cross the creek and walk across paddocks to the Spicers Gap road.

In ascent, walk north from the gate on the road at the western boundary of the state forest (signposted), then ascend any of the spurs on the north of Millar Vale Creek.

SPICERS PEAK TO TEVIOT GAP

(Walk 97) The mountainous terrain between Spicers Gap and Teviot Gap is the classic section of the Main Range and provides many of south Queensland's most outstanding bushwalks. It is often done in a single traverse with a long car shuttle. Extremely fit parties can complete this traverse in two days, although most people prefer to take three or even four days since this allows camping at the most spectacular campsites. If attempted in two days (a tough walk at grade 51/2), camp should be made at either Huntley saddle or Mt Huntley. On a 31/2 day trip (about grade 41/2), it is possible to camp near Mt Doubletop and at Lower Panorama Point and Lizard Point.

Alternatively, smaller sections of the Range can be done as circuits using the western ridges, or even a couple of eastern ridges. These routes are discussed later.

The terrain has many arduous ascents and it is not suitable for inexperienced bushwalkers. Navigationally the traverse is easier from north to south. The highest cliffs in this region tend to be on the northern slopes and, if walking north to south, most cliffs are encountered on ascent. The general rule is to contour right (westwards) to find the relevant cliff break. Some of these cliff breaks are much more difficult to find on descent i.e. when walking south to north.

The following notes describe the traverse route from north to south, but comments have also been provided on the south-north route where necessary.

Spicers Peak: The routes on the north of Spicers Peak have already been described. The descent on the southern side starts about 50m west of the cairn on the east summit. It is typically troublesome and tiring, with rainforest, thorny undergrowth and frequent small cliffs. If either descending or ascending, contour westwards to find any cliff breaks. Pack hauling is sometimes necessary, depending on your exact route. A typical time for the descent is 2 hours, although this is rather erratic and some parties have found much quicker routes. It seems to be best to head straight down for a while, then contour across to the east again.

The saddle at 420 909 is a useful campsite with water usually available a long way down to the west (about 15 minutes down, but allow an hour for the return journey). The knolls to the south of this saddle provide an excellent view of Mt Castle in the afternoon light.

Mt Doubletop: Proceeding south, you soon start climbing Mt Doubletop. When the route is eventually barred by cliffs, contour west, then ascend again until more cliffs are encountered. You can contour either left or right at these uppermost cliffs. The left hand route is steep and slightly exposed.

There are two lookouts on the northern summit of Doubletop, one looking north and the other south. The southern lookout has a tiny bivouac campsite for two or three people. It provides a superb view of the sunset over the Darling Downs in clear winter weather. Because the summit is covered in fragile sclerophyll heath, wood fires should not be used.

From Doubletop, descend south-east and follow the crest towards Mt Huntley, passing over several knolls and through patches of rainforest in the saddles. There are good eucalypt campsites at Swan Knoll (431 887), just north of the summit of Huntley Knoll (443 876) and at Mt Huntley saddle (443 872). In the rainforest saddle between Swan and Huntley knolls, there is an interesting section of ridge called the rainforest razorback. Nearby, at about 437 882, it is common to descend to the west slightly to avoid a vine entangled section of ridge, using a large open rainforest terrace just off the crest. Water can sometimes be obtained by descending along this terrace to a small lagoon on a natural slump shelf, although the water is usually very stagnant and would probably dry up quickly in dry weather.

Mt Huntley is a steep tiring ascent on slippery grassy slopes. When the cliffs are reached, contour west for a considerable distance, using care across the top of a slabby section. Contour around the north-west corner of the cliffs until a cliff break is found about 50m beyond one corner. The route up the cliff break may be difficult to recognise without previous experience of it. It follows a slight zigzag path, starting on the left of the break, traversing across to the right, then up to a large banksia tree. A 30m belay rope is recommended unless the party is experienced. From the top, ascend directly to the summit.

On descent, this cliff break can be extremely difficult to find, even if you have climbed it before. The best written direction possible is to proceed north-west from the summit and investigate the cliffs below large banksia trees for signs of footworn erosion. Sometimes the tree is marked with coloured tape, or you may notice an old blaze. A belay is strongly recommended. If the break can't be found, a time consuming alternative is by use of the western ridge, although this also has some difficulties. Another alternative is abseiling, but this would require a full length rope and considerable care.

There is a reasonably large camping area on top of Mt Huntley. The regrowth scrub immediately south of the summit was caused by surveyors clearing sight lines for a trig point in 1975.

Descent from Mt Huntley can be via the south-east crest, but most parties take the southern route through the water point in Tree Fern Gully. Descend immediately south from the summit into the rainforest, and proceed downhill for a considerable distance. Gradually tree ferns increase in number, this particular species (*Dicksonia antarctica*) being unique by their habit of winding along the ground in unusual shapes before growing upright. One has a trunk which loops in a complete circle. **Please treat these gently, do not knock the fragile fronds or trunks, and in particular, do not compact the earth by treading around the trunks or inside the circular fern**. This stand is one of the most unusual displays of this species in Queensland, although a section of the forest canopy was badly damaged in a storm a few years back.

The water point is reached after a long descent, just before a small cliff and waterfall. The water supply is permanent, although cups are needed to bail into water bottles. To regain the crest, contour eastwards for a considerable distance.

The crest between Huntley and Asplenium is mainly rainforest but there is one spectacular campsite. There are also several ridges of upjutting rock which regularly cause confusion to bushwalkers. The first major pinnacle should be climbed and the second bypassed on the western side.

Mt Asplenium and Panorama Point: To climb Asplenium, head upwards until the cliffs are reached, then traverse right to a cliff break. This cliff break is difficult to find on descent, although there is at least one other cliff break further west. The summit of Asplenium is rockstrewn rainforest and is not particularly suitable for camping.

Proceeding south-east from the summit, the ridge to Panorama Point, about 30 minutes away, soon becomes evident. It is actually possible for a very small party to camp on Panorama Point - a superb place on a clear dark night - but wood fires should not be used because of the fragile environment. A very large campsite where wood fires can be used lies just before Lower Panorama Point.

To descend south-east from Upper Panorama Point, initially travel south-west on a well-worn track, contouring right across the top of any cliffs. Eventually a fairly easy cliff break will be reached. Follow the base of the cliffs back around to the left for a considerable distance to regain the crest. The main ridge is again followed to Lower Panorama Point.

The descent to the saddle south from Lower Panorama Point is long and steep. On the final very steep slopes just before the rainforest, keep to the right since it is easy to allow the slope to divert you too far left. The ridge is now followed south over two knolls with good campsites to the foot of Mt Steamer. In between these two knolls is a very large thick patch of bracken which often obstructs progress.

Mt Steamer: Water is available in most cooler seasons 200m west of Mt Steamer's northern saddle at 460 814 (this water point is not reliable in very dry seasons). This saddle is also a good campsite. Mt Steamer is ascended from the saddle by climbing the steep grass slopes to the south.

If travelling north, care must be taken to commence the north-westerly descent of Mt Steamer from the eastern summit. Note from the topographic map that the correct ridge is fairly narrow and mostly eucalypt. It is separated from a broader rainforest ridge in the west by a creek.

To descend Mt Steamer on the south, it is necessary to again contour westwards to find a cliff break. After this, contour back east along the base of the cliffs to regain the crest. Watch your step from here on. From Mt Steamer to the unnamed peak west of Lizard Point (475 809 - sometimes called Mt Lizardback), there are several places where the ridge loosely overhangs 300m cliffs. Care is required at several places although there is no specific technical climbing difficulty.

Lizard Point is the name given to the spectacular rock shelf at 479 810. It is a reasonable campsite although wood fires should not be used, since the vegetation is fragile *Leptospermum* heath. Campsites are also available in the rainforest on the route just to the south.

To proceed south from Lizard Point, walk back westwards for about 150m, then turn south and contour across the slope to regain the crest. A track is usually present. From here to Teviot Gap, the route is mainly rainforest, with no readily accessible views.

Water is usually available by descending west from the saddle south of Lizard Point, near 479 808. Often a considerable descent is necessary.

Mt Roberts is easily ascended and descended on both the north and south ridges. There is a little scrambling and possibly some pack handling. Alertness is required at several places where the vegetation obscures your proximity to 300m cliffs, but there is no major technical climbing difficulty. Views from the summit are obscured by vegetation.

Mt Superbus to Teviot Gap: From the Roberts-Superbus saddle, ascend south-west to the Superbus shoulder at 474 784. From here, an old broken-down rabbit fence is followed down the ridge south-east to Teviot Gap. The route is steep and will be slippery in wet weather. An old forestry road is found at the end of the fence - turn right and follow it the final 700m to Teviot Gap.

In ascent, follow the old road north from Teviot Gap until about 200m beyond the wooden bridge at 488 773. The rabbit fence can soon be found by ascending to the left from anywhere in this vicinity (see also page 211).

SWAN CREEK VALLEY

WESTERN ACCESS ROUTES

The following are the main routes between the Swan Creek valley and the Main Range crest. The creeks which lie just north and south of Swan Knoll have not been mentioned but would probably also provide feasible descent routes.

Spicers Peak by South-West Ridge (grade 3): This ridge is best ascended from Hell Hole valley via the major spur at 399 895. There is a good lookout on the knoll at the top of this spur. Allow considerable time for the traverse between the west and east summits of Spicers Peak (see earlier description). The ridge is useful for both ascent and descent.

Hell Hole Creek: Much of the upper section of Hell Hole Creek near the boundary of the rainforest and sclerophyll forest is infested with nettles, although this may ease higher up. Consequently, the route may be feasible in descent, although it presents some difficulty on ascent.

(Walk 79) **Mt Doubletop by West Ridge** (grade 3): The ridge running west off the north peak of Doubletop is a good access route. It has one cliff to negotiate but this is not of major difficulty. The ridge is useful for both ascent and descent.

Mt Doubletop by South-West Ridge (grade 31/2): This ridge is most easily found from the junction at 403 868, where a private vehicular track turns off the Swan Creek road near the State forest boundary and ascends the ridge to the north (the very steep and rough track eventually crosses the ridge and descends to Hell Hole Valley, but vehicular access is restricted). Walkers can follow the ridge to the south peak of Doubletop. This route is slightly harder than others in this vicinity, since the latter section is quite steep and has some moderate scrambling difficulties. It would be easier in ascent.

Swan Knoll by South-West Ridge (grade 21/2): This is one of the quickest routes to the crest of the Main Range, starting at a creek junction at 413 873, near a popular unofficial campsite in the state forest. There are no difficulties in ascent but some navigation care is required in descent.

Huntley Saddle (grade 21/2 to 3): There is a reasonably easy descent route from Huntley saddle. Drop down a few metres below the lowest campsites, then contour to the south-west to the spur at 436 871, which leads down to the valley.

(Walk 79) **Mt Huntley by West Ridge** (grade 31/2): This is an excellent route. It is ascended via an old road up the spur at 417 870. The road reaches the ridge at the western saddle of Huntley (427 857), where there is a large camping area. From here there is a reasonably straightforward ascent of Mt Huntley, except for some cliffs which can be avoided by contouring along their southern base to a slippery cliff break. N.B. This cliff break can be difficult to find on descent.

DAY TRIP FEATURES

There are a number of day trips possible for parties base camping at Swan Creek. Details of most of the following routes have been given in the preceding pages.

Mt Doubletop: This peak can be climbed by either its western ridge (grade 3 for the return trip) or its south-western ridge (grade 31/2), or both can be used for an excellent circuit.

Mt Huntley via West Ridge (grade 31/2): This provides a reasonably energetic day trip, although very fit walkers may also be able to include a visit to Sentinel Point (see below).

Sentinel Point (grade 31/2): The western saddle of Huntley provides access to Sentinel Point, which is an excellent lookout. The cliffs at the east of Sentinel Point can be climbed via an awkward cliff break, or you can follow around the base of the cliffs on their southern side. It is also possible to include Sentinel Point in throughwalk itineraries crossing Mt Guymer and ascending from Barney Creek (refer to the description of the Emu Creek region on page 209).

Hell Hole Gorge (grade 2): Hell Hole Valley and Gorge are both on private land and permission for access should be obtained. The gorge is at the lower end of the valley and is an interesting half day trip. There is a constructed cattle track which bypasses the gorge on the north. A good circuit is to take the cattle track up into the valley, then rockhop down the gorge. In spring, the track has spectacular wildflower displays. In the gorge, it is common to encounter red-bellied black snakes, which are among the most beautiful of snakes (but still need to be treated with respect).

EMU CREEK VALLEY

WESTERN ACCESS ROUTES

The following are the main routes between the Emu Creek valley and the Main Range crest.

Sentinel Point via Mt Guymer (grade 4 to 41/2): Mt Guymer is an interesting *(Walk* eucalypt-forested mountain which can be visited on a day trip from Emu Creek, or *96)* on a throughwalking itinerary en route to either Mt Asplenium or Sentinel Point. It can be ascended from several ridges in the south but the ridge at 410 805 is likely to provide better glimpses of the Steamers. If walking to Sentinel Point, descent in the north is largely blocked by cliffs, but the very crest of the ridge north off the eastern summit (409 823) is possible. It is a long day (one way) from Emu Creek to the western saddle of Huntley, via Sentinel Point. The route from the saddle up the western ridge of Mt Huntley is described on page 208.

Barney Creek: Experienced parties could probably use this route for descent, although you would need to cross either Mt Guymer or Sentinel Point (both arduous climbs) to reach the main road access points in Emu or Swan Creeks.

Mt Asplenium by West Ridge (grade 3 to 4): This ridge extends out to Mt Guymer. Access to Mt Asplenium is blocked by cliffs at the top of the ridge, although the precise difficulty of these cliffs is uncertain. It is likely that a cliff break would be found by contouring around on the north side (at worse you would end up contouring to the normal cliff break used on ascent from the north). Do not be tempted to contour across the southern slope to Panorama Point, since this section is nettle-ridden and extremely slow.

Reedy Creek (grade 21/2 to 3) is quite trafficable although disturbed by logging operations in its lower sections. It is mainly used as a descent route from Panorama Point or the saddle to the south.

Davies Ridge (grade 21/2 to 3) is a good quick ridge with a spectacular view of the *(Walks* Steamers not far from the Main Range crest. You can also camp at this lookout, *75/96)* located at 445 824.

Lophostemon Spur (grade 21/2 to 3): The western ridge off the knoll at 456 815 has some superb box trees near the eastern end. It is disturbed by logging operations lower down the ridge but is readily trafficable.

Pinchgut Creek and Mt Steamer Creek: Experienced parties could probably use these routes for descent, but there is a possibility of logging disturbance.

The Steamer Range (grade 3 to 4) is a spectacular series of bluffs and pinnacles, *(Walks* named (from the west) the Prow, the Funnel, the Mast and the Stern. The range is *75/80)* normally ascended from Mt Steamer Creek. The best route is via a road to a small experimental pine plot at 428 800 (refer Emu Vale State Forest map). Aim to reach the ridge crest near the Funnel and contour on the north under the cliffs of the Funnel and Mast. Proceed further east under and to the north of the Stern, after which the ridge crest is regained at a small saddle. West of this saddle is the famous Steamers Lookout, which has excellent views but requires care. From here, journey east up and over Mt Steamer to its eastern summit. This latter section often takes longer than expected.

Menura Creek, which flows west from the Lizard Point-Mt Roberts saddle, is likely to be far steeper and rougher than other routes around Emu Creek, although parts are reportedly very pretty.

Mt Superbus Routes: There are two main routes between Emu Creek and Mt Superbus. See page 211 for full details.

DAY TRIP FEATURES

There are a number of day trips possible for parties base camping at Emu Creek.

Mt Guymer: This mountain could provide a variety of interesting day trips from Emu Creek. Details of the route have been given on page 209.

Lincoln Wreck: This would be a long day trip for experienced walkers (grade 4), or it can be visited on a throughwalk en route to Mt Superbus. Refer to page 211 for full details.

The Steamer Range: The trip to the Steamers Lookout would be about grade 3 1/2 when undertaken as a day trip from Emu Creek. Details of the route have been given on page 209.

MT SUPERBUS REGION

MT SUPERBUS

Mt Superbus (pronounced Superb-us, not Super-bus) is 1375m high, making it the highest peak in Queensland south of Innisfail. However, there are no views readily available and the main reason for climbing the summit is simply for the record. Much of the massif has been heavily logged.

The main summit actually lies about 400m west of the Great Divide crest, and so technically this particular summit is not the highest peak in south-east Queensland. The north summit of Superbus claims this honour. It is located on the Great Divide crest and is a few metres higher than the west peak of Mt Barney.

Mt Superbus Summit: The top of Mt Superbus is really a small plateau with a collection of high points, rather than one prominent peak. It is useful to identify a number of features before describing the various routes to the mountain. The main features are:

* The main summit (465 779).
* The summit saddle (467 780).
* The northern summit (470 784).
* The north-east shoulder (474 784).
* The southern summit (455 760).
* The southern spur, which extends out some 2 1/2km between the main summit and the southern summit.

Careful navigation is required on the summit plateau since there is a confusing combination of rainforest and old forestry roads. One old road crosses the summit saddle at 467 780, just east of the main peak. The south fork of this road eventually leads down into Emu Creek valley, although it is often overgrown (see the description of the Emu Creek route). Another old road lies just to the east of the main plateau, and initially takes a course along the southern spur before descending off down the eastern side (468 775).

Teviot Gap Route (grade 3 to 3½): This is the quickest route to Mt Superbus. In ascent, follow the old road north from Teviot Gap until about 200m beyond the wooden bridge at 488 773. You can ascend to the left from anywhere in this vicinity. An old broken-down rabbit fence will soon be found, leading up the ridge to the north-east shoulder of Mt Superbus.

In descent, carefully locate the Superbus shoulder at 474 784 (it is possible to miss it), then follow the ridge down to the south-east. The old rabbit fence will appear after a very short distance. The route is steep and will be slippery in wet weather. An old forestry road is found near the end of the fence - turn right and follow it the final 700m to Teviot Gap.

Mt Bell Route: The route between Mt Roberts and the Bell-Roberts saddle provides some unusual variations to throughwalk itineraries around Mt Superbus. It is described on page 213.

Emu Creek Route (grade 3½): It is possible to descend from the main summit of Superbus to Emu Creek, by following the old forestry track which descends south from the summit saddle (467 780). The route is often overgrown with raspberry and nettles, so gloves and long gaiters are recommended. Because of the unpredictable nature of the regrowth, the route is not recommended for ascent unless you have travelled it recently (regrowth is easier to push through in descent). This road eventually joins the Lincoln Wreck route, which is a preferred ascent route from Emu Creek.

Lincoln Route (grade 3½ to 4): The Lincoln Wreck is the remains of an R.A.A.F. *(Walk* Lincoln bomber, which crashed on the southern summit of Mt Superbus on April 9th, *80)* 1955. Tragically, the plane was flying on a medical evacuation from Townsville to Brisbane, with a sick baby aboard, when it strayed off course in bad weather. The baby, a nurse and four crew lost their lives. It seems especially tragic that the plane crashed only about 50m below the crest of the highest mountain within hundreds of kilometres of their flight path.

To ascend this route, start walking from the road closure at the end of the Emu Creek road (see road directions). It soon starts to climb steeply and narrows to a forestry track. After climbing for perhaps 1½ hours, the track divides. The left hand track goes to the main summit of Mt Superbus (this is often overgrown - see the previous description of the Emu Creek Route), while the right hand fork contours across the slopes towards the Lincoln Wreck.

Follow the right hand fork, crossing one creek, and then meeting a second creek. This second creek is marked by an old engine from the plane. At this point the route diverges from the road and follows the creek directly uphill. There may be remnants of a track but it is not essential to follow a particular course. Any route directly uphill from this point will lead to the southern summit, which is more like a broad plateau than a definite peak. The wreck lies just below a campsite on the extreme western end of the plateau. If camping in this locality, you will need to carry your own water. It takes between 1 and 1½ hours to travel from the Lincoln Wreck to the main summit of Mt Superbus.

TEVIOT FALLS AND MT BELL

This is a confusing region. The difficulty is caused by a profusion of logging regrowth in the upper parts of Teviot Brook, overgrown logging roads, the absence of views due to the rainforest canopy, the precipitous nature of some terrain and the apparent erroneous marking of the location of Teviot Falls on virtually all maps. Some older bushwalking guidebooks also give misleading information for this area.

The main day trip features in the region are Teviot Falls and Mt Bell. In addition, some bushwalkers visit the area on throughwalking itineraries in the Roberts/ Superbus region.

(Walk 50) **General Terrain:** It is worthwhile providing a general description of this region prior to giving specific route directions. Note that the Forestry Department's *Teviot Falls* map has a critical part of the creek obscured by printed information and is not recommended for trips in this area.

From Teviot Gap, a road travels north for about 700m until it crosses the south branch of Teviot Brook at about 488 773, on an easily recognisable wooden bridge. The south branch is an easterly flowing creek which drains the slopes of Mt Superbus. However, this is not the main tributary of Teviot Brook. The main tributary flows south from the Bell-Roberts saddle. For descriptive purposes this is called the north branch.

The majority of the catchment of the north branch, including the western slopes of Mt Bell, has been heavily logged and is badly infested with regrowth. The old logging road previously mentioned continues north from where it crosses the south branch (488 773), and eventually crosses the two north branch tributaries at 488 781 and 493 784 respectively. Although old bushwalking guidebooks recommend using this road, it is often badly overgrown with raspberry and nettles.

Teviot Falls: On all recent maps to the date of writing, Teviot Falls are marked on the south branch at 491 773. There is a waterfall at this point, but it is not the main waterfall, nor that evident from the popular lookout on the Teviot Gap road. These falls are on the north branch at 492 775. The falls on the south branch are barely visible from the lookout, but if you move downwards and to the right they can be seen originating from a narrow crevice, usually with a considerably lesser flow than the main falls.

To reach the south branch falls, follow the old forestry road until about 50m past the wooden bridge, where there is a left hand bend. At this point leave the road on the right and descend south-easterly, trying to stay parallel with the creek. At one point you may cross a side gully. It is best to keep high on the banks but if necessary you can descend along the creek. Eventually the cliff will be seen ahead, and you can descend to the creek and the falls.

From the south branch falls, you can traverse across to the north branch falls. Ascend to the north of the south branch and then contour across the steep slopes. A good instinct for bush navigation will help on this section. The aim is to traverse parallel with the cliff line, while remaining well to the west of it. If in doubt, stay high and follow a compass course in a general north-north-easterly direction. Descend when you either hear the falls or meet the northern creek.

There is a superb bathtub pool situated just in from the lip of the falls, with an impressive window view of Wilsons Peak. For reasons which will be obvious when you get there, swimming is not recommended after any sort of heavy rain or if you

212

think further landslides are imminent.

The return journey is the reverse of these directions, ascending to the forestry road after traversing within sight of the south branch. Don't be tempted to ascend up the slope south of the southern falls, since this terrain becomes extremely precipitous.

Mt Bell by South-West Ridge: This is an underrated peak. While the rainforest on the western slopes is infested with regrowth due to past logging operations, the eastern slopes are eucalypt forest with multiheaded grasstrees. The division between the forest types is very sudden, the line running a few metres east of the summit. It is possible to obtain some views from the peak. The main route to the summit is the south-west ridge from Teviot Falls (north branch).

The ascent to Mt Bell from the northern falls is reasonably straightforward, although there are several patches of logging regrowth. The worst regrowth can be avoided by contouring down on to the steep south-eastern flanks. Surprisingly, the ridge offers several good views through windows in the vegetation.

If descending from Mt Bell towards the northern falls, it is necessary to follow compass bearings in several places, since the ridge changes direction at least three times. One point of confusion is where the south-eastern ridge diverges off just down from the summit. Another area is in the final descent towards Teviot Falls.

Mt Bell from Mt Roberts: This ridge starts on the southern shoulder of Mt Roberts, where the Main Range crest makes a distinct south-westerly turn (482 797). It is initially very steep, thereby requiring careful compass work to descend the ridge (there are several parallel ridges, not all shown on the map, which can confuse you on descent). Otherwise the route is straightforward.

Other Features: There is some magnificent rainforest in the upper parts of the north branch of Teviot Brook, down from the Bell-Roberts saddle. In the past there has sometimes been a taped trail leading south off the ridge at about 491 794. It went up and down slopes without any apparent logic, before leading into a massive stinging tree forest with many trees several metres in diameter. This forest would be roughly at 491 789, although the trail may now be disused. Note that exit from this area would necessitate either use of the old Teviot Brook forestry road, which will probably be very overgrown, or a retreat back to the Mt Bell ridge.

EASTERN RIDGES

The main routes on the east of the Main Range are Panorama Ridge, Lizard Ridge and the ridge extending from Mt Bangalore to Mt Bell. These are discussed here. In addition, it is apparently possible to travel on several spurs running between Coulson Creek and the Spicers-Doubletop and Doubletop-Huntley saddles, but no information is available at the time of writing.

While Mt Bangalore offers day trip opportunities, Panorama Ridge, Lizard Ridge and the route from Mt Bangalore to Mt Bell are mainly used by throughwalkers. **Only very experienced parties should attempt these throughwalking routes**, since the terrain is extremely precipitous. Cliffs over 200m are common in some locations. Mt Bangalore is the only feature suitable for less experienced bushwalkers on the east of the range.

All routes pass through private grazing lands, and permission from landowners is essential. Landholders around Wild Cattle Creek in particular are likely to prosecute for trespass if bushwalkers do not obtain prior permission to cross their lands.

PANORAMA RIDGE (grade 5 to 5½)

This ridge extends north-east from Lower Panorama Point, and is the easiest of the three main routes which run from the eastern grazing country to the Main Range crest. There are no cliffs on the correct route although the ridge is often narrow and, at one point, forms a razorback bounded by extremely steep grass slopes.

On descent, considerable care is required with navigation, since it is very easy to confuse the correct ridge with a parallel ridge just to the north at 458 847. The latter leads to a large precipitous buttress. To find the correct route, proceed north-west from Lower Panorama Point for several hundred metres, until an easy cliff break is found leading down to the right (north-east). Follow the base of the cliffs back under Lower Panorama Point, **resisting the temptation to descend when the Point is initially sighted.** Note that the correct ridge initially runs directly east from Lower Panorama Point and then turns north-east. This is important because it is easy to descend too early on the wrong ridge and become cliff-bound. Once the descent is commenced, traversing between the two ridges is extremely steep and difficult.

On ascent, the ridge is easily followed, provided you start on the appropriate spur in the north branch of Wild Cattle Creek. When the final cliffs of Lower Panorama Point are encountered, simply contour right (north) for several hundred metres to an easy cliff break.

LIZARD RIDGE (grade 6½)

This is sometimes called Glucose Ridge because it is very long and tiring. The ascent can be tackled by any very experienced party but the descent definitely requires a leader who knows the route well. Otherwise the cliff breaks may be impossible to find.

The ridge can be climbed initially at Mt Neilson, but most people prefer to climb one of the spurs just west of this point. There are two precipitous areas on ascent. The first is only of moderate technical difficulty, but has some exposure and a great number of very large loose rocks. The second point is the ascent at the final cliffs.

At the base of the final cliffs, contour along to the north for perhaps fifteen minutes. Ascent is made at a cliff break just before an indistinct gully. There is a short section of cliff, some spear lilies and thick scrub, and another short pitch of cliff. A good belay rope is recommended. Once above the second pitch of cliff, the crest is easily gained. It may also be possible to ascend via the steep grass slopes further west from this ascent point, but the route appears exposed and dangerous.

MT BANGALORE

Mt Bangalore is variously spelled "Bangalore" and "Bangalora", but is known by most bushwalkers by the former name. Together with Mt Bell, it is part of a long ridge off Mt Roberts. Mt Bangalore offers a variety of day trip opportunities, or the two peaks can be used to travel between the Main Range crest and the eastern grazing lands. However, the full route is only suitable for very experienced parties.

Routes to the west of Mt Bell - i.e. in the triangle between Mt Bell, Teviot Gap and Mt Roberts - have already been discussed in the Mt Superbus section. The following notes describe Mt Bangalore and the route to Mt Bell.

Ascent Routes: This peak offers a range of bushwalking opportunities, from day trips of only modest difficulty (grade 2½ to 3) to far harder ventures. It is approached over private land, although to the date of writing gaining permission for access has not been difficult. The mountain is entirely eucalypt forest.

A road runs in near the foot of Mt Bangalore. Although not shown on most maps as a road, its rough path is marked by cadastral lines on the *Teviot* 1:25 000 sheet. It leaves the Teviot Gap road at 551 813, opposite a house 1.1km from the intersection with the main White Swamp road. It then proceeds in a slightly circular path to a locked gate at 531 807. Permission must be acquired to use this access route from the landowners who live opposite the gate, as well as those who live in a house located 500m back towards the White Swamp road junction (at about 554 817).

Access is apparently also possible via an old timber track which leaves the Teviot Gap road at 527 782. From this track you walk cross country to the southern part of the mountain.

The easiest route to climb the peak is from the north, leaving cars at about 538 814 *(Walk* and travelling north-westerly across grazing lands for about 2km before climbing the *68)* ridges. Crossing the foothill lands is time consuming because of the many gullies. However, after you cross the creek at 521 825, the ascent is straightforward.

Alternatively, **small experienced groups** can climb the very steep eastern slopes of the peak. Start out from the gate at 531 806 and initially contour north-westerly, then head straight up. The more northerly spurs are easier. On all these eastern spurs, great care must be taken not to dislodge rocks, because **rocks would quickly reach lethal speeds on the extremely steep slopes**. These routes are definitely not suitable for large groups.

Bangalore Gorge: This is an interesting dry weather route for descending the mountain. It is reached by taking the ridge south of the summit to the creek at 511 805. Descending this creek leads to a short but spectacular chasm. When the gorge is blocked by a sheer cliff, walk up the short ramp on the left. From the top of this ramp, a scrambling descent is made through scrub and loose rock, with considerable contouring to the left. You can then drop into the creek and walk upstream to the bottom of the gorge, where a small waterfall may be found after rain.

Although this route is not particularly difficult, it is only recommended for experienced bushwalkers since any navigational errors could lead to very precipitous terrain.

Mt Bangalore to Mt Bell: This route should only be tackled by experienced scramblers, since there is a section of climbing as you start to ascend from the Bangalore-Bell saddle towards Mt Bell. The exact difficulty of the climb is unclear, although it appears very steep when viewed from a distance. Belay ropes are recommended as a safety precaution.

Be careful to follow the correct ridge if descending from the summit of Bangalore to the Bell-Bangalore saddle. The correct ridge will be found by descending in a west-south-west direction, although initially there may be little sign of a crest. It is easy to take the more prominent southern ridge by mistake, leading to the Bangalore Gorge.

Apparently it is also possible to ascend Mt Bell by its eastern ridge (510 788).

N.B. Wood fires are now prohibited in all bush camping areas in Scenic Rim national parks. Machetes and similar brush cutting implements are also banned in national parks.

WILSONS PEAK REGION

Wilsons Peak is the classically shaped three-sided peak situated south of Teviot Gap, marking the junction of the Mcpherson Range and the Great Divide. It is a popular day trip venue, with some interesting circuit walks, and three ridge routes providing a variety of ascent options. Disappointingly, the peak provides few views, and border or rabbit fences must be followed on all three ridges. Nevertheless, the mountain has plenty of attractive forest and other features of interest.

Ascent Routes: The three ascent ridges are from the east (starting from the Boonah Border gate on the White Swamp road), north (ascending from Teviot Gap) and west (starting from the Teviot Gap road west of Teviot Gap). All are about grade 3 to 3$_{1/2}$. In all cases the ridges are followed to the upper cliff line, and then the base of the cliff is followed to a cliff break which lies a few metres west of the northern ridge. Although all routes are steep, none are of great difficulty unless rain makes the final cliff break slippery. Otherwise the greatest danger is tearing yourself on the barbed wire fence.

(Walk 66) The eastern route is the longest but gives the greatest variation of forest types. It passes through about 4km of superb open forest before reaching the steep rainforest ridge which leads to the summit cliffs. When the cliffs are reached, contour right until you reach the cliff break.

The other two ridges are almost entirely rainforest. If you wish, you can use both to provide a circuit walk. The north ridge is the easiest, and is found by ascending from Teviot Gap. Just after the start, there is a short patch of regrowth scrub at the national park boundary (496 760), before the ridge swings left towards a eucalypt knoll (502 755). This can be a little confusing. Simply make your way as best you can to the top of the knoll, then follow the ridge as it descends to the south-west. The rabbit fence will soon become evident when you re-enter the rainforest.

The western ridge can be ascended by following up the fence line where it leaves the road, about 3$_{1/2}$km west of Teviot Gap. It has more scrambling than the other ridges and for that reason may be easier in ascent. At the top, contour left to find the cliff break.

Killarney Gate Throughwalk: A good weekend throughwalk in this region is the trip between the Boonah and Killarney border gates, traversing the eastern and western ridges of Wilsons Peak. This would require a long car shuttle and follows the border fence most of the way, but has some inspiring sections.

(Walk 44) **Wilsons Creek Circuit:** This day trip circuit is about grade 3$_{1/2}$. It ascends the north ridge from Teviot Gap, then descends back to the road at the base of Teviot Gap via the east ridge and Wilsons Creek, which flows to the mountain's north-east.

After ascending the peak from the north, descend the eastern ridge until at the bottom of the steep rainforest slopes, where the first saddle is found (510 746). Wilsons Creek can be reached by walking about a hundred metres east of the saddle and descending to the north. The creek is a little scrubby initially, but soon opens up with several slabby sections and some impressive cascades. You need to pass the cascades via an open ridge on the east of the creek.

Keep descending the creek on the east until a short way below the junction at 515 759, then cross and find a ridge crest on the west bank, running parallel with the creek and initially about 50m in elevation above it (514 762). Follow this north-easterly to the Kinnanes Falls region. Descend back to the creek when you hear the falls. Care is required to get any sort of reasonable view.

To descend from Kinnanes Falls to the road, walk north-north-west over the ridge, then descend to the east when the cliffs are passed. Soon after you begin descending, you will notice "the Verandah" on your right (competent scramblers can explore this feature - see below). After descending to the Teviot road, the circuit is completed by following the road up to the Gap.

The Verandah and Kinnanes Falls: "The Verandah" is a narrow ledge which traverses all the way across the large cliff face to the north-west of Kinnanes Falls. It is particularly impressive when viewed from just below (refer to the route in the last paragraph). The feature is also visible from the foot of Teviot Gap just before the road climbs, from where both the Verandah and Kinnanes Falls can be visited on a short day trip.

Good scramblers with a head for heights can negotiate the Verandah, although it is very narrow and precipitous and requires considerable care. Any exploration should be from the northern end of the ledge, nearest the road. Do not try to locate the southern entrance from the ridge near Kinnanes Falls, since the terrain is loose and precipitous and the entrance is very difficult to find without knowledge of its location.

In the past, a few bushwalkers have crossed the creek above Kinnanes Falls, climbing the bluff to the east and then descending the ridge at 526 766. However, the exact nature of this terrain is unknown.

NEARBY AREAS

QUEEN MARY FALLS

This national park is mentioned briefly, since it has a pleasant picnic area and two interesting short track circuits. The falls are particularly impressive after autumn rains. A private camping park and kiosk is situated across the road.

DIRECTORY

QUEENSLAND NATIONAL PARKS AND WILDLIFE SERVICE

Cunninghams Gap: MS 394, Warwick. Q. 4370. Telephone: (076) 66 1133.

FORESTRY OFFICES

Warwick: P.O. Box 58, Warwick. Q. 4370. (Guy Street, Warwick). Telephone: (076) 61 2411.

PRIVATE CAMPING PARKS

Queen Mary Falls   P.O. Box 102, Killarney. Q. 4373.
Caravan Park: Telephone: (076) 64 7151.

15

THE MISTAKE MOUNTAINS
AND ENVIRONS

This chapter describes the broad sweep of mountain terrain at the north-western end of the Scenic Rim, extending from Cunninghams Gap to the Laidley/Gatton area. It is a region of complex geography and provides an unusual mosaic of bushwalking opportunities. Several mountain systems converge here - two arms of the Great Dividing Range (the southern arm being a major topographic feature and the north-western arm being relatively minor), the Mistake Mountains (named because the range was originally mistaken for the Great Divide) and the Little Liverpool Range. In addition, there are a number of interesting peaks on the high ridges that run off the Mistake Mountains to the north-west.

The region is a mixture of state forest, national park and private lands. The major mountain systems converge just north of Sylvesters Lookout, which is a well known view spot east of the state forest camping area at Goomburra Valley. The region is described here as follows:

• The central state forest area around Goomburra Valley and Sylvesters Lookout.
• The southern arm of the Great Divide which extends down to Cunninghams Gap. This is partly state forest and partly in the Main Range National Park.
• The Little Liverpool Range (mainly private lands).
• Laidley Valley (private lands).
• Mistake Mountains National Park.
• The North-West Ranges (private lands).

Left: Hole-in-the-wall, Mt Castle

SPECIAL NOTES

BUSHWALKING CONDITIONS AND HAZARDS

General Terrain: This region has a considerable range of topography. A few areas (in particular Mt Castle) are quite rugged and require good scrambling skills. However, many other walks don't require any scrambling abilities provided you have adequate navigation skills to stay on the correct route. As a general rule the region is slightly less rugged than other parts of the Scenic Rim, although it is advisable not to underestimate the terrain. Due to the abundance of large cliffs on the eastern scarp, some seemingly easy terrains could be quite hazardous if you ventured off the main routes.

Reasonably good fitness is required for off-track walking. The hill climbs aren't as steep and arduous as in the region south of Cunninghams Gap, but there are still many areas with strenuous ascents and descents.

Official Tracks at Goomburra State Forest Park and in the national park at Cunninghams Gap provide a variety of easy bushwalks. The remainder of the region is undeveloped. Old forestry and farm roads assist travel in a few areas.

Vegetation varies substantially throughout the region. The belt of mountains from Cunninghams Gap to Mt Mistake is mainly rainforest, but much of the remaining area is dry open eucalypt forest. Thick logging regrowth hinders off-track walking in many parts of the state forest. The private lands on the Little Liverpool Range and in other peripheral areas are used for grazing and are often partially cleared.

Climate and Water Availability: Walks on the official tracks are enjoyable at all times of year. However, since the region is relatively hot and dry, off-track walks are only recommended from May to September. Water would need to be carried in quantity on most throughwalking itineraries, and a few areas are almost totally devoid of surface water. In winter the nights are often very cold, but this is probably a less serious hazard than the risk of extremely hot day time conditions in the warmer seasons.

Navigation: The main navigation problems occur in the rainforest region between Cunninghams Gap and Mt Mistake, where compass skills are often required. Cliffs could also become a navigation hazard in a few areas if you ventured off the main routes.

Access on Private Lands: Many areas are on private lands or must be accessed across private lands. Bushwalkers need to make special efforts to maintain good relations with landowners since access conditions are quite sensitive in some areas.

FACILITIES AND CAMPING

There are two official camp grounds, one at Goomburra State Forest Park in the west and the other in the national park at Cunninghams Gap. The latter is beside a busy highway and is not highly recommended for weekend camping, but is suitable for overnight stops while travelling. Both camp grounds have toilets, picnic tables, barbecues and walking tracks, but not showers. The only other facility in this region is a council park which can be used for camping at the southern end of the Laidley Valley. Bush camping is allowed in most national park and state forest localities away from the official camp grounds and tracks. N.B. Campers should note that dogs and other domestic animals are prohibited at Goomburra State Forest Park, just as they are in national parks.

MAPS

The area is covered by good 1:50 000 and 1:25 000 topographic maps available from SUNMAP. The 1:50 000 sheets of *Rosevale* and *Cunninghams Gap* cover most of the area, although there is no 1:50 000 sheet for the north-western section around Junction View. The main 1:25 000 sheets are *Glen Rock*, *Townson* and *Cunninghams Gap*, with *Thornton*, *Rosevale* and *Junction View* necessary for certain walks in the north. In addition, the Forestry maps titled *Main Range* and *Mount Mistake* can be used for many walks. These are the only maps which show the location of the Goomburra walking tracks and the forestry roads.

ROAD ACCESS

The main access points are as follows:

Cunninghams Gap: Used for accessing the national park graded tracks. Directions are evident on any road map.

Goomburra Valley: This is the most common route for accessing the Mistake Mountains and nearby areas. Turn right at Gladfield 21km west of Cunninghams Gap, then hard right at the crossroads 10km further on. Follow this road for a further 25km, through various gates, grids and creek crossings (the latter section can be awkward in the wet). The camping area lies just beyond a fork in the road, at which you turn right. Follow the left hand fork if you are driving up to Sylvesters or Mt Castle Lookouts and the crest of the range. N.B. This latter road is usually closed in wet conditions by a locked gate.

Cunninghams Campsite No 6: This road is used to access the Mt Castle area via the steep south-eastern ridge of Boars Head. However, nowadays it is often difficult to obtain permission from the landowner to traverse the lands and it is very unlikely that camping would be allowed. To find the site, turn into Elizabeth Street in the centre of Aratula, just past the post office. Follow the road for 11km (passing Tarome State school on the right after 9 1/2km), then turn left along a road signposted "Cunninghams Campsite No 6". Pass through a gate, drive a further 2km, then turn hard right through an iron gate. From here, drive 500m along the fence to the campsite beside the creek. This last section is a dry weather road only.

Laidley Valley: This road can be used to access the Little Liverpool Range or various parts of the Mistake Mountains. Drive south from Laidley township for 2km, turn right and drive another kilometre, then turn left. From here it is about 16km to the community of Thornton (just a few houses around a road junction near Mt Beau Brummel) and another 10km to the end of the road. All access is on private lands and permission from the landowners is absolutely essential.

Main Camp Creek: This is used to reach Laidley Gap, although access is entirely on private lands. It is reached by driving west and then south-west from the road junction at Thornton (see previous description). There are several turns on the road. Refer to the topographic map for more details and ensure you obtain permission from the landowners to cross the private lands.

Junction View: This route south-west of Gatton is only used for trips on the private lands in the Mt Michael area. Drive west of Gatton for 3km and turn left into the Ma Ma Creek road, then drive 8km and turn left into the Junction View road. From this latter junction, it is about 25km to Junction View.

GOOMBURRA STATE FOREST PARK

There is a variety of walking opportunities in the Goomburra region, including track walks of various lengths and several more rugged day trips. Alternatively Goomburra can be used as an access route for throughwalks to Cunninghams Gap or to the Mistake Mountains National Park, both of which are described later in this chapter.

OFFICIAL TRACK WALKS

The official tracks in the Goomburra region are not designated as graded tracks, being somewhat rougher and steeper. The *Main Range* forestry map shows the locations of most tracks, although the *Mount Mistake* map is needed for the Winder Track.

(Walk 23) The two longest circuit walks - the Cascades Track and the Ridge Track - each provide trips of several hours duration. They can also be combined to make a single longer circuit. Both these walks leave from the camping ground.

The other tracks leave from the Mt Castle Lookout road which branches off just downstream from the camp ground and climbs to the crest of the Great Divide. One path leads to Araucaria Falls, which takes about 1 1/2 hours return. There are also two very short paths which branch off the top section of the road, leading to Sylvesters Lookout and Mt Castle Lookout. Both are inspiring view spots. The point where the Mt Castle Lookout track leaves from the locked gate at the end of the road is the junction of the Mistake Mountains and the Great Divide.

The other major walking path is the Winder Track. This follows an old forestry road from the end of the Mt Castle Lookout road, to the remnants of a logging winch (the winder) which lies on the crest of the Mistake Mountains to the north. The track is about 13km return. The winch is located near the state forest/national park boundary at a point where an old forestry road ascends from Laidley Valley (this latter road is now overgrown with raspberry and nettles - see page 228). A few hundred metres south of the Winder, water can be found by following a short side track on the west of the old road (not always easy to locate - see page 228).

It is intended to develop several other track walks at Goomburra in the next few years, possibly to features such as Point Pure and the Amphitheatre.

OTHER WALKS

(Walk 43) **Laidley Falls:** From the end of the Sylvesters Lookout track (394 050), it is possible to walk to Laidley Falls and the Mt Castle area. The trip to the falls and back takes about half a day and is a relatively easy off-track walk (grade 2 1/2). However, the section between the falls and Mt Castle is much harder, requiring scrambling ability and considerable care. It would also require a reasonably long day for the return trip (grade 4).

A rough path leads north from Sylvesters Lookout, initially taking you to a second view spot on a rocky spur to the north-east (397 051; this is considered by many bushwalkers to be the original Sylvesters Lookout). It then ascends to a rainforest knoll (398 053). Laidley Falls can be reached from this knoll by following the ridge which descends initially south-easterly and later north-easterly. There is often a vague foot pad, although navigation can sometimes be confusing around the knoll since there may also be a track leading off north-west to Mt Castle Lookout.

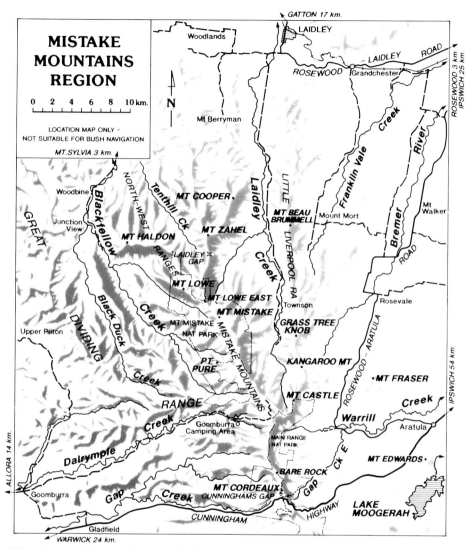

MISTAKE
MOUNTAINS
REGION

0   2   4   6   8   10 km.   N

LOCATION MAP ONLY –
NOT SUITABLE FOR BUSH NAVIGATION

MT.SYLVIA 3 km.

GATTON 17 km.

LAIDLEY

Woodlands

ROSEWOOD   Grandchester   LAIDLEY   ROAD

ROSEWOOD 3 km.
IPSWICH 25 km.

Mt Berryman

Creek

River

Woodbine

Junction
View

GREAT

Blackfellow

NORTH-WEST

Tenthill Ck

RANGES

MT COOPER

MT ZAHEL

MT HALDON

LAIDLEY –
GAP

Laidley

LITTLE

LIVERPOOL RA

MT BEAU
BRUMMELL   Mount Mort

Franklin Vale

Bremer

Mt
Walker

ROAD

MT LOWE

MT LOWE EAST

MT MISTAKE

Black Duck

DIVIDING

Creek

Creek

Creek

MT MISTAKE
NAT PARK

Townson

GRASS TREE
KNOB

Rosevale

Upper Pilton

MISTAKE MOUNTAINS

PT.
PURE

KANGAROO MT

ROSEWOOD – ARATULA

MT FRASER

IPSWICH 54 km.

RANGE

Creek

Dalrymple

Goomburra
Camping Area

MT CASTLE

Warrill

Creek

Aratula

MAIN RANGE
NAT PARK

CK E

MT EDWARDS

ALLORA 14 km.

Goomburra

Gap

Creek

BARE ROCK

MT CORDEAUX
CUNNINGHAMS GAP

Gap

HIGHWAY

LAKE
MOOGERAH

CUNNINGHAM

Gladfield

WARWICK 24 km.

There is a small campsite above Laidley Falls. The route from the falls to the Hole-in-the-Wall and Mt Castle is described later in this chapter in the subsection on Mt Castle (page 226).

Exploratory Routes: Blackfellow Falls (353 084), Point Pure (323 098) and the Amphitheatre (325 103) all provide exploratory ventures for experienced bushwalkers. The shortest routes to these features are probably from along the Winder Track, although there is thick logging regrowth in some places.

Blackfellow Falls can also be reached by a route which crosses the Great Divide downstream of the Goomburra camp ground (about grade 31/2 to 4). Ascend the ridge

223

at 340 057 (private lands) to the crest of the Divide, then descend to Blackfellow Creek via the ridge at 333 070 (national park). Follow up the creek to the junction then take the left hand fork to the falls. However, despite this being eucalypt forest, the bottom of the falls is difficult to reach due to regrowth scrub. The top of the falls can be reached from Blackfellow Creek by ascending the ridge at 340 078 until above the cliff line, then contouring around to the right above the cliffs. This version of the trip would require a long day (grade 4) but gives the best view of the falls.

SYLVESTERS LOOKOUT TO MT CORDEAUX

(Walk 71) This section of the Great Divide is not of classic appeal but is definitely worth a visit. If a lengthy car shuffle is undertaken, it can be walked in a long day provided care is taken with navigation. The trip is most commonly done as a weekend throughwalk, with a car shuffle from Cunninghams Gap to either Sylvesters Lookout (a relatively easy weekend walk) or Cunninghams Campsite No 6 (somewhat harder since it includes at least part of the rugged Mt Castle area, which is described in the next section). The route can be walked equally well in either direction.

Navigation is often confusing in this section. The route is entirely rainforest with no views between Bare Rock (394 995, at the end of the graded track north of Mt Cordeaux) and Sylvesters Lookout (394 050). It is important to stay close to the eastern escarpment if problems are encountered with either scrub or navigation. Any places where thick logging regrowth is evident should definitely be avoided by keeping east (for much of the route, the national park/state forest boundary lies just west of the crest). Water is obtainable from an easterly flowing creek at 386 012, just over an hour from Bare Rock.

Refer to page 201 (Chapter 14) for details of Mt Cordeaux and the graded track from Cunninghams Gap to Bare Rock.

LITTLE LIVERPOOL RANGE

The Little Liverpool Range is an offshoot from the Great Divide, stretching from Mt Castle to Laidley. It is almost entirely private grazing lands and as such has many cleared areas among its predominant covering of open eucalypt forest. While not as rugged or pristine as many other bushwalking areas, it nevertheless displays some classic qualities. For one, it is a long range with an inspiring sharp crest which gives excellent views of the surrounding country. The vegetation allows extremely fast travelling, and in fact a fast fit party can walk virtually the entire range in a long day. There are also some special vegetation features along the range, in particular masses of giant grass trees near Mt Beau Brummel.

Four main peaks provide the main attractions to bushwalkers - Mt Beau Brummel in the far north and Grass Tree Knob, Kangaroo Mountain and Mt Castle in the south. All can be accessed from Laidley Creek valley from where they make moderate day trips. However, Mt Castle can also be accessed from Sylvesters Lookout (via Laidley Falls) and Cunninghams Campsite No 6. For this reason, and because it is distinctly more rugged than the other features, it is discussed separately.

Relations between bushwalkers and landowners are sensitive in this area, particularly in the south of the Laidley Valley where the landholders insist on permission to traverse being sought prior to entry.

MT BEAU BRUMMEL TO KANGAROO MOUNTAIN

The *Rosevale* 1:50 000 topographic map is adequate for most bushwalking in this region. Most of the range north of Kangaroo Mountain provides relatively safe walking requiring no special equipment or precautions, although there is a short razorback section which requires care, as well as plenty of cliffs in the general vicinity. Provided care is taken and the party has experienced leadership, this area should be suitable for beginners. There are a number of interesting easy day trips available, including Mt Beau Brummel (grade 2 1/2 to 3). Alternatively, Grass Tree Knob and Kangaroo Mountain can be done as a joint day trip (grade 3). However, there is no water on the range in normal conditions and the area can be hot. If the full *(Walk* traverse from Beau Brummel to Kangaroo Mountain is attempted, it would be best *84)* tackled in early spring, since the winter days may be too short and summer would simply be too hot. Here is a description of the range, walking from north to south on a long day trip (grade 4 to 4 1/2).

Mt Beau Brummel: Virtually any of the ridges north of Mt Beau Brummel can be *(Walk* used for approach, although problems are encountered due to cliffs in some areas just *65)* to the south. Beau Brummel would provide an easy return day trip (grade 2 1/2 to 3) for a reasonably fit group. It is a very special mountain and there are masses of magnificent grass trees in the vicinity. Both peaks are worth visiting. The final approaches on a couple of routes are extremely steep, although there shouldn't be any climbing difficulties. It is also possible to approach Beau Brummel from Mt Mort, just to the east.

Walking south, the initial descent is very steep, but from here to the base of Grass Tree Knob the walking is fast and invigorating. It is open and partly cleared, and on some stretches you may find yourself following an old road. However, while much is fairly flat walking, the range narrows to a razorback in several spots. While these places are the only obviously hazardous locations, they definitely require care.

If attempting the entire range in a day, you should aim to be near Grass Tree Knob by lunchtime. Approach and descent on the west is barred by cliffs in many places along this section, although if you find your progress too slow there are descent routes at Grass Tree Knob.

Grass Tree Knob is easily ascended and descended by its northern and southern ridges. If approaching the mountain from the west, either of the two obvious ridges can be used, an old road being followed on one. It provides good views. As a day trip on its own, it would be about grade 2.

Kangaroo Mountain: Moving south from Grass Tree Knob, Kangaroo Mountain can be ascended firstly by following the ridge, and later by moving across a gully on the right. There should be no major difficulties if the correct route is selected. There are few views on the top and the undulating nature of the summit plateau makes it confusing to identify the true summit. However, it is useful to ensure you have crossed the summit to ease the difficulty of finding the descent ridge. For the best views, and to ensure you have crossed the summit, walk south-easterly until you encounter the cliff line.

To descend to Laidley Valley again, it is important not to miss the ridge which starts indistinctly at 416 104, since otherwise you may end up descending Surveyors Creek. To help pick out the ridge, stay on the western side as you cross back over the summit. The ridge starts just beyond a band of cliffs on the left. Once the start is found, it provides an easy quick route to the valley.

MT CASTLE

Mt Castle is distinctly more rugged than that section of the range to the north. While it provides several spectacular walking opportunities, the region requires care and many routes are not recommended for beginners. There are four different approach routes.

Other features of interest in the area include Boars Head, the Hole-in-the-Wall and Laidley Creek Falls. With an early start, an experienced energetic party would be able to visit all these features on a long day trip (grade 4 from Laidley Falls, and slightly harder from the Boars Head ridge).

The best views from Mt Castle are found south of the summit just before a dead end razorback. This razorback section requires considerable care.

Road Route (grade 3): The easiest ascent route is by following up Laidley Creek valley and approaching the mountain from the south-west. An old road (usually not too overgrown) zigzags up the slopes in the upper parts of the valley. It eventually ascends between the cliffs on the western side of the mountain, to a broad saddle a few hundred metres north of the summit.

Northern Route (about grade 4 to 5): If approaching from Kangaroo Mountain, Mt Castle can be climbed with considerable difficulty by a direct ascent from the ridge (there are some hazardous cliffs), or with less difficulty by traversing right into the major gully.

Boars Head Route (grade 4): Boars Head is the knoll immediately south of Mt Castle at 411 056. It is usually ascended from Cunninghams Campsite No 6 via the knoll's very steep south-eastern ridge. You need to cross farmlands to reach this ridge and there may be difficulty obtaining the landowner's permission for access.

The ridge connecting Boars Head and Mt Castle is partly a razorback. While it doesn't need any technical climbing skills, it is very sheer and requires considerable care. At the northern end of the razorback, direct ascent to the summit is blocked by a cliff line. On reaching the base of this cliff, contour around on the western side and then drop down to the road described above (see "Road Route"). Alternatively, it is possible to drop down to the road from the southern end of the razorback and thereby avoid all precipitous areas, but this route is considerably longer.

Laidley Falls Route (grade 4): If approaching from Sylvesters Lookout and Laidley Falls (405 054; see page 222), you can descend to the bottom of the falls by a scramble just to the west. Once below the falls, contour across to the east to the Hole-in-the-Wall. This is a unique cavity through the cliff visible in the late afternoon light from as far away as the road east of Cunninghams Gap. From the Hole-in-the-Wall, it is only a short distance to Boars Head (see description above).

Agile scramblers sometimes descend directly down the ridge from the Laidley Falls campsite to the Hole-in-the-Wall, but this route is exposed and not generally recommended.

LAIDLEY VALLEY

Laidley Valley offers day walking opportunities to the Little Liverpool Range (see previous description). In addition, it is also possible to undertake trips to two interesting features on the west of the valley.

TOWNSONS KNOB

Townsons Knob is the name of the knoll at 359 136. It is a good day walk destination (grade 2₁/₂), and also provides an excellent route to ascend the Mistake Mountains on throughwalks. Permission must be obtained to cross the private lands on the route from the landowner at the end of the Laidley Valley road.

The knoll is easily climbed by ascending the steep ridge to the west of the creek at the southern end of the road. It offers attractive views and interesting vegetation. Water can be obtained by descending to a small creek that lies west of the saddle between Townsons Knob and the crest of the Mistake Mountains. Further down this creek, there is a waterfall where it flows over the scarp (356 138). Care is required if descending directly from Townsons Knob to the waterfall.

LAIDLEY GAP AND MT ZAHEL

Laidley Gap lies just west of the property at the end of the Main Camp Creek road. Permission to cross the private lands is required. The Gap can be ascended and descended by either of two routes. The preferable option is the National Trail which climbs the ridge at 340 208 and approaches the Gap on a contouring course from the south. This path is usually marked. It is also possible to take a direct route between the farm house and the Gap, although some of the slopes are extremely steep and loose. The direct route is only recommended for ascent, and only then for small experienced parties.

Mt Zahel (grade 3) is easily ascended from Laidley Gap. There are two summits, the western summit being especially attractive with an unusual combination of rain-forest and dry eucalypt forest. The mountain can also be ascended by its eastern ridge, or both routes can be used to make an excellent winter day circuit (grade 3₁/₂). Permission from landowners is required on all routes. If using the eastern ridge, it is usual to ascend and descend via a spur south-west of the dam at 357 237, since it may be very difficult obtaining permission to cross the lands at the far eastern end of the ridge.

MISTAKE MOUNTAINS NATIONAL PARK

This national park is relatively difficult to access compared with most in south Queensland. It also has fewer spectacular attractions, and for these reasons does not receive heavy visitation. Despite this, it offers a range of interesting throughwalking opportunities. The main backbone of the Mistake Mountains is rainforest. Although parts of the national park were logged before the park was established, it provides pleasant walking conditions.

The main access routes are described in other sections of this chapter. They are (a) walking north from the Sylvesters Lookout forestry road; (b) ascending from Laidley Valley via Townsons Knob; and (c) walking south from Laidley Gap. Of these, Townsons Knob and Laidley Gap are the two most convenient access points if organising weekend throughwalk itineraries. Unfortunately, use of the Laidley Gap route may be questionable since it is currently very difficult to obtain permission to cross the private lands at Mt Lowe East (320 180 - see comments in the description of the North-West Ranges).

It would also be possible to walk to the national park from the North-West Ranges (see page 229), although carrying adequate water would be a major problem on this itinerary.

The main backbone of the Mistake Mountains provides relatively fast and easy walking conditions, since the Sylvesters Lookout forestry road extends north-westwards through the national park, almost as far as Laidley Gap. Nowadays the national park section of the road makes a surprisingly pleasant walking track, with the rainforest canopy meeting overhead and eliminating most of the unpleasant regrowth scrub which is normally encountered on old forestry roads (the track is no longer accessible to vehicles). The route is generally evident although good observation skills are required in a few places in the north where the path becomes faint. The vegetation changes from rainforest to open eucalypt forest near the national park's northern boundary.

The walk along the Mistake Mountains between Townsons Knob and Laidley Gap is a comfortable two day itinerary (grade 4). Note that the old Laidley Valley forestry road (marked on some maps on the ridge at 370 116) is now virtually impassable due to raspberry and nettle regrowth. The Townsons Knob route should be used to ascend the range instead. There is a water point near Townsons Knob on the upper part of the ridge (refer page 227).

There is also a water point just south of the Winder winch (see page 222), about 2km south of the top of the Townsons Knob ridge. The Winder is located at 355 109, at the point where the old Laidley Valley forestry road meets the top of the range (the top of this old road is marked incorrectly on the *Rosevale* 1:50 000 map but is shown in the right location on the *Mount Mistake* forestry map). A few hundred metres south of the Winder, try to find a rather overgrown foot track leading off to the west (not always easy to locate). It may also be possible to find water by descending westwards at several other places between the Winder and Mt Mistake, although no definite information is available. The chances of finding water probably reduce as you proceed north on the range.

Mt Mistake is a seemingly minor rainforest knoll at 343 162. It is a short side trip for parties walking along the range, but it requires some care with navigation. Allow several hours for the return journey from the knoll at 336 150. There are no views.

Exploratory Routes: Blackfellow Falls (353 084), Point Pure (323 098) and several nearby ridges and amphitheatres provide exploratory opportunities for experienced bushwalkers in this vicinity (refer to page 223). There has also been speculation whether any of the seemingly sheer north-eastern ridges from the Mistake Mountains (such as that off Mt Mistake) might provide access routes which could be used instead of Laidley Gap, but unfortunately no reliable information is to hand.

THE NORTH-WEST RANGES

(Walk
95)
This is the name given in this book to the series of long ridges which extend out north-west from the Mistake Mountains towards Junction View. The area offers several inspiring but little-known throughwalking opportunities. However, the region is mainly private land and most itineraries pass through several properties, so organisation of walks will usually require considerable work locating and approaching the relevant landowners. Great care would need to be taken with fire in drier seasons due to the thick grass cover.

The terrain is dry open eucalypt country, often with sharp ridge crests which provide a considerable sense of elevation. Considering that the country is private tenure and used for grazing, the extent of environmental modification and evidence of human visitation is much less than might be expected. There are many steep hills although progress is usually fast once on the crests. Campsites are reasonably common, but water must be carried in quantity. There is no water near the crests and the small creeks in the valleys are unreliable. Most throughwalks are only suitable for experienced bushwalkers with good fitness, partly for this reason.

Mt Michael to Laidley Gap: This is the main throughwalking itinerary (grade 41/2). It makes a reasonably energetic weekend trip but requires a long car shuttle. Alternatively, two parties walking in opposite directions can meet midway and swap car keys.

The route proceeds via Mt Michael, Mt Haldon, Mt Lowe and Mt Lowe East to Laidley Gap. At the time of writing there is some difficulty in obtaining permission to cross the section at the eastern end of the walk at Mt Lowe East (320 180), since the landowner has constructed a residence on Mt Lowe East and seems to wish to retain total privacy. However, it is possible to bypass the residence and, if permission can be obtained, the trip is an inspiring bushwalk. Alternatively, it may be possible to bypass the entire section near Mt Lowe East, by either dropping north to the valley or, if walking towards the Mistake Mountains, crossing the small valley in the south by a route just inside the national park boundary.

Mt Michael is usually ascended starting from an old road in the west (202 244). It begins behind the community hall, about 500m north of the school in Junction View village. Between Mt Haldon and Mt Lowe, there are several rocky knolls which require some care and scrambling ability. Some parties will find a pack hauling rope necessary for descending off one of these knolls (the name "Rocky Peak" is probably intended to refer to this knoll, although the name is used for different features on the various maps). There are good campsites in several saddles to the north and south of Mt Lowe.

To descend to Laidley Gap, you can choose to go directly down the main ridge along a steep recently constructed four wheel drive road, or you can descend further west. To descend east of the Gap, refer to page 227.

DIRECTORY

QUEENSLAND NATIONAL PARKS AND WILDLIFE SERVICE
Cunninghams Gap: MS 394, Warwick. Q. 4370. Telephone: (076) 66 1133.

FORESTRY OFFICES
Warwick: P.O. Box 58, Warwick. Q. 4370. (Guy Street, Warwick). Telephone: (076) 61 2411.

N.B. Wood fires are now prohibited in all bush camping areas in Scenic Rim national parks. Machetes and similar brush cutting implements are also banned in national parks.

16

THE BOONAH/IPSWICH PEAKS

The areas discussed in this chapter are all isolated peaks, and although most are located within the broad Scenic Rim crescent, they are not contiguous with the Scenic Rim or any other major natural region. The areas are well known for their excellent day walking opportunities, but are generally not suited to overnight ventures due to their small size.

Most of the peaks are relatively dry and rocky environments, vegetated by dry eucalypt forest or woodland with a heath understory. They offer superb wildflower displays in late winter and spring. Rock wallabies and koalas are also frequently seen here.

SPECIAL NOTES

BUSHWALKING CONDITIONS AND HAZARDS

General Terrain: The majority of the more popular routes are on rough tracks, which are generally suitable for less experienced bushwalkers given normal care and commonsense. However, considerable caution is required if undertaking any exploratory trips. Despite their small size, most of these areas are quite rugged, possessing numerous cliffs which could prove hazardous if inexperienced walkers ventured away from the recognised routes.

Vegetation: Usually the vegetation does not seriously impede travel, although the dry heath understories are often thick and scratchy. This may cause concern on some exploratory trips.

Navigation: With proper precautions and care, navigation is not normally a major difficulty in these regions, although bushwalkers should always carry a compass and an appropriate topographic map. Because of the relatively small size of the areas, 1:25 000 maps (or 1:10 000 if available) are essential to show any meaningful navigation detail.

Left: White Rock.

Some ridge routes are much more difficult to follow in descent than ascent, so care is often required to remember the descent routes. Cliffs are the major navigation hazards in these regions. Inexperienced walkers are advised to refrain from exploring unknown routes.

Water and Heat: Most of the areas are waterless, and they are often hotter than expected due to the open nature of the vegetation and the rocky environment. Always carry a reasonable water supply, especially in non-winter seasons.

FACILITIES AND CAMPING

There is a small national park camping area at Mt French, mainly suited for hike tents. Camping and day trip facilities include water, toilets, barbecues, lookouts and a few short graded tracks. The other main camping facilities in the region are private camp grounds in the vicinity of Lake Moogerah (see Directory). There is also an extensive picnic ground at Lake Moogerah, near Mt Edwards.

ACCESS AND PRIVATE LANDS

Most of the peaks are partly included in small national or environmental parks, but in no cases do the parks cover the whole of the feature. It is frequently necessary to acquire permission to cross private lands to gain access to the peaks. At the time of writing, access is freely available to White Rock and the main parts of Mts Edwards, French and Greville, but permission from local landowners is necessary to visit Mt Moon, Minto Crags and the Flinders Peak region. Bushwalkers need to make special efforts to maintain good relations with landowners in these regions. Enquire with the local national park rangers about how to contact the local landowners (if this fails, refer to the enquiry procedures in Chapter 2).

MAPS

The relevant topographic maps required for the various peaks are:
Mt Edwards: *Mt Alford* 1:25 000.
Mt French: Maps are not normally required, although the area is covered by the *Fassifern* and *Mt Alford* 1:25 000 sheets.
Mt Greville: *Mt Alford* and *Cunninghams Gap* 1:25 000 (both required).
Mt Moon: *Mt Alford* 1:25 000 (main map) and *Teviot* 1:25 000 (southern ridges).
Minto Crags: *Mt Alford* and *Teviot* 1:25 000 (both required).
Flinders Peak: *Flinders Peak* 1:25 000.
White Rock: *Woogaroo Creek* and *Spring Mountain* 1:10 000 (both required).

ROAD ACCESS

Mt Edwards is accessed from the Lake Moogerah picnic grounds. Roads are evident on any road map.

Mt French: Take the turn-off at the Dugandan Hotel, 400m south of Boonah. This leads to the picnic area on the north summit, the area known by rockclimbers as Frog Buttress.

Mt Greville: The areas around Mt Greville are private lands and access is restricted to one location. Drive out from Brisbane on the Cunningham Highway and take the turn-off signposted "Lake Moogerah" 5km beyond Aratula on the left. Ignoring any turns, follow the road for 11km, then turn right across a grid into Mt Greville Road. Drive a further 1.1km and park in the car park area on the right, at about 522 929. Alternatively, Mt Greville Road can be reached from Moogerah Dam by taking the road around the lake. This turns off south 1km from the picnic area. From here follow the directions below:

Odometer	Feature/Directions	Distance Between Features
0	Turn off onto lake circuit road	
4.8	Turn right	4.8
6.4	Turn left	1.6
9.9	Junction of Coulson, Croftby and Moorgerah Roads. Turn right.	3.5
10.3	Turn left into Mt Greville Road	0.4

Mt Moon: There are various access points for Mt Moon, all of which require permission to cross private property. At the time of writing, the main access route is from the east, using the road which connects Mt Alford township with the Carneys Creek Road. Cars are left near the floodway at 580 909. Enquire with the QNPWS Ranger at Boonah for details about how to contact the landowner.

If permission from landowners can be gained, it is also possible to climb the peak from the north-west. You can walk to the north-west ridge from the Croftby road, leaving cars at any convenient location between its intersection with the Coulson and Moogerah roads (see road directions for Mt Greville) and a point near a quarry about 2.5km to the south.

Minto Crags: The landowner's permission to access the crags is not readily granted and, if permission is given, extreme care must be taken to stay within the correct lands (enquire with the QNPWS Ranger at Boonah; refer also to page 237). The main access route is from private property using the road at 599 890. Take the Carneys Creek road which turns west 16km south of Boonah, then drive a further 8km and turn right onto the Mt Alford road. The road into the private lands turns off right about 11/2km north of this junction.

Flinders Peak: Take the Boonah turn-off just west of Ipswich on the Cunningham Highway. Drive 11.6km and turn left into Mt Flinders Road, just before Peak Crossing township. Drive 6.4km along this road and park about 400m after a concrete causeway, just before a gate and creek crossing (788 258). Permission from the landowner is required.

White Rock: If driving from Brisbane, turn left off Ipswich Road at Goodna shopping centre, then follow Queen Street (which later becomes Redbank Plains Road) for 5km to the Redbank Plains shopping centre (do not confuse this with Redbank Plaza). Turn right, drive a further 2km, then turn sharp left on top of a hill into School Road. Follow School Road for about 3.2km and turn right on top of a hill (the road directly ahead is usually closed off by a gate). After a further 600m, there is a car park on the left on the crest of a ridge (851 385). Leave cars here.

THE BOONAH-MOOGERAH DISTRICT

MT EDWARDS

(Walk 22) The easiest of the Moogerah peaks, Mt Edwards is climbed from a track which starts on the opposite side of the dam wall from the Lake Moogerah picnic area. The route is well worn and straightforward, although you should watch for any offshoot tracks during ascent which could possibly confuse you on descent. The route can be completed easily in half a day and is about grade 11/2.

An alternative and harder walk on Mt Edwards involves walking around the dam on the south side of the mountain and ascending the peak from the west. The route needs the best part of a day and is rated about grade 3. It should not be attempted in hot conditions, during rain or after particularly wet weather. Enquire with the QNPWS ranger at Boonah about how to contact the owner of the private lands which must be crossed south-west of the mountain.

The route starts by crossing the dam wall and walking the first hundred metres or so along the normal track. Then turn off the track on the left and make your way across the slope and then down to the north-western shore of the lake. Take care near the lake edge as the rocky shore is often slippery. Follow the lake shore around in an anticlockwise direction to where a creek enters the head of an inlet at 547 991. There is a small waterfall in this vicinity, and above this waterfall are several pools suitable for swimming in wet seasons. Follow the creek upstream for about 700m, then walk north-westwards across paddocks to a small earth dam at 534 999. Ascend to the north-east about a hundred metres past this dam and climb the steep gully at 538 004 (the most northern of two gullies in this vicinity). The gully gives good views towards the Main Range but care is needed as some slabs are very steep (in wet conditions these slabs could be quite dangerous). If conditions are suitable, it is best to stay in the gully until it begins to turn to the left at 544 007, then leave the gully and ascend through scrub to the summit. Descend back to the picnic area using the main track.

MT FRENCH

Although it offers only minor bushwalking opportunities, Mt French is an extremely interesting mountain and a notable peak of the Moogerah region. It is probably Queensland's most popular rockclimbing area and its cliffs display dramatic vertical fissuring. In addition some of the foothills are covered in a form of dry rainforest of great interest to botanists.

The road leads to the north summit, which is the region known by rockclimbers as Frog Buttress. A picnic area has been developed and several short graded tracks lead to lookouts which give good views. **Never throw rocks from the cliff-tops** - climbers frequent the cliffs below and several serious accidents have been caused by sightseers dislodging rocks. Similarly, if you decide to walk below the cliffs, pass below any climbers briskly in case rocks are accidentally dislodged.

MT GREVILLE

Mt Greville is a remarkable mountain of both scenic and biological interest. Located directly across Lake Moogerah from the picnic area, it makes a picturesque reflection in the waters. It is mainly vegetated in open eucalypt forest and wildflower heath, but it also has several major gorges which contain numerous palm trees. The mountain has a unique profile. Viewed from one place high on the Cunninghams Gap road, its humped summit and craggy spires have a remarkable resemblance to the shape of a feeding wallaby.

South-East Ridge: The peak provides many day walking opportunities. The main route to the summit is via the south-east ridge (515 935 - about grade 2½), which is found by taking the track leading directly uphill from the car park. This track is an official access route. There is a short band of rock and scree low down on this ridge, and some sections higher up where the track is vague, but otherwise the route is straightforward. The ridge is renowned for its wildflowers in early spring, the track often winding between heath on open rocky shelves. *(Walk 38)*

About two-thirds of the way up the south-east ridge, the track goes past the top entrance of Palm Gorge (see below). Just beyond here, the route joins the final summit ridge, and there is an excellent lookout just off the track (at about 509 939). Here it is possible to view a great expanse of the Scenic Rim, stretching from north of Cunninghams Gap to east of Mt Maroon. However, this part of the mountain is very precipitous and considerable care is required around the lookout.

Scrub obscures views from the summit of Mt Greville, but by crossing over the summit and descending through the scrub, views can be obtained from a lookout which lies above the northern cliffs.

There is also a lookout on the south-east ridge which overlooks Waterfall Gorge, although some searching is required to locate it (see later description).

Mt Greville Gorges: Either side of the south-east ridge lie the two principal gorges of the mountain - Palm Gorge (on the south) and Waterfall Gorge (on the north). Both can be used for either ascent or descent, and unless the conditions are wet are of only moderate difficulty (grade 3). Some people may experience problems negotiating the waterfall in Waterfall Gorge, but this section can be avoided if you wish. The gorges are particularly recommended as ascent routes if the weather is hot.

Palm Gorge: The easiest gorge route to locate is the descent via the southern gorge, since the track on the south-east ridge actually crosses the top entrance at about 511 938 (about two-thirds of the way to the summit). There are no major difficulties although there is some rockhopping and scrambling. Once out, pick up a track near the gorge entrance which leads northwards across the slopes to the south-east ridge route. Ensure you keep well clear of any farmlands below the gorge.

To find the ascent route up Palm Gorge, initially follow the south-east ridge track for several hundred metres, then follow a signposted side track which contours across to the left. The entrance to the gorge is marked by, and also partly obscured by, a large patch of lantana and scrub.

Waterfall Gorge is perhaps best done in descent, although it can also be used for ascent. To descend this northern gorge, you firstly need to locate the top entrance.

Starting from the top entrance of Palm Gorge, contour northwards for a considerable distance, trying to stay at the same elevation. At one point you should cross either a small gully or a narrow cleft in the rock, depending on your exact route, but eventually your progress will be blocked by the northern gorge. Move uphill until the gorge entrance is found at about 513 941.

For the most part, descent is of the same degree of difficulty as the southern gorge. However, near the bottom, the gorge becomes narrow with smooth slabs on either side and (usually) some small rock pools. At this point there are two options.

Competent scramblers can proceed down through the narrow section to the top of a waterfall some 15m high, which is bypassed by a sloping zigzag ledge on the right (south). This ledge is not difficult but requires a basic level of scrambling ability. The gully then leads out through scrub to the road. Alternatively, an easy exit from the gorge can be found by backtracking a few metres at the crevice before the waterfall, and climbing an obvious slope to the south. From here, the south-east ridge track can be easily reached by contouring.

Scramblers can also ascend the northern gorge by following up the scrubby gully just to the north of the car park, starting at a signposted track several hundred metres up the south-east ridge. On this route the waterfall is bypassed using the ledge previously mentioned. The entrance to the gorge from higher up on the south-east ridge (the easier route previously described) can also be used but is difficult to locate on ascent without prior knowledge of the route. Ascend the south-east ridge for a short distance until above the small scree slope, then contour right. After the gorge stops you from traversing further, climb up again and search for the entrance around some minor rocky outcrops. Once at the top of the northern gorge, you need to contour to the left for a considerable distance to reach the normal route to the summit.

Waterfall Gorge Lookout: This lookout is actually a rocky spur on the north side of the south-east ridge (possibly located at about 516 934). It is a short side trip from the south-east ridge and gives a dramatic view of Waterfall Gorge, although some searching is required to locate it.

MT MOON

National park covers only a small part of this mountain and it is necessary to cross private lands to access the peak. From the bushwalking viewpoint it can be approached from many directions, but unfortunately there is often difficulty in obtaining the co-operation of local landholders when seeking permission to cross their lands.

Mt Moon is a craggy peak where route variations can be made by exploring different gullies and crags, or by taking different gullies to avoid steep sections or scrub. Care should be taken on all trips on the mountain. A moderate degree of experience and judgment is required on most routes, and there is also a considerable loose rock danger in some areas. Unlike most other peaks discussed in this chapter, Mt Moon has few tracks to assist with navigation.

Eastern Route: The main access route at the time of writing is from the east, leaving cars near the floodway at 580 909. Enquire with the QNPWS Ranger at Boonah for details about how to contact the landowner. To climb the peak, walk along an old road which turns off just south of the floodway, then ascend the ridge which starts between the two tributaries at 574 904. It is critical to have a good topographic map and to clearly locate the start of this ascent route, since the ridges on either side of these tributaries lead away from the mountain.

The return trip to the summit takes the best part of a day and is rated about grade 3½. In descent the ridge described above is difficult to locate although alternative descent routes are available further north.

North-West Ridge: If permission from landowners can be gained, it is also possible to climb the peak from the north-west, leaving cars on the Croftby road (see directions on page 233). When using this route, some people scramble across to the saddle near the rocky tooth at 554 899, on the west of the summit before the final climb.

Other Routes: The southern summit can be ascended by its southern and western ridges, although at present it is difficult to obtain permission to cross the relevant private lands.

MINTO CRAGS

Mt Minto, popularly known as the Minto Crags, is a volcanic ring dyke. This string of rocky knolls lies in a semicircular mass just east of Mt Moon. All access to the crag system is across private lands and permission for access may be difficult to obtain. The best place to enquire about the name and address of the landholder is probably the QNPWS ranger at Boonah (although the crags are not in national park). If access is allowed, extreme care must be taken to stay on the property which covers the more northern crags. The southern-most crag lies on a separate property, and in the past the owner has made it very clear that visitors are not tolerated.

The Minto Crags can be traversed in a reasonably easy day trip (3/4 day, grade 21/2 to 31/2 depending on the route). Starting from the road at 599 890, walk firstly to the saddle at 613 886. A fair amount of exploration is required from here on, and care is necessary in places. While the summits of most crags can be traversed, people unused to climbing and scrambling will prefer to walk around the bases of many crags. After traversing in a semicircle to the final crag at 595 900, the road to the south is easily regained.

THE IPSWICH DISTRICT

FLINDERS PEAK

This is the major peak in the Ipswich-Logan region and, although only 679m high, *(Walk* its rocky profile dominates the skyline between Ipswich and Jimboomba. Its *63)* imposing character inspires considerable interest in climbing the mountain. However, it lies almost entirely on private land and permission from the landowner must be obtained to access the peak. Enquire with the QNPWS Ranger at Moggill for details about how to contact the landowner (if this fails, refer to the enquiry procedures in Chapter 2).

The peak is possibly more imposing from a distance than when upon it. There are cleared farmlands around much of its base, lantana on some of the slopes and a communications tower on the summit, so the area is hardly in pristine condition. Nevertheless, the peak gives good views of the Scenic Rim crest to the west, south and south-east, and there are areas of attractive sclerophyll forest on the ascent route. A rocky razorback just before the final summit climb provides additional interest.

Flinders Peak is usually climbed by its north-west ridge, which has only a few minor difficulties (grade 3). Walking along the road from the gate at 788 258, there are two creek crossings in the first few hundred metres. An old road turns off right near the second creek crossing, while the main road turns left and continues up the creek. Possibly the easiest way of accessing the north-west ridge is to follow the old right hand road up the slopes on the southern side of the creek. After a hundred metres, leave the road and ascend to the south-east (it is also possible to continue along this

Sandstone cave at White Rock

old road, which veers left after about 700m and regains the ridge at about 799 248; the cadastral lines marking the road are shown very faintly on the topographic map).

The north-west ridge can also be accessed by ascending south-easterly from the road which proceeds up the creek (refer map). Almost any spur within the first 1 1/2km can be used, although lantana may be encountered on some of the earlier ridges. The spur at 802 254 is an excellent route for both ascent and descent.

N.B. While climbing Flinders Peak is not particularly difficult, the rocky tooth just east of the summit has been the site of a fatal accident and should only be explored by experienced climbers. It is also important not to ascend any of the ridges east of the tributary at 812 254, since these lead onto this tooth.

Nearby Features: Ivorys Rock lies north-west of Flinders Peak at 788 282, and is clearly visible from Mt Flinders Road. Park about 3.8km from the main Boonah road, and approach the Rock initially from the south-west before exploring around the final pinnacle. Other peaks in this area, such as Mts Goolman, Perry and Blaine, can also be explored, but note that much of this region is badly infested with lantana. Access conditions are the same as for Flinders Peak.

WHITE ROCK

(Walk 36) This area is close to Brisbane and provides a variety of easy part day ventures (1/2 to 3/4 day; grade 1 1/2 to 2). Because of the availability of highly detailed maps (1:10 000), the area is also suitable for learning basic navigation skills.

Much of this region was once used for army exercises and live ammunition is still found occasionally. Do not interfere with any old ammunition but report it to the police or army.

To reach White Rock, walk along the road from the car park at 851 385. After crossing under the power lines, you pass through Six Mile Creek Environmental Park - marked as an oddly shaped L-block on the 1:10 000 map. Continue on and cross over a major gravel road at about 853 375 (not marked on the map). This road goes to a quarry just up from the small dam at 865 371.

From the road crossing at 853 375, there are several ways to climb White Rock. Possibly the best is by following the north-west ridge which starts just south-east of the road crossing. Alternatively, cross over the quarry road and continue 800m south along a minor road, then turn left up the valley to the west of White Rock (860 365). A disused vehicular track (one of many in this area not marked on the topographic maps) can be followed to the top of this valley.

The summit of White Rock itself is ascended by a gully on the east and provides interesting views. Probably the most impressive features in the area are the large smooth coloured sandstone cliffs and bluffs surrounding the pinnacle. The cliff on the south-eastern side of White Rock is particularly spectacular. From the knoll at 862 358, 700m to the south-west of White Rock, it is possible to see Mt Lindesay and other peaks of the Scenic Rim.

There are lots of other interesting features in the White Rock region, the area being sandstone and riddled with small caves. There are several caves on the southern side of White Rock's north-west ridge, while the minor knoll just north of this ridge, at 862 369, is riddled with caves on its eastern side.

Woogaroo Creek Environmental Park lies on the rectangular block to the west of Woogaroo Creek at 870 380. From the western corner of Woogaroo Creek Environmental Park, it is possible to follow the power lines back to the car park.

DIRECTORY

QUEENSLAND NATIONAL PARKS AND WILDLIFE SERVICE
Boonah: PO Box 121. Boonah. Q. 4310. Telephone: (074) 63 5041.
Moggill: 55 Priors Pocket Road, Moggill. PO Box 42, Kenmore. Q. 4069. Telephone: (07) 202 0200.

PRIVATE CAMPING GROUNDS
Moogerah Dam: A G Muller Caravan and Camping Area. M.S.F. 461, Kalbar, Q. 4309. Telephone: (074) 63 0141.

Yarramalong Recreational Centre. MS 461, Kalbar. Q. 4309. Telephone: (074) 63 7369.

The Gorge Camping Reserve. Telephone: R. Adams (07) 399 6672.

17

THE GRANITE REGIONS

The granite regions lie slightly to the west of south-east Queensland, but are popular destinations with south-east Queensland bushwalkers. Typically they are rolling areas of open eucalypt forest, dominated by granite domes and balancing rocks. Such topography is most classically represented at Girraween National Park south of Stanthorpe, and at Bald Rock, which is located on the border adjacent to Girraween but is normally accessed from New South Wales. This chapter also describes two nearby areas of lesser granitic character - Sundown National Park south-west of Stanthorpe and the Boonoo Boonoo River in New South Wales (approximate pronunciation "Bunna Boonoo"). All regions are located near the Queensland-New South Wales border.

Most of these regions don't have the same style of jagged relief typical of the Scenic Rim areas to the north-east. In general they offer relatively easy bushwalking without massive ascents and descents, although some remote localities in Sundown are exceptions to this principle. Sundown is dramatically different from all other bushwalking areas near south-east Queensland, with stark hillsides and dramatic red gorges reminiscent of landscapes in central Australia.

For people wishing for a greater insight into the nature and beauty of the granite regions prior to their visit, or wanting to preserve their memories afterwards, Errol Walker's book *Granite Wilderness* is highly recommended. It is an excellent photographic portrait of this natural region.

SPECIAL NOTES

BUSHWALKING CONDITIONS AND HAZARDS

General Terrain: In normal circumstances most of these regions provide reasonably safe bushwalking opportunities. The main hazards to be wary of relate to weather conditions or unusual conditions. Nevertheless some localities still require caution. In particular the more remote parts of Sundown have many rugged localities, with

Left: Granite arhitecture, Sphinx Rock.

extensive cliffs, loose rocks, thick scrub, heat and lack of water combining to cause serious hazards for inexperienced walkers. Even at Girraween and Bald Rock, areas of rugged cliffs and gorges lie among the rolling topography, and many granite slabs are quite precipitous.

Climbing and Scrambling in the granite regions is popular because the granite normally provides very good grip, and it is quite thrilling to dash up the long open slabs and scramble about in the crevices. However, when the rock is wet, much of the granite becomes extremely slippery. This is due to minute algae growing between the tiny out-jutting rock crystals, swelling up to cover the crystals and forming a smooth greasy surface. It is all the more treacherous since it is in such great contrast with its normal character. If rain is approaching or conditions wet, avoid exposed localities.

Navigation may be slightly confusing initially because the granite features often appear rather similar, but you soon learn to differentiate between the landmarks.

Vegetation is predominantly woodland and heath. While most vegetation allows easy walking, there are local patches of thick vegetation in many remote parts of Girraween and Boonoo Boonoo. In the upland regions of Sundown, there are extensive areas of thick scratchy undergrowth which can be very obstructive.

Heat and Cold: All these regions have highly reflective rock and vegetation, and can be very hot and dry in summer. In contrast, at night the areas are often the coldest in Queensland, the frosts being particularly severe in winter. Generally the most pleasant bushwalking times are March to May and August to October, with spring having the additional attractions of wildflower season. However, early winter is the recommended season if throughwalking away from the main river at Sundown, due to this region's particularly hot dry environment. Great care is required if venturing away from the Severn River at other times of year, or even in winter if the year has been dry.

Water can be a problem in very dry seasons, even in the Boonoo Boonoo and Severn Rivers. Both of these rivers contain numerous massive pools, ideal for swimming when the rivers are flowing well, but often rather stagnant in drier times. Check the water situation with the rangers before any trips, since the rainfall patterns some-times differ markedly from those in areas further east.

Lack of water can be a particularly serious problem in the more remote parts of Sundown, particularly in the non-winter months. Considerable caution is necessary if undertaking throughwalks away from the Severn River - see comments above.

Storms: Thunderstorms and hailstorms are frequent in late spring and early summer in all the granite areas, and can be surprisingly ferocious. It is advisable to carry wet and cold weather clothing even in summer. If lightning is threatening, avoid the open slabs and high domes.

FACILITIES AND CAMPING

Base Camping: The Queensland National Parks and Wildlife Service operates an excellent camping ground at Girraween, with good facilities. Booking is essential at holiday times and long weekends. There are also national park camp grounds with more basic facilities at Bald Rock, the southern end of Sundown and the southern end of Boonoo Boonoo. It is advisable to check camping conditions beforehand with the NSW National Parks and Wildlife Service if you intend to visit Bald Rock or Boonoo Boonoo in holiday times.

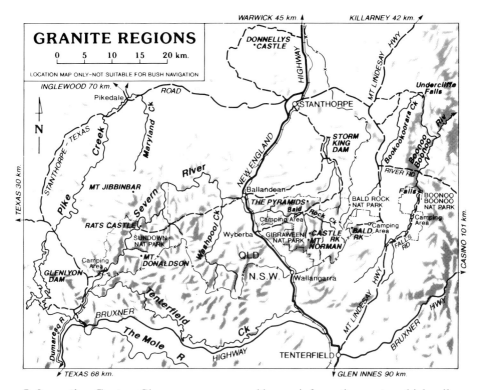

Information Centre: Giraween camp ground has an information centre which sells maps of Girraween and Sundown National Parks.

Throughwalk Camping: There are few camping restrictions for overnight bush-walkers in these areas. However, bush camping is restricted at some localities in Girraween, these mainly being areas close to the walking tracks, roads and official camping and picnic grounds.

BIOLOGICAL FEATURES

For the south-east Queensland botanist, the granite regions hold a special interest. The wet coastal regions have been left behind and you are into the first of the drier plant communities which lie further west. A totally different array of eucalypts inhabit these regions, with colourful spiralled barks and gnarled trunks. There are areas of pink flowering ironbarks and several species of silver-leaved ironbarks. Other plants rare or unknown in south-east Queensland also exist here, and wildflowers are profuse in spring.

Birdwatchers value the areas because of the many birds which don't occur further east. Sundown is particularly notable in this regard, with species such as the red-winged parrot, turquoise parrot and painted honeyeater. Some eastern species also occur at Sundown unexpectedly, such as the satin bower bird, which is normally considered a rainforest species.

While the granite regions are far from their best for recreation in dry conditions, they

243

provide good wildlife watching opportunities since the wildlife concentrates around the waterholes. Sundown and Boonoo Boonoo are particularly notable, and bush-walkers have frequently reported seeing dingoes, quolls, wedge-tailed eagles, water dragons, rock wallabies, platypus, white-winged choughs, lorikeets and many other birds close to the waterholes.

MAPS

Girraween and part of Bald Rock are reasonably well mapped on the QNPWS 1:25 000 map of Girraween, although unfortunately the map lacks both a grid and contours. Minor roads data is also often inaccurate (some minor roads shown are nonexistent), but this is not a serious problem. At Sundown the QNPWS 1:50 000 map is recommended, being much superior to the *Stanthorpe* 1:100 000 topographic sheet. In addition, the NSW 1:50 000 sheet titled *Wallangarra* is useful for Sundown and much of Girraween. For Boonoo Boonoo the best maps are the *Bookookoorara* and *Liston* 1:25 000 sheets (NSW issue), although the *Drake* 1:100 000 sheet may suffice if you only intend trips along the river. The *Bookookoorara* sheet also covers most of Bald Rock National Park, although some areas recently added to the south of the park are covered by the 1:25 000 sheet *Boonoo Boonoo*.

ROAD ACCESS

Girraween: The main camping area and national park office is found by turning east off the highway at the Wyberba turn-off (signposted), about 25km south of Stanthorpe.

A variety of roads exist near Girraween. If you continue eastwards along the road through the park, you will arrive at a junction after about 5km. The main left hand road will take you out of the park towards Storm King Dam and Eukey, while the road on the right (usually called the Mt Norman road) goes back through the park, past Mt Norman, to Wallangarra. The trafficability of this latter road is best checked with the QNPWS before use. It is classified as four wheel drive only, but if trafficable it allows day trip access to many features. A number of other minor roads are marked on the map in this area, but most have been legally closed and are blocked by locked gates. Some are used by the QNPWS for service purposes, and these make good walking tracks, although others are completely overgrown.

Bald Rock: Either follow the Woodenbong road (Mt Lindesay Highway) into New South Wales from Rathdowney (a slow winding route), or take the road to Amosfield which turns off in the northern outskirts of Stanthorpe. The park turn-off is on the right (west) about 22km south of Amosfield (7km south of the Bookookoorara Bridge).

Sundown: To reach the main QNPWS camping grounds, take the road towards Texas from Stanthorpe. Watch out for kangaroos and other wildlife if driving this road at night. After about 34km you will reach a junction where you keep left, and after another 29km another junction where you leave the Texas road, taking the left hand fork towards Glen Lyon Dam. The turn-off to the national park is about 15km south of this latter junction (at 582 993). After the turn-off there is one further Y-junction at which you should take the left hand fork. Do not drive this route without a reasonable supply of petrol.

Alternatively the north-east end of the park can be reached by taking a road west from Ballandean, a town on the New England highway 19km south of Stanthorpe. However, this is not recommended unless you are able to drive the latter part of the very bumpy road in a four wheel drive vehicle, or the weather is cool and you don't mind walking this section. In either event you will need the QNPWS map. The road turns off west at Ballandean and is initially marked "Ballandean Gun Club". After 400m turn left, then drive for about 5km. Turn left into Sundown Road about 600m beyond the end of the bitumen, just after a grid. After another 5 or 6km you will arrive at a deserted farmhouse - the old Sundown homestead. The very bumpy four wheel drive track to Burrows and Reedy Waterholes on the Severn River starts about 100m back up the hill from the farmhouse. There are a number of offshoot tracks from this road and it is not possible to describe them all, but you should be able to solve most difficulties by referring carefully to the QNPWS map and taking careful note of progress and direction. Ensure you have a reasonable petrol supply.

Boonoo Boonoo: The main access is via the Boonoo Boonoo Falls Road (not to be confused with the Boonoo Boonoo River Road). Boonoo Boonoo Falls Road is marked on the east side of the Mt Lindesay Highway about 27km south of Amosfield (5.5km south of Bald Rock National Park). The road and creek crossings have recently been upgraded. It is approximately 9km to the Cypress Rest Area, where basic car camping facilities are provided, and another 4km to the end of the road near Boonoo Boonoo Falls. Enquire with the NSW National Parks and Wildlife Service regarding camping prior to your visit.

The Boonoo Boonoo River can also be reached downstream of the falls by taking the Boonoo Boonoo River Road (signposted) which turns off the highway 11.5km south of Amosfield (3km north of the Bookookoorara Bridge). This is a dry weather only access. Base campers often set up where the road crosses the creek on a rough causeway, although the site is unofficial and has no facilities.

Undercliffe Falls is reached by turning east at Liston just north of Amosfield. Travel 5km to a major road junction, take the left hand fork, and travel another 4 or 5km until you see the falls turn-off marked on the right side of the road (refer to the *Liston* 1:25 000 map). You have to drive through some paddocks here. While people do camp at Undercliffe, the area is very open, has no facilities and is often crowded. It is not highly recommended as a camping area.

GIRRAWEEN NATIONAL PARK

Girraween National Park protects some of the best examples of granite geology in Queensland, with numerous monoliths and balancing rocks, and domed summits flanked by sweeping slabs. Most of Girraween can be adequately covered on day trips from the national park camping area. A number of off-track trips are possible, but first-time visitors are advised to initially explore the many interesting features accessible from the official track system.

OFFICIAL TRACK WALKS

Main Features: First Pyramid, Castle Rock, the Eye-of-the-Needle, Mt Norman, *(Walks* Sphinx Rock, Turtle Rock, Underground Creek, Dr Roberts Waterhole and The *16/17)* Junction can all be reached from the official track system, and provide sufficient scope for several weekends. The walking tracks are relatively safe and easy given common sense and dry rock, although it is necessary to take great care if the rock is wet (see warnings on page 242). If you are especially afraid of heights or have young children, it may be wise to avoid the final climb of Mt Norman (see description below), and possibly also Castle Rock and First Pyramid. Note that the Mt Norman track continues past the peak to picnic grounds on the Mt Norman Road to the south (if you prefer, it is possible to ascend the mountain by following the trail up from the picnic grounds). The Eye-of-the-Needle, an impressive rock structure, lies on the Mt Norman track just north of the summit cliffs.

Mt Norman Summit: There is plenty to see around Mt Norman, and many people visit without undertaking the final summit scramble. Those wishing to climb to the summit will find the ascent route marked by a signpost beside the walking track about 300m south of the Eye-of-the-Needle. This climb requires some previous scrambling experience (about grade 4), and would be dangerous in wet conditions. The first awkward section can actually be bypassed by seeking an alternative route on the other side of the rock, although it is immediately followed by a second more exposed section where it is necessary to scramble around a tree into a wide chimney. A climb up the chimney then leads to the first summit, from where the main summit is easily ascended. The climb becomes easier as you proceed higher.

OFF-TRACK WALKS

The Aztec Temple lies on a hill about 800m directly south of the Underground Creek - simply follow the ridge marked on the map. It has many interesting features, including massive rock formations and some unusual vegetation.

Slip Rock is a large expanse of sloping granite visible north-east of the Pyramids. It gives excellent views of both Pyramids, although the walk requires some cross country navigation skill. It can be reached by walking overland, starting either from Second Pyramid or from a service road which branches off the main road south of Slip Rock.

Billy Goat Hill is the name of the eastern dome near Racecourse Creek on the Mt Norman road. Another granite dome lies just to the west. Both domes are worthy of exploration.

Mt Norman Circuit: Experienced walkers with good navigation skills can make a long day circuit (grade 3 to 31/2) by combining the Mt Norman track with a descent of the tributary of Bald Rock Creek which lies just east of Mt Norman. Initially this tributary is extremely scrubby, but later it provides easy walking along open banks. It joins Bald Rock Creek just downstream of Dr Roberts Waterhole, and just upstream of an impressive set of cascades. From the junction it is best to return to the camp ground either by the walking track to Dr Roberts Waterhole, and then by the road, or by walking cross country to the road a short distance downstream of the cascades. Avoid walking further down Bald Rock Creek since the scrub becomes very thick.

Second Pyramid (grade 51/2) is recommended for experienced scramblers only. It is ascended via a chimney and some exposed slabs on its northern side. It is potentially dangerous, especially for beginners. A rope is recommended, but as there are no anchor points, the rope must be handled by an experienced belayer. The starting point can also be confusing if you don't know the route.

South Bald Rock is reached by firstly driving to the locked gate near the sharp turn on the Mt Norman road, about 1km south of the Paling Yard Creek crossing (refer

QNPWS map). From here follow the old trails marked on the map to a point directly west of the Rock. The Rock is easily ascended from the point where the road crosses the base of the slabs. N.B. The roads in this area can be a little confusing unless you take care with navigation, since not all roads marked on the map are distinct or correctly shown.

West Bald Rock is relatively easy to scale on its western side (grade 2 to 2½), but **Middle Bald Rock** is only recommended for experienced scramblers. It is climbed via a slight zigzag route up a very exposed steep slab on its western side (about grade 5½).

THROUGHWALK ITINERARIES

Throughwalking trips at Girraween can be arranged around the above points of interest, camping near one of the many creeks in the area. It is necessary to enquire with the QNPWS well beforehand since camping may be restricted in some places and seasons. The terrain favours fast travel if you are careful with your navigation. One good throughwalking itinerary proceeds via the Underground River, Aztec *(Walk* Temple, Bald Rock, South Bald Rock, Middle Bald Rock, West Bald Rock and Mt *60)* Norman, all in one weekend. This trip would be rated about grade 4 (or 5½ if Middle Bald Rock is included). South Bald Rock provides an acceptable overnight campsite on this itinerary. Similar trips can be arranged to combine other attractions.

Western Ascent of Bald Rock: Although normally accessed from New South Wales (see below), Bald Rock can also be climbed from Girraween on throughwalking itineraries. It is a reasonably easy ascent from a high point on the border fence service road (between the border trigs marked "55" and "60" on the map). You may have some difficulty negotiating the scrub in the lower section but the upper slabs are fairly easy in dry conditions.

BALD ROCK NATIONAL PARK

Bald Rock is a superb national park providing excellent examples of granite *(Walk* landscapes and vegetation. The rock itself is a massive dome, with two walking *18)* tracks ascending to the summit from the camp ground. Attractively coloured and gnarled eucalypts grow among the boulders and crevices on the rock, while the surrounding forested slopes also have a variety of interesting vegetation features. The park is ideal for a weekend base camp and is suitable for walkers of all levels of experience.

SUNDOWN NATIONAL PARK

Sundown is distinctly different in character from all other bushwalking areas in the broad south-east Queensland region. It has a relatively arid environment, rocky hill sides and dramatic red cliffs reminiscent of features in Central Australia and the Flinders Ranges. Dissecting this landscape is the broad fast-flowing Severn River.

This area has not received the intensive bushwalking exploration that has occurred over many years in other regions, but recent discoveries have revealed a remarkable bushwalking potential. Several trips are truly classic throughwalks comparable to the best walks at Lamington, Mount Barney and the Main Range. However, considerable care is required, since Sundown is a hot glary environment and water is absent in much of the higher country. Some localities could be hazardous to visit except in cool weather, and only then after a rainy season. For this reason early winter is recommended if attempting harder throughwalks, although base camps and easy river throughwalks are enjoyable from April to October. The river can be awkward to cross if the water level is high, and rockhopping can become quite difficult after rain.

A number of old dingo fences cross the park and run along the park boundary. These fences are about 11/2m high and are easily recognised. Since most are marked on the Sundown map, they can be of considerable assistance with navigation. Care should be taken not to damage the circumference fence since it assists in fauna management. The fences inside the park are no longer maintained.

BASE CAMP DAY WALKS

The official national park camping ground in the south provides the main base camping opportunities, although if you can drive into the north of the park by four wheel drive vehicle, it is possible to base camp at either Burrows or Reedy *(Walks* Waterholes or Red Rock Falls. Popular day walks from the southern camp ground *32/33)* include trips along the river, or to features such as McAllisters and Ooline Creeks. Day trips in the north of the park include Rats Castle (680 073), Red Rock Falls (744 081), Red Rock Gorge and the bottom section of Blue Gorge (653 077). All these features are described later in this chapter.

It is also possible to camp at the old Sundown homestead in the park's north. This has two wheel drive access but the only day walk readily accessible would be Red Rock Falls.

THROUGHWALK ITINERARIES

(Walk **Easy Throughwalking Trips** at Sundown tend to concentrate around walking up the *52)* Severn River from the QNPWS camping grounds, to points of interest such as Blue Gorge and Rats Castle. While wading is necessary at most river crossings, it is relatively easy walking in normal conditions, with ample camp sites along all stretches of the river. From the QNPWS camping ground to Rats Castle and return is an easy to moderate weekend walk with packs, or a long day trip for a fast party. A three or four day trip is recommended if you wish to explore the various side gorges of the Severn River. N.B. The river can be awkward to cross if the water level is high, and rockhopping can become quite difficult after rain.

Harder Throughwalks: Numerous possibilities exist, but three classic circuits are described later in this section. The latter two can be combined into one four day circuit:

• Mt Lofty/Red Rock Gorge/Red Rock Falls (2 days, grade 31/2).
• McAllisters Creek/Mt Donaldson (2 days, grade 4 to 41/2).
• Blue Gorge/Ooline Creek (3 days, grade 51/2 to 6).

RATS CASTLE

Despite being dynamited by vandals some years ago, Rats Castle is an interesting feature which can be visited easily in a half day's walk from Burrows Waterhole. It is a high pinnacle on the ridge top, overlooking a particularly dramatic bend in the Severn River. It is best approached from Sundown Creek on its eastern side.

MT LOFTY/RED ROCK FALLS CIRCUIT (2 days, grade 3 1/2)

This makes a good introductory throughwalk, visiting some of the best features in the *(Walk* north of the park. It starts and finishes at Sundown homestead, which has conven- *73)* tional vehicle access. Alternatively, individual features can be explored on day walks.

Mt Lofty: From Sundown homestead, follow the road down across the creek. Continue for about a kilometre to a point at about 764 099, then follow the fence which diverges west towards Mt Lofty. The ascent of Mt Lofty is open walking, and there is a fence junction near the top (743 095). The true summit lies just to the south-west, but offers no views. Some views can be obtained from the top of the cliffs further to the south-west.

From the fence junction (743 095), follow the north-westerly fence for about 800m, then leave the fence and follow the ridge west-north-west to the Severn River. Around July the lower parts of this ridge system produce brilliant displays of wattle flowers. Some sections require careful navigation as the ridge diverges in several places, but once on the hill at 727 103 it is an easy descent to the river. The river can be followed downstream to scattered camp sites below the junction of Red Rock Creek, in the vicinity of Red Rock Waterhole (715 101).

Red Rock Creek: On the second day, follow Red Rock Creek up to the gorge and falls. The rockhop up the creek is usually relatively easy but could be awkward after rain. The water supply in the creek is unreliable above Carpenters Gully, so be sure to carry water if in any doubt. Often the falls are reduced to a soak, but even then the cliff of red granite is an impressive sight.

The falls are climbed by a steep but straightforward scramble which leads up the northern bank. From the top of the falls it is possible to ascend to the road (747 081), from where you can descend via a creek in the north-east back to the Sundown homestead road.

McALLISTERS CREEK/MT DONALDSON CIRCUIT
(2 days, grade 4 to 4 1/2)

This is one of the most impressive walks in the park, with McAllisters Creek *(Walks* displaying spectacular gorges of red rock, and Mt Donaldson providing perhaps the *74/100)* best views in the region. As well as the two day throughwalk, much of McAllisters Creek can be explored on day trips from the QNPWS camp grounds. It is preferable to walk the circuit in an anticlockwise direction, since several waterfalls on McAllisters Creek could prove awkward on descent. These should be the only major difficulties if you follow the correct route.

McAllisters Creek: The McAllisters Creek junction lies across the Broadwater from the main camp ground in the south of the park. If the water level is high, the best place to cross the Severn River is downstream of the Broadwater. McAllisters Creek is usually dry at the junction, but forms rapids and pools higher up (except in very dry seasons).

There are occasional small rapids along McAllisters Creek, but the first major obstacle is Split Rock Falls. It appears possible to climb these falls at several places, but progress is then blocked by a pool and gorge just upstream. Although the latter can sometimes be bypassed on the left, most parties will find it easier to bypass both the falls and the gorge in one long traverse on the right. The bypass route starts by ascending a ridge on the southern bank a few metres below the falls. Climb steeply on loose slopes, taking great care to avoid dislodging rocks, then contour upstream when the ridge starts to level out. Descend back to the creek just upstream of the gorge.

A short distance further on lies Double Falls, situated in a spectacular chasm of red cliffs. These are again bypassed by a route high up on the southern bank. Start the ascent a few metres below the main falls. This bypass is harder than the Split Rock Falls bypass, and extreme care is needed to avoid dislodging loose rocks.

Double Falls to Mt Donaldson: The creek is then followed toward Mount Donaldson. It often flows in spectacular chasms with sheer red cliffs on both sides. You may have to carry water if the higher parts of the creek start to dry up. There is one major fork high up in the creek where it important to follow the left hand branch (679 009). Since the ridges are very scrubby in this area, it is probably best to follow the creek as far as possible, and aim to camp near or upstream of this fork. Mt Donaldson is then climbed early on the second morning. It may also be possible to bivouac near the summit, although the summit offers no comfortable camp sites.

Mount Donaldson Creek: To descend Mount Donaldson Creek, carefully navigate west-south-west from the summit until you meet a gully (don't be tempted to descend Stony Creek since this is strewn with large boulders). The descent along Mount Donaldson Creek is straightforward until progress is obstructed by a massive cliff just after crossing an old dingo fence. Despite the size of this cliff, it is relatively easily bypassed by ascending the right hand (northern) ridge. Here you will again meet the old dingo fence. To return to the camp ground, follow the ridge crest to the Severn River (leaving the fence after a short time). The camp ground lies a couple of hours downstream. Alternatively, if you intend to walk upstream, follow the dingo fence to the Stony Creek junction.

BLUE GORGE/OOLINE CREEK CIRCUIT (3 days, grade 51/2 to 6)

(Walk 100) The lower parts of Blue Gorge provide easy side trips when throughwalking along the Severn River, but at the time of writing few parties have completed the full ascent. Therefore much of the gorge is poorly known, and the information included here is based on a single trip in 1988. As it is further explored, better route information may result in the gorge being given a slightly lower grading, but at this stage it should only be attempted by experienced parties with good navigation and scrambling skills. Some parts of the route are not only quite exposed, but are also easy to lose. There are no tracks to help indicate where obstacles can be bypassed (other than old goat trails, which often meander in any direction), and several creek junctions may cause navigational confusion. The gorge shouldn't be attempted after rain.

Nevertheless Blue Gorge provides a rare opportunity in south-east Queensland - the chance to explore a rugged feature where few have been before. It is probable that there are both easier and harder variations of the following route, with the possibility of other discoveries in some of the side gorges higher up.

Itineraries: Blue Gorge and Ooline Creek can be tackled on a three day trip, the first day being an easy walk up the Severn River. The gorge starts just upstream of Turtle Waterhole, which makes a convenient campsite. Alternatively they can be linked with the McAllisters Creek/Mt Donaldson circuit to make a four day trip, which would surely be regarded as Sundown's premier throughwalk. This extended circuit has the potential to become one of the classic throughwalks in south-east Queensland, although its attractions are quite different to those of the wetter mountain areas elsewhere in the region.

Cliffs in the gorge extend higher up the creek than the national park map indicates. Most parties would require either a light belay rope or pack hauling rope to complete the ascent. It may also be possible to descend the gorge, but obstacles would be unpredictable and abseiling gear (including at least one full length rope) should be carried.

Water: Since the top section of Ooline Creek would be dry in most seasons, water must be carried from either the Severn River or somewhere in Blue Gorge. A dam just outside the park at 616 067 provides a useful emergency water supply.

Ascent of Blue Gorge: There are many small cliffs and waterfalls to negotiate in Blue Gorge, but initially these don't cause significant problems. One waterfall which appears to block the way can be negotiated by a short rockclimb on the right hand (northern) bank, or by a longer bypass downstream - pack hauling may be necessary. The most rugged area lies above the gorge's first junction (650 080), which can be identified by a huge chockstone in the main creek. At this junction it is tempting to take the southern fork, but this is actually a side gorge. The chockstone is bypassed on the left.

Climbing higher up the creek, there are a series of minor obstacles, but eventually you reach a point where a high steep slope on the right is climbed to bypass some waterfalls. This may be unnerving for some people although it is not difficult. The top of this slope provides a superb view back down the gorge.

Later there is a second major junction (647 083), where a side creek drops steeply down the northern bank. Just up from here, the main creek (the southern branch) appears to be blocked by a cliff in a short chasm. This is bypassed by a route high up on the left (southern) bank. Although you descend back into the creek after this traverse, almost immediately there is another traverse on the south bank to bypass a waterfall. This traverse is quite easy, but is longer, higher and more exposed.

The gorge continues for some distance upstream, but at this point it is easy to exit at an obvious place at the top of the traverse. This leads up to the ridge tops near the map spot height "844" (645 079). From here, walk westwards to the national park boundary fence. This section is very scrubby, and navigationally it is harder than it appears from the map. Persevere until you meet the boundary fence.

Boundary Fence: When you reach the park boundary, it is tempting to cross the fence since the scrub appears easier on the other side. However the situation soon reverses, so it is better to stay inside the boundary. Take care not to damage the fence, since it is used for stock and fauna management. The boundary is followed south-westwards for several kilometres, partly with the assistance of an old fire trail.

Descent of Ooline Creek: Descend to Ooline Creek at any convenient point where the map shows it running close to the boundary fence. It is reasonably fast walking along Ooline Creek upstream of the main gorge (marked "numerous falls and cascades" on the map), although navigation is a little confusing. Water is unreliable except after very wet weather. There are several camp sites for small parties.

If conditions are wet or the party wishes to avoid further climbing, it is possible to bypass the gorge on Ooline Creek by a long traverse on the eastern bank, crossing over the head of the side gully at 625 020. Once below the gorge, it is a relatively short walk back to the Broadwater camping ground.

FURTHER EXPLORATION

There are numerous exploratory possibilities at Sundown, and no doubt more features will be discovered with continuing bushwalking exploration. However, some words of caution are required:

• Many smaller creeks are dry except immediately after rain.

• There is some doubt about the water quality of Little Sundown Creek below the old arsenic mine.

• Stony Creek is reportedly potentially dangerous, due to the presence of huge boulders which have fallen from the cliffs of Mt Donaldson.

BOONOO BOONOO REGION

Walking along the Boonoo Boonoo River is open easy going for the most part, with some rockhopping in the upper reaches just downstream from the Boonoo Boonoo Falls. It is ideal country for both easy base camps and lazy mid-season throughwalks. There is an official camping area in the national park above the falls, while throughwalkers will find ample campsites along the length of the river between the falls and the Bookookoorara Creek junction. Some people also base camp at the road crossing midway between the falls and Bookookoorara Creek (201 188), although this is not an official site.

Most of the lower river stretches are on private lands, although to date there do not appear to have been problems of bushwalkers being refused access. The upper section near the falls is mainly in national park and state forest. Enquiries regarding camping permits at Boonoo Boonoo should be made to the NSW National Parks and Wildlife Service at Glen Innes (see Directory).

BASE CAMP DAY WALKS

(Walks 39/40) **From Boonoo Boonoo Falls Region:** Above the falls there is a series of magnificent pools ideal for swimming and liloing. For more energetic activities, rockhops down the river provide some of the most delightful ways to pass the time, or you may prefer to undertake trips to Mt Prentice (155 123) or Hairy Mans Rock (226 135). Both these features offer good views and are relatively easy cross country walks (grade 2 to 21/2), although they require basic navigation skills.

From Boonoo Boonoo River Road: From the road crossing on the river at 201 188, stretches of rapids and large pools are easily accessible, starting about 3km downstream from the crossing and continuing up to the falls themselves. It would be possible to walk to Boonoo Boonoo Falls and back in a long day.

THROUGHWALK ITINERARIES

Walking along the Boonoo Boonoo River is an idyllic delight. While little of it is grandly spectacular country, every bend has a new surprise - rapids, pools, slabs or wide sandy stretches. Campsites abound.

(Walk 56) With a long car shuffle, it is possible to undertake a very easy three or four day throughwalk between Undercliffe and Boonoo Boonoo Falls (grade 3 to 31/2). To reduce the length of the car shuffle, you can leave cars on the highway about 2km south of the Bookookoorara Bridge, and complete the last section of the walk

overland across Mt Prentice. However, it is probably necessary to gain permission to cross the private lands west of Mt Prentice.

From Undercliffe Falls, it is easier to walk to the Boonoo Boonoo River via the ridge just to the east of Bookookoorara Creek, rather than rockhopping down the creek itself. It is possible to glimpse Mt Lindesay in the distance from one part of this ridge (at about 213 257).

RIVER FEATURES

Boonoo Boonoo Falls are some 200m high. From the car park above the falls on the eastern bank, the descent route to the bottom of the falls starts out as a constructed walking track which proceeds down to a lookout. After the lookout, the track gradually becomes a steep but relatively easy scramble, leading down into a tributary about 50m from the main river course.

To ascend Boonoo Boonoo Falls when walking upstream, take a steep but definite track which starts about 50m up the side creek to the east of the falls (on your left as you are looking at the falls). Once you reach the lookout about three quarters of the way up, you can either ascend to the road and car park along the track, or traverse down near the top of the falls and walk up the river again. The latter route passes several magnificent pools.

Rockhopping: In wet conditions, the boulders below the falls can become extremely dangerous. Rockhopping gradually gives way to bank walking about a kilometre downstream.

Navigation at Rocky Island: At Rocky Island (184 170), the creek bed widens out and becomes a series of billabongs and sand bars strewn among the scrub. Take care to follow the correct river course in this region. To avoid any difficulties, stay near the west bank.

DIRECTORY

QUEENSLAND NATIONAL PARKS AND WILDLIFE SERVICE

Girraween:	Wyberba, via Ballandean. Q. 4382. Telephone: (076) 84 5157.
Sundown:	via Glenlyon Dam Road, MS 312, via Stanthorpe. Q. 4380. Telephone: (067) 37 5235.

NSW NATIONAL PARKS AND WILDLIFE SERVICE

Bald Rock &	P.O. Box 281, Glen Innes, NSW. 2370
Boonoo Boonoo:	(404 Grey Street, Glen Innes). Telephone: (067) 32 1177.

18

THE CONONDALE RANGES

Although bushwalking localities in the Sunshine Coast hinterland are not as extensive or numerous as in most other parts in south-east Queensland, there are special scenic and biological features here of immense interest to bushwalkers and naturalists. The most outstanding region is the Conondale Ranges, which lies roughly in the middle of a triangle between Maleny, Kenilworth and Jimna. This is an area of rainforest and eucalypt covered ranges split by delightful cool running creeks and streams. After the southern part of Fraser Island, the Conondale Ranges is the most outstanding natural area in the broad south-east Queensland region that has not been included in the national park estate. The region is extremely valuable biologically, being the habitat for several rare and unusual species of fauna.

The most notable feature in the Conondale Ranges is Booloumba Creek, which has superb waterfalls, gorges and pools only bettered in southern Queensland by creeks at Lamington National Park and nearby areas of the Scenic Rim. However, a number of smaller creeks in the Conondales also have considerable value for bushwalkers and naturalists.

N.B. To the date of writing, several waterfalls in Booloumba Creek have not been given either official or popular names. To avoid confusion in the written route descriptions, this book has applied names to these features, although it may be that other names will be officially adopted in the future.

SPECIAL NOTES

BUSHWALKING CONDITIONS AND HAZARDS

General Terrain: Several graded tracks in the region provide opportunities for short but interesting forest strolls. However, most bushwalking opportunities involve off-track day trips. Rockhopping trips along the creeks are the most popular ventures, although enjoyable bushwalks are also available in other areas.

The region is not of extreme ruggedness, the creeks being the only localities where cliffs are common. In other areas the main bushwalking difficulties result from logging regrowth, which is often both thick and extensive.

Left: Artists Cascades

The Conondale Ranges are crisscrossed with forestry roads, so the area is not normally recommended for throughwalks. In any event, campsites are very rare along the creeks once you venture away from the official camping areas, although it is intended to develop a number of overnight track walks in the region during next few years.

Rockhopping in the creeks requires considerable scrambling agility, although difficulties vary with the conditions and season. While much of Booloumba Creek presents relatively easy rockhopping in drier seasons, it is much harder and more treacherous when the rocks are wet. In particular, the upper section of Booloumba Creek requires frequent scrambling and climbing to negotiate waterfalls and the Booloumba Gorge, and some of these obstacles could be of extreme difficulty if the water level was high or if any other adverse conditions were encountered. An additional hazard is that many slopes beside the creeks are steep and very loose, so that exit from the creeks is sometimes much more difficult than is initially apparent.

It is necessary to swim through one pool to complete the trip through Booloumba Gorge, so large plastic bags will be required to wrap gear if you intend to tackle this particular venture.

Vegetation types include rainforest, wet sclerophyll forest and dry sclerophyll forest. There is widespread lantana infestation and other regrowth throughout the region, so garden gloves and gaiters may be advisable for some off-track trips.

Navigation: When rockhopping, it is recommended that you constantly monitor your progress by correlating creek bends and tributaries with the map. Otherwise it is easy to lose track of your position. Logging regrowth is the other major navigation difficulty in the region, although forestry roads are frequent so it is unlikely that bushwalkers would remain seriously disorientated for very long.

FACILITIES AND CAMPING

The lower part of Booloumba Creek has a system of state forest camping and picnic areas. Four separate areas along the creek are numbered 1 to 4 for easy identification (located between grid references 647 533 and 648 527).

Camping is also possible where the Maleny-Kenilworth road crosses Little Yabba Creek (690 550), and at Charlie Moreland Park (652 558), which lies upstream on Little Yabba Creek (refer to road directions).

Facilities at the camp grounds include barbecues, reticulated water and toilets but do not include showers. However, there are plenty of swimming holes in the creeks.

MAPS

Topographic maps are available from SUNMAP for all areas. The *Kenilworth* 1:50 000 map, and/or the combination of the *Mt Langley* and *Conondale* 1:25 000 sheets, are recommended for bush navigation. In addition, the 1:50 000 sheets of *Jimna, Moore* and *Kilcoy* are useful if travelling further afield.

These maps show good topographic detail, although they do not identify many features which were not well known or had not been developed at the time of their publication e.g. roads, camping facilities and various waterfalls and creek features. For these reasons this chapter provides extensive grid reference information.

ROAD ACCESS

FORESTRY CAMPING AREAS

Booloumba Creek Campsites: Driving from Maleny to Kenilworth, the turn-off to Booloumba Creek is well marked on the left of the road, 13.8km beyond Conondale township and 500m before Little Yabba Creek. From this turn-off, it is about 5km to the four picnic and camping areas, the first area being located at the sharp bend in the creek at 647 533, on the right of the road.

Charlie Moreland Park: A left hand turn just north of Little Yabba Creek (on the main road 500m north of the Booloumba Creek turn-off) leads to Charlie Moreland Park.

FORESTRY ROADS

Most of the forestry roads in this region are shown accurately on the topographic maps, even though the maps fail to name many features. One road not shown on all maps is a more recently developed route approximately connecting the points 607 487 and 616 474 (see comments below). Most of the forestry roads are trafficable by two wheel drive vehicles in dry weather.

Booloumba Falls Car Park: Continuing south along the Booloumba Creek road beyond Camping Areas 3 and 4 (648 527), you climb steeply and then follow the top of a ridge, arriving at a T-junction after about 6.5km (636 476). To reach features in the headwaters of Booloumba Creek, take the right hand road at this T-junction (access to the left hand fork is not permitted). After a further 1.7km, you will reach a sharp left-hand bend (624 486). This is the site of the old Booloumba Falls car park, which is a starting point for some trips. The new car park (622 483) is located about 300m beyond the old site, with a graded track leading to the falls.

Other Forestry Roads: If you continue to drive along the road, a major junction is reached about 3km past the Booloumba Falls car park (616 474). At this point you have the choice of (a) turning right on a relatively new forestry road and crossing over to the Sunday Creek road (597 497), and from there either back to Little Yabba Creek or on to Jimna, or (b) turning left and following various forestry roads to Bellthorpe and eventually out to Woodford and Caboolture. These are two of the more interesting scenic drives in the Conondale Ranges.

EASY WALKS

Mt Allan: From the state forest campsites on Booloumba Creek, it is a quick ascent to the summit of Mt Allan via its eastern ridge (about 2 hours return; grade 2). There is a good track, which is steep in parts but has no major difficulties. The start of the track is signposted in Picnic Area 2 (650 527). The fire tower on the summit of Mt Allan gives good views. *(Walk 26)*

Gold Mine Circuit: This track circuit is about 3km long. The start is signposted in Camping Area 3 (648 527). While primarily an easy stroll with creek and rainforest scenery, it also visits an old gold mine site of some interest.

Booloumba Falls and The Breadknife: An easy and very pleasant walk in the Conondales is the trip to Booloumba Falls, situated above Booloumba Gorge at the junction of Peters and Booloumba Creeks. This locality is also known as "The

Breadknife", the name given to an interesting ridge of rock situated amid the cascades. The site lies only a short distance from the road and is accessible by a graded track from the new Booloumba Falls car park (see previous road directions). An hour is ample for the return trip from the cars, although many will wish to linger longer and take a swim.

A large pool is situated among these cascades and is ideal for swimming, while the nimble can scramble to better vantage points to view the top of the Booloumba Gorge. However, caution is required, and tight control would need to be kept on children, since the rock slopes away awkwardly in many places.

BOOLOUMBA CREEK ROCKHOPPING TRIPS

Various rockhopping trips are possible along Booloumba Creek between the forestry campsite and the area around Booloumba Falls. In good conditions, this part of the creek offers plenty of swimming in idyllic clear green pools, as well as several spectacular waterfalls and an impressive gorge. However, good scrambling skills are necessary to negotiate the upper parts of the creek, and it is necessary to swim through a pool if you wish to complete the full trip through the gorge.

It is useful to consider this stretch of the creek in two sections. The lower section can be regarded as extending from the forestry camping areas upstream to Artists Cascades (about 3km). This section is relatively gentle in gradient and has only occasional small cascades. The upper section, which is much steeper, can be considered to extend from Artists Cascades to Booloumba Falls.

The following descriptions refer to various features along the creek that are not marked on the topographic maps. The grid references for these features, together with several unofficial names adopted by this book, are as follows:

- Booloumba Falls (the Breadknife) - at 622 492, at the junction of Peters and Booloumba Creeks.
- Booloumba Gorge - at 624 491, between Booloumba Falls and Kingfisher Falls.
- Kingfisher Falls (unofficial name) - the main double waterfall on the sharp bend in the creek at 627 490, just downstream of Booloumba Gorge.
- Frog Falls (unofficial name) - the broad 12m waterfall on the bend in the creek at 626 496.
- Artists Cascades (unofficial name) - the picturesque cascades at 628 497.

SUGGESTED ITINERARIES

The area is mainly suitable for day trips since there are virtually no campsites on the creek between the forestry campsite and Booloumba Falls. Note that there are only a few routes recommended for access to and exit from the creek (see "Access Routes" on page 259).

Itineraries from Forestry Campsite: The longest itineraries involve rockhopping up from the forestry campsite. There are three main options: (a) exiting from the creek at Frog Falls, which provides a relatively easy trip; (b) exiting from the creek just below Kingfisher Falls and walking up a steep ridge to the old Booloumba Falls car park; and (c) rockhopping the full distance to Booloumba Falls, which involves considerable scrambling and an obligatory swim through the gorge. All these routes are described later.

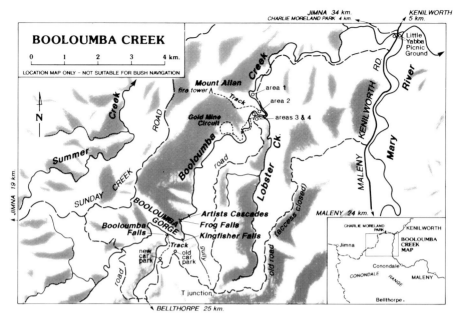

BOOLOUMBA CREEK

0   1   2   3   4 km.

LOCATION MAP ONLY - NOT SUITABLE FOR BUSH NAVIGATION

JIMNA 34 km.
CHARLIE MORELAND PARK 4 km.
KENILWORTH 5 km.

Little Yabba Picnic Ground

N

JIMNA 19 km.

Mount Allen fire tower

Gold Mine Circuit

area 1
area 2
areas 3 & 4

Summer

SUNDAY

Artists Cascades
Booloumba Falls
Frog Falls
Kingfisher Falls

MALENY 24 km.

new car park
old car park

Track
Gully

T junction

BELLTHORPE 25 km.

CHARLIE MORELAND PARK
KENILWORTH
BOOLOUMBA CREEK MAP
Jimna
Conondale
CONONDALE
MALENY
Bellthorpe

In all cases, it is necessary to either arrange a car shuttle beforehand or walk back to the camping grounds along the forestry roads (approximately 81/2km of road walking from the old Booloumba Falls car park site). The full circuit up to Booloumba Falls and walking back along the roads is a long day trip even for fit parties, and should only be attempted in good rockhopping conditions.

Itineraries from Booloumba Falls: Alternatively, it is possible to make a number of convenient circuits visiting only the upper section of the creek, leaving cars near Booloumba Falls and starting and finishing the walk at the same place. One popular option is to descend to the creek at Frog Falls and then scramble up through the gorge to Booloumba Falls. However, if you wish the gorge can be omitted, and you can both descend to the creek and return to the cars by the Frog and Kingfisher Falls routes. These routes are described below. *(Walk 85)*

Grading: In normal conditions, most of these trips would be rated around grade 31/2 to 41/2, depending on the exact itinerary, water level and the wetness of the rocks.

ACCESS ROUTES

Only a few points are recommended for starting and finishing trips on Booloumba Creek (other routes are possible but are unpredictable due to loose slopes and lantana). It is useful to note these routes because many of the slopes around the creek are more difficult to ascend than they appear, and problems could arise if a party needed to exit from the creek and underestimated the rough terrain. The main access and exit points are:

Forestry Campsite: This involves rockhopping upstream from Camping Area 3. Full details are given in the description of the lower section of the creek (see over page).

Frog Falls Route: This is mainly used as an access route when doing circuit trips in

259

the upper section of the creek, although it is also useful as an exit route, especially when walking upstream from the forestry campsite. To descend to the creek, follow the road directions to the old Booloumba Falls car park (624 486). From here, walk back up the road (eastwards) for about 100m and locate an old forestry track branching off to the north. Follow this down the ridge to the north-east (628 488). At about 630 489, both the ridge line and the main forestry track end at a steep slope. There may be a vague remnant of a track descending to the right, but if you stay on a minor crest on the left it is possible to descend without major difficulty for another 50m or so, before veering right into a gully (630 491). If you wish, you can descend down this gully to meet Booloumba Creek just downstream of Kingfisher Falls, but with a little searching you should be able to locate a partly constructed track on the opposite bank of the gully. This provides an easier route, crossing onto the ridge at 628 495 and zigzagging down to the top of Frog Falls (626 496). The track may be overgrown in places although it is not normally too difficult to follow.

In ascent, the exit route from the creek will be found on the eastern bank at the top of Frog Falls. The track can either be followed back to the old car park site, or if you wish you can leave the track where it starts to contour, climbing directly up the ridge to the forestry road at 637 493. The latter route is shorter if you intend walking back to the forestry campsite along the road, although some patches of lantana may be encountered.

Kingfisher Falls Routes: The gully route just described can be used to ascend or descend from just downstream of Kingfisher Falls. It is also possible for small parties to ascend the steep south-eastern slope above Kingfisher Falls. Considerable care is needed due to the loose nature of these slopes, and it should not be used for descent. The slopes eventually lead up to the old forestry track previously described (628 488). To use this route, you firstly need to climb around the bottom section of the waterfall to a small rocky outcrop overlooking the middle of the falls. For details of the route around the waterfall, refer to the description of Kingfisher Falls in the next subsection.

Booloumba Falls/Gorge Route: This route involves difficult scrambling in the gorge below the Breadknife. Full details are given in the next subsection.

CREEK FEATURES

Lower Section: To commence trips up the creek from the forestry camping area, start out by following the Gold Mine Circuit from Camping Area 3. Walk to the track junction on the upper part of the track (642 520), and then start following the creek upstream.

There is sometimes thick lantana on the banks in this area, so some wading may be necessary. This section of the creek is not recommended if you can't stand soggy boots (although at the time of writing most of the lantana near the creek has been cleared out by flood waters).

There are several sharp bends along this lower stretch which can help you monitor your progress. The best creek scenery begins about an hour upstream, and it gradually becomes more spectacular as you approach Artists Cascades.

If necessary, it is possible to exit from this section of the creek by climbing any of the spurs on the east bank. These eventually lead up to the forestry road. However, many of these spurs are unpredictable due to lantana and steep slopes, so normally it is best to exit using one of the routes further upstream.

Booloumba Gorge

Frog Falls and Artists Cascades: This part of the creek is a delight, with numerous small clear pools ideal for quick dips on a hot day. If you are accessing the upper creek using the track to Frog Falls, Artists Cascades are well worth a side trip, being found about 20 minutes downstream. There are no major obstacles. Frog Falls can be readily bypassed by an easy scramble on the eastern bank.

Kingfisher Falls: When travelling upstream, the scrambling difficulty increases significantly when you meet the main double waterfall just downstream of Booloumba Gorge (627 490), referred to here as Kingfisher Falls.

To negotiate the lower part of the waterfall when rockhopping upstream, climb the slippery grassy slope on the left, then contour across to a small rocky outcrop overlooking the middle of the waterfall. Considerable care is needed due to the loose nature of this slope. It should only be attempted by small parties.

If you wish, you can exit at this point by climbing up to the south-east, as previously described. To proceed on to the gorge, climb down to the middle of the waterfall, then cross the creek and climb the upper section by some slabs and ledges on the opposite bank. This is not too difficult in normal conditions, although it should not be attempted if the water level is high. From the top of the falls, a short section of rockhopping will take you to the start of Booloumba Gorge.

Booloumba Gorge: To negotiate the gorge, you need to swim through the first pool, so an air bed or several large plastic bags will be necessary to float gear. At the top of this pool, there is a small waterfall to climb. Shortly after this waterfall lies the major pool of the gorge, seemingly blocked at its upper end by two massive boulders jammed in the gorge.

The larger pool is bypassed by a scramble on the right hand (northern) bank. For details of the route, it is most appropriate to refer to the description supplied by Ross Scott of Kenilworth, who seems to capture the true essence of the adventure: "On the right hand side of the deep pool below the two rocks jammed in the gorge, are a few Piccabeen palms. Scramble up the sloping rock behind the palms and do the goanna glide under a tangle of vines and bushes. Go down the other side and onto a log which bridges a gap and then up two more huge boulders which have plenty of hand holds and you are then on the northern side of the Breadknife and the rest is easy". This description is accurate, although note that reasonable scrambling skill is required to climb the "two huge boulders". N.B. The log has since been washed away in the 1989 floods, but this causes no real difficulty.

Once above the "two huge boulders", rockhop around the west side of the Breadknife, then ascend to the Booloumba Falls Lookout. From here, either follow the graded track back to the new car park, or ascend the ridge directly above the graded track to the old car park.

Descent into Booloumba Gorge: It is possible to climb down through Booloumba Gorge, although the descent route is more difficult than the ascent and should definitely only be tackled by competent scramblers. From Booloumba Falls, walk up Peters Creek for 50m or so, until you can make your way around on the north of the Breadknife. From here, descend by following the reverse of the gorge route just described.

OTHER TRIPS

Other good creek trips in this region include Summer, Tragedy, Lobster, Peters and Bundaroo Creeks. Summer, Tragedy and Lobster Creeks contain many falls and cascades although they only have part of the water volume of Booloumba Creek. Summer and Lobster Creeks, located at 610 546 and 650 510 respectively, can be explored for most of their lengths on circuit walks by using forestry roads to access their headwaters. Tragedy Creek is usually done as a return walk from the road at 622 436. Peters and Bundaroo Creeks can be done in a circuit from the Breadknife, using the road which traverses the ridge between the creeks to complete the circuit. They are very pretty in sections. The road crosses the creeks at the approximate locations 607 488 and 614 472.

DIRECTORY

FORESTRY OFFICE
Kenilworth: P.O. Box 52, Kenilworth. Q. 4574. Telephone: (074) 46 0925

19

THE GLASS HOUSE MOUNTAINS

The Glass House Mountains are among the most memorable landmarks in south-east Queensland. They present dramatic profiles, rising abruptly from the flat coastal plain and clearly visible from the Bruce Highway just north of Brisbane. For this reason the peaks are popular for bushwalking and climbing.

To be fair to other bushwalking regions, the mountains appear far more striking from a distance than when upon them. All the national parks are tiny and the views from the summits are largely of pineapple farms and exotic pine forests. The highest summit is 556m, which is only about half the elevation of the high peaks around the Scenic Rim. Despite this, the mountains have a spectacular appeal. Many also have distinctive features e.g. Mt Tibrogargan has caves on its sheer eastern face which give it a resemblance to a human face with craggy eyebrows, while Mt Coonowrin has a distinctive leaning pinnacle that has earned it the nickname "Crookneck". A number of endemic plants add further interest to the peaks.

This chapter describes the three "major" peaks and the five "minor" peaks which provide the main bushwalking and climbing opportunities in the Glass House Mountains. Experienced energetic bushwalking parties have sometimes been known to climb all or most of these eight peaks in a weekend. Four of the peaks are included in national parks, while the remainder are mostly in state forest. N.B. From the geological perspective, many of the surrounding hills can also be regarded to be among the Glass House "mountains".

SPECIAL NOTES

BUSHWALKING CONDITIONS AND HAZARDS

General Terrain: The routes described here are the easiest ascent routes for each peak. The five minor peaks provide relatively easy ventures (mostly between grade 1 and 2), and are interesting and attractive walks despite their low height. While the three major summits (Beerwah, Tibrogargan and Coonowrin) are all potentially dangerous if caution is not exercised, only Coonowrin requires a notable level of technical climbing skill. Both Beerwah and Tibrogargan can be considered to be of intermediate bushwalking difficulty, but note the warnings which follow about the dangers on these peaks.

Left: Mts Beerwah and Coonowrin from Wild Horse Mountain.

Hazards: Overconfidence is probably the greatest hazard, since the dramatic nature of the peaks makes it easy to overlook dangers. This is particularly the case at Mts Beerwah and Tibrogargan, which are popular with tourists and novice bushwalkers. Although these peaks are not of great difficulty on a bushwalker's "scale of things", it is often necessary to scramble on sloping rock overlooking cliffs, a circumstance where carelessness can lead to disaster. There have been a number of fatal accidents on all the major peaks. Some scrambling experience is recommended and caution is required at all times.

Wet rock has also contributed to several serious accidents. All the major peaks should be avoided in wet conditions since the rock becomes quite greasy when wet.

Loose stones are common on most peaks and there is a major erosion problem on the main tracks. The route on Mt Tibrogargan is particularly dangerous since falling rocks are funnelled directly down the track.

Rockclimbing and Exploratory Routes: The three main peaks are popular rock-climbing areas and there are many harder routes than those described here. However, **novices should refrain from exploring unknown routes**, since this has been one of the major causes of fatal accidents. Neither are the Glass House Mountains recommended as sites for learning rockclimbing techniques. The rock here is typically smooth, and the absence of fissures means that a good knowledge of anchoring techniques is necessary to climb safely. Novice rockclimbers are advised to learn their skills at places such as Frog Buttress (near Boonah), in the company of experienced climbers.

Water: Carry all necessary water supplies. There is no water on any of the peaks and water from the creeks in the region is not recommended due to the prevalence of pesticide spraying.

Access to State Forest Areas: Access is freely allowed to Mt Beerburrum. For Mts Tunbubudla and Tibberoowuccum, telephone the Beerburrum Forestry Office before your visit to check if a permit is required.

FACILITIES AND CAMPING

There are two commercial caravan and camping parks close to the mountains (see Directory). In addition, there is a State Forest campsite at Coochin Creek near Pumicestone Passage (see road directions given later). Coochin Creek is brackish at the campsite but a small water tank has been provided. It is good site for canoeing trips on Pumicestone Passage as well as for trips to the Glass House Mountains.

National park picnic areas with toilet facilities are located at Mts Beerwah and Tibrogargan (camping is not permitted in these picnic areas). Mt Ngungun and Coonowrin National Parks have marked parking areas. The other peaks are mainly undeveloped state forest lands.

ENVIRONMENTAL AND SCIENTIFIC FEATURES

All the Glass House Mountains are old volcanic plugs. From the biological perspective, the main ti-tree species in the region (*Leptospermum luehmannii*, commonly called the Ngungun may bush) is noteworthy. This species, endemic to the Glass House Mountains, has become a popular garden specimen due to its attractively spiralled and gnarled trunks. It flowers about January, the population on the Ngungun plateau providing a particularly beautiful floral display.

The normal range of bushwalking environmental ethics apply with regard to litter and the like. As the areas are heavily used, additional effort is needed to avoid causing vegetation damage and erosion. Care is required with fire throughout the area.

MAPS

The *Woodford* 1:50 000 topographic sheet covers all the peaks, while the *Glass House Mountains* 1:25 000 sheet covers all peaks except Mt Coochin. The latter map is useful for navigation on Tibberoowuccum and Tunbubudla, and both maps give excellent outlines of the roads, creeks and other topographic features of the region as a whole. In other respects the maps are only of minor use for bushwalking navigation, since most peaks are simply too small for the maps to show much detail.

ROAD ACCESS

Road access is from Glass House Mountains Road (the old highway), usually radiating from Glass House and Beerburrum townships (refer locality map). Specific directions to individual peaks are given later in this chapter.

To find the Forestry Department campsite on Coochin Creek from the Glass House region, turn east off the new highway 2km north of Coochin Creek bridge into Roys Road. Drive along Roys Road for 5km, where a sign will direct you to the campsite along a side road on the right. This campsite is not far from Pumicestone Passage and Coochin Creek is quite broad here, so it is a good spot for canoeing and fishing. Coochin Creek is brackish at the campsite but a small water tank has been provided.

Alternatively, the Coochin Creek campsite can be found from the old highway by turning east just south of Beerwah township into Roys Road. After a short distance, the road splits into three. Keep left here and follow the predominantly bitumen road for 6km to the new highway. Carefully cross the highway and then follow the directions above.

THE MINOR PEAKS

Most of the five "minor" peaks are relatively easy walks which take between 1 and 3 hours. Although there are a few places where you walk close to cliff edges, you can avoid most dangerous locations using normal care and commonsense. Care needs to be taken not to dislodge rocks as much of the terrain is steep and loose.

MT BEERBURRUM (280m; grade 1/2; 30 to 45 minutes return)

The easiest of the eight main peaks, Mt Beerburrum has a state forest fire tower on the summit and overlooks Beerburrum township. The short ascent track is easily followed, starting from a picnic area located at the foot of the mountain. This is reached by turning off west just south of the township (a short distance north of the junction of the Woodford Road).

MT NGUNGUN (253m; grade 11/2; 1 to 2 hours return)

(Walk 25) This is a delightful mountain just west of Glass House township. From the town, drive south-west, turning right into Fullertons Road after about a kilometre. After a further 1.4km a road turns off right, leading to a car park on the south of the mountain. The peak is easily scaled by a track which leads up a gully from the car park. There is a plateau near the summit which has a profuse stand of *Leptospermum luehmannii*, providing a floral delight in the summer flowering season. National park covers 49ha of the mountain.

MT COOCHIN (240m; grade 11/2; 1 to 2 hours return)

This small twin peak lies north of Ngungun beside Old Gympie Road. It can be climbed via any of the ridges which don't require access across private property, the easiest being from an obvious spot on the road in the west.

TUNBUBUDLA (The Twins - 296m and 338m; 11/2 to 3 hours return)

This twin summit is the hardest of the Glass House Mountains "minor" peaks and has the potential to present some danger to inexperienced parties. It is reached by driving west of Mt Beerburrum along the Beerburrum-Woodford road (refer locality map). There are no tracks and a topographic map is recommended when exploring the mountain. The main east peak is relatively easy to ascend and descend by either its northern or eastern ridges (grade 2). However the route down from the east peak to the saddle is only suitable for small agile parties, since it is steep and extremely loose. The west peak is somewhat harder (grade 31/2+, depending on the route) and should only be attempted by experienced scramblers. It can be climbed from the west with some difficulty, or from the saddle via a cliff break on the southern side. If descending from the west peak to the saddle, contour right (south) when cliffs are apparent, descending in a spiral clockwise course to the southern cliff break. The descent from the saddle to the road is a pleasant stroll through open forest. *(Walk 29)*

MT TIBBEROOWUCCUM (220m; grade 11/2 to 2; 1 to 2 hours return)

This peak lies just west of Tibrogargan. There are cliffs on the eastern face but it can be easily climbed from the west, beginning on the fire trail which starts on the corner of Old Gympie and Marsh roads. This junction can be reached by turning west off the old Bruce Highway 3km north of Flinders Park, and following Barrs and McBride Roads beyond Mt Tibrogargan into Marsh Road. Alternatively, drive north from Tunbubudla along Old Gympie Road for about 3km. The fire trail passes through pine forest before reaching the mountain's western slopes, which can be climbed at any point. At the eastern end of the mountain, just before the summit, the ridge forms into an interesting but relatively easy razorback. A topographic map is recommended when exploring this mountain. *(Walk 27)*

THE MAJOR PEAKS

The three highest peaks are distinctly harder than most of the smaller mountains. While good technical climbing skills are only required on Mt Coonowrin, all peaks can be dangerous. Tibrogargan and Beerwah are not difficult on an experienced bushwalker's "scale of things", but it is often necessary to scramble on sloping rock overlooking cliffs, a circumstance when any overconfidence or foolishness can lead to disaster. There have been a number of fatal accidents on all the peaks. Some scrambling experience is recommended and caution is required at all times.

A rope and good rope skills are considered necessary on Coonowrin, and descents on all routes are more difficult than the corresponding ascents. **Avoid all peaks in wet weather.**

MT BEERWAH (556m; grade 21/2 to 3; 3 hours return)

This is the highest and most imposing of the Glass House Mountains. Drive west from Glass House township for 4km along Coonowrin Road, turn left into Old Gympie Road, then drive 400m and turn right. From here a predominantly sign-posted route leads between Mts Beerwah and Coonowrin and eventually terminates at a picnic ground just north of Mt Beerwah. Ignore roads to the left if not signposted. Walk up the track to the beginning of the slabs, which can be scaled either directly *(Walk 28)* or by an easier route up a gully on the left. An obvious route leads up to the base of the northern cliffs. From here turn right and follow the track up and around the mountain's western shoulder. Care is required on descent. The size of the national park is 245ha.

MT TIBROGARGAN (364m; grade 3 to 3 1/2; about 2 hours return)

From the old highway, turn west into Barrs Road 3km north of Flinders Park. Drive 2 1/2km to the Tibrogargan National Park picnic area on the west of the mountain (940 216). A track leads up the western ridge to the summit. The first 20m of the cliffs is awkward and can prove difficult for inexperienced scramblers, but after that the deeply eroded track is not technically difficult. However, **extreme caution is required to avoid dislodging loose rocks**, since any rockfall will be funnelled down along the track. The size of the national park is 291ha.

MT COONOWRIN (Crookneck, 377m, grade 5 1/2 to 6)

This peak should only be attempted by experienced and capable climbers. A belay rope is recommended, at least until above Salmons Leap. Follow Fullertons Road west from Glass House township, leaving Ngungun just to the north, until Old Gympie Road is reached. Cross over and continue along Fullertons Road, past a farmhouse, to the end of the road. From here a track leads uphill, curving left and climbing steeply to the base of the cliffs on the south of the peak. The route then proceeds up a steepish slab after which it turns left across to Salmons Leap (named after Bert Salmon, a well-known bushwalker and climber very active some decades ago). This traverse, as the name implies, involves a long step, and is recognised by a piton anchor in a hole and a boulder that leans out from the cliff-face. Above Salmons Leap, the going becomes easier, although care must still be taken. While most of the route is well worn by the marks of previous climbers, it is still possible to diverge from the route in several places. The size of the national park is 113ha.

DIRECTORY

QUEENSLAND NATIONAL PARKS AND WILDLIFE SERVICE
Beerwah: Roys Road, Beerwah. Q. 4519. Telephone: (074) 94 6630.

FORESTRY OFFICE
Beerburrum: c/o Post Office, Beerburrum. Q. 4517. Telephone: (074) 96 0166.

PRIVATE CAMPING GROUNDS
Mt Tibrogargan Relaxapark: Glass House Mountains Road, Beerburrum. Q. 4517. (Located on the old highway, about 1 1/2km north of the Beerburrum township turn-off and a few hundred metres south of Flinders Park, on the opposite side of the road - refer locality map). Telephone: (074) 96 0151.

Log Cabin Caravan Park: Glass House Mountains Road, Glass House Mountains. Q. 4518. (Located on the old highway, about 1km south of Glass House Mountains township, on the opposite side of the road - refer locality map). Telephone: (074) 96 9338.

20

THE COASTAL SANDMASSES

Brisbane probably has a greater variety of bushwalking landscapes within easy reach than any other capital city in Australia. Rainforests, rugged mountain terrains, spectacular granite features, deep wet canyons and stark arid vistas provide some of the major contrasts. However, the variation of landscapes could not be displayed more dramatically than by the unique and stunningly beautiful scenery of the coastal sandmasses.

South Queensland has five major sandmasses formed from the northward drift of sand from the northern New South Wales river systems. These are Fraser Island, Cooloola, Bribie Island, Moreton Island and the Stradbroke Islands. Of these, Fraser Island, Cooloola and Moreton Island provide the main bushwalking opportunities.

In favourable conditions, the beauty of many features in these coastal regions is almost beyond belief. While all areas have high levels of visitation which robs them of some (but not all) of their wilderness qualities, their natural scenic values are outstanding. If you make a special effort to explore some of the most beautiful locations in reasonable quiet and privacy, it soon becomes evident that the scenery is equal to that in Australia's major world heritage areas, including famous bushwalking localities such as south-west Tasmania.

Dawn and dusk are among the best times in these regions. Photographers who stroll around some of Fraser Island's lakes in the low early morning light are often greeted by stunning reflections in the calm quiet waters. If you canoe at sunrise on the placid Noosa River, you can paddle peacefully under spreading melaleuca branches in almost perfect silence, without even the disturbance of the wind's whisper. Swimming quietly in the early morning at a secluded lake, you will feel invigorated and enlivened by the cool touch of the water on your skin. On the beaches, dawn brings vibrant richness to the coloured sands. Nothing compares with these experiences.

Despite the large numbers of people who visit these regions, it is possible to organise many enjoyable bushwalking trips, including trips where you can experience some of the most beautiful localities in peace and solitude. Improvements in visitor management may also reduce the occurrence of overcrowding in the future. However, because of the heavy usage, you need to make special efforts to use minimum impact bushwalking practices, not only to reduce your own effect on the environment but also to set an example to others.

Some information in this chapter is of a more general nature than in other chapters in this book, particularly with regard to road access and some of the more unusual bushwalking routes. *Bushpeople Publications* is intending to pub-
* lish a full visitor guide to the coastal sandmasses in August 1991, with details on a wide range of visitor activities as well as additional bushwalking information (see inside back cover).

SPECIAL NOTES

BUSHWALKING CONDITIONS AND HAZARDS

Bushwalking in Sand Regions differs considerably from walking in other terrains. You do not have to contend with cliffs or scrambling obstacles and the hills aren't as steep or as frequent as in other regions discussed in this book. However, there is a variety of more subtle difficulties which can prove quite demanding if you are unprepared for them. In particular note that bushwalking on sand can be very hard on the feet, partly because you tend to cover relatively long distances and partly because the loose nature of the sand causes increased rubbing inside your footwear. Reasonably good footwear is recommended for longer walks and some people find that a high ankle line is advantageous to keep out sand. The type of walking also stresses different muscles than walking in terrains with firm soil underfoot. Walking rates are slower, depending to some degree on whether you are in inland areas or on beach sand. Walking in dry loose sand, or along the beach at high tide, is very slow and tiring and requires good fitness.

Vegetation: Most of the walks described here are either on well-used tracks or in reasonably open vegetation. A considerable number of off-track walks are also possible, but you need to be wary of the nature of the vegetation and take special care with route planning. While some coastal vegetation allows easy walking, some areas are horrendously dense. The worst vegetation types are probably those heath communities where the plants become bound together by dodder vine. In these areas, bushwalking travel can sometimes be slowed to less than 500m/hour. There are few things more painful than forcing a path through scratchy heath with sunburnt legs, and it is wise to carry long pants and long sleeved shirts. The thickness of the heath varies with recent bushfire history.

Navigation: Navigation can sometimes be confusing in coastal landscapes due to the similarity of the landmarks, the density of the vegetation and the difficulty of estimating walking rates. Some areas also have mazes of old roads which are not marked on the available maps. It is useful to note that the interior sand dunes tend to lie roughly parallel in a south-east to north-west orientation, reflecting the prevailing winds.

* *see changes on*
  inside back cover.

Water: Although water is plentiful in most areas, don't assume this is the case everywhere. Parts of the north of Fraser Island, the central-southern section of Moreton Island, and even parts of Cooloola, are largely devoid of surface water except in very wet seasons. Check your map.

Water in the sand areas is normally reddish-brown, the colour of weak black tea. This is caused by tannins from the surrounding heath vegetation and is not harmful. However, some of the water may smell a little in swampy areas. It is best to avoid this since it indicates lack of aeration.

Heat and Sunburn: Despite the large number of visitors who flock to Australia's coastline during the summer heat, these regions are probably at their best in winter, especially for bushwalking and photography. Heat, glare and sunburn can be extreme in all regions during summer, due to the open nature of the vegetation and the reflective environment. In addition, summer is the peak time for flies and insects. Even in winter, you always need to ensure you have plenty of sunscreen and a good hat. Winter is the best time for photography due to the lower angle of the light.

Swamps are a major feature of these coastal regions and can present major difficulties for off-track bushwalkers. Always plan your walks carefully in wetland areas. Most swamps are adequately marked on the relevant topographic maps.

Fauna Hazards: Despite some people's belief to the contrary, snakes occur in all regions. However, snake bite incidents are extremely rare. The most common fauna hazards are mosquitoes and sand flies, and fine mesh mosquito nets are recommended in all areas. There are also various types of bush rats which occasionally chew holes in tents and equipment in search of food, especially if items are not packed up at night. At Moreton Island and Cooloola, wild pigs are sometimes encountered, although it is unlikely that they would ever be a threat to humans. Wild horses occur in all areas and have caused a number of serious injuries to people who have become too inquisitive. It is important not to feed any wildlife, especially dingoes and brumbies.

Camping: You need to be prepared for rainy conditions, and sometimes unexpected storms occur at night. It is also often windy, and normal tent pegs will be inadequate if you intend camping on sites where the sand is particularly loose e.g. many beach camp sites. Peg length is more important than width for obtaining good anchorage, since extra long pegs are able to reach down into the firmer wetter sands.

Not everyone favours camping in sand conditions. You need to be mentally prepared for the sand "getting into everything", and a gradual introduction to sand camping is often better than immediately setting off on an extended holiday. Throughwalkers often carry a rag to sweep out tents (an old cloth hat can double for this purpose).

FACILITIES AND CAMPING

Always enquire with the relevant national park offices for latest details of camping localities, facilities and conditions. In most areas it is essential to book sites on long weekends and school holidays, and booking may also be necessary at other times.

Fraser Island: Fraser Island is the most populated of the three sandmasses discussed in this chapter, with considerable tourist development. The island has settlements and shops at four main locations along the east coast - Eurong, Happy Valley, Cathedral Beach and Orchid Beach. These sell petrol, groceries and various services. Naturally there is a limit to the range of stock and prices are somewhat higher than on the mainland. There are resorts and/or rental accommodation at all of these locations.

There are six major camp grounds with facilities. In the southern lakes region, three state forest camp grounds are located at Lake Boomanjin, Central Station and Lake McKenzie. The standard of facilities is generally toilets, cold showers and reticulated water. In the north, there are national park camp grounds at Dundubara (east of Lake Bowarrady) and Waddy Point on the eastern beach and Wathumba on the west coast. Facilities include toilets, hot showers, reticulated water and supplied firewood. Bush camping is allowed along much of the beach and in some inland areas, but not within 200m of any lakes. In addition, there is a hiker's camp with basic facilities at Lake Allom, inland from Cathedral Beach.

Cooloola: The only facilities within Cooloola National Park are the various camp grounds described below. However, adjacent to the park in the north, Rainbow Beach township has the normal range of shops and facilities that would be expected in a small seaside town.

Cooloola has three main camp grounds operated by the Queensland National Parks and Wildlife Service, at Freshwater and Double Island Point in the north and at Harrys Hut on the Noosa River in the south. The standard of facilities is generally marked sites and toilets, although Freshwater (the largest camp ground) is provided with hot showers. You need to carry your own drinking water if staying at the Double Island Point camp site. There is also a privately operated camp ground within the national park at Elanda Point on Lake Cootharaba. In addition, the Noosa North Shore region has several commercial camp grounds on the outskirts of the national park (see Directory), and Rainbow Beach township has two caravan parks.

Bush camping is regulated along the Noosa River, where camping is restricted to Fig Tree Point and ten sites upstream from Harrys Hut, and on the Cooloola Wilderness Trail. Other beach and bush camping is allowed in specified areas.

Moreton Island: The island has three main settlements, all on its west coast. These are Kooringal in the far south, and Cowan Cowan and Bulwer towards the north. All are relatively small quiet communities. Both Kooringal and Bulwer have small shops, but the range of supplies is limited. In addition, Tangalooma tourist resort is located midway along the west coast, and at the time of writing there is a small community of squatter's dwellings at North Point in the island's north-east (the future of these dwellings is uncertain).

There are three national park camp grounds in the central and northern parts of the island. These are Ben-ewa, just north of Tangalooma on the west coast, and Eagers Swamp and Blue Lagoon on the east coast. The general standard of facilities is marked sites, toilets and cold showers. Another camp ground may be developed at North Point in the next few years. Bush camping is also allowed along most of the beach and inland areas, with some beach sites being closed periodically for regeneration.

ENVIRONMENTAL CARE

These coastal regions have outstanding scenic and biological values. Unfortunately all have suffered greatly from abuse by irresponsible visitors. It is critically important that bushwalkers adopt minimum impact practices in these areas. In the past, much of the worst damage has occurred around unofficial beach camp sites, where vegetation has been killed to provide firewood and poor sanitation practices have left filthy surrounds. Tins and bottles have also been discarded in these areas, not only degrading the places, but causing a hazard to people with bare feet. Some particular issues of concern are discussed below.

Camp Fires: At the time of writing, wood fires are still allowed in all the coastal sandmasses, but it could be argued that this management policy is well out-of-date. Wood fires have done enormous damage to these areas, especially at unofficial beach camp sites where vegetation has been denuded to provide firewood. Camp fires have also been responsible for some of the disastrous bush fires in these regions (see page 78). At Moreton Island camp fires are currently allowed provided campers bring their own firewood onto the island, but this practice has increased the risk of introducing cane toads (Moreton Island is the only coastal area in Queensland that is currently cane toad free).

It is recommended that bushwalkers make a general practice of not using wood fires in these regions, except in developed camping areas where firewood is supplied. Always take extreme care with fires. **Extinguish all fires with water, not by covering with sand (see page 78).**

Lakes and Waterways: Please take special care to protect these features. Don't use soap or detergent near any lakes or streams, and don't light camp fires on lake beaches since, unlike the ocean beach, the charcoal will remain for many years and mar the beautiful white sands. On the Noosa River, help prevent erosion by tethering canoes instead of dragging them up the banks. Power boats are banned on the lakes and on the Noosa River upstream from Harrys Hut, and they are strongly discouraged on the Noosa River upstream from Fig Tree Lake.

Pristine Areas: Bushwalkers exploring some of the more remote parts of the coastal sandmasses occasionally find lakes and other areas not accessible by road and which do not show obvious signs of visitation. Treat these as rare gems indeed, and make every effort to preserve their pristine qualities.

MAPS

Fraser Island: SUNMAP have an excellent 1:125 000 tourist map of Fraser Island. Although not intended for bushwalking navigation, it is adequate if walking on official tracks such as the southern lakes circuit. For off-track walking, the best maps available are a series of three 1:50 000 forestry maps. In addition, SUNMAP have three standard 1:100 000 topographic maps (*Waddy Point, Happy Valley* and *Wide Bay*). These are useful for off-track navigation although the information on roads is out of date.

Cooloola: SUNMAP have a good tourist map of Cooloola, which is adequate for bushwalks on official tracks. The other main map available is Dennis Gittoes' privately published black and white map titled *Cooloola Coast*, which can be used both as a tourist map and for much off-track navigation. Take care that you are not confused by its unusual scale of 1:80 000. In addition there are several old 1:50 000 topographic maps (*Wide Bay, Cooloola, Wolvi* and *Kauri Creek*), which may be of some use for secondary reference purposes.

Moreton Island: Three good 1:25 000 topographic sheets are available for bushwalking navigation - *Moreton* (covering the northern segment), *Mt Tempest* (covering the central part of the island) and *Kooringal* (covering the south). However, some information on roads, buildings etc on these maps may be out of date. They are best used in combination with the SUNMAP 1:50 000 tourist map *Moreton Island - A Natural Place.*

ACCESS AND ROADS

Much road access in these regions requires four wheel drive vehicles, but this doesn't necessarily mean you have to own or hire a four wheel drive to visit. All areas have four wheel drive taxis which can assist small groups with transport (economy depends on group size and distance), and many tour operators are able to transport larger groups. In addition, there is two wheel drive access to various parts of Cooloola, and at Moreton Island many bushwalking trips can be organised around the barge landing points.

N.B. (1) Serious vehicle accidents are unnecessarily common on both the beaches and forestry tracks of the coastal sandmasses. If you are driving in these regions, note that speed limits and normal road rules apply in all areas, including the beaches. (2) Permits are necessary for both vehicular access and camping at Fraser and Moreton Islands. At the date of writing, only camping permits apply at Cooloola. (3) Prior booking for taxis is normally required (see Directory). It is best to discuss your proposed itinerary and the various cost options with the taxi operator at the time of booking.

Fraser Island: There is a very extensive road network on the island, and virtually all roads are four wheel drive only. The major roads and tourist circuits are clearly delineated on the SUNMAP tourist map. The main barge and ferry services cross from Hervey Bay to various points on the island's west coast (including Wanggoolba and Urang Creeks), and from Inskip Point north of Rainbow Beach township to the island's southern end (see Directory). One of the best ways for bushwalking parties without transport to visit the southern region is to arrange for the Eurong four wheel drive taxi to transport them from the Wanggoolba Creek ferry (see later description). It is also possible to hire the taxi from Rainbow Beach on the mainland, but this is usually much longer.

Cooloola: There is a bitumen road to Rainbow Beach township just north of the national park, and good road access to the camp ground at Elanda Point in the south. Aside from four wheel drive access along the beaches, the other main vehicular access routes are to Freshwater camp ground in the north and the Noosa River camp site in the south. The former is marked on the side of the main road 4km south of Rainbow Beach township. It is mainly a four wheel drive route, although it is trafficable by two wheel drive vehicles as far as the Bymien picnic area (refer to later descriptions). The dirt road to the Noosa River camp ground is normally suitable for two wheel drive vehicles, although parts near Lake Como may flood after heavy rains. The other major road in the region is the Cooloola Way, which is a very rough dirt road linking the Pomona-Kin Kin district to the Gympie-Rainbow Beach road. It can be used as a short cut when driving to Rainbow Beach from the south, although it is typically slippery and boggy after rain and occasionally may be impassable to two wheel drive vehicles. Refer to the *Cooloola Coast* maps for all road navigation details.

Rainbow Beach has a four wheel drive taxi which can assist with transport and sightseeing trips.

Moreton Island: Four roads cross the island - two in the north, one in the south and one across the middle of the island (the latter appropriately called the *Middle Road*). All are four wheel drive only. Refer to the topographic and tourist maps for details of locations.

At the time of writing there are two main barge services, with the *Combie Trader* running between Scarborough and Bulwer, and the *Moreton Venture* running between Whyte Island (at the mouth of the Brisbane River) and Campbell Point (just south of Kooringal). The *Moreton Venture* also operates to The Wrecks just north of Tangalooma. See the Directory for telephone numbers and other details. A four wheel drive taxi operates from Bulwer (see above and the Directory).

FRASER ISLAND

Fraser Island, located on the Queensland coast east of Maryborough, is the largest sand island in the world. It has a total length of 124km and is 25km wide at its widest point. The total coastline is 290km and its highest point is 240m.

The island possesses truly remarkable scenery, including magnificent beaches, spectacular coloured sands and possibly the most outstandingly beautiful array of freshwater lakes in Australia. There are also superb rainforests, rich eucalypt forests and a wide variety of wildflower heaths. The richness of the rainforests once confounded ecologists since sand has no natural mineral fertility. Many trees display aesthetic shapes and bark patterns, notably scribbly gum, paperbark, Moreton Bay ash, blackbutt and satinay.

The island has two types of lakes - perched lakes, which are formed on basins of compressed organic "clays" above the water table, and window lakes, which occur where the water table emerges between the dunes. In addition, several creeks are considered to be among the island's natural wonders. In heath areas the lake and creek water is usually stained a rich red colour by organic tannins, providing spectacular effects prized by photographers. In rainforest areas, the waters are often brilliantly clear.

Scenic Attractions: There is so much to see at Fraser Island that most visitors like to have the help of a "short list" when planning trips. In the southern lakes region, the most famous features are Lakes Boomanjin, McKenzie, Wabby and Birrabeen, as well as Wanggoolba Creek and Pile Valley. Along the beaches, the coloured sands at the Pinnacles and Cathedrals are spectacular, although Eli Creek, the *Maheno* wreck, Indian Head, Waddy Point, Sandy Cape and the beach itself are major attractions. In the central and northern regions, notable features include Lake Bowarrady and various other smaller lakes.

Planning Walks: It is possible to organise successful weekend bushwalks on Fraser Island, the greatest difficulty for most people being the travelling distance. For this reason longer trips are preferred. Both throughwalks and base camps are possible using taxi or charter transport. In addition, visitors with their own four wheel drive vehicles are able to undertake combined bushwalking/camping trips visiting different parts of the island.

To appreciate Fraser Island properly, it is preferable not to be too ambitious with your itinerary e.g. fit throughwalkers can walk the entire southern lakes track in two long days, but such a quick visit hardly does justice to the scenery.

SOUTHERN LAKES

(Walk
53) The southern lakes region has the greatest concentration of scenic features, and at the time of writing it is also provided with the main official walking track system. The track system starts at the ocean beach at Dilli Village, then proceeds via Lake Boomanjin, Central Station, Basin Lake and Lake McKenzie to reach the beach again east of Lake Wabby. This distance could be covered in a weekend by a fit throughwalking party (grade 31/2), but there is hardly any point. There is simply so much to explore and marvel at along the way that many parties take a week or more for this trip. Throughwalkers are able to undertake the trip using taxi or charter transport from the ferry at Wanggoolba Creek to and from the starting and finishing points. Base campers often stay at Central Station, since this is the most convenient point for undertaking day walks. If you have your own vehicle, Lake Wabby can also be visited in a short side trip from the beach. Allow several hours for the return trip and swim.

All lakes provide excellent swimming opportunities. There is also considerable rainforest in this section, with Pile Valley and the upper part of Wanggoolba Creek being special attractions. To really appreciate the lakes, try circumnavigating some on foot. Or wake up early before the crowds arrive, jog along the forest roads to raise a sweat before breakfast, and then splash in for an early morning dip. Depending on water levels, Lakes Boomanjin and McKenzie are the best suited to circumnavigation, although they may require light footwear in places and several short obligatory swims (pack your gear in several layers of plastic garbage bags).

OTHER TRIPS

North-South Traverse: It is possible to walk the entire length of Fraser Island, largely by inland routes, in two to three weeks. However, at the time of writing the route is still largely exploratory. Walking in the central section would include considerable road walking (see below), so the trip would not necessarily appeal to everyone. The southern lakes region and the far north of the island provide the main opportunities to get away from the island's road network.

Central Fraser Island: North of Lakes McKenzie and Wabby, much bushwalking would make use of the forestry road system. These roads tend to pass more to the west, through drier and lower heath vegetation. There is also less surface water, so walking could be a hot dry sunny activity. It may be possible to walk directly through the rainforest belt further east, without the use of roads, but at the time of writing the terrain in this region is unknown. The section between Wathumba and Lake Bowarrady can be walked either along the western or eastern beaches, or by taking a disused forestry track down the centre of the island. Enquire with the local national park ranger regarding the condition and location of this route. Lack of surface water is a major problem in this region.

Northern Region: North of Waddy Point, the vegetation tends to be low, dry and scrubby, and most lakes are broad and shallow. For the most part the dense scrub makes cross country bushwalking very difficult, but a fire trail near Ocean Lake allows bushwalking access. Travelling anticlockwise around Ocean lake on the official walking track, the old road can be found turning off right after a swampy stretch on the lake's north-west. The track is in relatively good condition, taking a course just to the east of Lakes Minker and Carree. There is also another old road which takes a south-easterly course from a point on the north-west coast a kilometre or two west of the lighthouse reserve, but access to this region is very difficult.

COOLOOLA

Cooloola is located on the coast between Noosa and Fraser Island. For descriptive purposes, the sandmass can be considered as two major topographic units - the high dunes in the east and the Noosa River basin in the west. The high dunes region is composed of south-east to north-west orientated dunes which often extend right to the beach i.e. without the usual line of beach foredunes that run parallel to the coast behind most other ocean beaches in south Queensland. The ocean's erosion of the high dunes has created Cooloola's best known trademark - the steep faces of coloured sands on Rainbow and Teewah Beaches. In addition, this eastern region has two spectacular unvegetated sandblows, one in the north adjacent to Rainbow Beach township (the Carlo Sandblow) and one in the south (the Cooloola Sandpatch).

To the west of the high dunes lies the Noosa River basin. For the most part this is a broad and relatively flat area of sandy swamp plains which drain into the Noosa River and its associated lake system. However, the river also drains an area of low infertile stony hills west of the sandmass. The Noosa River is a superbly beautiful feature and ranks as one of south Queensland's most outstanding natural wonders. On the southern boundary of the national park, the river drains into Lake Cootharaba, one of the largest natural perennial lakes in Queensland.

Cooloola has a broad variety of vegetation types, including impressive wet eucalypt forests, majestic rainforests, beautiful scribbly gum forests, wallum plains and many different types of heaths.

Scenic Attractions: Cooloola's outstanding scenic attractions are its beach scenery and coloured sands, the Noosa River, the various lakes and wetlands and the region's wildflowers and forests. Other major attractions include Double Island Point, the Cherry Venture (a shipwreck on the beach south of Double Island Point), the two sandblows, Lake Cootharaba and the Sir Thomas Hiley Information Centre located on the northern shore of Lake Cootharaba.

Bushwalking Conditions: Of south Queensland's coastal national parks, Cooloola has the most extensive system of developed bushwalking tracks, providing opportunities ranging from easy half day strolls to extended treks. There is also an extensive system of old forestry roads. Consequently, most bushwalking routes follow major paths, where there should be few navigation difficulties provided a good map and compass are carried. However, if any off-track walking is attempted, take care that the profusion of swamps and heath vegetation does not cause navigation problems, especially in the Noosa River basin. Some off-track areas are very scrubby.

COOLOOLA WILDERNESS TRAIL

The Cooloola Wilderness Trail is a 46km walking track through the western part of *(Walk* Cooloola National Park. It provides a comfortable 3 day walk (grade 3), although fast *51)* fit parties may be able to complete it in two days. Alternatively, four road access points along the route allow segments to be used for day and weekend trips.

The route extends from Elanda Point in the south to Mt Mullen East on the Rainbow Beach Road in the north. The two intermediate road access points are at the Noosa River (Harrys Hut) camping area and the crossing of the Cooloola Way.

Camping Areas: There are five main camping areas on the route - the private camp ground at Elanda Point, and national park camping sites at Fig Tree Point, Harrys Hut, Wandi Waterhole and Neebs Waterholes. To preserve the wilderness nature of the trail, there is a strict limit on the number and size of overnight parties allowed to camp at the Wandi Waterhole and Neebs Waterholes sites. It is advisable to apply for camping permits well before your trip.

The Wandi and Neebs Waterholes sites are undeveloped bush camp sites, with no facilities provided. To camp at Fig Tree Point, you will need to carry your own fresh water supplies since the Noosa River is saline at this point.

Nature of Terrain: The terrain in the various segments may influence your choice of itinerary. The southern section between Elanda Point and Harrys Hut travels through the rainforests of Kin Kin Creek and the wetlands around Lake Como. These areas are attractive but may become extremely waterlogged, especially in the wetter months of late summer and autumn. Before setting out it is advisable to check the condition of this section of track with the national parks office.

The northern segment is drier and more open than the southern segment, and provides superb wildflower displays in early spring. It travels through scribbly gum forests, wildflower plains and the low stony hills of the Noosa River's western catchment. The two sets of waterholes are special highlights. However, because of the open nature of the vegetation, many parties will prefer to avoid this northern segment during peak summer heat.

Itineraries: Although there are a few hills in the northern section, most of the terrain is reasonably flat and in good conditions the track allows fast travelling. Distances for the various segments are as follows:

Elanda Point to Harrys Hut camp site: 15.5km (not including Fig Tree Point).

Harrys Hut to Wandi Waterhole: 9.5km.

Wandi Waterhole to the Cooloola Way: 4.7km.

Cooloola Way to Neebs Waterholes: 7.7km.

Neebs Waterholes to East Mullen: 8.8km.

On a three day trip from south to north, it would be normal to camp at Harrys Hut and Neebs Waterholes. If going north to south, Wandi Waterhole and either Harrys Hut or Fig Tree Point would be good camp sites. Wandi Waterhole is the camp site nearest the midway point for parties aiming to complete the walk in two days. Alternatively, easier weekend itineraries are the walk from Elanda Point to the Cooloola Way (camping at Harrys Hut), or the trip from East Mullen to Harrys Hut (camping at Wandi Waterhole). All these itineraries require car shuttles. Wandi and Neebs Waterholes also provide interesting day trips from the nearby road access points.

Elanda Point to Harrys Hut Segment: The trail starts north of the kiosk at Elanda Point and initially follows the walking route to Kinaba. After about 2km there is a fork in the track where the Kinaba track turns off to the right. From here the wilderness trail proceeds to a bridge crossing Kin Kin Creek, then follows the creek downstream before veering north to Harrys Hut. Fig Tree Point can be conveniently visited on a short side trip.

The section of track beside Lake Como (i.e. between Fig Tree Point and the Harrys Hut road) is usually the first and worst section to be affected by waterlogging.

However, it can be avoided by use of a service road which joins the Harrys Hut road about a kilometre west of the walking track.

Harrys Hut to Mt Mullen Segment: This section is well marked and should not involve any navigation difficulty. The Cooloola Way is crossed approximately midway between Harrys Hut and Mt Mullen.

DAY WALKS FROM ELANDA POINT

A number of interesting day and half day walks are possible from Elanda Point, starting from the Cooloola Wilderness Trail. Despite a major infestation of exotic groundsel in the section between Elanda Point and Kin Kin Creek, the walks provide a range of interesting ventures. They are best in drier seasons since the tracks often become saturated after rainy weather, especially in late summer and autumn.

All the following walks can be made into joint walking/canoeing ventures if your party is able to split into two groups, with one group walking to the destination and the other canoeing, then swapping for the return journey. Normally you would need at least four people to arrange this type of trip.

Kinaba Information Centre (13km return): This walk takes from 3 to 5 hours, depending on party fitness and the condition of the track. It provides the only land access to the Sir Thomas Hiley Information Centre and passes through a number of interesting vegetation types.

Kin Kin Creek (between 4km and 8km return, depending on the route): This is an easy half day stroll in drier seasons.

Fig Tree Point (16km return): A relatively long day walk, but passing through a considerable number of vegetation types.

WALKS IN THE HARRYS HUT AREA

Harrys Hut to Wandi Waterhole (19km return): This is an excellent walk, providing an energetic day for most parties. Highlights include superb scribbly gum forests, wildflower plains and the Wandi Waterhole. The walk could also be organised using a car shuttle to the Cooloola Way.

Harrys Hut to Fig Tree Point (17km return): This is a reasonably energetic day walk, traversing through the wetlands of Lake Como using the Cooloola Wilderness Trail. It can also be done as a joint walking/canoeing venture if your party is able to split into two groups, with one group walking to Fig Tree Point and the other canoeing, then swapping for the return journey. This would also allow a visit to Kinaba Information Centre. The Lake Como track is often very badly waterlogged, but it can be avoided by using a service road which joins the Harrys Hut road about a kilometre west of the walking track.

Harrys Hut to Campsite 3 (14km return): This walk involves crossing the Noosa River by either boat or swimming. Once across, walk up the eastern side of the river to Campsite 3, travelling through wildflower heath, scribbly gum and bloodwood forest. This is another trip which can be made into a joint walking/canoeing venture if your party is able to split into two groups.

Campsite 3 to Cooloola Sandpatch (12km return): This provides a relatively easy day for canoeing parties camping at Campsite 3. There is a good walking track which travels through some of the best of the wildflower areas. Start by walking east on the old road which leads into the camp site. After approximately a kilometre, you will see a signposted turn-off on the right which leads south to the Sandpatch.

(Walk 70) **Harrys Hut to Cooloola Sandpatch** (26km return): The combination of the above two trips provides an inspiring bushwalk, but it is a long day and only suitable for very fit parties (grade 31/2 to 4). The walk may be easier if you canoe to Campsite 3.

Cooloola Sandpatch/Kings Bore Circuit (2 to 3 days; approximately 47km): This is an energetic weekend circuit for very fit parties. An early start on the first day will be necessary to enable you to reach Campsite 3 for morning tea and the Sandpatch for a late lunch (see details above). Then descend to the beach and walk north to Kings Bore (10km). There are several beach camp sites in this vicinity. Beach soaks provide a reliable water supply, although it may be advisable to boil the water due to the sanitation risk caused by heavy camping pressures. From Kings Bore the recommended route back to Campsite 3 is via the old forestry roads through the Ramsey scrub (refer to the *Cooloola Coast* map), with superb wet eucalypt forests, patches of rainforest and wildflower plains. Alternatively you can walk via Lake Cooloomera, walking mainly on flat plains. Although less hilly, the latter option is slightly longer and probably less interesting than the Ramsey scrub tracks. N.B. This trip may be easier if extended to either three or four days, staying at Campsite 3 for at least one night to reduce the length of one or both day's treks.

CENTRAL COOLOOLA WET EUCALYPT FORESTS

Freshwater Camp Ground to Kings Bore (approximately 24km one way): The high dunes between the Ramsey scrub and Freshwater camp ground have some of the best wet eucalypt forests in Cooloola. There is a maze of old forestry roads in this region, providing a variety of bushwalking opportunities. Most walking trips would be best organised as either extended throughwalks (three days or longer) or with a car shuttle or some form of vehicular support. If a vehicular shuttle can be organised, the route between Freshwater and Kings Bore can be done as a long day trip.

The route is entirely along old forestry roads, most of which are clearly marked on the various maps. Unfortunately, past logging activity has resulted in some confusing areas along the route, and a few of the side roads have virtually overgrown. Consequently, care is required with navigation. Do not attempt the route without plenty of time available and some experience in bush navigation. Check the tide times if relying on vehicular support.

If walking south to north, start by taking the track which runs uphill in a north-easterly direction just east of Lake Cooloomera. If walking from Freshwater, start by taking the walking track on the south side of the lake, then take the old vehicle track which branches off on the south of the walking track about half way along the lake. Turn left again after about half a kilometre.

NORTHERN WALKS

The northern part of Cooloola between Freshwater camp ground and Rainbow Beach provides some of the most outstanding bushwalking opportunities in the region, with superb rainforests and scribbly gum forests as well as inspiring beach scenery. A number of official walking tracks can be combined to provide an array of day and overnight bushwalking itineraries.

(Walk 20) **Rainbow Beach Township to Double Island Point Camp Ground** (full day; 21km circuit): Often called the "old telegraph track" or "high dunes track", this runs south-east along the top of the dunes. It passes through some of the best scribbly gum forest in the region and has two superb lookouts over Wide Bay and the coloured

sands. The old telegraph posts are still evident along the route. While mainly on official walking tracks, not all the route is signposted so some care is required. It also involves 2km of road walking. The distance from Rainbow Beach township to Double Island Point camp ground is about 12km (including the 1.5km side trip to Burwilla Lookout). Unless you are able to organise a car shuttle, there is a further 8km walk back along the beach and a kilometre through the town's streets to complete the circuit. There is no water on the route.

The track starts at the end of Double Island Drive in Rainbow Beach township. Murrawa Lookout is reached after 2km. After another 2km, the track divides, the right hand fork being signposted "Bymien Picnic Area, Lake Poona and Lake Freshwater". The left hand track, unmarked at the time of writing, should be followed to Double Island Point. After about a kilometre it reaches the Freshwater road, which is followed for 2km to the Burwilla Lookout car park. Here signposts clearly mark the tracks to the lookout and to Double Island Point camp ground.

If undertaking the walk in the reverse direction (e.g. because of tidal conditions), the track to Burwilla Lookout and car park is easily found adjacent to the toilet block in Double Island Point camp ground. The unmarked turn-off to Rainbow Beach township off the Freshwater road is approximately 2km north-west of the Burwilla car park. The track turns off right and ascends a hill at a point where the Freshwater road veers left and begins to descend (if you go too far along the road, you will soon start to enter rainforest).

Rainbow Beach Township to Bymien Picnic Area (14.5km return): Follow the "old telegraph track" as described above, but take the right hand track at the junction 4km from the township. Soon after this you enter rainforest, and about 2km further on you meet and cross over the Freshwater road. The track is usually clear and well signposted, although after heavy rains the section just before the Freshwater road may become submerged and difficult to follow. It is well worth extending the walk to include Lake Poona (see below).

Bymien Picnic Area to Lake Poona (approximately 2km): There is two wheel drive access to Bymien picnic area, which has several short walks through the surrounding rainforest. The most notable is the track to Lake Poona, Cooloola's most beautiful lake.

Bymien Picnic Area to Lake Freshwater (12km return; 15km if extended to *(Walk* Freshwater camp ground): This route follows an old road through some of Cooloola's *19)* most outstanding rainforests, providing some of the best opportunities available for birdwatchers to spot noisy pittas. The track eventually joins the Lake Freshwater circuit track on the west of the lake.

Overnight Walks: The above routes can be combined to provide a number of throughwalking itineraries. For example:

• The walk to Double Island Point via the high dunes track, and returning via the beach, is a relatively easy weekend walk (but carry all your drinking water).

• The circuit from Rainbow Beach township, via the dunes track to Lake Poona and *(Walk* then to Lake Freshwater, and returning to the township along the beach, provides *55)* a comfortable three day walk or an energetic two day walk (grade 31/2). Alternatively, this itinerary can be made easier by organising a car shuttle between Rainbow Beach township and Bymien Picnic Area (two wheel drive access).

GRAND COOLOOLA CIRCUIT

(*Walk 94*) Fit and experienced bushwalkers would be able to organise a superb eight or nine day circuit to experience the full range of Cooloola's unique landscapes and spectacular attractions in one trip. Depending on the exact route, the total distance would be between 120km and 160km. Many itinerary variations are possible, but in principle it would combine one of the best sections of the Cooloola Wilderness Trail (Noosa River camp ground to Neebs Waterholes) with the walking routes along the high dunes (i.e. from Rainbow Beach township to the Noosa River via Lake Freshwater and Kings Bore). These routes are described here. Walkers would need to arrange a method of crossing the Noosa River.

The remaining part of the circuit, between the north of the Cooloola Wilderness Trail and Rainbow Beach township, can largely be done on old forestry tracks. It may be possible to include a short section of cross country walking from Mt Mullen South to the Cooloola Way, but the nature of this terrain is unknown at the date of writing. It is intended to provide more details of this circuit in *Bushpeople's Visitor Guide to* * *Fraser Island, Cooloola and Moreton Island* (intended for publication in August 1991; see inside back cover).

NOOSA RIVER CANOEING

The Noosa River is one of the natural wonders of south Queensland, renowned for its deep red waters and their brilliant reflections of overhanging scribbly gums and bloodwoods. Luxuriant natural vegetation lines the banks for its entire length. Canoeing is without doubt the most enjoyable way to appreciate the river's tranquil atmosphere. On its silent waters you can pass within a metre of flowering swamp banksias, or paddle peacefully under spreading melaleuca branches. In the early morning, photographers become ecstatic over the reflections of the gnarled scribbly gums and bloodwoods leaning out over the ripple-free waters.

Like bushwalking or any other exercise, canoeing can be a little tiring if you're not used to it, but persistence pays off. Once you have experienced the river by canoeing in the quiet of the early morning or late afternoon, the noise of motorised boats will always seem offensive in such a peaceful setting. The tranquil waters provide some 20km of freshwater canoeing, enabling trips up to three or even four days in length. The placid nature of the river does not require previous canoeing experience, although naturally some safety and preparatory measures are recommended to ensure an enjoyable and carefree trip.

Hiring Canoes: You don't have to buy expensive equipment to go canoeing. You can hire Canadian canoes from Elanda Point, Boreen Point or from any of a myriad of places in Brisbane and other centres.

Canoeing Itineraries: There are two main sites for launching canoes - Lake Cootharaba (Elanda Point or Boreen Point) and Harrys Hut. Depending on your choice, a variety of itineraries are possible. A typical two day trip from Elanda Point would involve paddling up to Campsite 2, 3, 4 or 5, although inexperienced paddlers may prefer the slightly shorter paddle to Campsite 1. A trip of comparable length from Harrys Hut would be the paddle to Campsites 8 or 9. Starting your upstream paddle from Harrys Hut cuts out the hardest work, but also much of the prettiest country.

Use of the Noosa River camp sites upstream from Harrys Hut is strictly controlled to prevent overuse, and it is always necessary to book camp sites before your trip. Most

284

* *see changes on inside back cover.*

are bush camp sites designed for 4 to 8 people, although Campsite 3 is developed for larger groups. Alternatively, you may prefer to base camp at Harrys Hut and undertake day canoe trips either up or down the river. This would allow a visit to the Noosa River everglades and Kinaba Information Centre. The everglades is one of the prettiest stretches of the river, with interesting vegetation changes as the river proceeds from freshwater to saline.

An adventurous alternative itinerary is available by launching canoes at the headwaters of Teewah Creek. This provides a two day trip to Harrys Hut and a three day trip to Elanda Point. However, since almost the entire first morning on Teewah Creek is spent portaging and dragging canoes over fallen logs, it is only for adventurous light weight parties who don't mind a few scrapes on their canoes. A lengthy car shuttle is necessary.

Safety and Preparation: The basic points are:

- Life jackets are essential for all canoeists on the open waters of Lake Cootharaba. Non-swimmers should wear life jackets at all times.
- Don't have too many loose items aboard, and keep valuable items safe in case of capsize. Wrap all equipment in multiple layers of plastic bags to keep it dry. This is especially important if travelling across Lake Cootharaba.
- Don't attempt to cross Lake Cootharaba if the weather is very choppy (see below).
- Take ropes to tether canoes (often ropes are not provided with hire canoes).
- Always have a large hat that can't be blown off, as well as plenty of sun screen.
- Take care when alighting from canoes since some of the banks of the Noosa River are rather steep and awkward.
- Be alert for underwater logs and "snags" when canoeing, and never dive or jump into the dark waters without thoroughly checking for underwater objects first.

Crossing Lake Cootharaba: If you start your trip from Elanda Point or elsewhere on Lake Cootharaba, the hardest haul will almost certainly be the paddle across the lake to the QNPWS Information Centre at Kinaba. This often takes over an hour. It can also be a little unnerving for inexperienced canoeists, so it is recommended that inexperienced canoeists travel in the company of other canoes and that life jackets always be worn. Usually confidence and proficiency are quickly acquired.

When travelling towards Kinaba, it is easiest to paddle straight out from Elanda Point for about 300m (Lake Cootharaba is very shallow in places), then turn left and paddle through progressively deeper water towards the Cooloola Sandpatch. After a while Kinaba will become visible as a white dot amongst the foliage on the far side of the lake, just to the left of the Sandpatch.

A frequent scenario on weekend trips is that the initial crossing of Lake Cootharaba on Saturday morning is calm, but that the return trip on Sunday afternoon is somewhat rougher. Usually by this time paddlers have gained sufficient proficiency to know how to handle the more difficult conditions. However, in rare cases when the weather is extremely bad, it may be necessary to either wade the canoes back to Elanda Point (very slow) or leave them tethered at Kinaba and travel back via the walking track. In case you ever have to take this action, it is useful to limit your gear and include a rucksack and appropriate footwear as a safe guard.

Navigation in the Everglades: The Everglades is one of the most enchanting sections of the Noosa River, but navigation may be a little confusing if you try to relate the map with the actual terrain. From Kinaba Information Centre, follow the nearby channel for a short distance to Kin Kin Creek, which is relatively broad and deep. Turn right to follow the main route to Fig Tree Lake and the upper Noosa River. Fig Tree Lake is about 800m across but quite shallow - canoe across to the Fig Tree Point jetty on the far north-eastern shore. Here there is a camping and picnic area but no fresh water.

To travel upstream from Fig Tree Lake, locate a shallow reedy channel just east of Fig Tree Point. This leads to the Como Reach (a long straight broad reach of water, almost like a canal). The main course of the Noosa River joins the Como Reach on the east (right) about half a kilometre upstream, via yet another indistinct reedy channel. The water turns fresh about a kilometre upstream. You then enter "The Narrows", a stretch where the banks shelter the water's surface from the breezes, often providing brilliant reflections. In order to rehabilitate past bank erosion, landing is prohibited between Fig Tree Point and the Harrys Hut camp ground.

MORETON ISLAND

Moreton Island is located 30km off the coast north-east of Brisbane. It is 38km long and 9km wide at the widest point, with a total coastline of 85km and a highest point of 280m. There is a wide variety of vegetation types, from stunted heaths and foredune vegetation to tall eucalypt forests. Unlike Fraser Island and Cooloola, there is no rainforest vegetation. The north of Moreton Island has extensive areas of wet lands, the majority of lakes being of the "window" type. However, there are also several perched lakes in remote areas in the north.

The island has a special appeal that is difficult to define. Its lakes and forests could not be considered as spectacular as those at Fraser Island and Cooloola, but despite this it has a feeling of simplicity and pristinity that the other places lack. Moreton has fewer roads and less commercial development than the other coastal regions, and bushwalkers feel more of a sense of wilderness.

The island's bushwalking opportunities are varied, ranging from simple beach and road walks to exploratory trips in scrubby terrains. Because many itineraries are possible, this chapter does not attempt to provide comprehensive descriptions of all possible walks. Rather, several major trips are outlined, with suggestions for exploratory off-track walks for the benefit of experienced bushwalkers.

Water: While there are large freshwater lake systems in the north, it is important for bushwalkers to note that the southern half of the island is almost entirely devoid of surface water, except for several swamps and springs near the Big and Little Sandhills.

Vegetation: Much of Moreton's heath vegetation is extremely thick, and bushwalkers should not attempt exploratory trips unless they are prepared for particularly scrubby conditions.

SOUTHERN SANDHILLS CIRCUIT

(Walk 54) Although many people consider that the northern half of Moreton Island is the most outstanding section, the southern part has a distinctive landscape that provides unusual attractions. The two areas of unvegetated sand dunes are the major land-marks, and in clear weather are quite visible from the buildings of Brisbane. The

Little Sandhills cross the island from east to west about 6km north of Kooringal. The Big Sandhills are located a few kilometres further north, extending to the west coast but separated from the ocean beach by a narrow band of vegetation.

It is possible to visit this region on a relatively easy two day throughwalk (grade $2_1/2$). The trip does not require any taxi charters, since you can make a convenient walking circuit from the barge landing point just south of Kooringal township. The 1:25 000 topographic map Kooringal is used on the circuit. Since the initial part of the trip is along the surf beach, it is best to avoid stormy weather or particularly high tides when walking this section.

Kooringal to Little Sandhills: From Kooringal township, cross to the ocean beach via the dump road, then walk northwards along the beach for about 6km. Continue up to the Little Sandhills, the most easterly of which (414 796) provides a view well worth the climb. Despite their name, the Little Sandhills are quite large and extensive, and the stark white sands provide a spectacular landscape. There is often a small lake just west of the large eastern dune.

Big Sandhills: Continue north along the beach for a further $2_1/2$km, then try to locate a track leading through the scrub to the west to the Big Sandhills. The main track lies just south of a small coastal dune (marked on the map at 414 816), which may act as a marker. Other routes are possible if you are unable to find this track, although some are scrubby. N.B. If crossing from west to east, note that there are two tongues of unvegetated sand which extend east from the Big Sandhills. The main track to the coast starts at the eastern end of the northern tongue of sand, at about 410 817.

The Big Sandhills have a distinctly different character from the Little Sandhills. Much of the sand here is darker, and immediately west of the band of coastal vegetation (about midway across the island) is a large open "bowl" where the rain and wind often form interesting colour patterns on the ground. Further west lies the Big Sandhills' most impressive dune, a hill which rises gradually on the east with a steep lee slope dropping down to the western shore. Possibly the most unusual features here are the ironstone formations, which are a type of red sandstone forming many unusual shapes (they are not always visible, being periodically covered by sand). These formations are very fragile, so be careful not to break them when you walk on the dune. It is suggested that visitors walk in bare feet to ensure everyone takes appropriate care to avoid the formations.

It is possible to camp in the Big Sandhills amid the nearby surrounding scrub. In wet years there is a small lagoon just south of the large western dune, but drinking water is usually obtained from a spring on the ridge south-east of the dune. Look for a small isolated patch of trees in a tiny gully at about 404 817, about 300m to 400m south-east of the lagoon. Follow the gully up to a tiny waterfall. The water here smells slightly but has been used by visitors for many years without ill effects.

Other features of interest in this area include some old World War II gun bunkers just north of the Big Sandhills, visible from the ocean beach.

Big Sandhills to Kooringal: From the Big Sandhills, it it a pleasant half day walk down the west coast to Kooringal. There is a variety of vegetation, including patches of mangroves. Other features include the Toulkerrie oyster farm and various Aboriginal middens. Take care not to disturb any middens, which have revealed much archeological evidence about past Aboriginal occupation and life styles.

The Swamp Track: An alternative and slightly longer route to Kooringal is via the swamp track, which runs south from the Little Sandhills to just north of Kooringal air strip. Cross from the western beach to the middle of the Little Sandhills. The start of the track can be located at the end of the southern tongue of sand (412 786). It winds through attractive scrub and wet lands, eventually meeting the road which runs north of Kooringal.

To locate this track when walking northwards, stay on the road leading north from Kooringal until you pass the end of the air strip. The road takes a slight twist away from the western beach at this point (the air strip may be partly obscured by trees). Continue walking along the road, and carefully estimate when you have walked 800 metres. At this point a clear but unmarked foot track leaves the road at an angle on the right, leading inland over some low sand dunes.

NORTHERN AND CENTRAL WALKS

There are two main types of bushwalks in the northern and central regions of Moreton Island. Some itineraries mainly involve road and beach walking, but there is also a variety of off-track exploratory options. The relevant topographic maps are the 1:25 000 sheets titled *Moreton* and *Mt Tempest*. Here are some trip suggestions:

Blue Lagoon-Cape Moreton Circuit: This is an easy three day circuit (grade 3), following the road across the island from Bulwer to Blue Lagoon, then north on the ocean beach to Cape Moreton and returning to Bulwer via the picturesque north-west beach. Most of the route is straightforward, although there are several options for side trips. The first night's camp site is Blue Lagoon and the second camp site is on the north-west beach between North Point and Heath Island. However, water needs to be carried for the second night's camp. Try to plan the walk to avoid high tides on the beach sections.

A short side trip on the first day is the track to the south-western shore of Blue Lagoon, leaving the main road at 427 029 just before you reach Honeyeater Lake. If you wish you can use this track as a short cut to the Blue Lagoon camp ground, but normally you would need to wade along the shore of the lagoon in water that is sometimes waist deep. If the wading route is attempted, you should aim for the point where the sandblow meets the eastern lake shore (436 030). The camping area lies just east of here in the foredunes.

On the second day, the Spitfire Creek inlet (447 054) is well worth exploring, having several impressive Aboriginal middens (please ensure these are undisturbed). If you wish, the north bank of the creek can be followed upstream all the way to Lake Jabiru (a half day side trip), but travel is very slow due to the extremely scrubby vegetation (refer to page 290). Water is usually collected from Spitfire Creek for the second night's camp site. The section of the creek nearest the coast is often strewn with rubbish, but the water is clean a short distance inland.

In winter and early spring, migrating humpback whales can often be seen from Cape Moreton. The route across the cape to North Point is via the lighthouse roads marked on the maps. At North Point, fresh water can sometimes be obtained from squatter's tanks (with permission), although it is best not to rely on this supply.

In calm sunny conditions, Moreton's north-west beach is one of the most beautiful on the island, and it is not uncommon to see turtles, rays and porpoises close to shore. It makes a superb walk, especially when the vehicular traffic is light. You can choose to walk on either the ocean side or inland side of Heath Island, but the ocean side is usually preferable. Just west of Heath Island, it is necessary to wade to cross a creek outlet. There are usually several locations for crossing, some deeper than others.

N.B. (1) The western section of the north-west beach sometimes becomes impassable in particularly high tides and/or stormy weather. (2) It is possible to complete this trip as an extremely long two day circuit, in which case it would be best to walk in a clockwise direction and camp at Blue Lagoon.

Western Beach-Eagers Swamp-Mt Tempest Circuit: This is an energetic two day circuit from Bulwer (grade 3), again involving beach and road walking. On the first day, walk south from Bulwer on the western beach to Ben-ewa, then take the Middle Road across the island to the ocean beach. Camp overnight at the Eagers Swamp camp ground, which lies about 1 1/2km north along the beach.

On the second day, walk back to the Middle Road, turning off on an old track on the right about half a kilometre inland (418 955). This is the "old telegraph track". After about 2 1/2km, a signposted foot track turns off at a twist in the road (405 976) and leads up the ridge to the south-west to the summit of Mt Tempest. This is an excellent side trip (1 to 1 1/2 hours return). Reputedly the highest coastal sand dune in the world (280m), the summit provides superb views of the surrounding terrain.

The remainder of the trip involves following the old telegraph track north-westwards and then northwards until it reaches the Bulwer-Blue Lagoon road at about 401 039. This section of the old telegraph track is closed to vehicles. Due to heath regrowth, the old track is not always easy to follow, and sometimes considerable care is required not to lose the route. Water is usually available where a small creek crosses the track at 386 017. Just over a kilometre north of here, Hutchinson Peak provides a short but scrubby side trip.

Blue Lagoon-Mt Tempest Circuit: The old telegraph track can also be used to make a two day circuit via Blue Lagoon, Eagers Swamp and Mt Tempest, starting and finishing either at Bulwer or the eastern beach (the latter with the assistance of taxi transport).

Other Circuits: In addition to the trips already described, various itineraries can be planned using taxi transport from Bulwer.

Exploratory Trips: There are various off-track exploratory walks available, mainly in the Lake Jabiru and Smiths Peak regions. However, you need to be prepared for extremely scrubby conditions. A number of old mining survey roads still exist in some places. Aerial photos and older topographic maps are the best clues to the location of these old tracks.

SOUTH-NORTH TRAVERSE

It is possible to walk the full length of Moreton Island in about five to seven days *(Walk 92)* (grade 4 to 4 1/2). The following is a summary description of one of the many possible itineraries, walking south to north. The route zigzags up the island, providing a full insight into the mosaic of forests, sand blows, lakes, wet lands, heath lands and different types of beach landforms that make up Moreton's superb diversity of landscapes.

At the time of writing, you can start this itinerary by taking the Moreton Venture from the mouth of the Brisbane River to Campbell Point south of Kooringal. If you plan the trip appropriately, you can return to Brisbane using the same barge on its run from The Wrecks, between Ben-ewa and Tangalooma. However, always obtain up to date information on the ferry's operating days.

Day 1: This is a reasonably easy day, walking north from Kooringal and camping overnight at the Big Sandhills. It is suggested that you use the Swamp Track route previously described in the outline of the Southern Sandhills Circuit. If you wish you can choose to walk beyond the Big Sandhills to shorten the next day's walk, but since there is no water between the Big Sandhills and Ben-ewa, a great quantity of water would need to be carried. See below for more details.

Day 2: This is a long hard day (20km) requiring an early start and steady pace. The main difficulty is the complete absence of surface water on this part of the island. The suggested route follows an old four wheel drive track (the Rous Battery road, now rarely used by vehicles) through the centre of the island to Tangalooma.

To start, follow the directions given previously from the Big Sandhills to the ocean beach, then walk northwards along the beach for between 2km and 2 1/2km. The start of the Rous Battery road can be located in this vicinity, with the gun bunkers visible high on the hill to the north. However, there are several confusing roads leading inland as well as a number of bunkers, so some exploration may be necessary to find the correct route.

The Rous Battery road provides a pleasant walking track, with various vegetation transitions as you walk north-westerly. Sometime in the afternoon you will reach a junction with a major road (381 920). There are two options here. The shortest route is on the right, following vehicle tracks to the beach near Tangalooma and then to Ben-ewa camp ground (refer to the topographic map). Alternatively, you can take the left hand fork to The Desert, then pick up a foot track on the far side of The Desert which leads to the beach near Tangalooma. This takes slightly longer but is a more interesting bushwalking route.

Day 3: This is a relatively easy day, walking from Ben-ewa to Eagers Swamp via the Middle Road.

Day 4: A medium day travelling from Eagers Swamp to Blue Lagoon. It is possible to do this by walking along the beach, but the recommended route follows the old telegraph track past Mount Tempest, as previously described on page 289.

Day 5: There are two route options from Blue Lagoon to North Point. The easier route follows the ocean beach, which is only a half day's walk. An alternative route for experienced bushwalkers travels via Spitfire Creek to Lake Jabiru. This is initially extremely scrubby, although the going becomes easier after you reach the lake. Follow the eastern lake shore northwards, then locate an old track leading from just east of the northern part of the lake to the north-west beach. Regardless of the route taken, water needs to be carried for the camp on the north-west beach. For more details, see page 288.

Day 6: Walk to Bulwer via the north-west beach, as described on page 288. Here you can hire the Bulwer taxi (prior booking is necessary) to take you to the landing point of the *Moreton Venture* near The Wrecks, just south of Ben-ewa camp ground. Alternatively, you can choose to walk this section of beach or you can catch the *Combie Trader* from Bulwer to Scarborough (always obtain up to date information on the ferries' operating days).

DIRECTORY

QUEENSLAND NATIONAL PARKS AND WILDLIFE SERVICE

Fraser Island/North Cooloola: P.O. Box 30, Rainbow Beach. Q. 4581.
Telephone: (074) 86 3160.

Southern Cooloola: Kinaba Information Centre, via Elanda, MS 1537,
Tewantin. Q. 4565. Telephone: (074) 49 7364.
Also:
(074) 85 3245.

Moreton Island (Ben-ewa): via Tangalooma, Moreton Island. Q. 4025.
Telephone: (07) 408 2710.

FERRY AND BARGE TRANSPORT

Fraser Island (River Heads - Wanggoolba Creek):	Telephone: (071) 24 1900.
Fraser Island (Hervey Bay - Urang Creek):	Telephone: (071) 24 1300.
Fraser Island (Rainbow Beach):	Telephone: (074) 86 3227.
Fraser Island (Rainbow Beach):	Telephone: (071) 27 9122.
Moreton Island (Moreton Venture):	Telephone: (07) 895 1000.
Moreton Island (Combie Trader):	Telephone: (07) 203 6399.

FOUR WHEEL DRIVE TAXIS

Fraser Island (Eurong):	Telephone: (071) 27 9188.
Northern Cooloola (Rainbow Beach):	Telephone: (074) 86 3235.
Moreton Island Tourist Service (Bulwer):	Telephone: (07) 408 2661.

N.B. Some taxi services and ferries are also able to offer advice on bus charter transport.

PRIVATE CAMP GROUNDS - COOLOOLA

Elanda Point: Cooloola National Park, via Noosa. Q. 4567.
Telephone: (074) 85 3165.

Noosa North Shore
Wilderness Camp: P.O. Box 11, Tewantin. Q. 4565
Telephone: (074) 49 7955.

Lake Cooroibah
Holiday Park: P.O. Box 220, Tewantin. Q. 4565.
Telephone: (074) 47 1706.

21

ISOLATED AREAS

This chapter describes a potpourri of locations which don't fit readily into other chapters. They offer bushwalking opportunities which range from short graded track walks, to very challenging ventures that involve abseiling and difficult scrambling.

MT TAMBORINE

Mt Tamborine is a lush green plateau in the Gold Coast hinterland. It has considerable housing development, although there are also nine small national parks totalling approximately 650ha. These include Queensland's first national park, Witches Falls, which was declared in 1908 and is one of the mountain's greatest claims to fame.

Road access to the mountain is evident on any road map, while the Queensland National Parks and Wildlife Service's information sheet describes the facilities and locations of all the national parks. There is an information centre on the mountain near the corner of Beacon and Tamborine Mountain Roads.

For the most part the national parks offer opportunities for graded track walks, picnics, barbecues and creek swimming. The longest track walks can be done in a few hours. However, experienced bushwalkers who study the topographic maps of the area will find that there are also some interesting off-track exploratory ventures.

BACK CREEK AND KILLARNEY GLEN

Back Creek drains part of Beechmont, flowing north to meet the Coomera River near the Canungra-Nerang road. Part way along the creek is Killarney Glen. For several years prior to the time of writing, the latter location has been the subject of some

Left: Abseil at Denham Falls

293

controversy, with land being resumed by the Department of Defence and counter proposals being made for the future use of the area as national or environmental park. Killarney Glen offers opportunities for easy strolls and swimming in several superb pools, while the descent of Back Creek from the Beechmont plateau provides an adventurous day trip for experienced bushwalkers. On current trends the latter is likely to become one of the most popular abseiling excursions in south Queensland in future years.

Currently the land at Killarney Glen has been resumed by the Department of Defence, but Mr Fitzgerald (the previous owner, popularly known as "Paddy") continues to reside there with the approval of the Commonwealth government (he and his family are in receipt of ministerial advice that they have "a continuing interest" in the property). It is possible that the Department of Defence may be sensitive about large numbers of bushwalkers using this region, due to the various controversies and because the area is close to some army lands to which public access is prohibited. However, the fact is that the Back Creek descent is rapidly becoming a popular bushwalking trip and that there is already much public usage. The information here is merely intended to describe the features in the area and the bushwalking routes around the various obstacles, not to advocate for or against the different proposals for future land use.

Water Quality: Back Creek drains the Beechmont plateau where there are many houses and considerable grazing land. Consequently the drinking quality of the water is uncertain, especially in the upper section of the creek. On the descent route, it may be advisable to carry your own water, particularly if the creek level is low.

KILLARNEY GLEN

Road Access: When driving from Canungra to Beechmont, there is a sharp U-bend in the road approximately 5km after the James Sharp Memorial Park at the Coomera River crossing. Just before the guard rail prior to this bend (i.e. when driving uphill), there are two dirt tracks turning off on your left. These tracks lead to a small car park area (avoid the bottom track in wet weather). This is the limit of vehicular access. From here the walk to Killarney Glen only takes about 15 minutes, although it is quite steep, following the obvious dirt road down the hill to the east. Mr Fitzgerald is usually happy to receive day visitors, but to check latest access details, telephone the family either at Killarney Glen (075-33 3534) or in Brisbane (07-372 4258 or 07-372 6561). N.B. Public vehicles are definitely not allowed on the four wheel drive road leading down the hill from the car park area near the main road.

Features: The area around Killarney Falls is ideal for easy strolls, swimming and picnics. There are superb swimming holes at both Killarney Falls and the Emerald Pool, the latter lying 20 minutes easy stroll upstream. One of the remarkable aspects of the area is the sculptured rock at the base of Killarney Falls. This is reached by swimming up through a small gorge, which is another delightful feature of the area.

DESCENT OF BACK CREEK

(Walk 87) **General Terrain:** The terrain in the upper section of Back Creek is rugged and the usual route involves at least two abseils. It should not be attempted after substantial rains or if the water level is very high. Considerable scrambling experience is recommended. It is difficult to grade the trip precisely, although a grading of about 5 would probably be appropriate on the basis of the abseiling pitches.

However, if it is possible to descend without any abseiling, it is likely that the route would be about grade 4.

The creek has many features of interest, including five picturesque waterfalls and numerous swimming holes. There is also a variety of unusual basalt features, including a large number of caves. The latter are often formed underneath the waterfalls.

Maps: The *Canungra* 1:25 000 sheet is the preferred map for bushwalking navigation, although the *Canungra* 1:50 000 sheet can also be used.

Length of Trip: The descent to Killarney Glen takes a full day and most parties are advised to get an early start. The section from Denham Falls to Twin Falls takes about 2/3 to 3/4 of a day, while the rockhop from Twin Falls to Killarney Glen usually takes 2 to 3 hours, depending on the conditions.

Abseiling Equipment: The abseil at Denham Falls is just over 30m, so two ropes of normal length are required to provide a double rope abseil. Most other waterfalls can be negotiated with a single 50m rope (doubled to make a length of 25m), although the drop at Rainbow Falls may slightly exceed this length (depending on the location of the abseil anchor point). However, Rainbow Falls can be easily bypassed without abseiling.

Other Equipment: The Portals, which is a gorge just upstream from the Emerald Pool near Killarney Glen, is usually negotiated with a short swim, so carry several large plastic bags in which to wrap your gear.

Fauna Care: Some of the basalt caves in this vicinity have considerable numbers of bats. As well as following normal minimum impact bushwalking practices, visitors are asked to take special care not to upset these animals. Bat colonies are easily disturbed and excessive curiosity from visitors could have disastrous results. Unless you are a zoologist, it is best to refrain from entering the bat caves.

Road Access: A car shuttle is required, with a proportion of vehicles being left at the entrance to Killarney Glen (see previous description). The top of Back Creek is reached by driving to Windabout Road on Beechmont, which turns off the Canungra-Beechmont Road approximately 10km past James Sharp Memorial Park on the Coomera River crossing (i.e. about 5km up the road from Killarney Glen). After driving along Windabout Road for a very short distance, turn left at a junction, then drive to a second junction and turn right into Doncaster Drive. Leave vehicles at the bottom of the hill about 50m down. Here there is a small creek in a gully, which leads eastwards for about 150m to Back Creek. This is a public access route, the top section of Back Creek being a scenic reserve.

Denham Falls to Twin Falls: Denham Falls (188 903) lies about five minutes down Back Creek. They are normally negotiated by a 30m abseil from a tree on the east side of the falls. Despite the length of the drop, much of the cliff is not sheer, so the abseil is not too difficult. It is also possible to locate a scrubby bypass route by walking back up the creek a short distance until you can easily ascend to the **west** (i.e. the side of the creek nearest Windabout Road). From here, follow the top of cliffs along for a considerable distance until you can descend down to the creek again. Considerable route-finding care may be required.

As you rockhop down the creek below Denham Falls, the amount of rainforest gradually increases. After some time you reach Lip Falls (also called Gins Lip Falls - 190 904), which are easily bypassed by a track on the right (east) of the creek.

Continuing downstream, the next major feature is Cavern Falls (190 905), so named because of a major cavern underneath the rim of the cascade. They are usually negotiated by a 20m abseil on the east of the falls, with an overhang providing a free fall of about 8m. Considerable care is required not to dislodge rocks around the abseil point. There is reportedly also a bypass route on the west of the creek, although it may involve some difficult scrambling. Cavern Falls lies at the end of a small gorge which blocks most routes out of the creek.

Proceeding downstream, Rainbow Falls is the next major feature (193 907). In certain lighting, a rainbow can sometimes be seen at the bottom of this waterfall. The falls can be bypassed by a route which is easily found on the left of the creek (the west bank).

From Rainbow Falls to Twin Falls (194 908), massive boulders in the creek often cause slow progress, forcing you to take lengthy and sometimes scrubby detours up on the bank (usually the west bank). However, Twin Falls are perhaps the most picturesque of all the waterfalls, so the effort is worthwhile. Twin Falls are readily bypassed on the western bank.

Twin Falls to Killarney Glen: Soon after Twin Falls, the creek flows out into a large clearing of old farm lands, strewn with regrowth. This continues for about 1 1/2km and would be extremely uncomfortable if conditions were very hot. At one point an army road descends to the creek on the western bank. Access to this road is prohibited, although it is useful to remember for emergencies since it leads back to the sharp U-bend in the main road near Killarney Glen.

An unusual small gorge called the Portals (205 928) lies about 500m downstream from the point where the army road meets the creek. This is usually negotiated by a short swim (you will probably have to wrap your gear in large plastic bags). A short distance further downstream lies the Emerald Pool (203 935), after which it takes only about 20 minutes to reach Killarney Glen.

CROWS NEST FALLS REGION

Crows Nest Falls is one of several small national parks located near Perseverance Dam north-east of Toowoomba. The terrain in this region is dry eucalypt forest, with cascades, swimming holes and various boulder formations in the creeks. There are several interesting off-track bushwalks available, but the most popular trip is the day walk from Perseverance Dam to Crows Nest Falls. This is the route described here.

Maps: Most of the walking route is shown on the *Crows Nest* 1:25 000 sheet, although the *Ravensbourne* 1:25 000 sheet is also required to get a complete coverage.

Road Access: To reach Perseverance Dam from Brisbane, it is usual to drive via the Esk-Toowoomba Road. Turn right about 30km from Esk, then turn right again about a kilometre further on. From here it is about 8 to 10km to Perseverance Dam. N.B. All distances are approximate.

Alternatively, you can drive to Perseverance Dam via the Toowoomba-Crows Nest Road. Turn right at Pechey, which is 5km south of Crows Nest township.

To drive to Crows Nest Falls National Park, follow the road signs from Crows Nest township.

Water: In drier seasons, parts of Crows Nest Creek can become stagnant and it may be preferable to carry all your water supplies. The region can be very hot in warmer months so a good quantity of water may be necessary.

Private Lands: Some of this walk travels across private lands. To check access conditions, contact the local national park ranger (see Directory).

Grading and Hazards: The walk described here is about grade 2 1/2 to 3. Some rockhopping difficulty would be experienced in wet conditions and basic navigation skills are required (a topographic map is necessary).

Route: Leaving cars at Perseverance Dam, there are several routes down to *(Walk* Cressbrook Creek below the dam spillway. One route follows the ridge north of the *37)* car park (133 812) into a gully, which leads down to the creek (there are several gullies, some rougher and steeper than others). Another route starts on a dirt road at 136 814, branching off after several hundred metres to follow a ridge system northwards and then westwards, meeting Cressbrook Creek at 128 823.

Once in Cressbrook Creek, it is easy travelling down to the junction of Crows Nest Creek, which joins on the left. From the junction, rockhop up Crows Nest Creek for a short distance, passing a number of good swimming holes. After about 400m of rockhopping, look for a major gully which descends on the right (127 842). This marks the ascent route to the Valley of Diamonds Lookout (124 843), which is located on the obvious large bluff that can be seen rising up on the north bank of the creek. Either climb the gully or the slopes just to the north-west (i.e. upstream), then traverse west-north-westwards across the ridges to the lookout. N.B. It is important not to mistake this gully, which lies east of the bluff, for the extremely steep gully which splits the bluff.

From the lookout, a system of graded tracks leads through the national park to various cascades on Crows Nest Creek, and then to the main picnic area. The return route is basically the reverse of the above. There is also an alternative return route which uses a system of tracks and old roads on the slopes and ridges south of Crows Nest Creek, leaving from the small concrete pedestrian bridge at the cascades and meeting Cressbrook Creek at about 132 828. However, public access on this route is normally restricted. As there are several tracks and old roads in this vicinity, some navigation care would be required if access is granted.

DIRECTORY

QUEENSLAND NATIONAL PARKS AND WILDLIFE SERVICE

Tamborine: Knoll Road, North Tamborine. Q. 4272.
Telephone: (075) 45 1171.

Crows Nest: P.O. Box 68, Crows Nest, Q. 4355.
Telephone: (076) 98 1296.

OTHER TELEPHONE NUMBERS

Killarney Glen: See route description.

APPENDIX 1
DIRECTORY OF MAJOR
GOVERNMENT OFFICES

N.B. Addresses of government offices in regional areas, including local offices of the Queensland National Parks and Wildlife Service, are given in the Directory on the last page of each chapter. All addresses are as at March, 1991.

QUEENSLAND NATIONAL PARKS AND WILDLIFE SERVICE

Head Office: P.O. Box 155, North Quay. Q. 4002. (160 Ann Street, Brisbane). Telephone: (07) 227 8185.

Southern Regional P.O. Box 42, Kenmore. Q. 4069. (55 Priors Pocket Road,
Centre: Moggill). Telephone: (07) 202 0200.

QUEENSLAND FOREST SERVICE

Head Office: 160 Mary Street, Brisbane. Q. 4000.
   Telephone: (07) 234 0111

SUNMAP

Head Office: P.O. Box 40, Wooloongabba. Q. 4102. (Sunmap Centre, corner of Main and Vulture Streets). Telephone: (07) 896 3111.

City Office: Anzac Square, Adelaide Street, Brisbane.
   Telephone: (07) 227 6892

APPENDIX 2
NOTABLE PEAKS OF SOUTH-EAST QUEENSLAND

N.B. All elevations have been interpreted from topographic maps. Some may not precisely reflect the latest surveys.

THE HIGHEST PEAKS

	PEAK	ELEVATION	REGION
1	Mt Superbus	1375m	Main Range
2	Mt Superbus (North Peak)	1362m	Main Range
3	Mt Barney - west peak	1359m	Barney/Ballow
4	Mt Barney - east peak	1351m	Barney/Ballow
5	Mt Roberts	1336m	Main Range
6	Junction Peak (Mt Ballow)	1310m	Barney/Ballow
7	Mt Superbus - south peak	1303m	Main Range
8	Mt Asplenium	1294m	Main Range
9	Nothofagus Peak	1280m	Barney/Ballow
10	Bald Rock	1277m	Girraween/Bald Rock
11	Mt Norman	1267m	Girraween/Bald Rock
12	Double Peak (Mt Ballow - Central Peak)	1265m	Barney/Ballow
13	Mt Huntley	1264m	Main Range
14	Mt Barney - north peak	1260m	Barney/Ballow
15	Gwyala Peak	1260m	Barney/Ballow
16	Mt Lizardback	1250m	Main Range
17	South Bald Rock	1244m	Girraween/Bald Rock
18	Wilsons Peak	1231m	Main Range
19	Burrajum Peak	1230m	Barney/Ballow
20	Spicers Peak	1222m	Main Range
21	Mt Steamer	1215m	Main Range
22	Mt Guymer	1204m	Main Range
23	Savages Point	1200m	Barney/Ballow
24	Durramlee Peak	1200m	Barney/Ballow
25	Mt Bithongabel	1195m	Lamington
26	Mt Wanungra	1192m	Lamington
27	Mt Toolona	1190m	Lamington
28	Mt Lindesay	1177m	Border Ranges
29	Mt Hobwee	1175m	Lamington
30	Sentinel Point	1175m	Main Range

OTHER NOTABLE PEAKS

Main Range Region

Bare Rock	1170m	Mt Mitchell	1161m
Mt Doubletop	1150m	Mt Cordeaux	1144m
Mt Castle	970m	Kangaroo Mt	756m
Grass Tree Knob	750m	Beau Brummel	707m
The Prow	1040m	Mt Zahel	880m
Mt Bell	1082m	Mt Bangalore	831m

Central Scenic Rim

Mt Ernest	960m	Leaning Peak	1138m
Mt Clunie	1150m	Isolated Peak	919m
Big Lonely	1155m	Toms Tum	767m
Mowburra Peak	1166m	Midget Peak	946m
Minnages Mt	1025m	Barrabool Peak	1151m
Mt Philip	715m	Mt Maroon	966m
Focal Peak	1050m	Mt May	833m
Montserrat Lkt	1007m	Mt Gillies	647m
Mt Glennie	980m	Mt Tanna	795m

Eastern Scenic Rim

Mt Gipps	790m	Tweed Pinnacle	919m
Mt Nungulba	955m	Mt Warning	1156m
Tweed Trig	1025m	Bar Mt	1140m
Pt Lookout	1085m	Paddys Mt	950m
Mt Throakban	1125m	Mt Cougal	694m
Mt Widgee	1096m	Best of All Lookout	1100m
Mt Worendo	1142m	Bilbroughs Lookout	960m
Mt Wupawn	1100m	Springbrook Mt	947m
Mt Razorback	1045m	Turtle Rock	500m
Pyramid Rock	655m	Egg Rock	451m

Moreton and Fraser Islands

Mt Tempest	280m	Mt Bowarrady	280m
Storm Mt	274m	Jessie Peak	178m

D'Aguliar Ranges and North Coast

Mt Samson	690m	Mt D'Aguilar	725m
The Summit	765m	Northbrook Mt	659m
Mt O'Reilly	526m	Mt Beerwah	556m
Mt Tibrogargen	364m	Mt Coonowrin	377m

Other Peaks

Flinders Peak	679m	Mt Greville	770m
White Rock	182m	Mt Moon	786m
Mt French	598m	Mt Edwards	634m
Minto Crags	335m	Knapps Peak	651m

SPECIAL SUBJECT INDEX

This index contains selected references to special subjects e.g. topics relating to safety, environmental conservation, skills, equipment, people and book titles. Because of the nature of the book, it is not possible for this index to be comprehensive, but most of the more important references have been chosen.

INDEX TO
BUSHWALKING FEATURES

This index is intended to help readers quickly find descriptions of bushwalking features and routes. Because of the size of the book, the index does not include passing references (e.g. a brief mention of Mt Lindesay in, say, the chapter on Boonoo Boonoo). As a general rule, towns and road names have also been omitted.

305

AMENDMENTS AND NOTES

North-East Ridge of Spicers Peak (Page 202): Since the first printing of this edition, this route has deteriorated due to erosion and removal of vegetation caused by a combination of frequent usage and recent drought conditions. Some sections are likely to be difficult and dangerous, particularly when the route is slippery due to either wet or very dry conditions (in dry conditions, loose crumbly soil can accumulate and cover many holds). People are advised to avoid the route unless they are very experienced scramblers. A belay rope is recommended. Revised grading: Grade 4 to 5+, depending on conditions.

Notes: ....

....

....

....

....

....

....

....

....

....

....

....

....

....

....

....

....

....

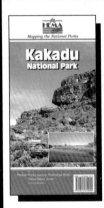

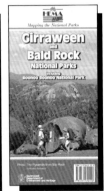
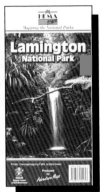
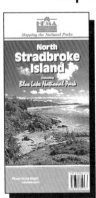